Sentinel Under Siege

SENTINEL UNDER SIEGE

The Triumphs and Troubles of America's Free Press

STANLEY E. FLINK

WestviewPress
A Division of HarperCollins*Publishers*

Copyright © 1997 by Stanley E. Flink

Published in 1997 in the United States of America by Westview Press, 5500 Central Avenue, Boulder, Colorado 80301-2877, and in the United Kingdom by Westview Press, 12 Hid's Copse Road, Cumnor Hill, Oxford OX2 9JJ

A CIP catalog record for this book is available from the Library of Congress.
ISBN 0-8133-3344-X

The paper used in this publication meets the requirements of the American National Standard for Permanence of Paper for Printed Library Materials Z39.48-1984.

10   9   8   7   6   5   4   3   2   1

For Joy,
wife, friend, and critic

CONTENTS

ACKNOWLEDGMENTS

I have always been uncomfortable with the idea of acknowledgment. It seems haughty and condescending on the one hand, timid and sanctimonious on the other. I trust that those I am about to acknowledge will understand that what I mean to express is gratitude in its most felicitous form—with astonishment. I have been the recipient of more generous assistance and support in producing this book than I had thought possible.

When I completed the first draft of the manuscript, I asked several distinguished scholars who are also—as is often the case—accomplished writers to read my work. Sociologist Kai Erikson and political scientist Joseph La-Palombara were the first to do so. They supplied, along with useful criticism, the strong encouragement so crucial to self-editing and completion.

I then turned to historians C. Vann Woodward and Peter Gay, who commented thoughtfully, each in a frank and distinctive manner both specific and helpful.

Yale law professor Akhil Reed Amar not only examined my reporting on the Constitution but invited me to attend his seminar on the Bill of Rights. I learned there much about the legal history of the First Amendment that enlarged earlier research and clarified the boundaries between the law and the media.

My colleague at New York University, Professor William Burrows, made persuasive suggestions regarding sequence and emphasis, advice he communicated at the cost of interrupting concentration on a book of his own. I am in his debt.

Outside the academy, I consulted a number of gifted people whose professional schedules are formidable. That they responded so quickly and constructively was a remarkable largesse.

James Hoge, former newspaper writer and publisher, currently editor of *Foreign Affairs,* provided the endorsement of an experienced practitioner who has contemplated the fate of a responsible press while at its center.

William F. Buckley Jr., founder of *National Review,* columnist, television commentator, and novelist, wrote a characteristically deft and knowledgeable analysis of the case I seek to make, commending its purpose and its promulgation.

Joan Ryan, once a columnist for the *Washington Post,* followed the evolution of my manuscript in segments, commenting wisely and raising useful questions.

Charles Kelly, an astute observer of the media and its paladins, challenged my arguments whenever he perceived digressions or inconsistency.

Donald Lamm gave unexpected support and guidance at the most propitious moment.

Add to this list of considerate and candid readers my wife, to whom this book is dedicated. She has read all the incarnations of the text and listened to the author's explications with suitable skepticism. Such discipline is priceless.

A deep sigh of appreciation for Marlene Brask, who patiently transformed handwritten paragraphs and audiotape dictation into word-processed manuscript. This she ultimately transferred to a wafer-thin disk, smaller than the palm of my hand. It contains five years of work, hundreds of pages. Incomprehensibly to me, this disk is put into the publisher's computer and emerges—give or take—as a book. Thus I migrate to the digital world.

My workplace at home has suffered from my inclination to file books and papers in stacks—on tables, on chairs, on the floor. The patient Marion Thomas has skillfully kept these stalagmites in place.

Most sympathetic concerning my befuddlement during this procedure is a golden retriever named Sam who silently appears when I am tediously searching for a source note and speaks to me consolingly with his eyebrows.

Stanley E. Flink

INTRODUCTION

The concept of the free press as the sentinel who guards democracy has been deeply rooted in American history. The Founders of the United States supported that concept eloquently and without exception.

Accordingly, the press was the only commercial enterprise given specific constitutional protection—the First Amendment.

The press was expected to alert the public to the abuse of power by government officials and expose corruption in the private sector.

At the end of the twentieth century, after more than 200 years of growth and technological evolution, the free press—print and electronic—is facing a time of crisis. Public trust is eroding, and the instruments of cyberspace are fragmenting the distribution of information that was for so long controlled by press organizations.

In recent years the mainstream press, once freestanding, has been acquired in great part by corporate entities whose diverse interests may conflict with the independence of news reporting.

At the heart of this dilemma is the belief that the constitutional protection of the press carries with it an *obligation* to provide a responsible and accountable information service in the public interest. If that service is compromised by competing corporate priorities or special interests of any kind, the possibility of government intervention increases.

In the coming years, responsible journalism can enlarge public confidence and sustain its economic viability, no matter how varied the distribution systems, by voluntarily generating *self-regulated* ethical standards.

There is no way the press can be policed from the outside without diminishing its freedom, but if the sentinel becomes a mere subordinate of powerful corporations, it will no longer be a guardian of public rights and could become a threat.

No democracy has survived without a free press. No despotism can permit a free press to exist.

Who, then, guards the sentinel?

This book is the product of a journalist's (and most recently a journalism teacher's) lifelong interest in and concern for a free and responsible press. Formal research and the assembling of editorial materials began in 1991, the two-hundredth year of the First Amendment. In the process, interviews were taped with more than forty men and women who have held significant positions in the media, education, and the law. Many of these people are briefly quoted at the beginning of each chapter, but their extended comments deserve a separate account. Most of the themes that were discussed resonate throughout this book.

I have also stood on the shoulders of a large number of public figures, writers, and scholars who, in one way or another, have themselves stood on the shoulders of those extraordinary early Americans whose philosophy and prophetic imagination envisioned a sentinel over public rights.

What emerged from this research was the remarkable discourse that flows into modern media issues directly from the Founders' letters and speeches—and from the political views that appeared in the small newspapers of the eighteenth and nineteenth centuries, produced wherever American printers could secure a subsidy or enough subscriptions to cover costs. The core conviction was, and continues to be, that prior restraint on speech or press is anathema. Less common were commitments to accuracy, accountability, and nonpartisanship. The challenge faced by the press editorially, and in due course legally, has been the central theme of America's political system—the rights of individual citizens in conflict with the powers of a federal government. This theme became narrowly focused during the colonial administrations of British governors, and fledgling newspapers were vital to the expression of discontent that led to the independence movement. Once the Constitution was adopted, and soon thereafter the first ten amendments, the stage was set for the political conflict in the 1790s concerning sedition in a democracy.

How much invective did a government have to tolerate from its constituents? Sedition (any public criticism of official actions) was an issue in 1798 but not fully resolved until 1964. Because the right of the people to rein in their public servants needed the amplification of a free and independent press, the most significant Supreme Court cases concerning that right are discussed early in this book. The historical roots of those cases include a blight too often ignored by the press—racism. The inescapable, systemic brutality of racism was not effectively confronted by the major media until the 1960s. If the media believed its role was to hold a mirror before the larger society, a case could be made that the civil rights movement was a primary image. *Life Magazine*, the *New York Times* and CBS News were the mirrors of greatest influence at that time, but defending the legal rights of black Americans provoked the energy and courage of editors and reporters in growing numbers. The underlying social racism, as always, received far less scrutiny.

Looking at the development of the early American press makes it clear that the modern media has only enlarged and complicated the issues of privacy, national security, and the watchdog role of the press—not invented them. The media, however, in its delivery of news and public discussion, has now become so powerful and omnipresent that governance and politics have had to change so as to accommodate almost instant shifts in public opinion, driven by the effect of television.

Enormous power has not bred self-discipline in the press as a whole, and vast revenues brought in through advertising have not inspired widespread ethical responsibility. These cosmic concerns are not only philosophical. They are essential to the stability of functioning democratic nations.

During the month before the remarkable 1996 Russian election—the first in Russia's history—I participated in a United States Information Agency–New York University program that permitted me to visit in Russia with journalists and academicians in various parts of the country. There were in their minds, and in their media, a great many issues and debates that virtually echoed, in the 1990s, what a youthful United States had debated in the 1790s. Government subsidies, rule of law, privacy rights, partisanship, autonomy, and ethical standards in and of the press were at the center of Russia's political discussion, just as they were in the late eighteenth century when some Americans feared that George Washington might become a king and other Americans gave impassioned support to a strong central government. The differences, of course, attend to the astonishing rapidity with which modern exponents and nay-sayers may reach mass audiences and the compression of time and reflection that denies the makers and critics of public policy a chance to weigh and balance their options before acting or speaking.

The call for higher standards in the media, anchored in ethical principles, and the need at the same time for vigilance over abuse of power by government and business have been familiar subjects in magazines and symposia since the early part of this century. What has not received much thoughtful attention during that time is the day-to-day necessity of news as a prerequisite of democracy—that is, fundamental, reliable, and useful information for the body politic. James Madison wrote 200 years ago: "A popular Government without popular information, or the means of acquiring it, is but a Prologue to a Farce or a Tragedy, or perhaps both."[1]

The idea that information on public affairs is as important as law and order, or drinkable water, to a free society has been neglected. The *negative* liberty of the press—Congress shall make *no* law—has been the preoccupation of the privately owned news media companies. The *positive* liberty of serving the public interest with news and information, gathered and presented within the constraints of time and competition, clear and accurate as possible, with a second thought for fairness and taste—is a liberty worth taking far more seriously.

To that end I submit the following book.

1

IN SEARCH OF A ROLE

I've been around a lot of places. People do awful things to each other. But it's worse in places where everybody is kept in the dark. It really is. Information is light. Information, in itself, about anything, is light. That's all you can say, really.

—Tom Stoppard, *Night and Day*

Predicting the future of the news and public information business is probably more difficult than anticipating developments in other institutions upon which society depends for order and enlightenment. By its very nature the news media changes rapidly, uses and discards its basic products, and ceaselessly adjusts to consumer tastes. If most of the information human beings need and look for becomes digitalized, economic concerns, which have for so long driven the purveyors of news, will surely become more complex, and many companies will rise and fall in the process. To begin with, the question of ownership and control of information will have to be examined and, no doubt, litigated. Whatever finds its way to the "computer nets" conveyed without wire will be, to a substantial extent, up for grabs. Digital communication is capable of being reliably accurate, inexpensive, ecologically sound, and easy to master. It will also stimulate much political and economic controversy. Where and how the profits will be made already consumes the corporate world. But how the essential information needs of human society will be served all over the planet—a population that is expected to double in size by the year 2050—is far from clear.

The *Economist*, in autumn 1993, produced a collection of essays it called "The Future Surveyed." Eminent "writers, thinkers, and politicians" suggested the more likely developments of the next 150 years. Hedging their bets, the editors quoted that great coiner of caveats cinemogul Samuel Goldwyn, who wisely advised, "Never prophesy, especially about the future."

Having acknowledged the daunting nature of the task, the *Economist* pressed on with the help of distinguished guest colleagues to forecast world politics, business, finance, and science—all inescapably the stuff of *news*, and all dependent upon the movement of information. A certain hopefulness is focused upon the possibilities of a responsible, accountable press emerging successfully in the next century. However dramatic and mind-boggling the technical innovations may be in the communications business, the public requirement for information on which to make political judgments will not change—not, that is, if democracy is to survive.

One of the key issues in and of the future will be to determine the methodology for the protection of the public interest from serious limiting—which is to say unacceptable—actions by governments, corporations (including media conglomerates), and the courts. The incursions of technology are already visible and almost uncontrollable. Writer Michael Crichton in a speech to the National Press Club in Washington on April 6, 1993, said:

> The American media produce a product of very poor quality. Its information is not reliable, it has too much chrome and glitz, its doors rattle, it breaks down almost immediately, and it's sold without a warranty. . . . In part, it's a problem of near-sighted management that encourages profits at the expense of quality. In part, it's a failure to respond to changing technology. And in large part, it's a failure to recognize the changing needs of the audience.

Crichton went on to describe the potential of the fiber-optic highway and the artificial intelligence agents roaming the databases. The individual citizen who can afford access equipment will be able to "call up" those news stories and all the supporting information he or she may want in a manner and with an expansiveness no newspaper or television station or news magazine (in current configuration) could equal.

It seems reasonable to expect economical adjustments in the methodology of news operations—and *there* is the rub. The public interest is not served if the public is not adequately, openly, and widely informed on public issues. A mass audience, growing more massive each decade, can be reached only by mass communications. Computers provide information one on one. News, useful or frivolous, is conveyed to collectivities with all kinds of calibration. Ask the polltakers. As the gap between the very rich and the working poor widens and the middle class shrinks, the media becomes inexorably skewed, even if unintentionally, in the direction of the economically successful. An electorate cannot form opinions based on data "called up" by sophisticated equipment unless that capacity is cheaply and readily available in every household, library, and school and perhaps at specified public places. Even then we must presuppose the education level and the motivation to utilize such mechanisms.

The likelihood is that mass communication distribution of news will keep its foothold, no matter how tenuous, for a long time to come. If that is the case, how can we ensure an effective, principled, dedicated press in

America—let alone in other parts of the world? Demonstrably, the preponderant news source over the past several decades has been television—a primary supplier of headlines and brief accounts of the day's major events with the capacity for galvanizing emotional responses with powerful pictures of disaster, violence, military actions, agony, celebrity, and heroism. Russell Kirk has called our times the "age of conditioned response." The question remains: Can television ever match the value of informed, reflective writing about news and public affairs?

In a letter to the *New York Times* (September 30, 1993) concerning events in Somalia, elder statesman George Kennan commented on the distorting influence of network television news. He said, in part,

> No one would deny, I think, that without the preceding television coverage of the situation in Somalia, the support for the action in the Congress and the public would not have been what it was. In pointing this out, I did not mean to "blame" television. Television was what it was and was only performing its accepted task. . . . Fleeting, disjointed, visual glimpses of reality, flickering on and off the screen, here today and gone tomorrow, are not the "information" on which sound judgments on complicated problems are to be formed. Television cannot consult the rich voice of prior experience, nor can it outline probable consequences, or define alternatives, or express the nuances of the arguments pro and con.

A response from TV news producers might point to hour-long news specials, to the PBS *Newshour* each weekday evening, to investigative reporting by weekly shows such as *Sixty Minutes* and *20/20*, and to the occasional appearances of distinguished scholars who enhance the evening news with brief but knowledgeable analyses. Local newscasts, budgetarily constricted (despite widespread profits), have less to boast about. At issue here, as with any study of the media, is not so much the public's *right* to know but the public's *need* to know.

The Press and Public Policy

The earliest perceptions of the New World and its challenges produced a gradually emerging definition of a new culture—the American culture. It was and may still be an incomplete experiment. George Washington offered a vision of a "new race." He said, "The bosom of America is open to the oppressed and persecuted of all Nations and Religions." John Adams, who succeeded Washington as president, pointedly insisted that emigrants "must cast off the European skin, never to resume it."[1]

But the American dream of the Founders seemed to be colored white—like their European skin. The darker-skinned peoples—the Native Americans, African Americans, Hispanic Americans, Asian Americans—were not considered full participants in the forging of a new nation—nor, for that matter, were women of any color until 1920. Emigrants from Europe brought with them many prejudices—often leveled at each other but almost universally based on the Old World assumptions of the white man's superiority.

America's vaunted cultural heritage, "strength through diversity," and what the historian James Bryce called "the amazing solvent power" of American institutions are now confronted by the cults of ethnicity. Ethnic ideologues—rarely speaking for more than a fraction of their constituents—have denounced the "melting pot" as a conspiracy to homogenize America. As Americans of all kinds approach the end of the twentieth century, for the first time in their history a great many of them do not believe that life will be better for their children than it has been for them. The agitated passions of ethnic identity seem to mount as confidence in the American dream diminishes. If the United States is to sustain a leadership role in dealing with the predicaments that lie ahead for all of humankind, it will have to begin with redefining itself as a nation. Can a diverse and divided citizenry in America today agree on common principles? Is a "national community" possible? Theodore Roosevelt admonished Americans in 1915 that "the one absolutely certain way of bringing this nation to ruin, of preventing all possibility of its continuing to be a nation at all, would be to permit it to become a tangle of squabbling nationalities."[2]

Has the experiment failed? Is the Constitution as a "living document" adequate to the task a vastly changed society asks it to perform? Citizens of Hispanic and Asian background will compete in greater number with African and white European Americans, and that reality taken in itself will force the restructuring of news and the reporting of public issues. The nourishing of democratic commonalities depends upon an independent, *responsible* media. It is the mucilage of a free society.

The pursuit of a civic conversation—that is, the news of public affairs and the robust discussion of evolving views—will require the highest quality journalism this nation has ever known. The serious media, which informs public opinion and thus affects, in a substantial way, the formation of public policy, should be the primary concern of First Amendment defenders—and above all of the "citizen-critics." Those sovereign citizens who were conceptualized by the Framers as the holders of power under the Constitution seem to have forgotten their inheritance, or have chosen to neglect it. In *Happy Days Were Here Again*, William F. Buckley Jr. deplores the lack of appreciation for the patrimony enjoyed by "those of us who live in the free world. The numbing, benumbing thought that we owe nothing to Plato and Aristotle, nothing to the prophets who wrote the Bible, nothing to the generations who fought for freedoms activated in the Bill of Rights; we are basket cases of ingratitude, so many of us."[3]

The drift away from the awareness of citizenship has diminished social responsibility in the media. The best way for the press to protect its own freedom of speech is to speak and write about significant public issues grounded in constitutional awareness. The press can bring public servants into line, Jefferson ruminated in a letter written to Lafayette in 1823, "but the only security of all is in a free press. The force of public opinion cannot be resisted."[4] This applies to both the "citizen-critic" and the "citizen-journalist." Dialogue, debate, and discovery are all inherent elements of a living constitution, but those elements are lost to the press when it forgets the obligation to its audience and emphasizes instead commercialism and careerism. The pernicious by-product then becomes the public perception that too much power is in the hands of the news media.

Two centuries of judicial interpretation and legislative statutes have left the First Amendment on shaky ground. Since Justice William Brennan's departure from the Supreme Court in 1990, no justice has stepped forward to serve as point man (or woman) for the First Amendment's laconic forty-five words. There has been, in the meantime, considerable nibbling at the edges of journalistic freedom. The nibbles are washed down by a brew of general skepticism about the ability of ethical standards in the press to survive the pressure of advertising revenue and about the consolidated financial controls imposed by the managers of conglomerates. All the same, low esteem for the press, measured by public opinion surveys, can be misleadingly skewed. The American public has rarely lavished praise on *any* of its institutions. Self-government is a political principle that asks the citizen to subdue autonomy in favor of law and community traditions. When the citizens are skeptical of government, they are not easily persuaded.

Eighteenth-century political essayists in England, such as John Trenchard and Thomas Gordon (*Cato's Letters*), were far more influential in early America than in their native land or on the Continent. They were chiefly concerned with the conflict between individual liberty and political power. No other watchdog, they declared, could protect liberty so effectively as an independent press. In that endeavor the evolving mass circulation press became its own worst enemy. Too often it forgot its purpose in the rush to sleaze, sensationalism, entertainment, and profits. A public already ill-disposed to participate in politics—to listen, to debate, and to read—was provided the added disincentives of contempt and complacency. The electorate set itself against the elected. "Don't confuse us with the facts," voters seemed to be saying; "we already have our opinions." If the journalistic dispenser of facts can be characterized as unreliable, uninformed, or self-serving, the inclination of the public to subject its own opinions to dispute, or to consider alternatives, becomes even less likely.

The *bottom line* in all of this is too often the *bottom line*. Profit-seeking and social responsibility are extremely uneasy companions. Like good cops who are reluctant to report the misdeeds of bad cops, reporters and editors rarely remonstrate with their bosses when economic well-being is at issue. Alexander Meiklejohn, a First Amendment scholar, recommended to citizens and the press alike that by every consideration of honesty and self-respect they should practice what they preach and preach only what they practice.

For teaching the press to avoid self-censorship and helping the proprietors to find the resolve and the methodology that will make good journalism more profitable than bad journalism, there are no simple prescriptions. There is, however, the remarkably rich and revealing history of free expression in America that began in colonial communities and, despite many indications of fragility, survived a revolution, a civil war, and many conflicts in far off places without irretrievably losing its way. It has benefited from, and been wounded by, the statutes and court decisions that seemed at times to build a cage around the sparse language of the First Amendment. The press, nonetheless, has encountered and triumphed over a number of serious threats to its constitutional independence, and it has very slowly but steadily learned to criticize itself and adopt some of the same ethical standards it has insistently demanded of public officials.

Self-Regulation

The Fourth Estate must now face the overwhelming influence of globalization, corporate aggrandizement, "virtual reality," and political manipulation by the various voices of spin-artistry and pressure groups. If enlightened proprietors are to accept the quintessential importance of a free press to the survival of freedom itself, there must be more extensive, imaginative, demanding education for journalists. On-the-job training will not do. The moral issues, the cultural complexities, the rise of religion and nationalism as social and political forces, the environmental concerns, and the technological evolution are but a few of the subjects that require sophisticated intellectual preparation.

Academic programs ought to be designed for critiquing and reporting on the media in all its forms. The lines between entertainment and public debate, between soft journalism and political analysis, between thought and feeling, grow fuzzier as information (true, false, and partial) seeks new markets on digital conveyor belts. News reporting was once called the first draft of history. There are now innumerable and contradictory first drafts ready to be summoned by computer.

If so many people in America do indeed get their only news from television, they are not likely to feel the gravitational pull of self-government; nor will they understand the complex issues of public policy. Television newscasts were never meant to be the essential source of information for "citizen-rulers"; nor can television be expected to perform such a role. In roughly twenty-two minutes each evening, dominated by visual effects and containing fewer words than those printed on the average front page of a daily newspaper, context cannot be provided. For their relatively small audiences,

C-Span, public television, and the ubiquitous CNN (which may soon face some round-the-clock emulators) are indisputably helpful, but television news generically could benefit from an independent commission on free and responsible broadcasting. According to the Pew Research Center for the People and the Press, fewer Americans are reading daily newspapers, and dramatically fewer are watching television news. The new (1996) figures gleaned from a national survey indicate that only 42 percent regularly watch one of the three nightly network newscasts. The number is down from 48 percent in 1995 and 60 percent in 1993. Furthermore, it would appear that network, local, and CNN news audiences are diminishing most rapidly among those people who are thirty years old or younger, followed by those thirty to forty-nine years of age. The number of regular viewers among those fifty years and over is about the same or slightly lower.

The printed press has responded to critical pressure in recent years by voluntarily—if not always enthusiastically—moving toward the appointment of ombudsmen, more acknowledgment of errors, and the hiring of more media reporters and columnists. These measures are not universal, and what has been done is often flawed; but taken together, such developments have set in motion an aspiration that is not likely to dissipate.

America's constitutional protection *for* the press should obligate responsible behavior *by* the press. As to the difference between publishers and owners of broadcasting facilities, Chief Justice Warren Burger described that margin as follows: "A broadcaster has much in common with a newspaper publisher, but he is not in the same category in terms of public obligations imposed by law. A broadcaster seeks and is granted the free and exclusive use of a limited and valuable part of the public domain; when he accepts the franchise, it is burdened by enforceable public obligations. A newspaper can be operated by the whim or caprice of its owners; a broadcast station cannot."[5]

Two basic realities are shared by print and broadcast, however, and are presumably understood by both groups. First, as Walter Lippmann observed long ago, when public anger or disapproval becomes sufficiently heated, the press had better regulate itself effectively or one day Congress will rely on "that legalized atrocity, the Congressional investigation, where Congressmen, starved of their legitimate food for thought, go on a wild and feverish man-hunt and do not stop at cannibalism."[6] It was true in the 1920s. It is no less likely today.

Second, the value of private news enterprises has become increasingly vulnerable to the proliferation of other information sources and the means of tapping into them. The independence of journalism, once defined as freedom from government interference, can survive only if credibility, competence, and integrity are the norm. The quality and reliability of news reporting in the next era will also determine profits. Intellectual property created by talented and responsible journalists will be protected—even in the digitalized ecosystem—by economic realities *and* the First Amendment. Monitoring that property—on the page, on the air, or in databanks—cannot be done by outside groups. There are too many players, and the playing field is too large. Many journalists who rejected a monitoring agency in the past are less certain now. But the greatest promise lies *within* those corporations that publish and disseminate news (including the Internet), and they are beginning to understand the intrinsic value of responsible journalism. Keeping a solid wall between news reporting and special influence from any sector—politicians, advertisers, religious groups, or ideologists—needs vigilance. Freedom to do *bad* journalism will always be there unless the Constitution is ravaged. For the privately operated news organization, the freedom to do *good* journalism will be more profitable in the long run—where reputation counts.

News as Theater

In the overloaded coverage of O. J. Simpson's unfinished tribulations, there was much to contemplate regarding America's addiction to celebrity, but more significantly, there was the troubling influence of media overkill on the judicial process—particularly the pretrial purchase of potentially relevant information by the tabloids, print and electronic. Once millions of people were lathered with data about law and lawyers—along with the often dubious speculations of "experts"—the profitability of higher viewer ratings or a burst in newsstand sales inspired vivid elaborations, implausible conspiracy theories, and smug pontifications. These contributions were too rarely edited and even more rarely supported by hard evidence.

How many people listened to or read the thoughtful, reflective accounts that followed the plethora of "real-time" competitive reporting at the outset of the story is not easily calculated. Public perception, however distorted in the short term, will resonate over time in legislative debates regarding restraints on the media and in future judicial decisions shaped, at least in part, by the monitoring eye of television cameras in America's courtrooms. Whether there will be, finally, any kind of collective self-analysis prodded by the notorious cases that engage massive national television audiences is unclear. The effect of such intense, vicariously shared experiences on viewers (and readers) includes a perplexing mix of involvement and detachment. Whether responsible media organizations can ever ensure balance or restrain excess remains an important, possibly crucial, question for future journalism.

The Culture of Contention

Since the early 1970s media critics and scholars have documented the steady decline of the press away from its watchdog fiduciary role—and the concomitant rise in its capacity for contentiousness. News purveyors, in print and on television, have become players in the political game. Tom Patterson, author of *Out of Order*, a highly praised book about the news media and the political process, believes that "news coverage has become a barrier between the candidates and the voters, rather than a bridge connecting them."[7]

Surveys sponsored by both conservative and liberal organizations have found little partisan bias in mainstream reporting on issues but increasingly greater *cynicism* on all matters political. The kind of reporting that day in and day out characterizes political leaders as venal, evasive, and incompetent creates mistrust and confusion among the voters and inevitably erodes confidence in a democratic government. Presidents, obviously, suffer the most from negativism and suspicion in the press. The White House depends on public opinion more directly than the other centers of power. Even when the highest office in the land tries to put the best face on policies and achievements, there are times when the *best* face is the true face.

The top people in publishing and broadcasting who have become players—even celebrities—in the political process have begun to operate outside the reality in which the average citizen lives. From that height (call it sky-box journalism) it is tempting to look down contemptuously upon the frailty of public officials and to convey a picture of ineptitude and hubris. The countervailing analysis of accomplishment and dedication, of vision and leadership, has become so infrequent and parsimonious that the electorate is bound to back away.

In 1994 the election attracted only 37 percent of registered voters. They were almost evenly split between parties but punished the incumbents (seen as Democrats) and showed a preference (small but consistent) for new faces (seen as Republicans). The press, oddly enough, often used the word "earthquake" to describe the results. They must have felt like a quake to the Democrats, but in total numbers they did not constitute much of a tremor. Apathy is not a seismic event.

The voters might respond to more responsible news coverage, but it will be, in all likelihood, a very slow movement. What appears to be vanishing from the calculation is the public assumption that the press is a surrogate for public concerns. *Nothing really bad will be done that we won't hear about soon enough. Meanwhile, let the game go on.* Those feelings are being nudged by disenchantment and skepticism. The major press, and the networks, are regarded as part of a new establishment. The media, no longer messengers, are becoming manipulators. This new establishment seems to have enormous power because it can create instant notoriety, bring down presidents (and their wives), make box office, fill stadiums, and provide what Lippmann called "those pictures in our heads" that shape our sympathy, our disgust, and our anger.

The media, however, is not an entity that we trust; nor is it significantly influential among all the constituencies. We may enjoy it. We may find it useful now and then. We may even take advantage of it when publicity serves our own interest. To depend upon it for truth (or near truth), to look at it for guidance and affirmation, is not very likely. The separation between the media and the consumer at the higher levels of imagination and ethical perception is a matter to be considered urgently. The practitioners are contending for all kinds of prizes. They contend for the best assignments, the lead story on the evening news, the byline on the front page. They contend for career advancement, an anchor position, a Sunday column, an invitation to be a talking head. As with Brando in *On the Waterfront*, failure is in the words "I could have been a contender."

Out of contention comes tabloidization, sound bites, salaciousness, and an epidemic of *wounding* journalism—the practice of rationalizing that private matters are included in the public's right to know whether they want to know or not. In rampaging through the private lives of public figures, the press loses sight of what such hapless offenders may have done—and are still trying to do—for the common good. The wounding of politicians by innuendo, undocumented charges, rumor, and satire has become commonplace. It may demonize some; it dehumanizes others. Surely it discourages the temptation among talented citizens to commit to public service. The culture of contention has placed profit, career, and fame far ahead of reliable information, accountability, and the public interest. The legal interpretation of the press clause in the First Amendment may itself have to contend with these developments, not least in regard to libel.

The decision to use private affairs as news that is part of the public domain ought to be made with the greatest care. Private matters would not be *news* if they were not *damaging*. The most effective damage control is prior restraint. If that remedy ever becomes acceptable, irresponsible contentiousness in the media will have opened the door. One of the many enduring admonitions of the 1947 Hutchins Commission (see Chapter 20) was, "It is not enough that we report the facts *truthfully*, we must report the *truth* about the facts." That kind of truth-telling can begin only with the individual journalists closest to the story.

A New Canon

Reinforcing good journalism is a compelling goal for media critics, academicians, and public policy thinkers. Systematic recognition and publicity for excellence in reporting at all levels have never received enough attention. Ethicist Sissela Bok suggests that a serious effort be made to change incentives so that "gains from deception are lowered and honesty made more worthwhile *even in the short run*" (emphasis added).[8] The established awards—Pulitzer prizes, DuPont, and others—do not penetrate the public awareness deeply enough; nor are they effectively attached to the specific work product.[9] Deserving local and regional news operations are too rarely and too narrowly applauded. Ethical awareness, self-criticism, ombudsmen, accountability, and moral courage in taking stands not immediately congenial to public opinion (or advertisers) have been given little or no time in the spotlight. Unacceptable practices should be internally reprimanded swiftly, and responsible practices should be more frequently recognized externally at all levels.

The presentation of well-researched contexts for the fleeting headlines, the follow-up stories, and the inclusionary dialogue with the media audiences to determine what issues they believe need exploring are all areas that deserve acknowledgment and *recognition* from some credible, independent oversight body. Appropriate commendation should be given as well to managements who develop imaginative means of enlarging minority participation and upward mobility within their own staffs. A "seal of approval" could become bankable.

If there is a starting place for such reinforcement, it might well be a compendium of the enduring literature (i.e., the Hutchins report) that has explored and celebrated responsible reporting of news and public affairs. A second step could be the formation of an organization that can identify achievements, recommend recipients, and make timely awards to a more varied spectrum of newspeople regionally and locally. The advisory board of such a body ought to be composed largely of journalists, active or retired, but need not exclude business executives, scholars, and public officials. A national network of media "nominators" within their own towns and regions could be developed to watch for notable work in print and on radio and television and the Internet. Traditional awards and prizes inevitably become politicized. A wider net ought to be cast.

Over time, the capacity of the good to drive out the bad in the news business will be enhanced dramatically by technical accessibility to information, but a *commitment* to responsible reporting by major mass communications companies has to be seen by their managers as enlightened self-interest. Sleaze will not sell to an educated market; reliable, accurate, fair journalism will so long as dissent is heard. Accentuating and amplifying the best journalism at all levels is a cause that should enlist the support of those who care about the First Amendment.

William Hocking, a member of the Hutchins Commission on a Free Press, believed that self-judgment of the press would benefit from the work of a society or a school in which professional standards are determined. "If there were a specialized social organ," Hocking suggested, "for collating and *announcing* the upshot of such experience, enjoying the respect both of the press and of the public, the psychological effectiveness of standards would be greatly increased; at the same time the nature of the standards themselves would become clearer, and the line between the *achievable* and the *impossible* more evident" (emphasis added).[10]

Hocking's objectives *and* their limitations have not lost meaning. If the owners and managers of large multi-interest media companies perceive an advantage in operating their news divisions as indispensable to political freedom and the common good, the sardonic judgment that virtue is an insufficient temptation might be less persuasive. The high quality of the people who are drawn to journalism has always been more conspicuous among those newspapers, magazines, and broadcasting operations where a reputation for integrity has been achieved, however painstakingly. But such reputations take time and resolve that have become, under the lash of quarterly results, more elusive. When management wants to satisfy the stock analyst, short-term considerations dominate.

Reputation is a long-term thing. Encouraging management to stay in the game and to worship at a "higher altar" in the turbulent era of new technologies requires a new pragmatism as well. A profit-making business dealing in services that purport to truthfully inform the electorate must be held accountable. If the people seek assurance that their public servants and their corporate masters are not deceiving them or plundering their natural resources or bowing to special interests, they should seek that assurance from the purveyors of news and political debate. The plethora of computer systems will not replace responsible, talented journalists as guides, interpreters, and the voices of conscience.

The wishes of the greatest number are what the democratic political process presumably determines. Those wishes do not always constitute the truth, much less wisdom, and they can on occasion produce a tyranny of the majority over the few. It is essential that the press be vigilant about such tyranny and that it ensure diversity of opinion. The electorate may think it is aware of the sins of *commission*, but without dissenting voices it will not learn of the sins of *omission*. When and if speech or press are regulated by government, Alexander Bickel urged that the public be assured that "the judgment that speech should be suppressed is made by the full, pluralist, open political process, not by someone down the line, representing only one or another particular segment of the society; an assurance that the judgment has been made closely and deliberately, with awareness of the consequences and with clear focus on the sort of speech the legislature wished to suppress."[11]

The Meaning of Autonomy

In a 1993 speech to the Radio and Television News Directors Association, veteran newsman Ed Bliss looked back over his long career and stated unabashedly, "Respect and credibility are your greatest assets. And, finally, that in the midst of all the hullabaloo—the problems related to ratings, personnel and budget—that in the midst of all that, you have a professional soul. That you cannot escape how you are regarded by yourself."

It has been said that there is no generally perceived reality with which we can define "truth" in our justice system. Surely the same must be said of journalism. The news media has to create its own reality and set standards for that creation, and it must then be accountable for the product it delivers to the public. The reporter's ego—at every level and in every medium—may produce lyricism, evocative imagery, trenchancy and wit, but it may also, *inadvertently*, create the perceptions that are opposite to what the reporter sees as truth, perceptions that are tangential, unrelated impressions in the reader's mind stimulated by literary distractions that detached, careful reporting cannot accommodate. The reporter may not be a phantom, but first-rate reporting should make the event more important than the writer. It requires tact, training, and rigorous circumspection to achieve something close to truth-telling. Such heights are rarely reached, but ethical passivity and self-serving ambition among practitioners of journalism have made the slope more slippery. Telling the truth without concern for business reaction, telling all the pertinent truth available without shading to please some special interest, and doing it with fairness and accuracy are a tall order. The value is in the persistent attempt to achieve it. Consider Oscar Wilde's warning: "Truth is seldom pure and never simple."

The press itself is no substitute for the institutions a society depends upon—its schools, its judicial system, its arts and leisures, its industry, and what has been called the inns and resting places of the human spirit where reason and faith come together. The press can put a light on events affecting these institutions, illuminating now and then that which is hidden and ought not to be. But as Lippmann cautioned, human beings "cannot do the work of the world by this light alone. They cannot govern society by episodes, incidents and eruptions. It is only when they work by a steady light of their own, that the press, when it is turned upon them, reveals a situation intelligible enough for a popular decision."[12]

The light becomes incandescent when its power flows from principles thoughtfully and carefully defined, tested, and then held fast. Over the making and keeping of those principles, the free press can and must always be its own sentinel. If more Americans, ethnically hyphenated or not, are to be persuaded to participate in civic life and to learn the rules of civility in public debate, many institutions must collaborate—families, schools, and religious congregations at the center. But without a diverse, free, *and* responsible press, democracy may well be chained while its back is turned.

2

THE PRESS AND THE LAW

Here arises the necessity for the freedom of the Press, which is the happiest Organ of communication ever yet devised, the quickest & surest means of conveying intelligence to the human Mind.

—Richard Henry Lee to Edmund Pendleton,
Virginia, May 26, 1788

The core issues surrounding freedom of the press in the United States have remained essentially the same for more than two centuries. Now, as cyberspace becomes the newest form of distribution for information of all kinds—public and private—the questions asked by the Founders resonate even more urgently. Some cyberspace analysts suggest that the process should begin with a "magna carta" for the electronic community.

Can the press and other media be free if they are owned by partisan proprietors, influenced by advertisers, and generally devoted to profit? Can they be free if they are regulated in any significant manner by the government beyond obedience to the existing laws of the land? Can the people count on the press to tell the truth about public matters so that the democratic process will be based on reliable and accurate information?

To cope with the technological complexities of the modern media—and the dramatic growth of electronic information systems anticipated in the coming years—those who wish to protect and preserve freedom of expression in American life should look carefully at the seeds of a free press that were planted in colonial America and flowered thereafter as part of nation building.

The first step is to consider the historical record, which includes constitutional law. Such an account provides the foundation for understanding all that followed the Declaration of Independence, politically and economically, in that area of American free enterprise that has come to be called the media. As media forms diversify and proliferate, constructive discussion is needed on levels of competence, standards, ethics, and self-regulation if we are to understand prescriptions for the survival of an independent, free press. What needs the most intensive examination is the defining of *responsible* journalism.

The anomaly that inevitably enters into any concerned affection for or suspicious hostility toward the news media also remains largely the same as it did when the Bill of Rights was composed: There does not appear to be any way of enforceably diminishing excess and sensationalism without destroying the vitality, the courage, and the dedication of the sentinel over all our other liberties. The only alternative to private enterprise is government. The two may conflict, but if one achieves control over the other, the fundamental dialogue of a democracy withers.

If nonlegislative measures are to be identified as standards for a free and responsible press, the work is currently incomplete, if not disregarded. Skepticism and resistance are common when reformers eye the press, but that prerogative is at the heart of good citizenship. Despite vast demographic and social change in the next century, news and public information will remain central to democratic political life. At stake are the interests of the larger society—*of the People*, as the Founders envisioned us, and themselves.

The year 1991 will be regarded by historians as remarkable for a great many reasons. Russian communism—at least in its sinister, nuclear power form—abruptly halted its threatening global role. The superpower status of the USSR diminished rapidly as republics, once locked into communism, demanded and achieved independence. The Berlin Wall had been breached physically and politically, and a united Germany was the challenging result. All over Eastern Europe, nations once occupied by Russian troops asserted their rights to self-government. Then, in reaction to Iraq's invasion of Kuwait, the United Nations moved toward a more collaborative effort at peacekeeping, in itself an affirmation of earlier promises that might radically change global security and the burgeoning creation of mass-destruction weaponry.

Meanwhile, with increasing intensity during 1991, environmentalists aroused international concern for the planet's ecosystems and its natural resources. At the same time, organized industry opposed government regulations and excessive environmental zeal. Thus conservationists were pitted against entrepreneurs.

In the face of such cosmic developments, December 15, 1991, did not receive a great deal of attention as a benchmark in American history. For those who noticed, it was recalled—and here and there celebrated—that 200 years earlier, on December 15, 1791, the first ten amendments to the American Constitution were ratified. These carefully wrought political restraints had been composed chiefly by James Madison, a representative from Virginia who later became the fourth president of the United States. The amendments he adapted from more than 200 proposals were known as the Bill of Rights. The first eight amendments dealt, in one way or another, with individual citizen rights. The ninth stipulated that the *enumerated* rights in no way denied any others "retained by the people." And the tenth added that powers not given to the federal government would be reserved "to the States respectively, or to the people." Historian Forrest McDonald has observed sardonically that the Ninth Amendment sought to guarantee that the first eight would not be dangerous; and the tenth declared them to be unnecessary.[1]

Despite Madison's exhortations, the Bill of Rights was not given primacy over laws enacted by state legislatures. The amendments applied only to the federal government—Congress shall not . . . . This limitation was a grave disappointment for Madison, who had not really believed in the need for enumerated rights in the first place because it was his view that the citizens constitutionally possessed all rights not explicitly given to the federal government *and* the right to vote that government out of office. Many prominent colleagues including George Washington, Alexander Hamilton, Roger Sherman, and James Wilson shared Madison's skepticism. This position, however, had cost Madison an appointment as one of Virginia's two senators (senators were not required to be elected by the people until 1914, when the Seventeenth Amendment so mandated), and he had to campaign against much anti-Federalist maneuvering for a congressional seat. The anti-Federalists, who were seeking a second constitutional convention with the hope of changing the document so as to dilute federal powers, used the absence of a bill of rights as a political weapon. Without it, they argued (some of them disingenuously), the national government would be able to deny individual citizens their fundamental liberties.

Madison corresponded with Thomas Jefferson on this issue. Jefferson was then representing the United States as minister to France. He strongly advised Madison on the importance of creating a bill of rights to give the people confidence and quiet the critics of the Constitution. He further surmised that such a bill would provide the judiciary an essential "legal check," assuming the judiciary would be independent of the Congress and the executive.[2] Madison, therefore, as a political expedient, had promised his constituents that if elected, he would propose a bill of rights before the convening of the first Congress. He also suggested that the protections provided should not only restrain the *federal* government but also protect the people from their *state* governments. Though each state had its own constitution, each varied in many ways from the others. Madison believed the state legislators, often willing prisoners of very narrow interests, were a greater threat to individual rights than was Congress. When he was elected to Congress, he promptly went about the business of drafting proposals for a bill of rights. Among them he included, "No *State* shall violate the equal rights of conscience, or the *freedom of the press*, or trial by jury in criminal cases." This proposal put pressure on the anti-Federalists to get their state constitutions in line with the federal Bill of Rights.

In 1775 there were thirty-seven newspapers spread among the colonies, many of them opinionated and vituperative. Tom Paine's pamphlet *Common Sense,* which called for a complete separation from England, sold an astonishing 125,000 copies—reaching nearly everyone in the colonies who could read at the time—an estimated 60 percent of the white "citizens." Paine and others of like mind understood that the English concept of liberty was hierarchical—individual rights varied according to class, property, even location.[3] Certain English towns, for instance, were given special charters of liberties because of some past relationship to the Crown. A mere change in residence might secure greater freedom. American rights envisioned as early as 1620 in the Mayflower Compact and in the Pilgrim Code of Law in 1636 grew out of a consciousness of forming a new community with common values and common goals. The religious and philosophical traditions that had dominated the lives of most colonists led them to think first of the community and then of the individual, but the Founders wanted all branches of government to be limited by shared, permanent human rights that were "natural, inherent and unalienable." The necessary two-thirds majority of the House voted in favor of the Bill of Rights in 1791 as presented by James Madison. The Senate, however, for reasons that were never fully explained, did not provide a two-thirds majority. It was finally determined among the senators that the amendments were to be a restraint specifically on the *federal* government. Since the Senate discussions were secret, we do not know how they voted or why. Their decision, nonetheless, made it possible that the rights described in the amendments could be denied to some citizens. These denials, as Madison had feared, were inflicted on individual citizens by state and local governments. But even if the Bill of Rights had been given power over state laws in 1791, women, American Indians, and white men who did not own any property would still not have been allowed to vote and would not have had the full protection of the "highest law of the land," accorded to bona fide "citizens."

It took a long and bloody civil war seventy years later to bring into view new possibilities of extending the reach of the Bill of Rights to everyone. The Thirteenth Amendment was enacted in 1865, ending slavery forever in any part of the United States. The Fourteenth Amendment was added in 1868. It directed that "no State shall make or enforce any law" that denies citizens the "privileges or immunities" of the United States, including "life, liberty, or property" without due process, and it promised to all citizens equal protection under the laws of the nation. Though these provisions appeared to give the Bill of Rights authority over state laws, as Madison had proposed in 1791, the Supreme Court found reasons for ruling otherwise. It interpreted "privileges and immunities" as qualities of national citizenship (such as the right to travel across state borders) and not the same as those individual liberties cited in the Bill of Rights.

It was not until the 1960s that the Bill of Rights was actually declared applicable to all Americans in every state. Women had finally achieved the right to vote in 1920 with the Nineteenth Amendment. American Indians did not secure citizenship until 1924. But the "fundamental rights" that were to engage the people of America and the courts most passionately in the twentieth century were embodied in the First Amendment. It assured freedom of religion, speech, press, peaceable assembly, and petition. The prohibition of any law abridging these rights had been considered technically, for most of the new nation's history, as a restraint on Congress only.

The Press Before the Highest Court

In 1931, after hearing the Supreme Court case *Near v. Minnesota*, Chief Justice Charles Evans Hughes wrote:

> The administration of government has become more complex, the opportunities for malfeasance and corruption have multiplied, crime has grown to most serious proportions, and the danger of its protection by unfaithful officials and of the impairment of the fundamental security of life and property by criminal alliances and official neglect, emphasize the need of a vigilant and courageous press especially in the cities. The fact that liberty of the press may be abused by miscreant purveyors of scandal does not make any less necessary the immunity of the press from prior restraint in dealing with official misconduct.[4]

Near v. Minnesota involved a Minnesota law enacted in 1925 to silence a sleazy Duluth newspaper that had criticized public officials for their alleged connections with criminal activity. The statute was invoked again to suppress a Minneapolis publication known for its stridency and bias, the *Saturday Press*. Not without reason, the *Saturday Press* had also accused local politicians of helping underworld figures. The gangsters struck back, killing one of the paper's publishers. Governor Floyd B. Olson moved to close the paper down, and the Minnesota Supreme Court upheld the "gag law," an action that caused the improbable alliance of the American Civil Liberties Union and the notably conservative proprietor of the *Chicago Tribune*, Colonel Robert R. McCormick. The *Tribune*'s lawyers took the case to the U.S. Supreme Court and argued that the First Amendment right of the press to inform the public regarding the activities of elected officials should apply to any state laws that imposed prior restraint. The highest court in the land agreed, and publisher McCormick had some of Chief Justice Hughes's empowering words (previously quoted) carved into the marble facade of the *Chicago Tribune* building.

The Constitution as a living document now had a clearly expressed opinion that enlarged the Framers' concept of a free press from a statutory phrase to a defining principle—the public's right to know. How much and when the watchdog should bark remained questions that would be asked many times thereafter. Not all the answers could be given the lapidary reception of Justice Hughes's pronouncement, but several Supreme Court decisions crucial to the free press were made in the second half of the century. In a 1964 decision, *New York Times v. Sullivan* (see Chapter 3), the Supreme Court reversed a judgment of the Alabama Supreme Court. Justice William Brennan wrote: "We hold the rule of law applied by the Alabama courts is constitutionally deficient for failure to provide freedoms of speech and of the press that are required by the First and Fourteenth Amendments in a libel action brought by a public official against critics of his official conduct."[5] Thus the possibility of any state law eluding the provisions of the federal Bill of Rights suffered a clarifying setback. The process has not ended, however. The law is what the Court says it is, and the Court can change its mind.

The constitutional scholar Zechariah Chafee observed that the First Amendment "protects two kinds of interest in speech . . . individual interest, the need of many men to express their opinions on matters vital to them if life is to be worth living . . . [and] a social interest in the attainment of truth, so that the country may not only adopt the wisest course of action but carry it out in the wisest way."[6] University president and philosopher Alexander Meiklejohn added: "In that method of self government, the point of ultimate interest is not the words of the speakers but the minds of the hearers. . . . What is essential is not that everyone shall speak, but that everything worth saying shall be said."[7]

For America's free (and sometimes responsible) press the issue has become more complicated with each new generation. What is worth hearing, or reading? Who decides? In theory, of course, the people decide. The American experience of colonial repression created a revolution and the design for a new form of government. In Europe freedom was parceled out and controlled by a sovereign authority, a monarch. The American Founders made *the people* sovereign—"We, the People of the United States, in Order to form a more perfect Union . . . "—and the people granted certain authority to the government they chose. It had never been thus in the history of humankind. At the same time the rights of individual citizens were given unique importance. This provided what Meiklejohn called "that curious quality of paradox by which all interpretations of self-government are affected."[8]

When does individual expression—that autonomy which characterizes the American way of life—threaten the "social compact," the common interests of all Americans, and the obligations we have to each other? The

press stands (often shivering in fear of losing advertising revenue or suffering expensive libel suits) at the center of this paradox. In practice the free
press gives sovereign citizens a voice. In theory the free press also reveals
the misuse of power at the governing level so that the *governed* may correct
or restrain or change the governors in an orderly, peaceful manner. In 1788,
before the ratification of the Constitution, James Madison, Alexander
Hamilton (who became the first secretary of the treasury), and John Jay
(who became the first chief justice), wrote a series of essays about the vital
need for a federal government in America. These essays were first published
in newspapers—many of which had existed long before independence—
under the pseudonym *Publius* (Publius Valerius had established a republican government in Rome after the overthrow of Tarquin). Later the essays
became a compendium in book form known as *The Federalist*. The responsibility of the press, the Federalists seemed to believe, included the obligation to remind, over and over again, "We, the People" of our collective
duty to govern ourselves wisely or risk the loss of the very freedom we aspired to initiate with our Constitution.

The Modern Predicament

Without a recognition of common interests and shared values, "We, the
People" cannot communicate with each other, cannot make intelligent political judgments, and surely cannot understand the "just powers" of the
government we have established. It is clear that the values of American society are no longer shaped by a New England consciousness inherited from
Great Britain. Contemporary values are more likely to be influenced by the
ethnic, religious, or social groups to which American citizens belong than
by the national community in which all share. The increasing diversity of
American society at the national level has triggered an emphasis on special
interests at the local level. That development has often produced apostles of
hate and envy who attack whole groups indiscriminately. Social fragmentation works against the common traditions on which the nation was built—
a society nourished by individual freedoms that attracted immigrants from
all over the world. It will be the most crucial challenge to the serious
media—"the responsible press"—in the third century of the Bill of Rights
to report the issues, illuminate the ideas, and give voice to disparate views.
Rapid change and social metamorphosis threaten the respect for the core,
those ethical principles to which every American may turn for hope and
confidence, and above all threaten the knowledge, if not the wisdom, with
which to find common purpose. In the words of Judge Learned Hand, "The
spirit of liberty is the spirit which is not too sure that it is right. . . . The
spirit of liberty is the spirit which seeks to understand the minds of other
men and women."[9]

It has been said that since the founding of the United States popular consent and vigilance are the essential protections for American citizen rights. John Adams, when he was second president of the United States, bluntly acknowledged that "the free press is sacred . . . the only means of informing people of their rights and giving them common principles on which to act."[10] The question in the next century must be how to define and support common principles in a society composed of diverse ethnic and racial groups—each citizen with an agenda and each part of a minority. In that effort, the free press—if it deserves the continuing protection of the First Amendment—must take heed.

The Price of Public Esteem

There is much conflict in the attitudes of "ordinary" people toward the media. Since the 1950s public opinion surveys made by reputable organizations have consistently found a very low regard for "the press" (described as newspapers and magazines) and "the media" (described as print *and* electronic reporting). The National Opinion Research Center of the University of Chicago has asked diverse groups of Americans each year since 1951 how they feel about their institutions—such as medicine, the military, education, Congress, trade unions—along with the press and television.

Americans are not awestruck by *any* of their institutions. Few achieve positive ratings of even 50 percent when the question is asked in the form of "Do you have a great deal of confidence in . . . ?" That question is admittedly general, perhaps loaded. The replies reveal, for instance, that Americans have little confidence in Congress as a whole but may have a high regard for their own representatives because of some local project or a personal favor or because they know him or her and like his or her style. In that kind of context we may say we do not trust "the press," but we may look upon our own local paper with considerable approval because it led the way in keeping municipal taxes in line or reported on the high school soccer team for which one of our children plays.

The press—and by extension television news—has never been given much public affection. The confluence of events in the 1990s, however, which took place so swiftly in Eastern Europe, Berlin, the USSR, and in the Middle East, produced a high standard of journalism in American newspapers and news magazines. As for television news, CNN has been almost Orwellian in its ubiquitous "real-time coverage." But CNN and the major networks, faced with military restraints on the press during the conflict with Iraq, took a page out of Walter Lippmann's *Public Opinion* (1921) by seeking help from experts rather than trying to collect fleeting, kaleidoscopic information entirely on their own. Military figures, academics, and think-tankers contributed much to public understanding by appearing on network evening news and talk shows—and on CNN. The *New York Times* sent more than thirty reporters to the emerging nations in Eastern Europe after the Soviets announced their planned withdrawal. The *Washington Post* and the *Los Angeles Times* were not far behind. The media—print and electronic—unexpectedly became players in the political transformation that would affect international relations and global economic and environmental concerns more dramatically than the most experienced observers had believed possible.

The "media as player" works in mysterious ways. The extended technological reach of information distribution involved FAX machines, VCR cassettes, desktop publications, and radio—unjammed after forty years of Communist resistance. For better or worse, world leaders of every stripe were beginning to perceive that a society could not survive—let alone flourish—without access to information of all kinds and that such information was no less immune to political borders than the weather, the fallout from Chernobyl, or holes in the ozone layer.

How much Václav Havel depended on videocassettes in Czechoslovakia's "velvet revolution," how much of the psychic upheaval in East Germany had drawn its yearning from West German television programs, and how many samizdats circulated in Russia before Mikhail Gorbachev declared perestroika and glasnost will be revealed gradually in the years ahead by reflective journalistic accounts and the biographies of major leaders. The most important revelation, however, is that massive change took place precipitously and the media was a powerful influence in that process.

Watching the Watchdog

The power of the press has been examined and analyzed since the seventeenth century. The printing press in its crudest form was introduced in 1440, but two centuries passed before printed matter could be turned out quickly enough to reach a body politic whose literacy was by then sufficiently widespread for opinions to be formed and responses organized. John Milton's essay *Areopagitica*, which addressed the subject of "prior restraint," was printed and distributed in 1644. (Areopagus is the hill outside Athens where the Greek tribunals met to pronounce their judgments.) It was the most eloquent attack of its time on censorship. Despite Milton's belief that truth would triumph through free expression in the marketplace—in the form of either speech or the printed word—he wanted to limit that marketplace to members of the Church of England. Nonetheless, his concept of a free press struck chords among thoughtful men everywhere the pamphlet was read. Milton may not have envisioned a tribunal of public opinion responding to a free press, but his contempt for "prior restraint" on commentary concerning public affairs was a meaningful contribution to the ideas that shaped the early American experience, and it found both enlargement and voice in the formulation of the Constitution and the Bill of Rights.

Scholars who have documented the development of the press in the United States usually identify the post–Civil War period as the beginning of national power for American newspapers. The urban population began to grow rapidly in those years. Diversity of background and accumulated wealth in the cities provided competition and entrepreneurial zest. City services—transportation, schools, police, firefighters—were needed as the numbers swelled. All the elements of popular news were available—violence, politics, culture, capitalism, crime, and despair. The audience for newspapers and magazines, even books, was in place and proliferating. Soon the "new journalism"—no longer dominated by political loyalties— took hold with "human interest" stories, on-the-scene reporting, dramatic escapades, and "exclusive" interviews. News was business, and advertising made it profitable. By 1885 there were five daily newspapers in New York City with circulations well over 100,000. By the turn of the century, several big-city newspapers built circulations of over half a million. In that economic climate the mission of informing the electorate on public issues (local and national) with accuracy and fairness so that the "sovereign citizens" could make wise decisions was easily distorted, if not abandoned.

The importance of reliable information for those who participate in the democratic political process means that *access* to information is as vital as the First Amendment right to *speak* or *write* it. Expression would be misleading or fanciful without the facts. It is on this principle that the ethical responsibilities of the modern media rise or fall. To understand how the role of the press may be determined in the years ahead—as one millennium ends and another begins—we can learn a great deal from the development of freedom *and* responsibility in the early American press before independence and during the period when the Founders were creating a constitution.

Franklin and Washington were the most renowned of the delegates to the Constitutional Convention. Franklin had spent twenty-five of the previous thirty years in Europe as an envoy and advocate. He had argued vigorously on behalf of Americans and their capacity to govern themselves. When he returned to Philadelphia he was entering his eighties and was suffering from gout. He could not sit comfortably in a horse-drawn carriage and had to be carried about in a sedan chair like an Oriental potentate—a description that would have displeased him. As Carl Van Doren put it, "For nearly sixty years he had devoted much of his time to drawing men together and negotiating difficult agreements."[11] He had organized many American cultural and political groups. The Albany Congress had adopted his Plan of Union in 1754. He had helped draft the Articles of Confederation, the Declaration of Independence, the treaty of alliance with France, and ultimately the treaty of peace and independence with Great Britain. He had also owned and edited a newspaper and developed strong views on the ethics of journalism.

During the Constitutional Convention a visiting clergyman from Massachusetts named Manasseh Cutler stopped by for tea at Franklin's home. He thought it certain that Franklin had the largest and best private library in America. He found the elderly philosopher-diplomat more interested in general learning than politics and observed: "He has an incessant vein of humor, accompanied with an uncommon vivacity, which seems as natural and involuntary as his breathing."[12] Shortly after the convention ended in Philadelphia, Benjamin Franklin was asked what kind of government would emerge. "We have given you a Republic," he replied wryly, "if you can keep it."[13] To keep it, the American people then required a free (though intensely partisan) press, just as they now require a free (though intensely competitive) media.

3

MALICE WITHOUT WIT

And people say, "Why are you poking your nose into somebody else's business?" My response is, "It's not somebody else's business. It's *your* business we're poking into, Aren't you interested in our finding out for you what's going on?"

—Arthur Sulzberger Sr., former publisher
and chairman of the board, *New York Times*

The 1964 Supreme Court Case *New York Times v. Sullivan* is a tale often told wherever journalism is taught, criticized, adjudicated, or reexamined in the context of the First Amendment. The simple language that prohibited Congress from making any law abridging the "freedom . . . of the press" had become the head of a pin on which numberless angels danced. The plasticity of the American Constitution may have been part of James Madison's vision, but the translation of "majestic generalities" into twentieth-century principles was given one of its most sweeping interpretations by Justice Brennan when he led the Court to a decision that institutionalized "uninhibited, robust and wide open" debate on public issues. The Court's watershed judgment overruling the Alabama Supreme Court decision— which had found the *New York Times* guilty of libel and placed a price tag of $500,000 on that alleged transgression—finally ensured the demise of the 1798 Sedition Act. "The attack upon its validity has," Justice Brennan wrote, "carried the day in the court of history."[1] It also set the compass for the turbulent future of free speech and press in America.

Remarkably enough, the issues were wrested not out of reportage but out of a full-page paid advertisement that had run in the *New York Times* on March 29, 1960. The ad was primarily an appeal for funds to pay the legal fees necessary to defend Martin Luther King Jr., support embattled black students in Alabama, and underwrite the "struggle for the right to vote." Civil rights demonstrators, said the ad, had been met "by an unprecedented wave of terror by those who would deny and negate that document which the whole world looks upon as setting the pattern of modern freedom."[2]

The text of the ad referred to events in South Carolina and other locations in the South, but the focus was on Montgomery, Alabama, and the attempts to "destroy the one man who, more than any other, symbolizes the new spirit now sweeping the South—the Rev. Dr. Martin Luther King, Jr." Despite the Civil War, emancipation, and the Thirteenth, Fourteenth, and Fifteenth Amendments, African Americans living in the South were denied basic constitutional rights with such stubborn regularity that many of them grew up, even in the middle of the twentieth century, without a hope of citizenship in any meaningful sense and with so many fastidiously sustained humiliations in regard to their schooling and job opportunities that repression seemed perpetual.

New York Times reporter Harrison Salisbury had gone to Alabama in the early 1960s to write a series of articles on the plight of black citizens. On April 12, two weeks after the controversial advertisement had appeared, a Salisbury piece headed "Fear and Hatred Grip Birmingham" was published on the front page of the *Times*:

> Whites and blacks still walk the same streets. But the streets, the water supply, and the sewage system are about the only facilities they share. Ballparks and taxicabs are segregated. So are libraries. A book featuring black and white rabbits was banned. A drive is on to forbid "negro music" on "white radio stations." Every channel of communication, every medium of mutual interest, every reasoned approach, every inch of middle ground has been fragmented by the emotional dynamite of racism, reinforced by the whip, the razor, the gun, the bomb, the torch, the club, the knife, the mob, the police, and many branches of the State's apparatus.[3]

Oliver Wendell Holmes had written of another case nearly a half-century earlier: "The case before us must be considered in the light of our whole experience and not merely in that of what was said a hundred years ago. ... We must consider *what the country has become* in deciding what the Constitution means" (emphasis added).[4] What the country had become in the land of Bull Connor, the Montgomery police chief, and his kind throughout the South was metaphorically a potbellied, rednecked kingdom of bigotry and intimidation against which so few voices were raised that the deep slumber of a decent conscience in the South became permanent. It was, indeed, the words "heed their rising voices" that set events in motion. A month before the ad appeared, the *New York Times*, after reporting on lunch-counter sit-ins in North Carolina, published an editorial recognizing "the growing movement of peaceful mass demonstrations by Negroes" and urging Congress to "heed their rising voices." Bayard Rustin and Harry

Belafonte decided to use that evocative phrase as the headline for a fund-raising campaign "to assist with Martin Luther King, Jr.'s rising legal fees."[5]

Alabama was, at the time, busily working every angle to keep the NAACP out of the state. Part of that effort involved characterizing King as a tax evader who had lied to the government. His financial records were and had long been in disarray, though he had not been accused of any criminal neglect; nor was there reason to suspect anything worse than inattention to record keeping. Accountants and lawyers, however, were exacting large fees in the process of straightening out his church finances. Because of this drain on King's resources, the fund-raising ad was placed in the *Times*. The page rate was $4,800, but the ad brought in many times that amount. The solicitation was signed by sixty-four prominent citizens and endorsed by twenty ministers, including four black churchmen from Alabama whose names were used without their knowledge or permission—though Bayard Rustin's assumption that the four would have agreed had there been time to contact them was reasonable. Nonetheless, the Alabama ministers, who would become widely known in the years that followed, were separately sued for libel simply because their names appeared in the ad. They were Ralph D. Abernathy, S. S. Seay Sr., Fred L. Shuttlesworth, and J. E. Lowery.[6]

The *Times* was sued by the police commissioner of Montgomery, L. B. Sullivan, who claimed that the ad published by the newspaper was defamatory. He also sued the four Alabama clergymen as "sponsors" and "publishers" of the ad. Two paragraphs of the ten that composed the text were the basis for the suits. The Alabama law of defamation was not unlike similar laws in most other states. Sullivan was not mentioned in the ad by name or office. He maintained that his administrative role was widely known, and therefore any reference to improper police behavior damaged his reputation. The Alabama law permitted criticism of public officials as "fair comment" provided the material used was based only on facts "established as true." Because several of the police actions described in the text were not entirely accurate, the Alabama prosecutor didn't even put the defamation issue to the jury. If the defendants could not establish the truth of *all* the facts in the ad, the general impression of defamation was not important. The jury could find the ad libelous automatically because of inaccuracies.[7]

The *New York Times* was guilty of defamation because it published a paid advertisement alleging police "brutality" and "harassment" of black people—and Martin Luther King in particular—using a series of descriptions that included some facts that were *not* entirely true. The fact that the *Times* and the four black ministers were unaware of the errors was not a defense under Alabama law. Defamation was virtually pro forma, but *punitive damages* required some proof of malice and/or the technicality that a retraction had been requested of the defendant and then refused. Sullivan had, indeed, demanded a retraction, and the *Times* had, indeed, quite understandably, refused. In the eventual U.S. Supreme Court hearing that refusal was considered to be a possible demonstration of malice.

One point made by the Alabama court was the judgment that the *New York Times* was "sufficiently engaged in business" within Alabama to subject it to state jurisdiction. The finding was based on the fact that of roughly 650,000 copies of the *Times* in which the ad appeared, 394 copies were distributed (not necessarily purchased or read) in Alabama, 35 of them in Montgomery County, the location of Sullivan's activity and the place where alleged harm to his reputation had been caused by the newspaper despite the fact that his name and position were not mentioned. It boggled the minds of most people who read about the case in 1964 how 35 copies of a newspaper could damage any reputation and, more puzzling, how any connection could be made between the descriptions of "police brutality" in various locations and the actions of one unidentified county commissioner.

Sullivan, as the nominal top cop in the county, maintained he was, "by inference," accused of

1. Ringing the campus of Alabama State College with police.
2. Arresting Dr. King for spurious offenses.
3. Padlocking the dining room to starve the students.
4. Bombing King's home.
5. Assaulting King.
6. Charging King with perjury.

The actual text of the two paragraphs cited by Sullivan as containing false charges is as follows:

In Montgomery, Alabama, after students sang "My Country 'Tis of Thee" on the State Capitol steps, their leaders were expelled from the school and truckloads of police arrived with shotguns and tear-gas and ringed the Alabama State College Campus. When the entire student body protested to state authorities by refusing to re-register, their dining hall was padlocked in an attempt to starve them into submission. . . .

Again and again the Southern violators have answered Dr. King's peaceful protest with intimidation and violence. *They* have bombed his home, almost killing his wife and child. *They* have assaulted his person. *They* have arrested him seven times—for "speeding," "loitering," and similar "offenses." And now *they* have charged him with "perjury"—a felony under which *they* could imprison him for ten years. (emphasis added)[8]

The "they" in the paragraph above is Sullivan—according to Sullivan. Law professor Harry Kalven, who wrote one of the most highly regarded scholarly essays on the case, comments: "There are statements invisibly published in plaintiff's community which refer to him only by a strained construction of their language and which, given the mood of the day, would not likely be considered defamatory by a Southern audience. It is this marginal harm that the jury added up to $500,000 damages."[9]

There were layers of irony in Sullivan's strategy. To prove that some of the charges were untrue, Sullivan's lawyers had to back away from earlier claims that the advertisement's references to police brutality were really aimed at Sullivan. Professor Kalven observes that Sullivan argued that the arrests of Dr. King took place before he, Sullivan, became commissioner, and as commissioner, he had nothing to do with indicting King for perjury. Backward whirled the wheels as Sullivan insisted that statements referring to an imprecise "they" actually referred to him, but then it couldn't be he because the statements falsely ascribed to him things he didn't do. Kalven is bemused by all this but notes that the U.S. Supreme Court did not try to pedal backward with the commissioner. What the Court *did* confront was the allegation of false charges. The inaccuracies attributed to the two paragraphs were as follows:

1. The dining hall was not *padlocked.*
2. The students did not *refuse* to reregister.
3. Not *all* students protested.
4. Student leaders were not *expelled.*
5. The police never *"ringed"* the campus.
6. The police came to the campus three times, in substantial numbers, but *not* because of the protest.
7. Martin Luther King Jr. was not arrested *seven* times. He was arrested *four* times.
8. The charge of assault was based on a "controverted instance of some years before."

One further error was the failure to notice that the students sang the national anthem, not "My Country 'Tis of Thee." There was, in fact, partial or substantial truth in all the allegations. Not *all* the students protested; most did. Dr. King *was* arrested. Four times can focus the mind as effectively as seven. Nevertheless, in terms of existing law, the falsity charges were not without weight. That Alabama saw an opportunity to severely punish one of those irritating, northern, liberal news organizations seemed obvious. In Anthony Lewis's comprehensive book on the Sullivan case, *Make No Law*, the intent of Sullivan and his lawyers is carefully documented. Their target was the American press "as an agent of democratic change."[10]

Lewis examines the role of national newspapers, magazines, and broadcasters in arousing public opinion against southern racism. Despite the school segregation decision in 1954, there were, in 1960, no blacks attending public schools or colleges with white students in Alabama, Mississippi, Georgia, Louisiana, or South Carolina. Less than 15 percent of blacks eligible to vote had been allowed to register in those same states. "Freedom Riders" protesting illegal segregation at bus and train stations in the South were roughed up by mobs. Salisbury's stories on these and other events stimulated further libel suits—$3,150,000 in damage claims against the *Times* and $1.5 million against Salisbury himself. This was just the beginning. Libel suits were being prepared against CBS and other media companies in an outpouring of anger and defensiveness calculated to silence the "outside" press by financial harassment. Lawyers and politicians in the South believed they had vast public support for any attack on the outsiders who dared to read the Constitution and the First Amendment as a rejection of any restraint on the criticism of public officials. Kalven and his colleague Meiklejohn were in full agreement that, to use Kalven's words, "political freedom ends when a government can use its powers and its courts to silence its critics. . . . The presence or absence in the law of the concept of seditious libel defines the society."[11]

By the middle of 1964, there were close to $300 million in libel actions against the press brought by southern officials. It was white supremacy arrayed against black civil rights. The justices of the Supreme Court would have to look at history, at the American experience, along with legal precedents. If southern justice, based on seditious libel, was allowed to stand, the press would either retreat or be crushed by fines and fees few could afford. School desegregation, decreed by *Brown v. Board of Education* in 1954, had been evaded, resisted, manipulated, and delayed with all kinds of charades and maneuvers. Alex Bickel, the Yale law professor who would represent the *Times* in the 1971 *Pentagon Papers* case, wrote an article in 1962 about schools in New Orleans, Little Rock, and elsewhere in the South. He noted that

> compulsory segregation, like States' Rights and like 'the Southern Way of Life' is an abstraction and, to a good many people, a neutral or sympathetic one. These riots, which were brought instantly, dramatically, and literally home to the American people, showed what it means concretely. Here were grown men and women furiously confronting their enemy: two, three, a half-dozen scrubbed, starched, scared and incredibly brave colored children. The moral bankruptcy, the shame of the thing, was evident.[12]

The same moral bankruptcy was evident in *Sullivan*, but behind it was another kind of bankruptcy lurking in the fiscal shadows—the cost of morality if subjected to seditious libel trials. The *Times* hired a Birmingham law firm known for its willingness to defend blacks in criminal cases. T. Eric Embry was the lead partner, and he was told that the *Times* would fight to the end. The first step was to get the case out of Alabama jurisdiction, if possible. Embry actually took his guidance in this effort from an article written by Walter Burgwyn Jones, "Alabama Pleading and Practice of Law."[13] Jones would be hearing the case as circuit judge of Montgomery County. Judge Jones's father, Thomas Goode Jones, fought in the Civil War with the Confederate army and carried the flag of truce from Lee to Grant at Appomattox.

Judge Jones had, during 1960 and 1961, issued a number of orders not calculated to give the *New York Times* any comfort. He was determined to hobble the civil rights movement in any way he could. He told the NAACP it could not do business in Alabama, he forbade the Freedom Riders to demonstrate, and he blocked the U.S. Department of Justice from examining voter-registration records. In the libel trial brought by the mayor of Montgomery against the *Times*—after Sullivan had won his first case— Jones declared that the trial would take place under the laws of Alabama, *not* the Fourteenth Amendment. His reverential first loyalty was to "white man's justice, a justice born centuries ago in England, brought over to this country by the Anglo-Saxon race."[14]

Using a technicality, Judge Jones unabashedly contradicted his own text on such matters and declared that the *Times* distribution of 394 copies of its newspaper within the borders of Alabama was enough "business" to bring it under the jurisdiction of state courts. If that was not supported by higher courts, then Jones decided that Embry's attempt to get the suit quashed was made in a "general appearance," rather than the "special appearance" technically necessary to protect the *Times* from being entangled by the state courts. Embry, who in 1975 was appointed to the Alabama Supreme Court in a clear indication of how the times can change, always believed but could never prove that Judge Jones actively participated in planning the libel actions by Sullivan and several others calculated to punish northern media invaders.[15]

Sullivan was one of Montgomery's three city commissioners. His assignment was to supervise the police and fire departments and the cemetery and scales departments. He and his lawyers (with or without Judge Jones's advice) maintained that the reference to "truckloads of police" sullied Sullivan's reputation. This injury to the commissioner was exacerbated, they said, by the inaccuracies in the advertisement regarding what the police did, how many students protested, and whether a dining hall was padlocked. These factors constituted Sullivan's case.

Meanwhile, the four Alabama black ministers had been defending themselves as innocent of any participation in writing the ad and as unaware of the fact that their names would appear in it. The jury took a little over two hours to find both the *Times* and the four ministers guilty of libel. Under Alabama law, Judge Jones had told them, a statement that was "libelous per se" was presumed to be "false." That presumption might be questioned, but the defendant would, of course, have to prove that every fact in the material under question was true. Since there were several *admitted* errors, no such comprehensive truth could be claimed, and the need for further deliberation was removed. The *Times* and the ministers were ordered to pay total damages of $500,000.

The *Times* had moved for a continuance and would, after considerable debate (which still seems surprising for its timidity), appeal to the U.S. Supreme Court, but the lawyers for the four ministers had not made a separate motion to this effect and were, therefore, told by the sedulous Judge Jones that they had forfeited the right to seek a new trial. He further directed that their property could be seized in lieu of cash to pay their fine. Reverend Abernathy immediately lost his aged Buick and a small piece of family land. The *Times* was sympathetic to the ministers and vowed to help them in every way possible. Its law firm hoped to achieve a reversal of the Alabama court's judgment and would seek a similar action for the ministers as well. The variable in their cases was hinged to jurisdiction—the ministers clearly came under Alabama law as residents, but the *Times* counted on escaping such a narrowed mandate. Judge Jones, not unexpectedly, denied a new trial. The *Times* appealed to the Supreme Court of Alabama. On August 30, 1962, the Alabama Supreme Court upheld all of Judge Jones's findings and further emphasized that any reference to agencies of the government automatically attached itself to "the official in complete control of the body" involved. The $500,000 fine, said the Alabama Supreme Court, was not inappropriate (though it was ten times higher than the highest fine the court had ever sustained) because the *Times* had shown "irresponsibility" by not checking its news files where it would, the court blandly assumed, have found ample evidence of falsity. Finally, the court took care of the First Amendment. It stated that "the First Amendment of the U.S. Constitution does not protect libelous publications." That observation was, for the moment, irrefutable.[16]

The progression toward the U.S. Supreme Court had engaged precedent as a matter of course, but history as a force was yet to have its say. The drama—it was the kind of political theater that might have been conceived by an Aristophanes—had many plot-building scenes before it reached the high court climax. The first player on stage had been Alabama governor James Patterson, who had his attorney general explore a lawsuit against the *Times* for libeling state officials—though not one of them was named in the ad. Sullivan's suit was followed by similar suits brought by another commissioner, by the mayor of Montgomery, and by a former commissioner—each asking $500,000. The governor wrote the *Times* and demanded a retraction. The *Times* gave him one—of a sort. It printed a statement that read in part: "To the extent that anyone can fairly conclude from the statements in the advertisement that any such charge [of wrongdoing] was made, the *New York Times* hereby apologizes."[17] That was not enough for Patterson. He sued anyway—for $1 million—and named Martin Luther King Jr. as one of the defendants. The complexity, costliness, and cynicism with which the laws can be employed were marshaled by southern politicians to continue the suppression of black aspirations and to whiplash criticism of white supremacy in the media. The *Montgomery Advertiser* reported: "State and City authorities have found a formidable legal bludgeon to swing at out-of-state newspapers whose reporters cover racial incidents in Alabama."[18]

The fact that this massive attempt to keep a whole state closed to scrutiny was, to a substantial extent, based on an advertisement for which the authors were not known scored no points for the *Times*. They had "circulated the libel" and that made them legally responsible. The jury in the first trial was all white, but Professor Kalven gives the devil his due. Kalven wrote: "Alabama did not create any separate rules of law for these defendants. It simply applied the existing principles of the law of libel."[19] The jury could and did decide that the unnamed, undesignated Sullivan was the target of the ad's references to the police. Sullivan could recover damages for any statements *tending* to harm his reputation even if no harm was demonstrated. Simply put, the existing libel laws were sufficient to threaten the survival of the *Times*, already reeling from labor strife and low profits.

Enter Herbert Wechsler, Columbia Law School professor and a highly respected legal scholar. He joined the *Times* legal forces and began to shape the case after the overwhelming defeat in the appeal process before the Alabama Supreme Court. Sullivan's lawyers were very confident. They saw no possibility of reversal unless more than a century of libel law was overturned—at least in regard to the freedom of the states to make their own rules without fear of the Constitution. "Wechsler," says law professor Lucas Powe Jr., "had a case with wonderful facts but no law. His job was to show the Court how to make the law conform to the fact."[20] Wechsler summoned the past, the history lessons he knew so well. He put together an argument that accused the Alabama courts of using seditious libel as the core of judgment—but without proving that the defendant had deliberately intended to bring a government official "into contempt or disrepute." To that shortfall Wechsler added the claim that the *Times* had no protection against double jeopardy—the *Times* was being sued and would be, or had been, fined again severely for the same alleged statement and punished with damages far beyond those amounts considered permissible under the Sedition Act (to be precise, a thousand times higher). The jury, Wechsler submitted, had taken a generalized and impersonal attack on a governmental agency (namely the police) and made it a defamation of one man (namely Sullivan). In this case, the libel law had "transformed the law of defamation from a method of protecting private reputation to a device for insulating government against attack." Many years later, Wechsler wrote in the *Media Law Reporter*: "If you feel that the environment is on your side, that legal trends are on your side, the problem of counsel is to present the Court with adequate materials to support that case."[21]

Ironically, Wechsler discovered that he had to begin by persuading his client that the case *could* be supported. He recalled his astonishment when he encountered skepticism at the *Times* about taking the case to the U.S. Supreme Court:

> As soon as I realized what was involved, my reaction was, first, to give them a sense of how the scope of the First Amendment had been progressively expanded by the Supreme Court in recent years, so that every one of the old shibboleths had gone—the idea that contempt isn't covered—and libel would logically follow. Second, I said that if the *Times* didn't make this argument, in what was overall a very sympathetic case, who could be expected to make it? I did tell them there was a substantial chance that the Court could decide the case on its individual facts rather than by a broad rule, but I pointed out that even to hold that factual shortcomings in a libel case could be a *federal Constitutional matter* would have large implications. (emphasis added)[22]

Wechsler knew that if he was to engage the Court's attention persuasively and secure a review of the Alabama verdict, he would have to demonstrate forcefully that the long-standing rules of libel would violate the First Amendment protection of speech and press if allowed to be used for the benefit of *one* public official such as Sullivan. One of Wechsler's associates suggested that the Alabama judgments were no less repressive than the Sedition Act of 1798, which had been widely considered as a violation of the First Amendment. Orville Dryfoos, then the publisher of the *Times*, liked the constitutional argument, and Wechsler was finally given the green light.

Wechsler's powerful petition to the Court, which would be the basis of his subsequent brief, made the point that unlimited libel damages such as those piling up in Alabama would diminish, if not prevent, the "free political discussion" that the Court had already agreed was "the very foundation of constitutional government." He also quoted from Justice Black's opinion in *Bridges v. California* concerning the essential right of the people to criticize "all public institutions." Thus the First Amendment points were made first, then the procedural points regarding the Alabama court's decision that it had jurisdiction over a New York newspaper company and the technicality invoked to deny the *Times*'s lawyers in Alabama the right to appeal.

Wechsler did not dwell on racism, which was, in fact, the central motivating force, except in one paragraph of his brief: "This is not a time when it would serve the values enshrined in the Constitution to force the press to curtail its attention to the racial tensions of the country or to forgo dissemination of the publications in the areas where tension is extreme. Here, too, the law of libel must confront and be subordinated to the Constitution. The occasion for that confrontation is at hand."

If the Supreme Court had rejected Wechsler's petition, it would have, in effect, permitted the South to secede from the Union a second time. There was the prospect of "intellectual secession" wherein the northern press would have been silenced and the South would have gone its way in defiance of constitutional protections without a critical press baying at its heels. Instead the Court scheduled the case, and political free speech, so long embraced and articulated by Alexander Meiklejohn, would have its day of reckoning. Government officials could expect no limitations—other than deliberate, malicious falsehood—on the criticism or evaluation of their *public performance* if the *Times* triumphed. And so it did.

Justice William J. Brennan wrote the key majority opinion. There were no dissents, but in addition to Brennan's opinion, Justices Black and Goldberg each wrote a concurring opinion in which Justice Douglas joined. The sentiment, however, was unanimous. Brennan took the position that the threat of libel suits brought by public officials could chill freedom of discussion. Reporters, editors, and public speakers wishing to make "factual assertions" on a controversial subject might think twice and then retreat—not because they did not believe in what they were writing or saying but because they could not be certain that they could prove the truth of their assertions to a jury's satisfaction. Brennan's opinion was drafted along the lines of Wechsler's brilliant brief, and as Professor Kalven remarks, "At various critical points, the opinion echoes the carefully precise language of the brief and the structure of the Court's argument reflects the structure of argument in the brief."[23] Wechsler had not accomplished this in isolation. Herbert Brownell, Thomas F. Daly, and several other distinguished lawyers worked with him as "of counsel."

Justice Brennan, in his response, expressed many deeply held convictions he had been promulgating in the recent past, not least his belief that strict legal rules by their very existence might cause *self-censorship*. He was, however, in the Sullivan case primarily concerned with the effect on public discussion of using libel laws to protect public officials. In Alabama there was a sobering demonstration of silenced debate, and without federal intervention the voices of dissent would never have been heard.

Having paid serious attention to the importance of "citizen-critics" to keep government honest, the Court devised a new set of guidelines to translate that concern into law. Public officials cannot "recover damages" even if criticism is *defamatory or false (or both)* unless it is proven that the statements were made with "actual malice" or with "reckless disregard" for the truth. Deliberate malice, however, must be proven with "convincing clarity." The jury cannot interpret criticism of underlings—or whole agencies—as attacks on the person at the top. And finally, judges at all levels, during trial or in considering appeal, must conduct an independent review to make certain that the evidence produced is constitutionally sufficient. Under these rules the Sullivan case (in Alabama) could have been reversed if only on the grounds of public officials not recovering damages without proof of malice and the jury being prohibited from transporting criticism of underlings (the police) to the level of administrative supervision (Commissioner Sullivan). Without these restraints, a jury determined to find libel might find a way to bend the facts.

How did this new approach to First Amendment cases alter the status of the dormant Sedition Act? Harry Kalven Jr. wrote his definitive essay on the subject for the *Supreme Court Review* in 1964. He saw *New York Times v. Sullivan* as a recasting of the "common law defamation by constitutional standards." The Alabama courts had violated First Amendment principles and, therefore, violated the Fourteenth Amendment. Racism was at the heart of the issue, and the civil rights movement had become, in Kalven's words, "an elaborate petition for redress of grievances"[24]—one of those fundamental rights protected by the First Amendment: "the right of the people to peaceably assemble and *petition the government for redress of grievances*" (emphasis added).

Kalven says, "The Justices directly confronted the question of the Constitutional status of the Sedition Act of 1798 and used 'history' to confirm a national consensus."[25] The act was repellent to most Americans because it made any criticism or remonstrance by the "citizen rulers" concerning their public servants libelous if a jury chose to regard those expressions as defamation. No malice was needed. No deliberate, calculated use of falsehood was needed. If a jury—or a judge, for that matter—could be persuaded to make a judgment of libel even when the speakers or the writers believed fervently that truth was inherent in their sentiments, then public discourse would lose its zest and its purpose. Democracy, as envisioned by the Framers, would wither. Hyperbole, the blood of debate, would become thin and go anemically into the night. The discussion of public issues, and the views about public officials, must be "robust." There was optimism in that word and faith in the ability of free, uninhibited political speech, on platforms and in print, to sort out the virtuous, the accurate, and the truthful by discourse. Wit without malice was the ideal state.

Kalven's thesis is that the Supreme Court of the United States considered the political lessons of history—in this case, the long, painful evolution of black civil rights—and found the "political realities" compelling. The Court did, indeed, decide to "heed their rising voices." To do this, it first "took the question of defamation away from the jury," where it had been anchored for more than two centuries in colonial America and then in the United States. The Alabama courts, Kalven repeats, did not "create any special rules of law" for the *New York Times* case. Alabama simply used what was on the books—but with relish. It was such relish that finally changed judicial taste at the highest level.

The ease with which an Alabama jury, in a little over two hours of discussion, connected police actions on site to an absent and unidentified commissioner; the almost instantaneous acceptance by Judge Jones of the plaintiff's assertion that the *New York Times* was doing sufficient business in Alabama to justify a status of being under Alabama jurisdiction; the blithe use of partial errors concerning the facts or the statistics (even the outright mistakes) in the advertisement as totally disabling to the defendant's case even if the essential facts were true; the Sullivan contention, on the one hand, that some accusations and inaccuracies maligned him but, on the other, that he could not have been responsible for the alleged offenses because he was not in office at the time; and finally, the swift buildup of other libel cases asking enormous damages that were calculated to drive independent judgment of Alabama's behavior toward civil rights out of the state (and out of business)—with all that in the background, the political importance could not be ignored.

The U.S. Supreme Court would then, Kalven observes, have to dismantle much of the "common law of defamation." It did so by rejecting the view of the Alabama Supreme Court that "libel is beneath constitutional protection." The state laws could not rule out "constitutional scrutiny" by the Supreme Court.[26] Wechsler, in his remarkable brief, put it this way: "Libel can claim no talismanic immunity from constitutional limitations. It must be measured by *standards that satisfy the First Amendment*" (emphasis added).[27] The Court accepted that Alabama was not fiddling with the existing laws "in order to call it libel." It also incorporated its own past decisions limiting certain kinds of expression. But it strongly affirmed that any and all expression of opinion or debate on "public questions" is secured by the First Amendment. On this point the Court referred to the Brandeis opinion in the *Whitney* case, adding to those words quoted earlier in this account: "a profound national commitment to the principle that debate on public issues should be uninhibited, robust, and wide open." The ad in the *Times* was "an expression of grievance and protest on one of the major public issues of our time."[28]

As to Sullivan's case, seen against the political background, the Court stated that the First Amendment did not require "any test of truth," and factual errors alone could not justify repression of speech or press. Injury to *official reputation* was not a justification either, nor was a *combination* of factual error *and* wounds to reputations. In this manner, Kalven writes, the Court disposed of any claim against the constitutional protection of the political advertisement in the *Times*, errors and all. The Court then turned, somewhat to Kalven's perplexity, to the size of damages. The fines imposed were far too large and would inevitably have an "inhibiting" effect. What is more, there was no evidence of financial loss—or, important to add, of loss in public support. It would be possible to prove that in racist Alabama, the charges against Sullivan (or those he supervised) were bound to enhance their popularity, not damage it. There remained, of course, a need to articulate a rule that "would permit good faith error in public discussion." The existing constitutional convention was that the plaintiff had to demonstrate that an alleged "falsity" was expressed with "actual malice." This had long been the rule for representatives, senators, and other public officials. They could say what they wanted in the various chambers or public forums so long as *malicious falsity* was not involved. The Court, in the *Sullivan* case, Kalven says, decided that the citizen as critic should not be treated differently from other "officials." On this point the Court went far beyond any earlier procedural regulation. It stated that judges must assess all the evidence in advance and determine for themselves whether that evidence was adequate for a trial by jury or a retrial by a higher court. In regard to Sullivan, the Court emphasized that the evidence was *inadequate* to connect the commissioner with the general accusations made in the text of the advertisement.[29]

With all of this in hand, Kalven suggests that *New York Times v. Sullivan* contains "the seed of important new doctrine." The elements of that new doctrine are these:

1. The free speech and press provision of the Constitution *rejects seditious libel as an offense.*
2. Constitutional history had relegated sedition to an outer pasture, but the "nagging question" of the constitutionality of the Sedition Act of 1798 had never been put to rest.
3. The opinion in the *Times* case had resolved the constitutional question and obliterated the Sedition Act.
4. The "clear and present danger" test, and all other attempts to balance one interest against another or differentiate between state laws and federal laws in regard to First Amendment cases, were either discarded or drastically diminished.
5. From *New York Times v. Sullivan* onward and upward, consideration of speech and press criticism of government would begin with the new rule that seditious libel and defamation no longer pertained—"rather than with the sterile example of a man falsely yelling fire in a crowded theater" (the Justice Holmes benchmark used in a World War I case).

In Kalven's view, a society "may or may not treat obscenity or contempt by publication as legal offenses without altering its basic nature. If, however, it makes seditious libel an offense, it is not a free society, no matter what its other characteristics."[30]

New York Times v. Sullivan disposed of the Sedition Act once and for all. The act had departed the "court of history" empty handed. This judgment gave the First Amendment its "central meaning." The protection of free speech was essential to democracy. There was no longer any doubt as to what speech was being protected and no doubt *why* it was being protected. Seditious libel could no longer be made the subject of government sanction. For the philosophers, this meant citizens had a *duty* to observe and criticize their representatives in government. Criticism of public officials was not merely a constitutional largesse, there on the table like the salt, to be used now and then.

Justice Brennan added considerable moral weight to all these points. Following many of Wechsler's arguments, he ticked off a number of clarifications. For example, it should be made very difficult—if not impossible—to go about transmuting criticism of government into a personal attack on one high-ranking official who might, theoretically, have had some influence over the situation. That would be creating a cause for action, a power not given to the state. If the "citizen-critic" feared such a maneuver, he would not criticize. As Meiklejohn had insisted, "These conflicting views must be expressed, not because they are valid but because they are relevant."[31]

Justice Potter Stewart, in a 1959 case involving a state ban on the movie version of *Lady Chatterly's Lover*, wrote another useful description of the Constitution's protection of free expression: "Its guarantee is not confined to the expression of ideas that are conventional or shared by a majority. It protects advocacy of the opinion that adultery may sometime be proper, no less than advocacy of socialism or the single tax. And in the realm of ideas it protects expression which is eloquent no less than that which is unconvincing."[32]

Moving on from there, Justice Brennan articulated protection for false statements of fact on public issues because in "robust" debate there was always the likelihood of error. The Court further emphasized the deterrent effect of placing the burden of proof on the critic of official conduct. Kalven sees the Court as requiring that speech be *overprotected* so as not to be *underprotected*. In that process, the fading "clear and present danger test" was virtually eclipsed. There was no danger in citizen criticism, no matter how harsh. The citizens are in charge. Wechsler had chosen *not* to argue the case for the *Times* on the basis of "clear and present danger," even if there was no evidence of any danger, with or without clarity. The Court reversed Alabama not because there was so little substantive harm in the text of the "heed their rising voices" advertisement but, says Kalven, "because the law looks too much like punishment for seditious libel."[33]

There remains, nonetheless, a limitation of sorts at the far side of the field. It is called "actual malice," and that intentional factor is sometimes embellished with "reckless disregard for the truth." Such a limitation is reserved for very deliberate, knowingly false expression. Justice Black rejected even *that* encroachment on freedom of expression. He believed that "there should be no libel or defamation law in the United States under the United States Government, just absolutely none."[34]

The question of how much privilege would be given to statements that were not true now became a problem for the plaintiff. Sullivan would have to prove falsity *and* malice, and the courts (through the judges) would have to review all the evidence to determine its validity before allowing a trial. The finding of malice is not, therefore, easily or deceptively made, but blatant falseness, calculatingly expressed, in contradiction of known truth, would not escape the charge of malice. What is more, there are certain kinds of speech and publication—presumably carefully defined—the prevention and punishment of which has never been thought to raise any constitutional problem. These include the lewd and obscene, the profane, the libelous, and the insulting or fighting words.

As noted earlier, Wechsler emphasized that "libel can claim no talismanic immunity from constitutional limitation," and the assumption might be made that obscenity, or provocatively insulting "fighting words," should have no fewer limitations. Defining obscenity or insult will never be a slide-rule calculation. Here the debate continues, but the place reserved for political speech, for citizen criticism, has been surveyed and mapped clearly by *New York Times v. Sullivan*. It can still be asserted that a member of Congress has greater speech privileges than a citizen-critic-ruler. The people's representatives may say what they please on the floor of Congress, with or without malice, and suffer no constitutional retribution. The citizen who speaks or writes with equal (and deliberate) malice can be punished. It is possible, Kalven theorizes, that the difference in protection grew out of an awareness of multiplicity. There are few officials, but many, many citizen critics. Are the outnumbered officials more vulnerable than the masses of citizenry?

It was not unlikely, in the view of many scholars, that reasonable protection for the press and the citizen-critic, the demonstrator and the petitioner, would expand inexorably to matters of public policy and public domain—such as art. When the arts were making political statements, would the First Amendment welcome them? Kalven thought Meiklejohn's thesis on this point regarding free expression was a prelude to that expansion. When Professor Kalven asked Professor Meiklejohn how he felt about the *Sullivan* decision, the latter did not hesitate: "It is an occasion for dancing in the streets."[35] That was a long way from the dancing on the head of a metaphorical pin, which is where this discussion began. He might have danced more enthusiastically had a few more loose ends been tied up. The political discourse rule was his muse: If it deals with public issues, it has constitutional protection. Shall we dance? If not, it is business unrelated to the Constitution.

4

POMP AND PROVENANCE

The Bill of Rights wouldn't pass, if they voted today. We started talking about the *Pentagon Papers*. That was *not* a very good First Amendment opinion by the Court. In the first place, there were nine opinions and one of the justices, White, was begging the government to prosecute all of us for criminal violation, even though he never read the Papers. None of them had read the Papers. The prosecutor didn't read them. Griswold says he didn't read them. But, you know, if you're confident enough about your country to take a really long view, the First Amendment is such a superb document that you have to think that even if the pendulum swings a little bit, it will be back.

—Ben Bradlee, former editor of the *Washington Post*

Despite the triumph made over seditious libel, the press as a sentinel was never in greater danger constitutionally than in the late 1960s and early 1970s. The federal government was the protagonist this time, and the press, represented by its most prestigious practitioners, contemplated its options and chose, finally, to fight. The issue was, as it may well be again in the years ahead, national security. The next battle will have to confront the vast dispersal of information resources and the phenomenon of "real time" reporting, the "first draft of history" happening live on camera and witnessed by millions of viewers. One aspect of national security, however, that is unlikely to change, whatever else may change, is the secrecy surrounding policy decisions, which will always be in play so long as there is a free press. No story embodies the contest between public information rights and official secrecy more dramatically than that attempt to write a second, contextual "draft of history" called the *Pentagon Papers*.

In the literal sense, it was a history of the Vietnam involvement, but it was, as its appointed organizer, Leslie Gelb, described it, "Not so much a documentary history as a history based solely on documents—checked and rechecked with ant-like diligence. . . . We could not get into the minds of the decision makers, we were not present at the decisions, and we often could not tell whether something happened because someone decided against it, or most likely, because it unfolded from the situation."[1]

The "ants" were all members of the Vietnam History Task Force. Their work was launched by Secretary of Defense Robert McNamara on June 17, 1967. He later said that his purpose was "to bequeath to scholars the raw material from which they could re-examine the events of the time. If historians are to make a careful examination, they need the raw materials. I simply asked that these be brought together, and I have no regrets for having done so."[2]

Ernest May, Harvard historian, joined the task force early on, but he regarded the finished report as less than distinguished. He thought it had the shortfalls of a hurriedly turned out product. There were, unsurprisingly, a variety of views on the value and reliability of the *Papers*—some suspecting the dovish bias of task force members, others ruefully acknowledging that the overall impression made things look better than they were. Such speculations were heatedly made at times, but however the substance of the *Papers* was ultimately judged, the exercise seemed inconsequential in the light of the larger story that overtook it: the right of the press to publish materials concerning national security matters possibly stolen or leaked from the government. Freedom of the press became the overriding issue, more so than the contents of the *Pentagon Papers*, which the press acquired and published. The government does not *own* the contents of its documents, cannot *copyright* anything, and cannot (in theory) *restrain* publication. In making these points, Yale professor Alexander Bickel, who represented the *New York Times*, emphasized that the government *does* have the power to protect security at the source. What it wants to keep secret, it can keep, barring leaks. Bickel said,

> The power to arrange security at its source, looked at in itself, is great, and if it were nowhere countervailed, it would be quite frightening—is anyway, perhaps—since the law in no wise guarantees its prudent exercise or even effectively guards against its abuse. But there *is* countervailing power. The press, by which is meant anybody, not only the institutionalized print and electronic press, can be prevented from publishing only in extreme and quite dire circumstances. The rule of the *Pentagon Papers* case calls for evidence of *immediate harm* of the *gravest sort* (typically loss of life or catastrophic injury to the national interest) flowing directly from publication before a restraint will be allowed. (emphasis added)[3]

In June 1969, a full two years before the *New York Times* published excerpts, there were fifteen sets of the *Pentagon Papers* ready for distribution. Leslie Gelb classified each copy as top secret in what he called "an absolutely routine decision"[4]—the Defense Department regulations having dictated that any compendium of documents bear the highest classification of any one part of the collection. If there was one top secret document, everything would be top secret. Of the fifteen sets, two went to the National Archives to be reserved for the Kennedy and Johnson libraries; two went to the State Department for Nicholas Katzenbach and William Bundy; one went to the office of Clark Clifford, former secretary of defense; one went to Robert McNamara (the set marked #1) at the office of the Bank for International Reconstruction and Development; and two went to the Rand Corporation in Santa Monica, California, where important research and analysis of defense matters was conducted. The remaining seven stayed in the office of the Secretary of Defense and were designated for use by such officials as Cyrus Vance, Paul Nitze, and Paul Warnke. Robert McNamara did not read the *Pentagon Papers*. "He couldn't bear to read them," said a close friend. That remains the case even though McNamara has written, at seventy-eight, a memoir on the war: *In Retrospect: The Tragedy and Lessons of Vietnam.*

Aside from Gelb, the only person who, within days of receiving them, read every page of the *Papers* was Daniel Ellsberg, who had worked on the task force and was continuing his research at the Rand Corporation. He had moved to California in 1959 with his wife and two children to join Rand, where he concentrated at first on the Soviet nuclear capability and the so-called missile gap.

Ellsberg, as a leading player in the *Pentagon Papers* pageant, brought impressive credentials. He was born in Chicago during the depression. His father, an engineer, moved his family to Detroit in search of work. Ellsberg was bright and self-assured as a boy, learned to play the piano and basketball and took up alpine climbing, skydiving, and debating. At Cranbrook School for Boys he was voted "most likely to make a contribution to human progress" and won a scholarship to Harvard, where he graduated in 1952. He seemed to move from strength to strength at the university, becoming president of the literary magazine, the *Advocate*, and a member of the editorial board of the *Crimson*, Harvard's daily newspaper. His senior thesis was on economic game theory, and it received the highest grade possible. It also won him a Woodrow Wilson fellowship to study economics at Cambridge, in England. When he returned a year later, he completed a master's at Harvard—again with the highest honors—and could have become a member of Harvard's prestigious Society of Fellows while he went on to get his doctorate. Ellsberg chose, instead, to join the Marine Corps for two years. In his junior year he had married a Radcliffe girl, Carol Cummings, the daughter of a marine colonel. The wedding was small, attended mostly by college friends, and took place in an Episcopal church. Ellsberg and his father-in-law, a widower, were close. The colonel on occasion went skiing with his daughter, Ellsberg, and their friends. The relationship influenced Ellsberg's interest in the marines, and the Suez problem in 1956 persuaded him to extend his military service. It also gave him his first top-secret security clearance, when his outfit went to sea in the Middle East.

He returned to Harvard after that adventure with a strong interest in the military, and while studying as a junior fellow, he became a part-time consultant for the Rand Corporation. With his doctorate almost completed, he finally moved to Rand full time. Rand sent him off to Washington frequently to work with the State and Defense Departments. For a while he served on the staff of Assistant Defense Secretary John McNaughton. He took the job because, as a consultant to the Kennedy administration, he had become increasingly involved in the Vietnam strategy. After a year of reading intelligence reports, he was convinced that too little was known about the reality on the ground.

Ellsberg's marriage had dissolved, and his curiosity about Vietnam had intensified. He asked for an assignment that would take him to the scene of action, and he got it. Periodically, Ellsberg would write articles for Harvard publications or open letters to his classmates "to communicate honestly some of the complexities and my own uncertainties."[5] Before he went out to Southeast Asia he spent some time, in 1965, lobbying for Johnson's policies on Capitol Hill and visiting campus gatherings. He was not a resolute hawk, but he thought America's basic policies in Vietnam were probably correct, and he defended them articulately.

In mid-1965, he traveled to Vietnam as an "apprentice" to Major General Edward Lansdale, who was going to work on what was called the "pacification program." In this role, Ellsberg developed a number of friends who would be significant in the following years as the story of the *Pentagon Papers* unfolded. One of them was a political scientist named Anthony Russo, who was doing research for Rand on the morale of the Viet Cong. Ellsberg also met and enjoyed being with several of the top reporters working in Saigon. He helped them whenever possible, and he listened to their views. Among them was Neil Sheehan, who was working for UPI but was later hired by the *New York Times*.

Lansdale admired his young aide from Harvard but worried about his sense of self-preservation. Ellsberg had become a crack marksman while in the marines and learned to fire a pistol very accurately with either hand. When he went on patrols in the Mekong Delta, he agreed to carry a gun. "If you didn't carry a weapon," he explained, "other people had to take care of you."[6] He was frequently involved in ground actions, came under fire, and fired back. As his doubts about America's Vietnam presence grew, he began to be uncomfortable about his own participation in combat exchanges. He also began to question the effectiveness of "pacification." The villages were not truly secure, and villagers cared little about who won the war. They wanted all foreigners to go, and they wanted to get on with their lives.

In 1967 Ellsberg was hit by a different enemy—hepatitis. Were it not for that serious illness, he believed he would have stayed on in Vietnam indefinitely. He was, instead, sent off to a hospital in Bangkok for treatment, and lying under a dextrose drip in Thailand on his thirty-sixth birthday, he conceived a long, philosophical piece for his *Harvard Fifteenth Anniversary Report*. It said, in part, "I'm proud to have served with Lansdale, and I've learned fully as much as I hoped: and learned to care deeply for this tormented country, Vietnam (whose countryside, I think, is the most beautiful in the world: a fact that rarely seems to be mentioned), its children, its people, and their future." He reaffirmed his faith in Lansdale's concepts of political education and counterguerrilla tactics but added sadly, "None of them are being applied, in any degree."[7]

When he recovered, Ellsberg went home to California, found a beach cottage in Malibu, and resumed working for Rand. As the highly charged political atmosphere, which would explode in 1968, began to simmer, Ellsberg underwent subtle personal changes—in outlook, in manner. His hair grew longer and he left it that way, and his military bearing relaxed. He maintained, all the same, his close relationship with Russo and with Henry Rowen, the president of Rand. He agreed to go back to Washington in late 1967 to become a contributor to the *Pentagon Papers*. He was there in early 1968 when Lyndon Johnson ordered the cutbacks in bombing and told the nation he would not run for president again. Ellsberg's continuing doubts about Vietnam were not yet turning him against American policy, but he was deeply troubled by the destruction and upheaval caused by intervention. When Henry Kissinger asked the Rand Corporation for a fresh analysis of policy options, Rowen assigned Ellsberg to the task. He spent four days at Richard Nixon's headquarters in New York's Pierre Hotel, reviewing the possibilities with Kissinger. The list included everything from total U.S. withdrawal to the use of nuclear weapons. Subsequently, he sent off questions to the State and Defense Departments and to the CIA, which produced close to 1,000 pages of comments. These were explained to Kissinger and Nixon after the Republicans won the election in 1968. There were no revelations and little change in policy. By 1969 Ellsberg was back at Rand. He believed that he was the only researcher given the assurance he would have personal access to all the *Pentagon Papers* at the earliest opportunity. Gelb remembered no such arrangement. Ellsberg was, indeed, designated courier for a large part of the material, carrying at least eighteen volumes of the *Papers* from Washington to Santa Monica.

Ultimately, as the story evolved, an affidavit was filed with the U.S. District Court in October 1969 in which Carol Ellsberg, no longer his wife, revealed that she had learned (apparently from their children) that he was making copies of documents, some of them stamped top secret. At about the same time, six of Rand's senior analysts, increasingly concerned that Washington was not allowing important information on Vietnam to be disseminated appropriately, joined in the composition of a letter to the *New York Times*. It stated categorically: "We believe the United States should decide now to end its participation in the Vietnam War, completing the total withdrawal of our forces within one year at the most." One of the signers was Daniel Ellsberg. The wheel had turned. The letter took strong positions on the hopelessness of military actions, the need to let the Saigon government rise or fall on its own, and the exaggerated nature of claims that the future of Vietnam was vital to American interests. The letter stated that the cost in lives and property "far outweigh any prospective benefits" of continuing intervention.[8]

Ellsberg attributed his shifting convictions to the reading of the *Pentagon Papers*, and he decided to go public with his conclusions. He was, as his colleagues recall, acting like a man with a mission. The hawk had clearly become a dove—an impassioned and eloquent, but controversial, dove. By 1970, he was eased out of Rand. There were several other organizations he could have gone to, but he chose the Massachusetts Institute of Technology's Center for International Studies. He moved to MIT at the same time that William Bundy, assistant secretary of state in Johnson's administration, arrived. The director of international studies, Everett Hagen, had wanted to create some diversity at his center by welcoming a full range of views. Bundy and Ellsberg would bring opposing positions on many matters, not least the Vietnam nightmare.

In August 1970, Ellsberg married Patricia Marx, daughter of an active Republican manufacturer of toys. Cambridge became Ellsberg's new home. He and his wife, who shared his feelings about Southeast Asian policies, were about to share another struggle of their own making. During his last months at Rand, Ellsberg had immersed himself in the *Pentagon Papers*, and the records indicated that he had access to all forty-seven volumes— and exclusive custody of twenty-seven of them. Ellsberg's study of the documents, he told all who would listen, convinced him that America had been wrong from 1954 onward. He said that the idea of North Vietnam aggression against the South was clearly contradicted by the *Papers*. He believed it was "our aggression entirely, our intervention. Ours is the Foreign intervention in that situation. The other intervention, even by the Chinese and the Russians, is just negligible by comparison."[9]

Ellsberg had become concerned about his own contributions, his "personal responsibility." He was convinced that he had to help end the war, and making the *Pentagon Papers* available to a wide audience would achieve that end or at least hurry it along. Anthony Russo had been fired by Rand in early 1969. He thought it was because he had written reports critical of the South Vietnamese government. Some of his colleagues thought he was embittered about his dismissal, but whatever the reason, he persuaded a girlfriend who ran a small, unsuccessful ad agency to rent her Xerox machine at night to Ellsberg. With the help of his two children, Robert and Mary, and Russo, Ellsberg copied thousands of pages of the *Papers*, masking the "Top Secret" or other classifications. Some of the pages were from drafts, some from originals, and some from the final *Pentagon Papers*. Not all were copied at the ad agency, but every page was returned to the Rand files. Most of this work took place toward the end of September 1969.

Ellsberg's first wife, the mother of his children, questioned him about the danger of indictment, even prison, for his copying activity. In her affidavit she reported: "My former husband at that time told me that he was very concerned about the War in Vietnam and that he was going to be actively working against it and that there were things that had not been disclosed which should be known. He then said that he would only give it [the copies] to authorized people like Senators Fulbright and Goodell."[10]

In November 1969, Ellsberg met with Senator Fulbright and some of his staff. The senator was disenchanted with American policy in Vietnam, particularly with the Gulf of Tonkin Resolution, which he considered a "functional equivalent" of a declaration of war against North Vietnam. Fulbright was skeptical about how the *Papers* would help stop the war, but he promised Ellsberg he would try to get them released. The excerpts he had been given were put in the Foreign Relations Committee safe in the new Senate Office Building, and Fulbright faithfully wrote a letter to Defense Secretary Melvin Laird. He stated that he had heard of the "history of the decision-making process on Vietnam policy covering the period from 1940 to April, 1968" and wanted copies made available to his committee for review purposes.[11]

Laird acknowledged receiving the letter at once but waited a month before writing a full response, which refused Fulbright's request. Explaining his refusal, he stated,

> In 1967 Secretary McNamara initiated a detailed history of the evolution of the present-day situation in Vietnam. It was conceived as a compilation of raw materials to be used at some unspecified, but distant, future date. On the basis of the understanding that access and use would be restricted, the documents were designed to contain an accumulation of data of the most delicate sensitivity, including NSC papers and other Presidential communications which have always been considered privileged. . . . Many of the contributions to this total document were provided on the basis of an expressed guarantee of confidentiality.[12]

Laird went on to insist that access to the *Pentagon Papers* was extremely limited and it was in the national interest to keep it that way. Fulbright was not ready to give up. He wrote Laird again on January 19, 1970, insisting that the issue involved was one of "Constitutional responsibilities."[13] The Senate's constitutional responsibility in regard to foreign policy and collaboration with the executive branch required access to background information. Fulbright added a reminder to Laird that the *Papers* had been commissioned by a former secretary of defense, not the president, and therefore the doctrine of executive privilege was not relevant. Laird did not reply.

Ellsberg went on with his pilgrimage. He volunteered to help Senator Charles Goodell, a moderate Republican from New York who introduced a resolution calling for U.S. withdrawal from Vietnam by December 1970. The senator could not find a cosponsor for the resolution, but it was widely publicized; and Goodell, in his frequent public statements on the subject, seemed to echo many of Ellsberg's views. Ellsberg did not let Goodell know that he had a copy of the *Pentagon Papers*. Instead he delivered 3,000 additional pages to Fulbright's staff. The senator considered their contents and understood the effect such records could have on the legislators and on public opinion. But he wanted them made available *officially* so that procedural controversy would not distract from the substance. He eventually tried writing Laird one more time. Silence.

Ellsberg went down every path he could think of, including a possible "war crimes" trial—authentic or academic. He would be a defendant or a witness. In either case, the *Pentagon Papers* might be subpoenaed. He urged lawyers he knew to initiate civil suits against the conduct of the war. And he went on writing and talking.

Meanwhile, American troops crossed into Cambodia, and National Guardsmen shot and killed four students in a demonstration at Kent State University. There was a mass march on Washington. Antiwar rallies grew in size and ferocity. Ellsberg had testified before the Foreign Relations Committee on May 13, 1970, at Fulbright's invitation. With considerable emotion he urged withdrawal from Vietnam. Fulbright's questions elicited answers that resonated from the still secret *Pentagon Papers*. Ellsberg referred to "the documents of a number of administrations." He described the influence of domestic politics on decisions made in Vietnam and then said of the actions ordered by the Nixon administration, "This administration is no less ready than earlier ones to incur escalating risks and domestic dissent to avoid or postpone . . . 'humiliation.'"[14]

Humiliation and its constant companion, embarrassment, were soon to become virtual personae in the *Pentagon Papers* case—the humiliation of defeat, the embarrassment of disclosure. But the helicopters were not yet evacuating frantic figures from the roof of the American embassy in Saigon. There was still hope in the White House that a peace with some honor could be negotiated.

Fulbright was probing relentlessly. Speaking of the *Papers*, he rhetorically commented to Ellsberg at the May 13 hearing, "Here is a study made at government expense, paid for by the tax payer, and withheld from the Committee [his committee]. I don't see any justification for such classification." His comment wasn't—except by intonation—precisely a question. But Ellsberg answered supportively and emphasized the vital nature of the information compiled in the *Papers* to the people who were making crucial decisions. "I would wish," Ellsberg said with a straight face, "first of all, that President Nixon could have access to the information in that study and in other studies that were done directly for Mr. McNamara."[15]

Fulbright found this dialogue with Ellsberg useful. He made the point that would survive all the shadings of controversy: "I can't subscribe to this extension of the *concept of classification* to prevent our knowing about the past. . . . It doesn't give democracy an opportunity to function at all" (emphasis added).[16]

Laird remained adamant. Even though some Senate staffers had read parts of the *Papers* and a left-wing think tank was examining and reading Ellsberg's copy, there was no significant public disclosure, no indignant media outcry, no spotlight suddenly piercing the somber discontent. Fulbright rose in the Senate three months later to declaim against Laird's judgment: "The Executive Branch—in what has become a reflex action—has slammed the door on Congress. . . . I hope the first enterprising reporter who obtains a copy of this history will share it with the Committee."[17]

In late November 1970, Ellsberg wrote a letter to the *New York Times* that was endorsed by several MIT faculty members. He attacked the administration's Indo-China policy vehemently: "Nixon's clearly announced and demonstrated strategy entails not only prolonging but vastly expanding this immoral, illegal, and unconstitutional war."[18] He continued to use the *Papers* as a resource for lectures and articles and at a short meeting with Henry Kissinger months before the letter to the *Times*. Kissinger, who had been involved in the actual planning of the *Pentagon Papers* project and had a copy available to him, said he had not read the *Papers* and, according to Ellsberg, gave as his reason that they were not important to the current situation. Ellsberg rejected that argument and urged him to assign a staff member to read them carefully. Reportedly, Kissinger then offered the task of analyzing the papers to Ellsberg himself, who turned it down. The two men met again at a Boston meeting sponsored by MIT and major business leaders to discuss foreign policy. It was late January 1971, and Kissinger, who was one of the main speakers, claimed that "there are no good choices left in Vietnam" and that "this administration has been the best protection of those who most loudly deplore our policy."[19] Ellsberg tried to question the secretary, but the meeting broke up. The next day South Vietnamese troops entered Laos supported by American airpower.

Ellsberg continued to write heated editorials against the Vietnam actions taken by the Nixon administration, but he did not spare the president's predecessors. He also persisted in his efforts to get a member of Congress to reveal the *Pentagon Papers* because the legal risk would be far less if the disclosure came from a constitutionally protected legislator. It did not appear that Fulbright was willing to shelter in that protection, so Ellsberg turned to Senator George McGovern. McGovern was a candidate for the presidency, and he feared a number of negative possibilities, including the accusation that he might be using the *Papers* for political purposes. He advised Ellsberg to try the *New York Times* or the *Washington Post*. McGovern's impression of Ellsberg was that "he was a hawk with a bad conscience."[20]

In retrospect, many public figures, including McGovern, agreed that had a member of Congress, earlier on, taken a copy of the *Pentagon Papers* to the floor and gone public with its contents—or some provocative part of them—the people would have been better served. As it was, Ellsberg had reached the end of his patience. He knew that Neil Sheehan, his friend from Vietnam, was now working for the *New York Times* in Washington. On March 28, 1971, the *Times* book-review section produced a piece by Sheehan reviewing a large number of antiwar books recently published. Sheehan's title was "Should We Have War Crimes Trials?" He suggested the possibility that if the law were seriously applied to American military conduct in Vietnam, "the leaders of the United States for the past six years at least . . . may well be guilty of war crimes."

In a sense, that speculation was the end of act one of the *Pentagon Papers* drama. The opening of act two took place in Cambridge, Massachusetts. Neil Sheehan and his wife, Susan, a *New Yorker* writer, journeyed to Cambridge about the same time that Sheehan's piece appeared in the *Times*. They stayed in a motel and returned to Washington shortly thereafter with a large package of documents that would become widely known several weeks thereafter as the *Pentagon Papers*. Ellsberg had not given Sheehan all the material. He excluded the four "diplomatic volumes" because he did not want to jeopardize any American negotiations. "I wanted," he said some time later, "to get in the way of the bombing and the killing."[21]

Act two was not as slow moving as act one, but its momentum was impeded by skepticism and lawyers. For the collectors of little-known facts, it should be noted that the first clue to the existence of the McNamara history project appeared in *Parade*, a Sunday supplement magazine that frequently printed advance fragments of newsworthy mosaics. The *Pentagon Papers* fragment was published in October 1970. In March 1971, Thomas Oliphant bylined a front-page story in the *Boston Globe* that carried the headline: "Only 3 Have Read Secret Indo-China Report: All Urge Pull Out." One of the three was, of course, Ellsberg, who told Oliphant that by assisting in the Vietnam policy, "I was participating in a criminal conspiracy to wage aggressive war." Inexplicably, the Oliphant piece caused no fuss; nor was it picked up by other publications.

At the *Times* an obstacle course had to be navigated by those who wanted to move ahead swiftly. Sheehan was no sprinter. He moved more deliberately and thoughtfully than some editors thought necessary. Others considered his "war crimes" piece as too strident. Not all *Times* men were that keen on antiwar stories. David Halberstam had resigned in 1967 to write independently and, subsequently, chided the *Times* for not having probed with greater initiative the decisions to escalate in Vietnam. But Sheehan had the Washington bureau chief, Max Frankel, on his side. Frankel wanted to step up the pace before the *Washington Post* or the *Los Angeles Times* could publish the story. There was a long history of leaked, classified materials in *New York Times* stories. No news organization of any size could stay the course without leaks. The process was a second guessing game: When is a leak a trial balloon or a political ploy or an act of vengeance? James Reston, the much-honored Washington reporter and columnist for the *Times*, had used leaks from the Eisenhower administration about the *Yalta Papers*, and he had also agreed to suppress leaks about the Bay of Pigs invasion of Cuba at Jack Kennedy's request. The former furthered Reston's career, and the latter came to be a decision even President Kennedy regretted. Kennedy, after the fact, speculated that had the full story been told in advance, he might have called it off and spared the nation a costly fiasco.

Reston, who later became a *Times* vice president, advocated publication of the *Pentagon Papers*. If the *Times* ducked he threatened to run the material in his own newly acquired *Vineyard Gazette*, which was published on Martha's Vineyard, an island off the coast of Massachusetts populated in the summer by more movers and shakers from Washington per square foot than any other confined area on the planet. Frankel and Sheehan examined the materials and agreed that they were a "gold mine." The New York hierarchy was briefed, including Jim Greenfield, who had been in Kennedy's State Department and actually sat in on many of the meetings described in the *Papers*. He decided to bring Sheehan and Frankel to New York. Abe Rosenthal, the managing editor, and Greenfield claimed to have read forty-two relevant books written by former government officials, including Arthur Schlesinger Jr., Ted Sorensen, and Roger Hilsman. *Times* staff members went through ten years of *Times* clippings on Vietnam. The books and the clippings confirmed that very few—if any—of the classified *Pentagon Papers* had not been publicly reported, discussed, even debated. Greenfield said finally that the "principle" of protecting classified information, specifically with regard to Vietnam "had become almost academic."[22]

Rosenthal asked his assistant, Peter Millones, to set up a secure workstation outside the office. A three-room suite was rented at the New York Hilton, and *Times* security guards were assigned to keep it off limits. Desks and equipment were shipped in, and Hedrick Smith delayed his departure for Moscow to join the team, along with Fox Butterfield (a reporter who had worked in both North and South Vietnam) and Ned Kenworthy from the Washington Bureau. They would all avoid the *Times* building and labor exclusively at the Hilton. They worked more than twelve hours a day and decided to focus on what was newsworthy in the *Papers* rather than follow a chronological order. Sheehan would do the first article, and it would be about the Johnson years, the covert warfare, and the bombing of North Vietnam.

Meanwhile, the internal debate ran on. Harding Bancroft, who had once served in the State Department, was publisher Arthur Sulzberger's second in command on the administrative side. He was impressed by the advice of Herbert Brownell, who represented the *Times*'s outside law firm, Lord, Day and Lord. Brownell and Louis Loeb, another Lord, Day and Lord partner and a former general counsel of the *Times*, urged their client *not* to publish the *Pentagon Papers* in any part. They warned that the government would take legal action and most probably succeed. This view was not shared by a young in-house lawyer named James Goodale, who ran the legal department and became a vice-president of the *Times* company. Goodale identified with the editorial staff and knew many of the reporters. He had worked on strategic intelligence while in the army reserve and was familiar with the practice of using *New York Times* stories as footnotes in government reports, then classifying all the material involved. He said, "If, in fact, there was *New York Times* material in there [the *Pentagon Papers*], how could the government prohibit you from publishing what you had already published?"[23]

This was to be the case not only in regard to *Times* stories but similarly those eventually published in the *Washington Post* and other newspapers. Goodale put his arguments into a memorandum and lobbied hard, but he feared that Lord, Day and Lord would prevail. James Reston, Rosenthal, Frankel, and other editors were not ready to accept the fate predicted by Brownell and Loeb. The argument turned to procedure. Should the *Papers* be revealed in a series of substantial stories combining explication and actual documents? Should there be reporting only *about* the documents? Should there be one very large presentation—all of one issue of the Sunday magazine, for instance? Each approach had its advocates, but overwhelmingly the reporters and editors who wanted to publish preferred a series—and, for the fullest possible exposure of the facts, the inclusion of actual documents.

Then it became a matter of size and length. The Sheehan team wanted ten to twelve pages a day for about ten days. Publisher Sulzberger settled on six pages a day—perhaps to contain costs, perhaps to avoid overkill. He was about to depart with his family for England. On June 11, he met with his top people and agreed on six pages each day for ten days, documents to be included. The editors had already determined that they would avoid any sensational headlines. As a final precaution, Sulzberger insisted that Bancroft should be given a last look at all stories and have the authority to suggest changes. Presumably, if the suggestions were unacceptable to the editors, they would call Sulzberger in London.[24]

Rosenthal had taken an empty office on the ninth floor of the *Times* building, stripped it of all niceties, covered the walls with masonite, and moved in a page-proof press along with automatic typesetting perforators, a galley-proof press, makeup tables, and a paper shredder. Caution against any premature revelations was intensely enforced. The printers began type-setting before Sulzberger gave the green light. The dummy for the June 13, 1971, Sunday edition was prepared on Saturday afternoon, June 12. Sanford Ungar's account refers to "a gaping blank, four columns wide and five inches deep . . . on the front page, marked only with the word 'Neil.'"[25] The six inside pages agreed upon were positioned late on Saturday, and Neil Sheehan's low-key story about the *Pentagon Papers* as a whole was dropped into the empty space at the last minute. Rosenthal, still uneasy about the company's commitment and wondering what would happen if the government demanded that the *Times* cease any further publication, sought to reassure his boss in Europe. On Monday, two *Times* editors called friends at another newspaper to ask if they would send Sulzberger a congratulatory cable. They did.

How many different renderings this vignette might have if each of the principals put his recollections on a word processor would make an interesting footnote, but it is the consequences of publication that have endured. What happened on that Sunday when nearly a million copies of the *New York Times* were delivered to newsstands and private homes? Initially, very little. Neither Sheehan nor the top editors received any phone calls regarding his story that Sunday. Salisbury saw a great many people at lunch and dinner but heard not one word on the *Pentagon Papers*.[26] On Thursday, June 10, 1971, Robert Mardian, assistant attorney general serving John Mitchell as head of Internal Security, gave a speech in Los Angeles. His topic covered "lawlessness and the indifference to the obligations of citizenship." He accused the American news media of contributing to this trend. It was not until Monday morning, when he returned to Washington, that Mardian saw a copy of the *New York Times*. The Monday issue contained a second installment of the series on the *Pentagon Papers*, dealing with the decision to bomb the North Vietnamese. He phoned John Mitchell, who had known about the *Times* series for a day, but took no action. Secretary of Defense Laird had phoned Mitchell on Sunday and phoned him again on Monday because he was about to appear before Fulbright's committee and expected questions on the *Papers*. Mitchell told him to merely say the matter was under consideration at the Justice Department. Mitchell also requested of Laird a memorandum explaining what the *Pentagon Papers* were and how they had been prepared. No one at Justice knew anything about the *Papers* and no one at Defense had read them. Laird's memo, which was instantly stamped top secret, could describe only general suppositions about harm to national security.

In due course Republican politicians communicated their views. Senator Dole advised against going to court. He saw the attractive possibilities of great embarrassment for the Democrats. The *Papers* were apparently focused on Lyndon Johnson's administration, and it was known they *concluded* with documents pertaining to 1968. President Nixon therefore would be untouched, the Republicans assumed. On Tuesday morning, at a White House meeting with Republican leaders, Nixon also leaned toward the strategy of keeping hands off. Kissinger's office disagreed. The Pakistani government was just then helping to arrange a visit to China for the American president. Kissinger was also secretly negotiating with the North Vietnamese government at meetings held in Paris. Both of these critical initiatives could be threatened if the governments involved did not believe America could protect confidentiality. It was Kissinger's view that an injunction must be conceived and delivered. It would, of course, seek to stop publication and would be, by definition, a prior restraint. The long history of opposition to any prior restraint had only a month earlier been reaffirmed by Chief Justice Burger—not an admirer of the press—on May 17 in a decision on the distribution of leaflets in Chicago charging a local real estate broker with antiminority blockbusting. Burger, in his opinion, reiterated the "heavy presumption" against the "Constitutional validity" of any prior restraint on expression.

Nixon's administration had since 1968 been actively attacking the press—particularly the "Eastern establishment press." Vice President Spiro Agnew, who subsequently left office in disgrace, was the point man. He had shrewdly used Montgomery, Alabama—still smarting from Sullivan's defeat—as one location for a denunciation of the *Washington Post* and all its tributaries. He accused the *New York Times* of suppressing favorable news about the Nixon administration. Agnew used antiwar sentiment as a symbol of moral decay and media treachery. Meanwhile, Attorney General Mitchell issued 122 subpoenas for film or testimony from CBS and NBC reporters, achieving little more than costly annoyance. But he did *not* investigate the Kent State killings and rejected reports—including evidence developed by the FBI—concerning an "advance agreement among the Guardsmen" to fire on the student protesters.[27]

The meetings held on Monday, June 14, to discuss possible actions against the *New York Times* did not include Solicitor General Erwin Griswold, who would soon find himself representing the government's view on the *Pentagon Papers* before the Supreme Court. Ultimately, Mitchell and Mardian sent a telegram to the *Times* asking that all further publication cease and that the *Papers* be returned to the Department of Defense. The telegram stated that "publication of this information is directly prohibited by the provisions of the Espionage Law, Title 18, United States Code, Section 793."[28]

Nixon had called Mitchell at his Watergate apartment, where the telegram was being composed, and had the message read to him. He cleared it and Mitchell sent it to the FBI for transmittal to the *Times*. The first delivery went to a fish company in Brooklyn, but on a second effort it reached the newspaper. Mardian, as it turned out, had phoned the *Times* and read the telegram to Bancroft, who said he would get back to him in an hour. It was early Tuesday morning and the *Times* would go to press in about two hours. Louis Loeb, speaking for Lord, Day and Lord, vigorously recommended compliance. James Goodale, who had rushed into the office from his New York apartment, insisted, "We won't stop publication." Rosenthal demanded that they call Sulzberger at his London hotel. After the publisher had heard both sides, he decided to go ahead and publish. The Tuesday edition rolled, and Goodale knew this meant a legal fight. When he asked Loeb to prepare the defense, Loeb turned him over to Herbert Brownell, who had been Eisenhower's attorney general. Brownell was astonished that the editors would consider defying Mitchell, and he declined to represent the newspaper. This was, in effect, the end of the relationship between Lord, Day and Lord and the *New York Times*.[29]

A response to the government's telegram had been hammered out. It was phoned to James Reston in Washington for his comments. As fortune would have it, Reston was sharing a meal with Robert McNamara. There was a phrase in the *Times* reply saying the newspaper would abide by "decisions of the courts." This phrase was repeated to McNamara, who suggested dryly, "not the courts—the *highest* court." The *Times* apparently split the difference and settled for "We will abide by the decision of the court." The reply began by "respectfully" refusing the request of the attorney general and explained that "it is in the interest of the people of this country to be informed of the material contained in the series of articles."[30]

On June 15, the *Times* ran Sheehan's third article, but the major story on the front page was about the refusal of Mitchell's request that the *Pentagon Papers* be returned and publication cease. Goodale had seen Yale law professor Alexander Bickel the day before because Bickel, a constitutional scholar, was preparing an amicus curiae brief for a number of news organizations in regard to a reporter's right to confidentiality. The case involved *Times* reporter Earl Caldwell and would be in all likelihood on its way to the Supreme Court in the near future. The *Pentagon Papers* were also discussed, and Bickel had commended the *Times* for their decision to publish. He had indicated that the newspaper had the right to do so under the First Amendment. Bickel might well be the man to take up the argument Lord, Day and Lord had ducked.

Goodale phoned Floyd Abrams, who would become one of the leading First Amendment advocates in America over the next twenty years. Abrams had been a student of Bickel's at Yale, and he suggested that he and his colleagues at Cahill, Gordon would join the battle if Bickel agreed to lead it. The *Times* newsroom tracked Bickel to his mother's apartment on Riverside Drive in Manhattan, but it was after midnight before they made contact. He gave his consent and managed to reach the Cahill, Gordon office by the early hours of the morning. He and Abrams worked without a break to prepare a ten-page brief for a meeting with U.S. Attorney Whitney North Seymour.[31]

The *Pentagon Papers* litigation took a notably brief period of fifteen days. The process began in New York before U.S. District Judge Murray Gurfein. All that Seymour knew about the *Papers* he had read in the *Times*. Because the wrong part of the Espionage Act was cited, Judge Gurfein delayed until after lunch that day his response to the government's request for a temporary order restraining the *Times* from further publication. The judge had been very recently appointed to the bench by President Nixon and this was, by chance, his first case. The government insisted that further publication be prevented because of potentially serious damage to American diplomatic efforts and to the national defense. There were, however, no specific examples given. Professor Bickel pointed out that no American court had ever successfully enjoined the publication of a newspaper. He asked the judge if he wanted to be the first to do such a thing—especially in view of the government's generalized suppositions and lack of hard evidence. Judge Gurfein, appealing to patriotism, suggested the *Times* suspend further publication of the *Papers* voluntarily until the case could be more fully heard. Bickel rejected the request and stated that "a newspaper exists to publish, not to submit its publishing schedule to the United States government."[32]

Judge Gurfein issued a temporary restraining order, all the same, until the hearing he set for Friday—three days later. He did *not*, however, order the *Times* to return its copies of the documents. During the delay period the *Washington Post*, much disturbed by its inability to compete with the *Times* on a story that appeared to be the largest security leak since Stalin learned about the making of the atom bomb, finally put the pieces of the puzzle together.

The *Post* had hired Ben Bagdikian, a onetime media critic of great distinction who had known Ellsberg when both men were at the Rand Corporation. Bagdikian was at Rand for a short interlude, writing a book about mass communications. At the *Post* he became an assistant managing editor for national affairs. On Wednesday, June 16, he tried to reach Ellsberg, leaving messages wherever possible. The process took awhile but eventually paid off. The *Times* had that day not published any *Pentagon Papers* materials. The editors were able to shift gears and report on the philosophical and legal conflict between press and government. It was an issue that engaged more of the nation's press organizations than the first three installments of the *Papers*.

Not so the television news organizations. The electronic press had the FCC to reckon with, and the commission was now chaired by a Republican, Dean

Burch, who had, many critics believed, intimidated the networks ever since he was appointed. Whatever the source of their timidity, the networks moved very slowly, if at all, on the *Pentagon Papers* story. The first major break in their ranks occurred when Walter Cronkite managed an interview with Ellsberg at a secret location. The interview gave the *Papers*, and their dissemination, greater notoriety but produced no revelations of substance.

Bagdikian finally spoke to Ellsberg from a pay phone in Washington's Statler Hilton Hotel. There was widespread suspicion that the *Washington Post* telephones were bugged by the government, and Ellsberg had insisted on the outside communication. Bagdikian flew to Boston not long thereafter and endured a number of maneuvers designed to elude the possibility of surveillance by the authorities. He finally received a massive number of papers and packed them into a large cardboard box. Ellsberg was clearly upset by the *Times* acquiescence to Judge Gurfein's order. He wanted the publicity to keep its momentum—on television or in print. The *Post*, he later maintained, had promised "that they would give it a number of pages per day."[33]

There had been, for twelve days, no trace of Ellsberg and he had not yet been identified publicly as the source of the leaked *Papers*. By Wednesday, June 16, *Newsweek* had published an interview with Ellsberg, and the FBI was reportedly telling foreign journalists that Ellsberg was, indeed, the culprit. The St. Louis *Post-Dispatch* confirmed the Ellsberg role in its Thursday edition, the same day that Bagdikian arrived back in Washington with his cumbersome box held together by a piece of rope that had been used to restrain a dog. He had phoned Ben Bradlee from Boston, and it was agreed that he and the *Papers* would go to Bradlee's home rather than to the office. Bradlee gathered a band of editors, lawyers, and secretaries at his Georgetown house. He reckoned that he had two days at the most to cull the 4,400 pages Ellsberg had given Bagdikian. There would be a tense discussion in the living room and in the library between executives and editors. The *Post* was part of a large media company—magazines, television stations, news service, interests in a newsprint company and warehouses—and above all, a public offering of common stock had gone to the market on June 15. The *Post*'s lawyers, for reasons not dissimilar to those given by the former *Times* lawyers, Lord, Day and Lord, advised against publication. Among other points made, there was the charge that to publish the first story the next day—or at most the day after—was irresponsibly swift. After all, the *Times* had taken nearly three months to check out every possible danger to national security in the materials it had selected. Bagdikian argued vehemently against delay. They were not bound, he said, by the government's action against the *Times*. Furthermore, they should not cave in because it would appear "as though they were not supporting the *Times*." Sounding much like Alexander Bickel in his response to Judge Gurfein, Bagdikian declared, "The only way to assert the right to publish is to publish."[34]

Top reporters threatened to take early retirement or quit their jobs if the *Post* didn't publish something at once on the *Papers*, and many accused the *Post* management and attorneys of cowardice. Finally, Bradlee and editorial page editor Philip Geyelin called Katherine Graham. She listened and paused and then said, "Go ahead." The proprietors of both important newspapers, the *Times* and the *Post*, had decided to stand by their journalists. There was a last-minute delay at the *Post* based on a legal technicality, and Mrs. Graham had to decide a second time. She did not waver. Shortly after midnight the presses rolled and the morning edition featured a four-column headline: "Documents Reveal U.S. Effort in '54 to Delay Viet Election." The byline belonged to Chalmers Roberts, a veteran reporter who was an authority on the 1954 Geneva conference.

The government was taken by surprise when, on Friday, June 18, the *Post* entered the scene with its first article. It made Mitchell's case against the *Times* more difficult. A proliferating story was not as easily curtailed as an exclusive. Bickel would make the comment that the government had alleged *any* further publication would gravely endanger national security—yet "the republic stands. And it stood for the first three days." To some, it might seem naive that great danger could ever appear so quickly, but it was the principle that evolved out of Oliver Wendell Holmes's original "clear and present danger" concept. The government was forced to act against the *Post*—in this instance before Judge Gerhard Gesell. In confronting the *Times* and the *Post*, the government was hobbled by the fact that no one in any important position had read the documents. But it was possible that such ignorance could be obscured—at least from public knowledge. The first hearing was, as it turned out, *in camera*.

The problem of ignorance, however, was even greater than expected. The government offered an example of serious, immediate danger by adding a supplement to an affidavit given by Admiral Noel Gayler, director of the National Security Agency. He indicated that a certain document would reveal the NSA could intercept North Vietnamese communications and knew how to break their code. The technical adviser to the *Washington Post* lawyers was George Wilson, the *Post*'s defense correspondent. He knew the NSA document well. It had been published on page 34 of the 1968 Senate Foreign Relations Committee hearings on the Tonkin Gulf—an especially annoying burr under Senator Fulbright's saddle. Wilson had actually brought a copy of the record with him. He read it to the judges and to the government's attorneys. Their one example of a secret that the *Pentagon Papers* would expose to alleged devastating effect was already public information. The sound of the government's case collapsing may not have been audible, but everyone at the *in camera* hearing was aware of it.

On Wednesday, June 23, one court of appeals ruled against the *Times*, and another ruled in favor of the *Post*. Publication was officially restrained at both newspapers until Friday evening to allow the government a chance to appeal; but the split in the judgments assured a Supreme Court hearing.

The Supreme Court's so-called year was concluded, or very close to its end. Justice William O. Douglas had been at his summer home on the West Coast for a week. The other justices had a final conference scheduled for Friday, June 25, to tuck away any loose ends, but now they knew they would have to hear the *Pentagon Papers* case because they could not leave a newspaper of the stature of the *Times* in limbo while the *Washington Post* was free to publish a story the *Times* had begun. At the Friday conference it was, despite the conditions, a close run thing. The justices voted five to four to hear the two cases. They actually scheduled an unprecedented *Saturday* morning sitting and allowed twice the normal time for oral argument. Douglas flew back to Washington. He had phoned in his vote, which was *not* in favor of hearing the cases because he joined with Justices Black, Brennan, and Marshall in preferring that the *Post* be left in the clear and the *Times* be released from the restraint put upon it. As it turned out, the full Court convened on Saturday morning. Two briefs were prepared by each side—one to be open, the other confidential.[35]

More than 1,500 people stood in line outside the Supreme Court building that morning—for 174 seats. Solicitor General Griswold had filed a secret motion asking that all arguments be held *in camera*, but the first announcement Chief Justice Burger made to a very full courtroom was that the government's request for *in camera* arguments had been denied by a six-to-three vote. The voting on the "merits" of the cases was to be precisely the same—six to three. After hearing arguments, however, each justice wrote a separate opinion. The first to complete this task was Douglas, who flew west again on Monday. His colleagues were still composing as he left.

At 2:30 P.M., Wednesday, June 30, the Court reconvened, minus Douglas. Justice Brennan had drafted an opinion that was the opener. He emphasized that prior restraint requires convincing proof, and the government had not produced it. The same three justices who had dissented in the rejection of Griswold's motion for secrecy now dissented from the majority on the merits. Burger referred to the *Pentagon Papers* as "purloined" documents and caustically asked why the *Times* wanted immediate relief when they had taken many weeks to study the documents before publishing. Justice Harlan made a similar point about haste, saying the Court had been "almost irresponsibly feverish in dealing with these cases." Justice Harry Blackmun was convinced that serious harm would be caused by publication—perhaps prolonging the war, perhaps jeopardizing the release of American prisoners. Solicitor General Griswold had argued in the lower court that confidentiality of communication is as essential to the government as confidentiality of sources is to the press.

The classification policy had been set by President Eisenhower in 1953. It designated three categories: top secret, secret, and confidential. Pious statements were issued in both the Eisenhower and Kennedy administrations regarding "unnecessary classification and overclassification," but bureaucrats at all levels continued to use rubber stamps to deny access to information—some of which had already been published or openly discussed, some which had no bearing on security, and some which the stamper believed would look more important if it were classified. Out of this undisciplined freedom to classify emerged distortions, misuse, and venality. Illogical and harmful limitations were not in the public interest, but there was no clear means of limiting the limitations. Under such a system it was no surprise that Leslie Gelb would be required to brand *all* the *Pentagon Papers* top secret because a *few* of them might reasonably be considered potentially damaging to legitimate American interests or truly vital to national security and therefore required top secret classification.

A memorandum from one of the members of the Joint Chiefs of Staff, complaining that the top-secret classification was becoming excessive, triggered no corrective reform because the memorandum itself was stamped top secret. In point of fact, the Special Task Force on Secrecy, set up by the Pentagon's Defense Science Board in 1970, noted that "the amount of scientific and technical information which is classified could profitably be decreased by as much as *ninety per cent* by limiting the amount of information which is classified and the duration of its classification" (emphasis added).[36]

Against such a shadowy background Solicitor General Griswold, who would have to argue for the government in favor of restraining publication, soon learned that very few people on the government's side had read the *Papers* or knew what was in them. When he asked high-ranking officials to give him a short list of critical items, they produced a group of forty-one. He read the documents that were singled out and realized that they might be politically embarrassing, but they were certainly no threat to security. Griswold wrote an op-ed piece for the *Washington Post* in February 1989 stating that after he had been given a chance to review most of the *Papers*, he had concluded there was not a single document that could damage or impede America's security interests. However, he could see a great deal of embarrassing information pertaining to various public officials and to their decisions.

Griswold, returning to the Supreme Court hearing, had cut the list of forty-one items to eleven—one of them being the "diplomatic volumes" that Ellsberg had withheld anyway. Bickel, meanwhile, prepared his case for the *Times* with great care. He had not appeared before the Supreme Court before, but he had written and lectured on the Court extensively. He was only forty-six at the time, but he had delivered the Holmes lectures at Harvard Law School, and these had been expanded into a book called *The Supreme Court and the Idea of Progress*—a work that was widely discussed and influential in legal circles. Bickel was a colleague and close friend of Robert Bork, and they shared a view of the Court that opposed attempts to shape public policy or cross the line into areas best left to the political process. For the sake of his client, the *Times*, Bickel the lawyer (rather than Bickel the professor) plotted his strategy so as to win the support of at least one "swing justice"—Potter Stewart or Byron White. He provided a moderate rather than an absolutist approach. Ironically, Griswold had been one of his professors at Harvard Law School. Neither man was easily labeled in conventional liberal/conservative terms.

Griswold surprised legal experts by mentioning in his brief the dubious means by which the *Times* came into possession of the *Papers* and referred to "common law right of literary property" despite the fact that the government, as servant of the people, has no claim of copyright. As to the president's power to conduct foreign affairs and his role as commander in chief, Griswold declared: "To limit the President's power in this regard solely to punishment of those who disclose secret information would render the power meaningless: the harm sought to be prevented would have been irreparably accomplished."[37]

Bickel articulated the precedents for resisting "prior restraint" and added that any exceptions had to do with "the redress of individual or private wrongs"—that is, libel. The president, Bickel observed, "can discipline, he can discharge, and he can repossess government property"—but there was no legislation authorizing prior restraint as a means of dealing with security leaks. "Only when publication could be held to lead directly and almost unavoidably to a disastrous event," Bickel said again, can prior restraint be justified. Two district judges and two appellate courts had reviewed the government's evidence and could not find potential disaster. Delay by limitation becomes censorship, the argument went on, and the *Times* had been restrained for eleven days, the *Post* for seven. The *Times* brief ended with a historical overview:

> Press and government have a curious interlocking, both cooperative and adversary, relationship. . . . This has been the case, more or less, in this century since the extension of manhood suffrage and the rise of an independent rather than party-connected or faction-connected press. It is not a tidy relationship. . . . The greater power within it lies with the government. The press wields the countervailing power, conferred upon it by the First Amendment. If there is something near a balance, it is an uneasy one. Any redressing of it at the expense of the press, as this case demonstrated, can come only at the cost of incursions into the First Amendment.[38]

The *Post* was represented by William R. Glendon, not in the least professorial and known for his earthiness. He shrewdly attacked the Espionage Act, which Congress had amended in 1950, saying: "Nothing in this Act shall be construed to authorize, require, or establish military or civilian censorship or in any way to limit or infringe upon freedom of the press or of speech as guaranteed by the Constitution of the United States." Glendon ridiculed the notion that the *Post* could have gotten hold of the *Papers* by using the Freedom of Information Act. Simply put, the *Papers* could not be *declassified* by the authority of the Freedom of Information Act and therefore could not be ascertained. Glendon's clincher was to assert that the *Papers* were already so widely distributed that the "government's efforts to suppress the truth will not prevail. . . . Public revelations of this controversial history will continue apace until it will all become available to the American public."[39]

Chief Justice Burger made no secret of his skepticism about press behavior, but when he appeared at the American Bar Association convention nearly a month after the *Pentagon Papers* case had been resolved, he said in a television interview, "We can't do anything about the media. This is a matter of self-restraint. . . . We have just got to have a pervasive civility in dealing with all our problems."[40]

Friday night, June 25, a warrant for Daniel Ellsberg's arrest had been issued. He was charged with illegally copying and possessing government documents. At 10 A.M. on Monday, June 28, Ellsberg arrived by taxi at the post office building in downtown Boston. He told reporters and a crowd of onlookers—many of whom were there to support him—that he had indeed made the *Papers* available to Senator Fulbright and to the *Times*. He said he had done so on his own and would take responsibility for all his actions. He was placed under arrest by the FBI. The magistrate asked for his passport and granted a $50,000 personal recognizance bond that he wouldn't have to pay unless he failed to appear in court. A Los Angeles grand jury indicted him the same day. About forty-eight hours later, Ellsberg's lawyers could point to six Supreme Court opinions on the *Pentagon Papers* that in one way or another made the prosecution of Ellsberg seem less urgent.

Justice Potter Stewart had decided that the government's evidence was unconvincing, although he suspected there were some components of the *Papers* that would do damage if published. More significantly, he commented on the classification system: "For when everything is classified, then nothing is classified, and the system becomes one to be disregarded by the cynical or the careless, and to be manipulated by those intent on self protection or self promotion."[41]

Justice Hugo Black, however, remained a purist. "I believe," he said, "that every moment's continuance of the injunctions against these newspapers amounts to a flagrant, indefensible and continuing violation of the First Amendment." It was not the first time, or the last, that jurists who favored the closest possible reading of the Constitution, the "strict constructionist" view, would find themselves conflicted. Most of those who so believed were conservatives, and many were sympathetic to Richard Nixon or, at least, to the centrality of executive privilege. Justice Black was not their soulmate, but he was enunciating a constitutional philosophy they shared. Justice Black, of course, did not confine himself to the constitutional point. He elaborated eloquently: "Paramount among the responsibilities of a free press is the duty to prevent any part of the *government* from *deceiving* the *people*" (emphasis added). By uncovering government actions vital to the public understanding, Black noted, "the newspapers nobly did precisely that which the Founders hoped and trusted they would do."[42]

Justice Douglas turned the knife: "The dominant purpose of the First Amendment was to prohibit the widespread practice of government suppression of embarrassing information." Justices Brennan and Marshall echoed Alexander Bickel's theme that the Supreme Court should not be asked "to prevent behavior that the Congress has specifically declined to prohibit."[43]

As for Justice White, there was not much space between yes and no. He seemed to be straddling the issue, believing that the damage was probable but the government's case was too weak. He then suggested that the government might find a better way of doing it: "That the government mistakenly chose to proceed by injunction does not mean that it could not successfully proceed in another way."[44]

Among the strategies the government might have developed was one Chief Justice Burger described with considerable asperity, directed at publishers. He claimed to be astonished that "a newspaper long regarded as a great institution in American life would fail to perform one of the basic and simple duties of every citizen with respect to the discovery or possession of stolen property or secret government documents. That duty, I had thought— perhaps naively—was to report, forthwith, to responsible public officers. This duty rests on taxi drivers, justices, and the *New York Times*."[45]

During the summer of 1971, editor and publisher William F. Buckley Jr. filled almost an entire issue of his conservative magazine the *National Review* with a report called "The Secret Papers They Didn't Publish: Top-Secret Memoranda—1962–1965." These materials included a section on a Pentagon recommendation to Secretary McNamara that America should conduct a "demonstration drop of nuclear devices . . . followed by use of nuclear bombs and devices where militarily suitable." The *Times*, the *Post*, and other newspapers quoted the *National Review* story extensively. Not long after, Buckley convened a press conference and revealed that everything he had published about the "secret papers" was a hoax. He was widely criticized for being irresponsible, but the hoax was a revealing and instructive exercise. It took the skin off both government policymaking and journalistic behavior. Obviously, high-level government officials, and many editors, were unable to detect a deliberate send-up.

Meanwhile, the FBI and the Justice Department continued an almost obsessive search for Ellsberg's collaborators and the evidence to prosecute all concerned on criminal charges. There were intimations, not apparently discouraged by Deputy Attorney General Richard Kleindienst, that the 1972 presidential campaign might not focus on Vietnam or the economy "but [on] whether an *arrogant press* is free to undermine the security of this country without check"(emphasis added).[46]

Ellsberg's fate was to be decided before U.S. District Judge William M. (Matt) Byrne Jr., considered to be a civil libertarian. Hearings were scheduled to begin on January 6, 1972, but a grand jury escalated charges against Ellsberg and Russo for stealing, concealing, retaining, and conveying secret documents, among other offenses. A number of political developments in Washington interrupted the trial of Ellsberg and Russo, but it finally resumed on January 17, 1973. By then, the Watergate investigation was making headline news. The trial took place in Los Angeles, far away from the gathering Watergate storm in Washington. Between January and April 1973, testimony was heard regarding alleged threats to national security caused by the *Pentagon Papers* disclosures. Toward the end of April, the Watergate prosecutors learned that White House "plumbers," including E. Howard Hunt Jr. and G. Gordon Liddy, had conducted, in 1971, a burglary of a psychiatrist's office in Beverly Hills, looking for damaging personal information on Daniel Ellsberg. What they found was not significant, but it was clearly an illegal operation on every level. Judge Byrne resisted a dismissal in the Ellsberg trial until May 11, 1973, and then, reportedly exasperated by emerging wiretapping evidence, he threw out the charges against Ellsberg and Russo in their entirety. There was, however, no formal acquittal, and even twenty years later in a 1994 telephone conversation, Ellsberg explained that he would not discuss some aspects of the case because accusations remained technically on the books. In July 1974, John Erlichman and G. Gordon Liddy were found guilty of a conspiracy to violate the psychiatrist's civil rights. About a month later, President Richard Nixon resigned.

The publication of the *Pentagon Papers* (absent the "diplomatic volumes") had no significant effect on national public opinion. It didn't stimulate an outcry, a movement, or even that kind of debate and discussion that clearly reshapes political policies. The frantic search for guilty parties in Ellsberg's so-called conspiracy helped to keep the story alive. The Bantam book, made out of the ten *Times* installments, sold over a million copies, but many editors and publishers gradually became aware of a deeply ironic and sobering reality—they were better off before the Supreme Court opinions were handed down on the *Pentagon Papers*. Those in government who yearned for some means of restraining the press on security issues, at least while preparing for court hearings, rejoiced that there appeared to be a tacit assurance because publication *could* be stayed if the evidence supported a high probability of immediate serious damage to American interests. The fact that in the *Pentagon Papers* cases the government had failed to produce persuasive evidence did not mean that it could not one day, in a future case, convince the courts by using the *Pentagon Papers* opinions as precedent.

Alexander Bickel commented philosophically on the outcome of the *Pentagon Papers* cases in his book *The Morality of Consent*: "Before June 15, 1971, through the troubles of 1798, through one civil and two world wars, and other wars, there had never been an effort by the Federal government to censor a newspaper by attempting to impose a restraint prior to publication, directly or in litigation. The *New York Times* won its case, over the Pentagon Papers, but that spell was broken, and in a sense, freedom was thus diminished."[47]

Bickel, who died of cancer at the age of forty-nine, believed that "those freedoms which are neither challenged nor defined are the most secure."[48] His friend Judge Robert Bork, in a 1984 opinion that actually expanded First Amendment protection against libel, seemed to take Bickel's apprehension into account when he underscored the difference between "creating new constitutional rights" and trying "to discern how the Framers' values, defined in the context of the world they knew, apply to the world we know."[49]

The world we know has been conveyed to most of us, however imperfectly, by an unfettered press. The means of conveyance may be proliferating, but finding reliable contexts will be no easier. A nation besotted with fragments of information needs a frequent reminder of context to test alleged truth, to arouse moral reasoning, and to preserve its freedoms.

5

PRACTICING FREEDOM

What those guys back then 200 years ago tapped into was obviously something so elemental that you go to Kenya, or you go to Tibet or you go anywhere and you talk to journalists there who are not trained, never been to journalism school, maybe never even read an English language publication, but they start putting out little publications and they instinctively know that what they have to do is to help the people in their village or their town understand what is going on.

—Bill Kovach,
former *New York Times* Washington bureau chief;
curator, Nieman Foundation for
Journalism Fellowships at Harvard

The American experience, as it has been called, provided a unique set of circumstances—a seedbed for the growth of a freewheeling, undisciplined press in which flowering eloquence and farsightedness grew among the weeds of demagoguery and self-interest. The evolution of journalistic practice that accompanied the growth of the early American newspapers is, in many respects, a premeditation of responsible modern media.

In colonial America, and after independence, any man who could afford the equipment might become a publisher. The range of pamphleteering, partisan vituperation, monitoring of public officials, and reporting of legislative debates before and after 1776 inexorably developed a market for daily and weekly newspapers. Historical estimates of literacy in colonial America vary substantially, but there is general agreement that probably close to half the white adult males could read. The newspapers that appeared in the early years of the eighteenth century had very small circulations not only because of limited literacy but because publishers were concerned with an elite property-owning readership. In the southern colonies public speaking and printing were controlled to the point of censorship, particularly in regard to slavery. The northern colonies permitted greater diversity. Partisanship and individuality were developing characteristics in northern communities. The newspapers were amplified by word of mouth, church gatherings, tavern discussions, and visitors from other communities. Men who could read would read aloud at home to their wives and children and to friends and neighbors at taverns and meeting places. Artists of the early American period often depicted the reading of newspapers in their scenes of American life. The gradual proliferation of printers produced more opinions and less conformity. The urban marketplace for information became competitive by the 1720s. There were not many skilled craftsmen in the colonies, however, who could make paper, manufacture and set type, or repair the primitive machinery used in a print shop. Those who learned worked for printers who were not eager to produce books because long manuscripts required too much of their limited supply of paper, type, and press time. Publishers preferred pamphlets, broadsides, and, above all, newspapers. The same typefaces could be used one day, reset the next. Proprietors were interested in profitability then as now. It was cheaper to import books from England. There were only a few private book collectors in America during the first part of the eighteenth century—notable among them the theologian and prolific writer Cotton Mather.[1]

The Library Company of Philadelphia, started in the 1740s with the encouragement of Benjamin Franklin, was a model for libraries in Newport and Charleston and eventually most urban centers in the colonies. Some libraries levied subscription fees, but over time new associations were founded to support circulating libraries that loaned books free and often concentrated on key subjects to match public interest. By the 1770s there were at least 150 bookstores in the five largest colonial cities.[2] The ubiquitous Dr. Franklin—philosopher, diplomat, scientist, businessman, printer, publisher, educator—articulated the standards of a rising middle class composed of artisans, farmers, and shopkeepers. In his best-selling *Poor Richard's Almanac* the prolific Pennsylvanian advocated thrift, initiative, diligence, and other desirable attributes in the form of aphorisms ("Lost time is never found again"; "Fish and visitors smell in three days"; "Keep your eyes open before marriage, half shut afterwards.") Franklin was unique among the Founders. He understood and liked the common man, but he could sit among the aristocracy, at home and abroad, with equanimity and a very ready, ribald wit.

In 1719 Franklin had taken note of a newspaper in Philadelphia called the *American Weekly Mercury*. It was the only local newspaper being published at the time and Franklin said of it: "a paltry thing, wretchedly managed, in no way entertaining, and yet profitable. I therefore freely thought a good paper would scarcely fail of good encouragement." He acted on that supposition ten years later when he commenced publication of the *Pennsylvania Gazette*, which he had taken over in 1728. In 1729 he enlarged it to a four-page weekly. As a publisher he had strong notions about appropriate standards. "I carefully excluded," he said, "all libeling and personal abuse, which has of late years become so disgraceful to our Country."[3] He discovered that newspapers were delivered free by the post office, but the postmasters frequently owned or had a financial interest in one newspaper and denied delivery to all others. This was palpably unfair in Franklin's view, and when he became deputy postmaster general for all the colonies in 1758, he changed the rules so that every paper would be treated the same. Furthermore, it would cost each newspaper ninepence a year for each fifty miles of carriage given by the post office.

As a young man Franklin had worked for a paper in Boston, but when he launched the *Philadelphia Gazette* he wrote, edited, and printed the publication himself. He was known to write letters to himself as editor and then answer them. In 1731 under the title *An Apology for Printers*, he offered some of his convictions about journalism. Among them was the belief that when public men differed in their opinions, both sides should be given equal space in the press. He added, with deliberate irony, "If all printers were determined not to print anything until they were sure it offended nobody, there would be very little printed."[4] He knew the value of a printing press from design and mechanism to literary and propaganda purposes. Franklin was, among his many incarnations, an inventor as well. The lightning rod, rocking chair, and an enclosed stove resulted from his experiments. He also devised bifocal spectacles. In 1741 he introduced the *General Magazine and Historical Chronicle for all the British Plantations in America*. It was, in effect, the earliest literary digest in the new world.[5]

Newspapers, from the first decade of the eighteenth century until well into the nineteenth, engaged American writers, editorialists, and politicians in the adventure of free expression and the arousal of public opinion on a regular basis—with demonstrably swift results. There had been newspapers of a sort in England during the Restoration, but it was many years before journalism as a business was established and familiar. The colonies adopted the idea early and enthusiastically. Information and news were tailored to constituencies. Political records were frequently the basic product, especially in the earlier years—official notices, transcripts of debate and discussions in the state assemblies and other governmental materials. But editors soon added short bits of poetry, aphorisms, even general advice.

To help merchants and tradesmen, the colonial newspapers published shipping schedules and advertisements. What evolved was, for energetic, busy colonists, a resource that kept them abreast of the actions and opinions of those who were delegated to make decisions and carry out policies not necessarily born of popular consent. Politics was an entertainment of sorts, and newspapers were a source of amusement along with information. The building of a way of life on the foundations of individual freedom and the control of government by the citizens, were documented and circulated through newspapers in a manner that abided by no grand design or special philosophy. The process grew quite naturally out of the curiosity and needs of colonial Americans from many countries and traditions who had settled thousands of miles away from older societies given to class distinction and the omnipresence of some higher authority not of their choosing. These older structures were remembered with little affection.[6]

No printer in the colonies was more distinguished for articulating the independence and hunger for freedom that new arrivals in the colonies were to share than Isaiah Thomas. His career is herewith described in some detail because it represents the ethical values, the courage, and the risks inherent to the proprietorship of a *responsible* news medium in the early years of this nation. The principles involved remain the same two centuries later.[7]

Thomas was born in Massachusetts in January 1749 and brought to Boston at age six. So far as he knew, he had never been in a schoolhouse. There was in Boston in 1755 a printer named Zachariah Fowle who occasionally published ballads and small books. Fowle had no children and he promised Isaiah's mother, a widow of little means, that he would treat the boy as his own and give him a good education, teach him the art of printing, and allow him to choose at the age of fourteen whether he wanted to leave and seek his own fortune or remain as an apprentice.

A year later Fowle persuaded Mrs. Thomas to have Isaiah "bound over to him" as an apprentice. An indenture of apprenticeship was signed in June 1756. The apprenticeship was to continue until Isaiah Thomas was twenty-one, and the conditions of his service to Fowle and his wife were as follows:

> During all which said time or term, the said apprentice, his said master and mistress, well and faithfully shall serve; their secrets he shall keep close; their commandments lawful and honest everywhere he shall gladly obey; he shall do no damage to his said master, etc., nor suffer it to be done by others without letting or giving reasonable notice thereof to said master, etc.; he shall not waste the goods of his said master, etc., nor lend them unlawfully to any; at cards, dice, or any other unlawful game or games he shall not play; fornication he shall not commit; matrimony during the said term he shall not contract; taverns, alehouses or places of gaming he shall not haunt or frequent; from the service of his said master, etc., by day nor night he shall not absent himself; but in all things and at all times he shall carry and behave himself towards his said master, etc., and all theirs, as a good and faithful apprentice ought to do, to his utmost ability during all the time or term aforesaid.

In return for these extraordinary obligations Zachariah Fowle and his wife agreed to teach young Thomas the art of printing, and also to read and write. They further assured that he would receive sufficient and wholesome meat and drink, along with washing facilities, lodging, clothes, and other necessaries for such an apprenticeship. Upon the expiration of this agreement, they were to give Isaiah two suits—one for the "Lord's Day" and the other for working days.

From 1758 to 1761 Fowle had a partner named Samuel Draper who was an "intelligent and kind man." Draper did his best to teach Isaiah how to spell and write, but the partnership did not last and Draper left when Thomas was about twelve years old. Isaiah remained with the Fowles for about ten years. In one way or another he learned some elementary grammar and began to write what was described as good, plain English. He also became, at the age of seventeen, an accomplished printer. When he was eighteen he quarreled seriously with his master and fled in the middle of the night, taking passage on a boat to Halifax. He got a job with the *Halifax Gazette*, a government printer. Leaving Halifax a few months later, Thomas drifted from one job to another, for a while enjoying a position with a South Carolina printer who had an extensive bookstore, but he made his way back to Boston in spring 1770. He reluctantly formed a partnership with his old employer, and they commenced business on Salem Street in July 1770, publishing a small newspaper called the *Massachusetts Spy*. The partnership was dissolved within three months, and Thomas was able to buy Fowle's interest, including the press and type, with money loaned to him by a relative. In March 1771 he moved again, this time to Union Street, and enlarged the *Spy* to four full pages. He had a mere 200 subscribers; but the numbers rapidly increased, and within two years he had the largest subscription list in Boston. No paper exceeded 2,000 subscribers throughout the next century, so the largest list in Boston might well have been a few hundred. Such statistics were not reliably kept, though it is known that Benjamin Franklin, when he acquired the *Philadelphia Gazette*, had ninety subscribers.

Isaiah Thomas, at twenty-eight, became a printer, publisher, and editor. He found a number of good writers who supplied him with political essays, and he later wrote: "Common sense in common language is necessary to influence one class of citizens as much as learning and elegance of composition to produce an effect upon another: the cause of America was just, and it was only necessary to state this cause in a clear and impressive manner to unite the American people in its support."

The *Spy* achieved a level of excellence that attracted readers throughout the colonies. Copies of good papers mailed to distant communities were often excerpted and printed by another publisher. In one of Thomas's early issues an editorial appears as follows:

> Rulers are made for the people, not the people for the rulers. The people are bound to obey the rulers, when the rulers obey the law; and when the rulers are affectionate fathers, the people are bound to be dutiful children. . . . Rulers are appointed to be the representatives of God among men; when they imitate

Him in righteousness the people are under the strongest obligations to give them great honor and reward. The people always have a right to judge the conduct of their rulers, and reward them according to their deeds.

Among the contributors to the *Spy* was one who signed himself *Centinel*. There were those who suspected that John Adams was *Centinel*, but the truth was never learned. *Centinel*'s style was impressive and sounded like the thoughts of a highly educated man. His criticisms of the government, however, annoyed colonial governor Hutchinson. Even more annoying were the essays of Joseph Greenleaf, who wrote under the signature of *Mutius Scaevola*. Greenleaf, writing for the *Spy*, declared it wise "that the pretended governors were dismissed and punished as usurpers, and that the council according to charter, should take upon themselves the government of the province." This sentiment was described by the *Boston Evening Post* the following week as "from its nature and tendency, the most daring production ever published in America."

Isaiah Thomas became the subject of considerable attention from the colonial governor's staff. He was harassed in every way possible, but the governor and his council were unable to legally attack him. First, he had not appeared before them, wisely refusing to do so. If he had, his answers might have been construed as contempt. The council could not compel his appearance, and the attorney general was unable to find a basis for libel. The governor did get at Joseph Greenleaf and removed him as a justice of the peace for the county of Plymouth.

Thomas gave his paper and himself to the cause of freedom with outspoken vigor and fearlessness. Franklin had said the only way the colonies would ever coalesce into one united polity would be under British oppression. The course pursued by Parliament and the Crown did indeed bring the colonies into a kind of union of action and a recognition of their own power and strength. The colonies found that, as Montesquieu observed, "they had grown to be great nations in the forest they were sent to inhabit."[8] The colonial governor believed it was essential that the colonies be kept disconnected and independent of each other or the empire would lose them. In all of this the editorial tone of the *Spy* continued to be bitter, sarcastic, sometimes fierce, and always defiant. The *Boston Gazette* followed the same editorial policy, but in a style that was considerably less inflammatory. Isaiah Thomas generously wrote, "During the long controversy between Great Britain and her colonies no paper on the continent took a more active part in defiance . . . or more ably supported its rights than the *Boston Gazette*." Unhappily, the *Gazette* did not prosper economically and eventually collapsed.

Thomas became an active member of the Sons of Liberty, and many of its members would meet in his office. He knew he was on a list of proscribed anticolonial figures and he believed his life was in danger. He sent his family to Watertown and went himself to Concord to consult with John Hancock and other leading members of the Provincial Congress. Hancock and his friends advised him to get out of Boston, and on April, 16, 1774, he took his presses and boxes of type and "stole them out of town in the dead of night." They were carried first by ferry to Charlestown, and then on to Worcester. Hancock made sure that out of the limited supplies of paper available, enough went to Thomas so that he could continue printing the *Spy*. In the first issue published that May in Worcester, Thomas wrote, "I beg the assistance of all the friends of our righteous cause to circulate this paper. They may rely that the utmost of my poor endeavors should be used to maintain those rights and privileges for which *we* and our fathers have bled."

In the fall of 1775 the Continental Congress established a post office department for all the colonies and appointed Benjamin Franklin postmaster. Franklin selected Isaiah Thomas as his deputy for Worcester. In the year that followed Franklin was frequently at Worcester, and his relationship with Thomas flourished. The publication of the *Spy* was interrupted for more than a year during the Revolution because Thomas had to go to New Hampshire and support his family, who were living on a small farm in Londonderry. In the spring of 1778, however, he returned to Worcester, repossessed his press, and resumed publication. He was fortunate in being able to purchase some new type that had come over from England, and he found, again, many able writers who contributed to the columns of the *Spy*. In the 1780s the growth of his enterprise accelerated. New metal types and better paper were procured, and to the business of editing and publishing a newspaper he added that of printing, publishing, and selling books. It was not long before Thomas's business extended to nearly every state in the union. At one time he had under his control, along with his partners, sixteen presses, seven of them in Worcester. He had five bookstores in Massachusetts, one in New Hampshire, one in Albany, and one in Baltimore. Thomas and his publications editorially supported the adoption of the Constitution despite the majority opposition to it in his own state. In the process of inspiring a shift in that opposition, he printed everything George Washington said or wrote. Such material appeared to have some positive effect on his constituents.

As his success in publishing expanded, Thomas found it necessary to build his own paper mill, which then permitted him to print more books and establish a bindery. By the end of the decade he had become one of the largest book publishers on either side of the Atlantic. His work was praised for its accuracy and imagination by British historians, French cultural leaders, and others in Europe.

Thomas worked with Benjamin Franklin in defining rules for the publishing trade, and in October 1789 he led a welcoming group of citizens when

George Washington visited Worcester. One of Thomas's nephews was an apprentice in the business and remembered being introduced at the age of fourteen to the first president of the United States. Washington told him, "Young man, your uncle has set you a bright example of patriotism, and never forget that next to our God we owe our highest duty to our country."

In the years that followed, no man of any substance or achievement came through Worcester without calling on Thomas, and his contemporaries described him as a man of elegant manners and "great good looks." He had built a large house that he used for public events and the entertaining of the great and the near great who visited the community. The long war and the years of confusion and struggle that followed had taught Thomas the necessity of supporting a national government and helping to keep it stable and efficient. He believed this was the only way to survive as a nation, and his loyalties were primarily to the Federalists, though he did not deny space in his papers to opposition views. In 1802 he turned his business over to his son, Isaiah Thomas Jr., and retired into a very active and studious life—expanding his collection of books and writing his major work, *The History of Printing in America*, published in 1810 in two volumes. There is no record of his having had any interest in a political appointment. The Federalist principles he had adhered to were supported by only a minority of his constituency. Though he was a self-educated man, he belonged to many honorific societies, including the American Philosophic Society in Philadelphia and the American Academy of Arts and Sciences in Boston. When he died in 1831 he left most of his possessions to the Antiquarian Society, including the largest collection of early American newspapers ever assembled. He was and remains a practitioner who exemplifies the principles essential to a free and responsible press—including, in his case, a defiance of despotism that could have cost him his life or, at the very least, his vocation and his right to adamantly resist "padlocks on our lips and fetters on our legs" in the fight for constitutional freedom.

6

THE LIMITS OF LIBERTY

It also means that they're very responsible about what they're writing about because they do live in the community and they can't hit and run. They can't come in, write a story and then run and never have to go back and talk to that person again. And that's a two-way street, too, because sometimes, if you're writing about your friend and you find out your friend has been dipping into the till, you're reluctant to write about it.

—Polly Saltonstall, former editor and proprietor
of weekly newspapers in Maine;
writer for the Associated Press and
the *New York Times* News Service

Isaiah Thomas died before two of the most important developments in the growth of the American press—the invention of the telegraph and the onset of the Civil War. Thomas had set standards for himself and his newspaper during his country's earliest days. To seek a profit in the publication of news while accepting the protection of the First Amendment to the Constitution of the United States was not seen to invite any conflict of interest in 1791. That challenge, inherent to press responsibility, was one of many perplexing, contradictory aspects of the early American experience. It seemed axiomatic that private ownership of the press was the only alternative to government control. Prior restraint was one of the despised practices of tyrants. Unfettered private enterprise was the logical remedy. Or so it seemed. A troubling paradox, however, not unrelated to private enterprise and inescapably part of the American dialogue was slavery. Virginia, Edmund Morgan observed in his distinguished book *American Slavery, American Freedom*, was the "key to the puzzle" of explaining how "people could have developed the dedication to human liberty and dignity exhibited by the leaders of the American Revolution and at the same time have developed and maintained a system of labor that denied human liberty and dignity every hour of the day."[1]

The blatant contradictions appeared to be irreconcilable. When Thomas Jefferson wrote the words of the Declaration of Independence, his first and most important claim was that "all Men are created equal, and they are endowed by their Creator with certain unalienable Rights, that among these are Life, Liberty and the Pursuit of Happiness." But Jefferson—then and until the end of his life—owned nearly 200 slaves. George Washington owned approximately the same number.[2]

The southern Founders, as it was with many other slaveowners, were not contentedly at peace with themselves on the subject of slavery; nor were all slave masters indifferent to the well-being of their human possessions. But they did not feel responsible for the paradox. They had inherited slavery from others (including England's King George III), and those slaveowners who had been well educated had read Plato's *Republic* and Aristotle's *Politics*. Both philosophers had rationalized slavery as the natural fate of certain men and women whose capacities were limited to menial labor and whose rank in the society was appropriate and necessary.

Americans had needed arms and ships and ample supplies to wage a revolutionary war. They turned to other countries for help, particularly France. Tobacco was the equivalent of money in purchasing guns from abroad, and the crop was grown almost entirely by slave labor. Virginia, which gave the United States its military leader, Washington; its lyrical voice of liberty, Jefferson; and its designers of a government responsible to the people was the largest of the colonies. Virginia was also the home of 40 percent of all the slaves in America. Most of American tobacco was grown in Virginia, but the influence of its leading citizens resonated far beyond commerce. Virginia adopted the first state constitution with a bill of rights. Virginians drafted the Declaration of Independence, the U.S. Constitution of 1787, and the first ten amendments. During thirty-two of the first thirty-six years of the United States, Virginians were elected to the presidency. Every one of them owned slaves.[3]

The English government had insisted that colonists in Virginia could not vote for members of the preindependence House of Burgesses (which later became the state legislature) unless they owned land. Jefferson had, in fact, when compiling the Declaration's list of grievances against King George III, accused the Crown of imposing slavery on the colonies by demanding cultivation of the land and a crop production of such magnitude that the white settlers could not deliver without importing slave labor.[4] This grievance was eventually dropped from the Declaration—not improbably because an ironic expiation of slave labor would not find a comfortable setting in a document devoted to such high aspirations and righteous indignation.

In any event, from Jefferson's point of view, the use of slave labor not only produced wealth and freedom among the large landowners, which permitted them to pursue public service, but helped to establish common interests between Virginia's large and small planters, since both survived on the same crop. Common interest in prosperity made slave labor crucial to the plantations—large and small. Slavery also bridged the social gap and the early antipathies between the aristocratic Virginians and their less-educated, poorer neighbors. The patricians courted the common farmers in electoral contests with each other. The well-born did not want to antagonize the lesser freemen because stability and profit flowed from an amicable relationship. The large planters could rent some of their land to the freemen, but their major income depended on the labor provided by enslaved African men and women. Racism of this profitable nature further united the great planters with the small farmers in a common identity. As Edmund Morgan put it, "Neither was a slave, and both were equal in not being slaves."[5]

The most eloquent attack on the slave trade came from Virginia's venerable George Mason in 1785. Writer Carl Van Doren envisions Mason "tall, white haired, his black eyes burning," rising to speak in condemnation of "the infernal traffic" that the avarice of British merchants had prolonged even though Virginia made many attempts to end it. "Every master of slaves," Mason said, "is born a petty tyrant. They bring the judgment of heaven on a Country. As nations cannot be rewarded or punished in the next world, they must in this. By an inevitable chain of causes and effects, providence punishes national sins, by national calamities."[6]

Such impassioned remarks would have reached very few citizens unless they were published in newspapers. The Constitution itself was first printed for public examination in the *Pennsylvania Packet* on September 19, 1788. Mason published his concerns about the Constitution in the *Packet* on October 4, 1788. The introspection about slavery was not confined to ambivalent southern planters. There was more widespread abolitionist sentiment in the northern colonies, where fewer slaves were owned. Such virtue came at a lower price in the North. The economies of all the southern colonies were based on slave labor. It had become a way of life. Their newspapers were important marketing instruments for the slave trade. Typically, the Charleston *Evening Gazette*, in its July 11, 1785, edition, announced the arrival of a Danish slaver with "a choice cargo of windward and Gold Coast negroes, who have been accustomed to the planting of rice." Such announcements were common in the press of the southern and border states but not unknown further north.

British "republican" pamphlets that advocated a free press, greater individual rights, and protection of property had considerable influence in Virginia. These ideas resonated in the language of Virginia's constitutional documents. Pseudonyms were a precautionary device in the pamphlets and newspapers published during the years closely preceding the Revolutionary War and in the formative period after ratification of the U.S. Constitution.

Names such as Cato, Brutus, Agrippa, Publius were employed by writers who wanted to protect themselves, or enhance the credibility of their views without damaging their personal reputations, by avoiding the personal attitudes aroused when their names were known. In most of the writings of these pseudonymous authors, the questions of free expression and private property were mingled either overtly or presumptively.[7]

In 1732, the Virginia House of Burgesses had authorized a printer named William Parks to publish accounts of its voting and some of its discussions. A few years later Parks launched the colony's first newspaper, the *Virginia Gazette*. There were three newspapers in Virginia at the time of the Revolution—one of them edited by a woman, Clementina Rind. They provided stories borrowed from London newspapers, general essays, and, most important, a kind of printed forum for politicians—in and out of office—to debate matters of public interest ranging from transatlantic tobacco trade to specific local issues.[8]

The role of the press in ventilating competing views on political matters in the late eighteenth century was evolving throughout the colonies—much of it centering on the subjects of political freedom, personal liberty, and citizen participation in political activities. Slavery and its moral implications was not always neglected by the press, though most comment on this subject appeared in the northern cities. Antislavery reform did not emerge with any strength even in the abolitionist and church newspapers. By 1753, the British governor of Virginia was reporting to London that the House of Burgesses was sounding as if it was "very much in a republican way of thinking." The relationship of liberty and property (which included slaves) was already central to American politics.[9]

The movement toward independence among Virginians, despite a low level of literacy, was fueled by Park's *Gazette* along with pamphlets such as Tom Paine's *Common Sense*. Religion made its contribution as well. There were Quakers, Baptists, and Presbyterians among those who sought equality. Dissenters from the once-dominant Church of England founded the college called Hampden-Sydney—named after two "republican thinkers." The mucilage that held Virginians together in their journey toward republicanism, equality, and liberty (for white, landowning male citizens) was the shared agricultural economy, availability of land for the small farmers, and slave labor.[10]

In 1791, a free African American named Benjamin Banneker wrote angrily to Jefferson, accusing him of obvious inconsistency between his expressed views that African Americans and Indians were "culturally inferior" and those sentiments expressed in the Declaration of Independence. Banneker had been born in Maryland and educated by Quakers. President Washington had appointed him to work with Pierre Charles L'Enfant on the Commission to Design a New Federal Capitol along the Potomac River.

Jefferson himself had recommended Banneker, who had a reputation as a mathematician and astronomer and who was the publisher of an annual compendium modeled on Benjamin Franklin's *Poor Richard's Almanac*. Jefferson replied to Banneker's letter: "Nobody wishes more than I do to see such proofs as you exhibit that nature has given to our black brethren talents equal to those of the other colours of men, and that the appearance of a want of them is owing merely to the degraded condition of their existence, both in Africa and America."[11]

Confronted by economic concerns, however, the dim glow of idealism in dealing with slavery at the time of the Revolution faded. The freedom accorded former slaves was limited, and the northern states often behaved with greater callousness than the South. That indefatigable traveling political scientist and social critic Alexis de Tocqueville cut through the sanctimony when he observed in his much-quoted volume *Democracy in America*, "The prejudice of race appears to be stronger in the States which have abolished slavery than in those where it still exists; and nowhere is it so important as in those States where servitude never has been known."[12] How the constitutional philosophers of a new and unique nation shaded their vision of "disinterested" public service to accommodate racism (not exclusively southern) and a slave-based agricultural system was a question that continued to haunt the American conscience. In 1773 Benjamin Rush, a Philadelphia physician and politician who feared anarchy if the central government was too weak had exhorted his colleagues to abolish slavery. "The plant of liberty," he said, "is of so tender a nature that it cannot thrive long in the neighborhood of slavery."[13]

Would the southern colonies have abandoned the confederation that became the United States if slavery had been condemned? Was racism the price of a strong union and a new constitution? Finally, why did so many leaders of church and state remain silent when they might have utilized the press to ignite a sense of outrage—or at least forboding—about racial hypocrisy and its effect on the future? For nearly three centuries the depth of racist feeling below the surface of American life—and the volatile anger and frustration rising from it—demonstrated the destructive need of some Americans to find security in the subordination of others. In the distribution of political power—that process of establishing "place" and "station"—a ruling class made up of "gentlemen" to be supported willingly by the "yeomanry" began with a widely shared sense of superiority over African Americans. That led undeniably to suppression and exclusion in both policy and practice—self-serving, ill-informed, involuntary, or deliberate but deep running and persistent to this day.

The dilemma has been examined fitfully for more than 200 years in many contexts, by many voices—newspapers, pamphleteers, religious leaders, foreign visitors, scholars, and politicians. It lurks omnipresently behind every problem on the domestic agenda for the 1990s and into the next century. Belatedly, agonizingly, inside the newsrooms of the contemporary media, the presence of minority reporters and women has introduced reporting that reflects the demographic reality of America's cities, and inevitably editorial substance has become more inclusive. This trend brings with it the mystifications of "political correctness," multiculturalism, and economic imbalance. It pits the early American passion for individual autonomy against the needs of the community. A *multiethnic* society can accept and nurture an American culture. A *multiethnic* society can become Yugoslavia. Only the media can broadly illuminate the differences.

Madison's concerns about patronage and self-interest in the Congress were somewhat ameliorated by the gathering force of publicity. In 1789 the press began to cover debates in the House and print the texts of bills that had been submitted by individual representatives. The concept of political accountability embodied in printed public reports was taking hold. Many bitter criticisms of slavery as a violation of the most basic of republican and Christian principles were pronounced at the Constitutional Convention, but the northern anti-Federalists never formed a resolute policy on the subject. Whatever some of the southern anti-Federalists might have thought about slavery, not many were prepared to denounce in public a fundamental social and economic advantage in their region.

The unrelenting "truth-telling" of determined newspaper writers and outraged printers was too infrequently directed at the shame of slave labor in colonial America. Historian C. Vann Woodward, an eminent scholar and writer on the South, described one important consequence: "The New England colonies, founded in the interest of religion, became a seed bed of the capitalist spirit, while the Southern colonies, developed in the interest of business, generated a climate uncongenial to that spirit."[14]

Somehow, the entrepreneurial drive and the creation of wealth did not find a place at the center of economic development in the South. Plantation life was shaped to a kind of Old World aristocratic style—supported always by unpaid labor and numerous household servants. Eugene Genovese, in his book *The Political Economy of Slaves*, writes, "Southern ideals constituted a rejection of the crass, vulgar, inhumane elements of capitalist society. The slave holders simply could not accept that the cash nexus offered a permissible basis for human relations." Genovese nonetheless regards the great figures of Southern history—many of them Virginians—as socially responsible and personally honorable. Men like Jefferson, Madison, and Mason were not to be denied recognition as leaders and as individuals who were "noble, virtuous, honorable, decent and selfless in a ruling class." The Puritan ethic in the northern colonies, hard work and "the ascetic compulsion to save," made capital for investment available, in contrast to the southern ethic of leisure and paternalism.[15]

The learned, virtuous men of the South who were financially independent and, therefore, could be "disinterested" politically expected to be trusted by all their constituents. The "greedy" aspirations of merchants, artisans, and small landowners who wanted strong, narrowly focused representation in the state legislatures were inimical to the kind of republic envisioned by the authors of *The Federalist*. The greedy men were considered part of the "middling class." Melancton Smith, a prominent merchant who operated out of New York City and Poughkeepsie and was a member of New York's first Provincial Congress and later a delegate to the Continental Congress wrote many newspaper articles on the subject of the "middling class" using the pseudonym Plebeian—an unlikely choice for a man of his means. In one of his essays he observed: "A substantial yeoman of sense and discernment, will hardly ever be chosen. From these remarks it appears that the government will fall into the hands of the few and the great. This will be a government of oppression. They fancy themselves to have a right of pre-eminence in everything. In short, they possess the same feelings, and are under the influence of the same motives, as an hereditary nobility."[16]

Similar evaluations were not uncommon among anti-Federalists, and the perception was not without substance or merit. The "men of Philadelphia" were men of property. As representatives of leadership in each of their states, they were accustomed to the respect and deference of less affluent folk—the yeomanry, the tradesmen, mechanics, and laborers of the towns they represented. There was a basic respect for the recognized qualities of leadership: "visible forms of social, economic, educational superiority, and often in the advantage of a distinguished family name."[17]

If the esteem in which they were held, however, had anything to do with social position, it could be said also of almost all of them that they had earned it. There may have been an element of inheritance among them, but that did not eliminate the need to watch over their estates and financial interests. A recent view of the yeomanry has been expressed by historian Gordon Wood, who saw the acquisitive, competitive common men—small farmers and merchants and artisans—as having a prophetic outlook: "Thus in 1787–1788, it was not the Federalists but the Antifederalists who were the real pluralists and the real prophets of the future of American politics. They not only foresaw but endorsed a government of jarring individuals and interests. Unlike the Federalists, however, they offered no disinterested umpires, no mechanisms at all for reconciling and harmonizing these clashing selfish interests."[18]

Abolitionists published their views in the earliest days of the republic with little political effect. The Civil War, the Emancipation Proclamation, the Thirteenth and Fourteenth and Fifteenth Amendments, even religious awakenings, did not fully expunge the legacy of a Constitution that had been composed without finally confronting the hypocrisy of subjugation practiced by white men—the same white men who had rebelled angrily against far less severe restraints. The effect of humiliating, institutionalized inferiority suppressed and starved the ability of young black Americans, generation after generation, to seek self-improvement, to aspire, to expect justice, or to contribute to the body politic. The fact that some blacks—however small in number—were able to overcome such a disabling environment is in itself part of a story that developed in the shadows and very rarely made its way into the journalistic sunlight. Frederick Douglass, a former slave who became a publisher, described that light in a speech to a white audience gathered to celebrate the Fourth of July in 1882 at Rochester, New York: "The rich inheritance of justice, liberty, prosperity, and independence bequeathed by your fathers, is shared by you, not me. The sunlight that brought light and healing to you, has brought stripes and death to me. This Fourth of July is yours, not mine. You may rejoice. I must mourn."[19]

That such a speech could have been delivered by a former slave would not have surprised James Madison, who in *Federalist 54* had offered his ironic thoughts on slavery, published in the New York newspaper the *Independent Journal* on February 13, 1788:

> We subscribe to the doctrine, might one of our Southern brethren observe, that representation relates more immediately to persons, and taxation more immediately to property, and we join in the application of this distinction to the case of our slaves. But we must deny the fact that slaves are considered merely as property, and in no respect whatever as persons. The true state of the case is, that they partake of both these qualities; being considered by our laws, in some respects, as persons, and in other respects, as property. . . . Let the case of the slaves be considered as it is in truth a *peculiar* one. Let the compromising expedient of the Constitution be mutually adopted, which regards them as inhabitants, but as debased by servitude below the equal level of free inhabitants, which regards the *slave* as divested of two-fifths of *the man*. (emphasis added)

In regard to the "two-fifths of the man" reference, Madison is, sardonically it seems, describing the agreement to allow southern states the right to count each slave as "three-fifths" of an inhabitant for the purpose of determining congressional representation on the basis of population.

The debate over a population seen by some politicians as "fractional" creatures, neither human nor animal, did not engender, so far as the public record reveals—most of it in newspapers—much fervor about the corrosive ethical aspect of slavery. The discussions were primarily concerned with *property*. The philosopher John Locke was influential in those ruminations. He provided a convenient theory that men "being in slavery, not capable of any property, cannot, in that state, be considered as any part of civil society, the chief end whereof, is the preservation of property."[20]

The importance of the middle class was emphasized by Aristotle 2,000 years before the Constitutional Convention in Philadelphia. This Greek philosopher who became the first great political scientist organized his students at the Lyceum in Athens to make an analysis of government structures in 158 city-states. Aristotle's contemporary, Euripides, the often-quoted playwright and satirist, had already described Greek society as made up of three classes—the useless rich, the envious poor, and the middle class who could save states.[21]

Aristotle meticulously reported his more scientific findings in *Politics,* which recommended separating family governance from political governance, cited the necessity and motivational value of private property, urged that the consent of the governed be allowed to determine the authority of political leaders, and calibrated the mediating importance of the middle class. That mediating process, Aristotle warned, required constitutional laws—"reason unaffected by desire."

The educated elite in the 1790s hoped the press would help them reach less informed citizens with the Aristotelian wisdom that unless a republic could structure itself as a stable, lawful system, it would deteriorate into a hopeless "democracy"—indifferent to law, property, *or* individual rights. Regarding the service of a free press to the political process, Jefferson had written in 1786: "It is part of the price we pay for our liberty, which cannot be guarded but by the freedom of the press, nor that be limited without danger of losing it."[22] This prescription was not always easy to swallow. In 1789 Edmund Randolph of Virginia wrote to James Madison regarding letters that had appeared under the pseudonym of Decius in the *Virginia Independent Chronicle* between January and July 1789. These were bitter attacks on Virginia anti-Federalists, particularly Patrick Henry, who was accused of enriching himself at public expense. Randolph's letter said, in part: "The liberty of the press is indeed a blessing which ought not to be surrendered but with blood; and yet it is not an ill founded expectation in those, who deserve well of their country, that they should be assailed by an enemy in disguise, and have their characters deeply wounded, before they can prepare for defense."[23]

The pseudonym may have protected the author, but to the victim he was considered merely an "enemy in disguise." The aristocratic Federalists were asking the people to accept that their own best interests would be served by a central government stronger than individual liberty and guided by a wealthy elite. The price of admission was deference.

7

CRAFTING A CONSTITUTION

We can look to history for some of the right questions, and we can look to the Amendments for the principles that can help guide us. But each generation in American life must take the Constitution and make it live in the circumstances of that generation. And in no part of our life, I think, is that responsibility more complex than it is with respect to mass communications.

—Benno Schmidt Jr.,
former president of Yale University

In their discussions and the drafting of documents, the "demi-gods" (as Jefferson described them) of Philadelphia found themselves closeted, isolated from their constituents, and immersed in an enterprise sufficiently protected from the curiosity of the press to permit a kind of fraternal bonding even among men of widely differing views. The composition of the Constitution took place against the background of tension among Federalists and anti-Federalists regarding social and political authority, but the newspapers had no access to the resolution of tensions among the delegates until the texts of agreement were made public.[1]

Jefferson, in the Declaration of Independence, had reflected his own political and religious views, which were shared by other prominent participants—Benjamin Franklin, George Washington, John Adams, and George Mason among them. They were rationalists. Arbitrary governments were anathema. *Reason* and *experience* would form the judgments of individual citizens, producing "self-evident" truths beginning with the realization that governments are derived from "the just consent of the governed." Politics of reason, created for the benefit of all men, were bound to provide human happiness. Jefferson had, in fact, changed the familiar priorities of "life, liberty and property" to the phrase that has inspired yearnings for freedom all over the world—"life, liberty and the pursuit of happiness." Later in life, Jefferson wrote that the initial draft of the Declaration—composed with the agreement of Ben Franklin, John Adams, Robert R. Livingston, and Roger

Sherman, the other members of the drafting committee—was intended "not to find new principles, or new arguments . . . [but] to place before mankind the common sense of the subject in terms so plain and firm as to command their assent."[2]

For the men of Philadelphia, determining "common sense" in the format of constitutional articles required more rigorous argument and persuasion than determining a list of grievances against the British Crown. The quality of men who gathered as delegates from each of the states was, if not godlike, certainly distinguished. From Virginia came George Washington, James Madison, Edmund Randolph, George Mason, George Wythe (who had signed the Declaration) and others; from Pennsylvania, Robert Morris, Gouverneur Morris, James Wilson (who was to create the phrase "we the people"), and Benjamin Franklin; from Delaware, John Dickinson, leader of the strong centralized government faction; from South Carolina, John Rutledge and Charles Pinckney; from New York, Alexander Hamilton, Robert Yates, and John Lansing Jr. Hamilton was adamantly nationalistic, but Yates and Lansing fought for states' rights and went home before the vote, feeling they had lost. William Patterson represented New Jersey and later became a justice of the Supreme Court. Roger Sherman of Connecticut was the only delegate to have signed the Continental Association of 1774, the Declaration of Independence, the Articles of Confederation, and, ultimately, the Constitution. Rufus King represented Massachusetts and, the newspapers revealed afterward, surprised the other delegates as both tactician and orator.[3]

It was the Articles of Confederation that launched the debate in 1787. But that launch was delayed from May 14 until May 29 to allow for latecomers and to be certain a majority of the states were represented. On Friday, May 25th, the delegates from seven states elected George Washington as their president. A committee on procedure was appointed, and it recommended that all deliberations be conducted in secrecy. There was almost unanimous agreement that every delegate could advocate a position and then change his mind when persuaded to do so without facing charges of inconsistency. Newspaper coverage having been forbidden, the freedom to switch was assured. Nothing less draconian, the delegates believed, could have guaranteed a wide-open forum. In the first rounds each state was allowed the same single vote—provided two of each state's delegates were present along with a quorum of at least seven state delegations.

When a delegate to the Federal Convention found a copy of what was called the Virginia Plan on the floor outside the meeting hall, he gave it to George Washington for safekeeping. The first president waited for an appropriate moment and then rose to his feet and addressed the hushed gathering: "Gentlemen, I am sorry to find that one Member of this Body, has been so neglectful to the secrets of the Convention as to drop in the State House a copy of their proceedings, which by accident was picked up and delivered to me this morning. . . . I must entreat Gentlemen to be more careful, least our Transactions get into the *News Papers*, and disturb the public repose by premature speculations." A delegate wrote in his diary that Washington, following his admonishment, threw the document on the table and said, "Let him who owns it take it." Then he bowed, picked up his hat, and left the room "with a dignity so severe that every Person seemed alarmed."[4]

Some delegates had arrived with a resolve to merely tinker with the Articles of Confederation and resist any major changes. Others vowed to create a new form of government—most eloquently Hamilton and Dickinson. It was Connecticut's Sherman who devised the approach likely to win the day, as it did—a system part national and part federal, one branch of the government to "be drawn immediately from the people," the other to represent each state and to be chosen by the state legislatures. Thus was born the foundation of the Constitution—*the one* (executive), *the few* (Senate), and *the many* (House of Representatives). Aristotle had called it the balance of interests. Washington was pessimistic about getting any format adopted, but he provided a memorable and brief presidential comment: "If to please the people, we offer what we ourselves disapprove, how can we afterwards defend our work?"

Political journalists have asked that same question ever since with inevitable and growing cynicism. George Washington may have intuited the rising tide of anti-Federalist entrepreneurs who would threaten "disinterested" public service with personal ambition, profit-seeking, and what Gordon Wood sees as the precursor of modern American politics: "the scrambling of different interest groups, the narrow self-promoting nature of much of the law making [in the state legislatures], the incessant catering to popular demands. These were the hallmarks of what 'disinterested gentlemen' called the 'excess of democracy.'"[5]

The eight year Revolutionary War caused so many demands to supply 100,000 men under arms that, "the inexhaustible needs of the army—for everything from blankets and wagons to meat and rum—brought into being a host of new manufacturing and entrepreneurial interests, and made market farmers out of husbandmen who before had scarcely ever traded out of their neighborhoods."[6] The government issued paper money to purchase supplies during the war—an estimated $400–$500 million. Capitalism spread from the cities to the farm country and the plantations. The political behavior that followed in its wake was antithetical to what the Founders had envisioned—that rational, civilized community of happy people knowing their place and deferentially welcoming the governance of a disinterested, educated elite.

George Cabot, thought to be the wealthiest man in New England, believed society should be "a well regulated family." There was no such thing as equality. Cabot spoke of the "better sort" as the natural rulers. The "multitude" must be imbued with the desire to be subordinates, a task best performed by family, church, and government and aimed at what another Federalist called "a speaking aristocracy in the face of a silent democracy."[7] It is not illogical that an alternative to the "elite" Federalism and "greedy" anti-Federalism was articulated by Jefferson in a pronouncement that signaled a third party eventually called, odd as it may sound to American voters today, Democratic Republicans (also known as Jeffersonian Republicans). Jefferson believed in "an aristocracy of talent arising out of a democracy of opportunity."[8] The upward filtration of talent rising out of a democracy of opportunity was an ideal for government service that was not realized in Jefferson's time; nor has it been achieved in the nearly 200 years since his presidency.

The continuing role of the press in the development of a uniquely American concept of liberty, individual freedom, and political power based on the consent of the governed is significant for what it provided and what it did not. The journalistic surveillance of government seems to have drawn its energy as much from the curiosity and economic concerns of the readers as from any morally expressed editorial mission. Some owner-publishers ventilated their personal views or attacked perceived villains in public life, but the newspapers were discovering a commercial reality—paid circulation. Much of what the readers wanted in the first decades of the republic was the record of legislative activity at state and federal levels. Beyond that was the demand for essential information on matters of immediate economic interest. The larger philosophical issues were embodied primarily in essays and letters submitted by aroused citizens or purposeful public figures who, as already noted, used pseudonyms when they found it desirable to hide their identity from all but a few friends or associates. Only very rarely in the process during the early years was there a perception that the press was an important ethical resource—the Fourth Estate in theory—accustomed to largely unfettered freedom and therefore obligated to take *responsibility* for its influence.

Instead the journalism of that time was scattered over a landscape of special interests and operated largely as a tabula rasa for the spokesmen of those interests. Noah Webster, in a July 4 oration, warned his countrymen: "Never let us exchange our civil and religious institutions for the wild theories of crazy projectors; or the sober, industrious moral habits of our country for experiments in atheism and lawless democracy. Experience is a safe pilot; but *experiment* is a dangerous ocean, full of rocks and shoals."[9] The ocean was, of course, republicanism, and in the classic conflict between the Federalist "aristocracy" and the anti-Federalist "self-government," the press mirrored the views expressed by both sides—often tilting toward one or the other. But newspapers of the period did not report independently on events or legislative actions in a manner that attempted to interpret the facts or propound the opinions that might provoke a clamor for reforms above and beyond party loyalties. The newspapers as sophists in the marketplace, inflaming the rabble, were not an immediate issue. The space they gave to opposing views was something else altogether, and the First Amendment for more than a century offered little protection when the central government was sufficiently irritated.

Historian Gordon Wood describes William Findley—"that pugnacious Scotch-Irishman from western Pennsylvania"—as a powerful but typical populist voice against the "aristocracy." Findley came to America from Northern Ireland in 1763. He was twenty-two years old. "He had no lineage to speak of. He went to no college, and he possessed no great wealth. He was completely self-taught and self-made, but not in the manner of Benjamin Franklin who acquired the cosmopolitan attributes of a gentleman." As a representative to the Pennsylvania legislature, Findley epitomized the "rough upstart" and the inevitable conflict of his sort with the Federalist gentry. One of his opponents, Henry Brackenridge, had moved to western Pennsylvania to make his fortune and, as an educated gentleman, decided to rescue his uncultivated neighbors by bringing the press to the area. He helped establish a newspaper in Pittsburgh, called the *Gazette,* and wrote for it frequently. In one article he allowed that he had been singled out by the "Eastern members" of the assembly from among the "Huns, Goths, and Vandals" to represent the western interests. In 1786, at a dinner party in Philadelphia to which both Findley and Brackenridge had been invited, a political discussion took place and Brackenridge said at one point, in defense of Robert Morris's banking interest, "The people are fools; if they would let Mr. Morris alone, he would make Pennsylvania a great people, but they will not suffer him to do it."[10]

It was a remark bound to infuriate Findley, who took up his pen and wrote a letter to the Pittsburgh *Gazette* accusing Brackenridge of betraying the people's trust by changing his vote on certain fiscal matters and showing himself to be self-seeking. Brackenridge tried to defend himself, but Findley had so vehemently attacked his "pretensions as a virtuous, gentlemanly leader" that he never recovered. In 1788 Brackenridge the Federalist lost to Findley the anti-Federalist in the election of delegates to the state ratifying convention. Findley had also gone after Robert Morris, the patrician financier who had helped fund the rebellion against England. Morris was so pressured by anti-Federalist sentiment that he began to "renounce his interest in commerce" and in a vain attempt to realize the "classical aristocratic ideal of disinterestedness" lost his fortune, his mansion, and all his possessions and even went into debtors' prison. Findley had written pointedly of Morris: "The human soul is affected by wealth, in almost all its faculties. It is affected by its present interests, by its expectations, and by its fears." When Morris asked in reply why Findley pursued wealth, the anti-Federalist responded bluntly, "I love and pursue it—not as an end but as a means of enjoying happiness and independence."[11]

The point of these not uncommon exchanges was that the anti-Federalists had taken the position that the so-called ruling class was no different than the self-made man, or any more respectable. William Findley was a particularly feisty exponent of the widening view among American citizens that the elite should be denied the right to "simply stand and not run for election" on the turf of "disinterestedness." The newspapers provided the forum for these arguments, and Findley later wrote that his group had "learned to take a surer course of obtaining information respecting political characters" and would point out where the private interests of the aristocracy were "inconsistent with the equal administration of government." No clearer description of the press as watchdog could have been given. The watchdogs, however, were for the time being the active participants in the political process and not working journalists. Legislators could not be "just *for* the people, they had to be *of* the people as well" and able to write their views convincingly for public consumption.[12]

In his newspaper the *Farmer's Letter* and its successor, the *Scourge of Aristocracy*, Matthew Lyon attacked the Federalists unmercifully. He had come to America from Ireland as an indentured servant. He had fought with Ethan Allen's Green Mountain Boys, secured his freedom, and won election to Congress as a "republican" from Vermont. His editorial positions were pungently expressed. The Federalists constituted "a set of gentry who are interested in keeping the government at a distance and out of sight of the people who support it." They were, wrote Lyon, "an aristocratic junto" seeking to "screw the hard earnings out of the poor people's pockets for the purpose of enabling the government to pay enormous salaries."[13] (In 1992 very similar words appeared in the American press regarding the putative "Congressional bank.") The most unremitting attacks upon Federalism were appearing regularly in Republican newspapers and periodicals during the 1790s. The "republicans" were gathering into a political constituency called the Republicans. One of their newspapers promised to reveal the "origins, progress and alarming influence of that system in iniquity, robbery, bribery, and oppression, hypocrisy and injustice, which may be traced from the attempt of Alexander Hamilton to palm off upon the Constitutional Convention a monarchical constitution through the corrupted mazes of funding and banking, stock jobbing, and speculating systems, down to the alien and sedition laws, standing army and navy of the present day."[14]

The Republicans, in historian Robert Shalhope's view, "felt they must effect two integrally related revolutions: one economic and one political—both premised on the idea of equality."[15] Jeffersonian Republicans believed the prosperity of the ordinary farmer could ensure a stable democracy. Land, free trade, and improved agricultural techniques would give full expression to each man's economic nature and personal autonomy. The Federalists were outraged that "banditti-like" people were organizing to oppose Federalist policies. Those people, one Federalist wrote, are "butchers, tinkers, broken hucksters, and trans-Atlantic traitors." The idea that such men, no matter what their background, could "freely discuss and publish as we do or as they might choose, that the views of each might be made manifest" was intolerable.[16]

The Federalist "gentlemen" could stomach criticism from men of their own social class—and indeed they *had* for more than a century of colonial life—but the vituperation from social inferiors was unacceptable and, they decided, dangerous. The Federalists passed, therefore, the Sedition Law of 1798 (which was to resurface in 1964) to silence the rabble. It virtually prohibited criticism of any public official and could impose a fine of $2,000 in addition to imprisonment for two years. Truth should be determined by well-educated, reasonable men, vowed the Federalists. The Republicans, however, advocated that a wide variety of opinions about political philosophy and individual public figures should get a fair hearing—and truth or falsity could not be determined by judges or juries. Thomas Jefferson reiterated his support for the concept of an open marketplace of ideas. Opinions, he believed, true or false, malicious or benevolent, should "stand undisturbed as monuments of the safety with which error of opinion may be tolerated where reason is left free to combat it."[17]

James Madison joined the fray, observing of the free press that "some degree of abuse is inseparable from the proper use of everything. . . . Better to leave a few of its noxious branches to their luxuriant growth, than by pruning them away to injure the vigor of those yielding the proper fruits." The Federalists were, as always, dismayed by such opinions—particularly when they were articulated by "gentlemen." That any free man might be allowed to express a view, no matter how "scandalous" or "abusive," was unacceptable. Federalists remained loyal to their hierarchical structures while the Republicans continued to promote the free-market economy and the free market of intellectual competition as well. It should be noted that both Jefferson and Madison during their presidencies expressed deep annoyance and frustration with the press, and both used national security issues to circumvent the First Amendment. The conflict between a paternalistic, centralized system and a philosophy of individual opportunity followed by social mobility was inevitable. Historian Shalhope writes: "Under the pressure of rapidly changing socio-economic conditions, the independent republican producer—integrally related to the welfare of the larger community—gradually underwent a subtle transmutation into the ambitious, self-made man set against his neighbors and his community alike."[18]

Madison, speaking of the Republican pamphleteers and newspapers, reflected on points overlooked that might have been "many of the true grounds of opposition" to the Federalist Constitution. Madison had written to Jefferson in 1788: "The articles [of the Constitution] relating to Treaties, to paper money, and to contracts, created more enemies than all the errors in the System, positive and negative put together."[19] The Federalists (Madison was not, in the strict sense, always one of them, and he disagreed with his *Federalist* coauthors, Alexander Hamilton and John Jay, on many fundamental positions) had more important concerns than their "private interests" or social status. Gordon Wood believes "they were defending . . . a moral and social order that had been prescribed by the Revolution and the most enlightened thinking of the Eighteenth Century. . . . The Founders thus gave future Americans more than a new Constitution. They passed on the ideals and standards of political behavior that helped to contain and control the unruly, materialistic passions unleashed by the democratic Revolution. . . . Our yearning for examples of unselfish public service suggests that such ideals still have great moral power."[20]

Could the press, or some part of it, have ever engaged these subtle shadings among the day-to-day events—the classical ruminations (on paper and in public orations) of the educated, intellectually eloquent spokesmen who dominated the discourse on traditionalism—ruminations that also appeared among the opposition? Were there widely known pundits and social commentators on the staffs of late-eighteenth and early-nineteenth-century publications? Newspapers were still too small compared to those that began to appear in the cities during the decade just before the Civil War and with increasing momentum afterward. The most powerful voices turned to pamphlets and narrowly focused, low-circulation periodicals to distribute their views. In one such pamphlet Thomas Paine had proclaimed, "We have it in our power to begin the world over again." And in his implacable resistance to the need for a Bill of Rights, Alexander Hamilton wrote in a New York newspaper: "What signifies a declaration that the 'liberty of the press shall be inviolably preserved'? What is the liberty of the press? Who could give it any definition which would not leave the utmost latitude for evasion? I hold it to be impracticable; and from this I infer that its security, whatever fine declarations may be inserted in any constitution respecting it, must altogether depend on public opinion, and on the general spirit of the people and of the government."[21]

The Constitution—Hamilton would say—had no power to even discuss the press, so why limit by amendment that which did not exist?

8

SAFEGUARDING LIBERTY

There was a poll a few years ago about the Bill of Rights and I think the poll showed that most people thought it was a communist plot.

—Corliss Lamont, humanist philosopher,
Columbia University professor

A notable reply to Hamilton's skepticism came from Judge Samuel Bryan of Philadelphia in 1787. The judge confronted the assertions that Congress had no power whatsoever to deal with the press by citing what became Article 1, section 8, of the Constitution, which allowed the central government "to make all. laws that shall be necessary and proper." Who would say a limitation on the press was *improper*? While acknowledging the importance of a strong national government in such areas as defense and interstate commerce, Judge Bryan observed: "Universal experience demonstrates the necessity of the most express declarations and restrictions to protect the rights and liberties of mankind, from the silent, powerful, and ever active conspiracy of those who govern."[1]

Jefferson not only agreed with these sentiments but, writing again from Paris, he emphasized freedom of the press and religion and reaffirmed that, "a Bill of Rights is what the people are entitled to against every government on earth, general or particular, and what no just government should refuse, or rest on inference." Judge Bryan had referred to *universal* experience. The Constitution and the Bill of Rights were extracted from the uniquely *American* experience that had produced, from colonial rule and a war for independence, the understanding of liberty that needed constitutional protections legally enforceable through a Bill of Rights.[2]

It was the American Constitution, born out of the American experience, that for the first time in human history provided a legal basis for freedom of speech and press. Americans had, after all, been involved with their own representative governing bodies during more than 150 years of colonial life. James Madison's remarkable character and intellect were to leave their mark indelibly on the nature and adaptability of the "great rights of mankind." In the context of the written word, in the recording of ideas, and in the less precise realm of prophetic anticipation, he was a gifted, intuitive leader whose ruminations publicly and privately seem almost deferential to a vision of government he did more to create than any other participant. But he was, according to his friends, unwilling to accept any greater credit than that he persistently defended those principles he believed it would be foolish to forget.

Madison was only thirty-eight when he began the drafting of the Bill of Rights. His friends noted that he was very small, and his voice was soft. To see or hear him at important large gatherings required considerable effort, but John Marshall, who was to become a distinguished chief justice, mused that if eloquence is "persuasion by convincing, Mr. Madison was the most eloquent man I ever heard." Despite the inability of reporters to hear his speeches clearly and the sketchy accounts that resulted, the enduring power of his thoughts as presented at the conventions, at the meetings of Congress, and in ratifying debates is incontestable. Major William Pierce, a delegate from Georgia, kept notes on the attributes of his colleagues. He jotted down his impression of James Madison during the first days of the Federal Convention: "Mr. Maddison [sic] is a character who has been in public life; and what is very remarkable every Person seems to acknowledge his greatness. He blends together the profound politician, with the Scholar."[3]

When Madison offered the texts of his amendments to the Constitution, he kept his own shorthand notes of their purpose: "To limit and qualify powr. by exceptg. from grant cases in wch it shall not be exercised or exd. in a particular manner," which, translated loosely, expressed his desire to guard against excessive power in the legislatures. His other major concern was to restrain "the body of the people, operating by the majority against the minority." In other words, despite a system in which majority votes were considered central, Madison feared greatly the tyranny of the many over the few. In this apprehension the press was a vital defense force. If newspapers were free to publish the views of a minority—or even a "single voice," as John Stuart Mill would put it in 1859—and reveal the injustice of a majority opinion when demonstrable, the legislators might be persuaded to modify or the judiciary might be willing to reject.[4]

If *individual* rights were valid and defensible, such protections as Madison expressed in his amendments were essential—even though the Congress and the executive were not explicitly empowered to abridge those rights under the articles of the Constitution. Madison deliberately altered the language of previous declarations of rights going back to the Magna Carta. Many of those same rights were found in the documents composed by each of the American colonies before independence and adopted as state constitutions afterward. The most significant change Madison made seemed the smallest. He inserted "shall" in place of "ought," thus strengthening a recommendation by making it an imperative. If the people were sovereign, they would have to command their representatives. "In Europe," Madison wrote, "charters of liberty have been granted by power," the power being a king or queen. In America, he reminded the Framers, "Charters of power are granted by liberty." One of his Federalist colleagues compared the Constitution to a "great power of attorney under which no power can be exercised but what is expressly given."[5]

In the 1990s, as television cameras begin to enter the courtrooms, the perceptions may be altered—for better or worse. Justice as soap opera, theatrically trained lawyers, judges aware of a national audience, and juries worried about their profiles may transform the traditional concept of local citizens participating in the trials of neighbors (or at least people who live in the same geographical and social environment) into a complex, veiled process appealing more to impressionistic effects than to revealing, thoughtful judgments based on an inherent knowledge of time and place affecting the case in hand. The First Amendment's laconic reference to a free press was applied, over time, more sensitively to protection of unpopular views, lonely dissent, conscientious objection—the minority opinion in danger of assault from a presumptuous majority. But the fear of an unrepresentative government, of politicians with hidden interests, was the primary apprehension and was, indeed, the affliction most likely to be identified by the press.

In 1735, long before the vision of an American constitution had engaged colonial leaders, John Peter Zenger, publisher of the *New York Weekly Journal*, printed articles and satires attacking the colonial governor of New York, William Cosby. Zenger was charged under British law with seditious libel and spent several months in jail before his trial. He appeared to have no defense, since the law was explicit about any criticism of a public official. The verdict was considered inevitable. Zenger's lawyer, Andrew Hamilton (not related to Alexander), who came to New York from Philadelphia to defend the publisher pro bono, was determined to confound the law by arguing that if the criticisms were *true*, there was no crime involved. The press, Hamilton claimed, was not free if it was prevented from printing the truth. He put this theory to the court, and the judge rejected it swiftly with the argument that the law made it a crime to criticize a governor and damage his reputation—but the crime was even *more* offensive if the criticisms were true. Zenger could correct a falsehood in subsequent articles, but the truth would stand forever and the damage with it.

Hamilton took the case to a jury. The jury had been instructed to rule on one aspect only: Had Zenger published articles critical of the governor? If yes, the publisher was guilty. That, of course, was a given. The evidence was visible to all. Hamilton, however, forcefully repeated the argument the judge had rejected. Truth should be a defense. The jury should take the law into its own hands if that were the case. And so they did. Zenger was acquitted. The precedent set was enduring. A jury could acquit even when the defendant was obviously guilty, providing they believed the law to be oppressively unjust. The Zenger case made it unlikely that seditious libel would thereafter be used very often, if at all, to punish the press for criticizing public officials. The effect of Zenger's triumph was to permit the appearance of a great deal of critical opinion—some of it far from just—in the colonial press. The consequence of this inclination toward the rights of individual writers and speakers was the fading of preoccupation with the so-called structural role of speech and press freedoms.[6]

In 1798 the editors of several Republican newspapers were indicted under the Sedition Act. A Federalist paper in Boston editorialized approvingly: "It is patriotism to write in favor of our government—it is sedition to write against it." Jefferson was predictably outraged. He described the law as "a nullity as absolute and palpable as if Congress had ordered us to fall down and worship a golden image." When he became president, Jefferson pardoned, in 1801, all persons convicted under the Sedition Law and returned their fines. The law was permitted by Congress to expire that same year, but some aspects of it remained on the statute books of many of the states. Madison's apprehension that the state legislatures would ignore or evade the substance of the federal Bill of Rights was well founded. Newspaper publishers and writers of opinions offensive to the state governments were vigorously prosecuted under the sedition laws that survived in one form or another. Many of them were convicted of a crime if they criticized local government unless the writer could prove to a jury that the charges were true.[7]

In the 1830s, several southern states passed new laws that violated the First Amendment by forbidding any speech or publication in favor of abolishing slavery or contesting the "property rights" of slaveowners. The irony of protecting "property," which happened to be enslaved human beings, by denying freedom of speech and press to other human beings who dared to advocate the abolition of slavery was insidious. Abolitionist literature was not even accepted by the post office in certain southern states. The issues were, in fact, stripped down to one subject—economics. There was no clamor among publishers or legislators. The tocsin did not sound, even in the councils of northern abolitionists. The freedom of the press was not at risk. Congress had "made no law." Jefferson, in 1804, acknowledged: "While we deny that Congress has a right to control the freedom of the press, we have ever asserted the right of the States, and their exclusive right, to do so."[8]

The First Amendment was not of much interest to the Supreme Court for decades at a time. In 1842 Congress passed an act prohibiting the incorporation of "indecent and obscene prints, paintings, lithographs, engravings, and transparencies." In 1865 Congress prohibited the mailing of any "obscene book, pamphlet, picture, print, or other publication of a vulgar and indecent character."[9] Not one of the acts dealing with such censorial limitations was successfully overturned in the Supreme Court. The Court even confirmed the power of Congress to refuse the use of the postal service "for the distribution of matter deemed injurious to the public morals."[10]

Several points regarding these developments in the separate states and in the Court seem to suggest themselves to a concerned citizen looking back over the 200 years since the passage of the Bill of Rights. Who, it might be asked again and again, decides? What is *injurious* to public morals? What *are* public morals? One man's injury may be another man's freedom. Americans who had experienced the oppressions of colonialism, the turmoil of revolution, and the heady business of creating a free republic from the bottom up detested censorship and feared self-interested power accumulated by a central government. If obscenity offended everyone, it would need no restraints enacted by government, let alone sustained by the courts. Philosopher William Hocking, who became involved in a study of a free and responsible press (see the discussions on the Hutchins Commission in Chapters 19 and 20) offered this mordant view: "The effects of overemphasis on sex motives, of the destruction of reticence and normal shame, of the malodorous realism which claims superior candor and novelty for its rediscovery that man is an animal—what are the effects? Nothing at all that any eye can see; nothing but the slow unbalancing of emotion in the accepting mind, the disintegration of personality, the decay of taste, the gradual confirmation in the individual case of the hypothesis put before him that man is an animal—and nothing else."

9

ENLARGING THE FOURTH ESTATE

I would not want to work as a journalist for an outfit that was not profitable. ... If a publication is not owned by a company which is robust, it's going to become vulnerable on journalistic grounds, as well as financial grounds.

—Strobe Talbott, former Washington bureau chief,
Time Magazine; U.S. deputy secretary of state

The effect of the Bill of Rights—when it was finally enacted with the fateful limitations put upon it by the Senate to preserve independent powers for the separate states—was not immediately seen. What is more, despite hortatory speeches by many distinguished figures—Virginia's Patrick Henry most persistently, but many others, North and South—cautioning that a bill of rights was required if the Constitution was to stand, it took (as already noted) nearly three years for the states to approve the amendments. And despite some genuine conviction about "enumerated rights," they were not cited with any frequency or passion until the Civil War years.

What preoccupied the Congress and the states most vehemently during the first half-century of constitutional government was property, commerce, and an almost neurotic interest in limiting the central government's power. Patrick Henry, during the constitutional ratification debates, had risen to his feet indefatigably for twenty-three days, speaking for three or four hours at a time. He didactically described the potential horrors of federal taxation, takeovers by northern merchants, and forced payments to British creditors; above all, he pointed to the absence of guarantees for the rights of individual citizens. He wanted most to get a second constitutional convention (where fundamental changes might be made to protect private property and commercial interests more emphatically), but he got instead a bill of rights.[1]

Meanwhile, the Republicans extolled the virtues of the common man, using newspapers to spread their views. Getting votes inspired, early on, the use of propaganda in the press, a kind of spin that was to become endemic to the process. It would be a long while before editorial independence and balanced reporting found a place in the unlicensed, self-defining universe of journalism. There was, however, an important role to be played by the newspapers—getting the various political positions on the record. The footnotes of any scholarly work concerning early American history are speckled with references to specific "gazettes." (The word *gazette* was derived from a Venetian coin, the *gazetta*, which was the cost of a copy of a newspaper published in Venice around 1530.) Indeed, wherever popular movements took place, however the opinions of the general population were motivated, the newspapers were essential. Without them little knowledge of government—local, state, or national—would have reached the vaunted common man, though many "common men" could not read and depended upon the summations of those who could. In a manner of speaking, churches and taverns became newsrooms. Early in the eighteenth century Boston was able to provide a tavern for every 100 residents. Roughly the same numbers applied in and around other American cities. Newspapers were commonly available at inns and taverns, whose proprietors considered the reading and discussion of news as an enhancement of the drinking atmosphere. For those who had difficulty reading, the tavern offered a kind of broadcasting service and the opportunity to argue.

The first federal Congress was assembled on March 4, 1789, in New York City. The choice, Representative James Madison informed President George Washington, was either staying in New York or strangling the new government at its birth. By May 1789 most congressmen had found some kind of residence in New York and were settling into a normal routine. The small gallery space at meetings of Congress was usually filled and frequently raucous. Members were not always in town and did not attend every session if they were, but it was reported that they paid close attention to the records of debate as they appeared in the *New York Daily Gazette* or the *Daily Advertiser*.[2] Both carried excerpts of speeches made on the floor of Congress. Thomas Lloyd founded the *Congressional Register*, which did not appear until several weeks after the speeches it printed had been delivered. A publisher named John Fenno started the *Gazette of the United States*, receiving patronage and financial support from Alexander Hamilton, who expected a pro-Federalist tilt. Dismayed by the "hymns and lauds chanted" by this "paper of pure Toryism," Jefferson and Madison persuaded a New York editor, Philip Frenau, to launch a Republican paper in Philadelphia to be called the *National Gazette*. Jefferson assured Frenau that some government advertising would be placed in his paper.

In short order Frenau published vigorous opposition to Hamilton's plans. President Washington received angry complaints from Hamilton about Jefferson's hired gun on the *National Gazette*. The squabbling and political abuse that followed contributed to Jefferson's decision to leave the cabinet and return to Monticello. He left Madison in command of the evolving Republican party in Congress. Madison, in his quiet way, became a persuasive tactician who kept in touch with his friend at Monticello, and others outside the government. He and Jefferson had devised a cipher "code" for their correspondence to be used whenever sensitive matters were discussed in writing. The appointed local postmasters were not above the practice of "reading other people's mail" if political advantage could be gained, nor were they unwilling to discard the newspapers of which they disapproved.

The code had been agreed upon by Jefferson and Madison early in their fifty year friendship. The two men met for the first time in 1776 when both were delegates to the Virginia General Assembly. In 1782, Madison was in Philadelphia, a leader of the nationalist faction in Congress, and Jefferson, who had been governor of Virginia, was preparing for his voyage to France as the negotiator of a peace treaty. He was delayed and decided to stay in Philadelphia for a month, living in the same boarding house Madison had chosen for his residence during sessions of the Congress. Their collaboration flowered. They talked about books and libraries and, above all, constitutions. Madison compiled a list of approximately 300 books—largely philosophical and political treatises—he hoped Jefferson might acquire in Paris and London. They also agreed on the need for the rudimentary code to be used in their letters to protect the privacy of their observations on political figures or party strategy. Over the years that followed they communicated regularly and Madison was such a frequent visitor to Monticello that the Jefferson family named a bedroom after him.

"A popular government without popular information, or the means of acquiring it," Madison wrote in a familiar passage, "is but a Prologue to a farce or a tragedy; or perhaps both. Knowledge will forever govern ignorance; and a people who mean to be their own Governors, must arm themselves with the power which knowledge gives."[3]

Whether more "professional" politicians seeking reelection would provide greater information for the people—by maximizing access and candor—than one-term public officials was a question newspaper editors did not examine until later in the century. In the formative years newspapers were relied on to publish the minutes of state legislature and congressional sessions and to replicate speeches or essays written by men in office or by the principal advocates of evolving political philosophies. In selecting materials, publishers more often than not avoided the views that disagreed with those they found congenial. The process was frequently stenographic. Policy was the proprietor's choice. The relationship between the publishers and the individual politicians was based on shared beliefs. When passions were ignited, broadsides, pamphlets, or letters to the editor gave vent to slander and distortion that, although extreme at times, had very limited distribution. Circulation figures were not systematically recorded, but for several decades the size of newspapers and their profitability remained small. According to Clarence Brigham's meticulous index of American newspapers published between 1640 and 1820, there were 2,120 different newspapers in the colonial territories and in what became the states. Of these the largest number appeared in the six middle-Atlantic states, ranging from New York to Maryland. New York City alone produced 138 papers over the period; Philadelphia, 107; and Boston, 73.

The economic realities inflicted high losses, and few papers endured. Of the more than 2,000 attempts, 1,118 papers went out of business in less than two years. Approximately fifty papers lasted fifty or more years. The *Pennsylvania Gazette* published for eighty-seven years—the longest run of all. Brigham commented on his extensive research and statistical compilation:

> The newspaper is omnivorous. Not only political history, but religious, educational, and social history find place in its pages. Literature, especially essays and poetry, was constantly supplied to its readers. If all the printed sources of history for a certain century, or decade, had to be destroyed save one, that which could be chosen with the greatest value to posterity would be a file of an important newspaper.[4]

It is significant that Brigham cites the file of an *important* newspaper. He was not anticipating such aberrations as the modern "supermarket" papers, let alone television "tabloid news," but he was mindful of a consideration that will be examined more fully later in this book—the border (ill-defined as it may be) between serious, principled news reporting (print or electronic) and the realm of sensationalism, innuendo, and shameless opportunism of "yellow" tabloids and the other forms of cynical "licentiousness" that have presumed constitutional protection. Nonetheless, in the nineteenth century (as in the colonial years) there was no other way for literate citizens to find out what actions were taken or what opinions had been expressed in Congress than by reading the gazettes. Second- and third-hand reports at dinner tables were confined to the affluent urban few. Seats in the gallery were even fewer.[5]

There had been other printing presses in the Western Hemisphere before the birth of publishing in the American colonies. In the sixteenth century the Mexicans had actually produced their own paper made from the barks of trees and the leaves of a certain species of palm tree. Until the late seventeenth and early eighteenth centuries, however, printing presses in South America were largely, if not totally, devoted to religious materials. The first regular American newspaper was the *Boston Newsletter*, started in 1704 and owned by a postmaster; the second was also located in Boston and began in 1719; and the third, which appeared a day after the 1719 Boston debut, was published in Philadelphia. It was not until 1725 that a New

York City printer published a newspaper. The *Daily Advertiser*, which was one of the papers Madison, Hamilton, and Jay used to disseminate their Federalist essays, was not founded until 1785. Along the way dailies, weeklies, semiweeklies, and triweeklies were started, and failed, in large numbers, especially in New York City and Philadelphia.[6]

Henry Adams, the great-grandson of President John Adams, wrote the nine-volume *History of the United States of America During the Administrations of Thomas Jefferson and James Madison*, which is one of the most highly regarded works of its kind. It is still widely used in academe, particularly its opening chapters on American society in 1800. There are, however, scholars who find the material on that period inaccurate and in need of revision. One such historian, Noble E. Cunningham Jr., has written: "In surveying the intellectual life of the nation, Adams dismissed newspapers as worthy of little notice. 'Of American newspapers there was no end,' he wrote, and he thought that the education supposed to have been widely spread by them 'was hardly to be distinguished from ignorance . . . the student of history might search forever these storehouses of political calumny for facts meant to instruct the public in any useful object.'" Cunningham disagrees with Adams's tart assessment. He cites Pierre Samuel DuPont de Nemours, who wrote an essay in 1800 saying that American newspapers disseminated "an enormous amount of information—political, physical, philosophic; information on agriculture, the arts, travel, navigation; and also extracts from all the best books in America and Europe." DuPont further observed that "in America, a great number of people read the Bible, and all people read a newspaper," including fathers who read aloud, from the papers, to their children.

On one point nearly all historians agree—newspapers were widely available and avidly read. The reading of the Bible had, of course, encouraged literacy. Religion could not be promulgated without parishioners who could comprehend the text. The church-going citizens, who were in the majority, learned how to read as a necessary aspect of life in the New World, and they often learned much more than the Bible from ministers who had been educated at universities. When Noah Webster founded the New York *Minerva* in 1793, he told his readers, "In no other country on earth, not even in Great Britain, are newspapers so generally circulated among the body of the people, as in America."[7]

Adams's contempt for the intellectual content of newspapers led him to overlook the "popular culture" attributes of those proliferating publications. The best-selling "booklet" in the America of 1800 was Mason Locke Weem's brief *The Life and Memorable Actions of George Washington*— eighty pages in the original but replete with "anecdotes apropos, interesting and entertaining" that could be excerpted by newspaper editors. The booklet went through twenty-nine editions by 1825.

The interest in politics—people and policies—was accelerating. Contemporary media often shocks the American public with its breezy, sleazy, anecdotal coverage of public figures, blurring the line between private lives and public responsibility in a feeding frenzy that has given aid and comfort to those who want to shackle the press clause of the First Amendment. But the author of the Declaration of Independence suffered in his 1800 campaign for the presidency as many slings and arrows—taking into account the difference in technology—as any modern candidate. Jefferson was attacked in newspapers, pamphlets, and pulpits. The Federalists saw him as a muddled visionary who might make a good university professor but who was distinctly incapable of administering a national government. The *Gazette of the United States* thundered at all voters to ask themselves: "Shall I continue in allegiance to God and a religious President; or impiously declare for Jefferson—and no God." In contrast, the *Maryland Gazette* said his whole life had been a comment on the Declaration and he was the best "friend of the people." The Philadelphia *Aurora* printed a version of the Republican platform, and in parallel columns listed "things as they have been" under the Federalists and "things as they will be" under the Republicans.[8]

Jefferson won by the narrowest of margins and regarded the election "as real a revolution in the principles of government as that of 1776 was in its form." He reminded Americans that the process was not achieved by "the sword" but by the "peaceable instrument of reform, the suffrage of the people."[9]

What Henry Adams did not perceive in the collections of newspapers he examined was the deep-running significance of political activity and awareness in the American culture. Political campaigns were central to the passions, the concerns, and the entertainment of Americans in the early decades of the republic. Congressional debates were more fully reported in the newspapers of 1800 than they are today. This in turn provided the grist for ceaseless discussion among the people and the inclination to gather locally when issues were hot and debate positions that would be forwarded, upon achieving some semblance of consensus, to the duly elected representatives in Congress. Henry Adams in his history of the period did not see in Jefferson's election a validation of the party leader who attracts national support and provides a vision that a majority of the voters can share. The press was robust, irreverent, and multivoiced but preponderantly partisan. Nonetheless, over the course of his presidency, Jefferson built a substantial following in all parts of the country. His ideas were larger and more persuasive than sectional interests, party politics, or the polemics of newspaper proprietors. It might be that historians of America in the first part of the nineteenth century can find in the remarkable, primitive plethora of small newspapers that informed the electorate the evidence for Jefferson's faith that "every difference of opinion is not a difference of principle."[10]

The 1840s brought important changes to the American newspaper business. First, the so-called penny press evolved because growing circulations permitted the publishers to sell each copy for a penny. Railroads were being built rapidly enough to provide wider distribution, and telegraphy offered opportunities for reporting the news swiftly. Postage rates were lowered and the technology of printing presses improved to the point that large-circulation papers could print quickly and get the news out while it was fresh. S.N.D. North, who wrote *History and Present Condition of the Newspaper and Periodical Press of the United States* (1884), observed that there was by 1880 "no field of thought or labor which does not command its special organs of opinion and information." He cited community needs, marriages and deaths, business announcements, official government notices required by law, and local and foreign news among the headings that were either covered by the larger newspapers or found in special interest journals. The newspaper business had in 1840 been measured for the first time by the federal census. A few states did their own census covering newspapers and periodicals, but not comprehensively. North stated that newspapers "have come to rank side by side with the schools, the churches, and the libraries as an educating and elevating influence in society and *differ* from these civilizing institutions only in the sense that they are *private enterprises*" (emphasis added). North also reported that in 1870 the printing industry, book publishing, newspapers, and periodicals employed about 30,000 people and generated $40 million a year. The law had required a report on newspapers and periodicals because of their relationship to "the moral, social and intellectual condition of the people." The report revealed that in 1870, the smallest town in the United States with a daily press was Elko, Nevada—population 752. The smallest town with two daily newspapers was Tombstone, Arizona—population 973. The localized press was a unique resource in nineteenth-century America, and in many ways that usefulness persists.[11]

In 1881 the population of the United States was approximately 50 million, and there were 970 daily newspapers with a combined circulation of about 4.3 million. The average circulation was 4,400. Between 1870 and 1880, the number of employees working for newspapers in the United States increased from 30,000 to 65,000. Their wages increased over the decade from $8.1 million to $15.3 million. The 960 papers in the United States in the year 1870 outnumbered the 650 in Britain, the 545 in Germany, and the 539 in France. In 1880, the average annual subscription to a daily newspaper cost $7.20; though the dailies in New York City were charging 2.3 cents per copy, the national average was 4.5 cents per copy. The growth of advertising, for which there are few reliable statistics, can be measured best by IRS collections. Taxes in 1867 on newspaper income brought in $9.6 million; in 1880 the figure was $39.1 million. There was also intense competition for lucrative contracts to publish government announcements, and most of these awards depended upon the political affiliation of the publisher.[12]

The *New York Sun* was the first newspaper that attempted, in 1833, to become a penny press. By 1835 it needed steam power to run its equipment because of the growth in its circulation. The *Sun* was never quite on time until the invention of what S.N.D. North called "locking of the type upon the cylinder." There were seven six-penny papers in New York City that came out in the morning, four six-penny papers that came out in the evening, and five general one-penny papers. Some twenty years later, Civil War coverage increased the operating expenses of newspapers, and the penny press became the two-penny press. Copies of the early penny-press publications in library collections reveal that most of them were small, poorly printed, and short on news. The two-, three- and four-penny papers were of considerably higher quality and published extensive "digested" news. New York publisher James Gordon Bennett, who owned the *Morning Herald*, said of his penny paper, "We know what we are, but know not what we may be." Significantly, the penny press tended to be independent and catered to a poorer class of readers—or so the publishers believed. These readers were, by all indications, not political and wanted news of the day reported objectively.

The politicians in the big cities resisted this trend because they saw a loss of influence over the voters. The freedom from political obligation, however, among the cheaper newspapers taught the higher-priced, quality newspapers an interesting lesson—and they too became more concerned with news that was not slavishly partisan. The impact the penny press had on the newspaper business included larger circulation for the dailies and frequent changes in the style and character of editorial matter. (In a 1947 *Yale Record* parody of the *New York Daily News*, the tabloid was replicated with such visual authenticity that 25,000 people bought copies—not noticing at once that the "2 cents" price on the front page was replaced by "2 cents here, 2 cents there, it all adds up.")[13]

Whitelaw Reid, the publisher of the *New York Tribune*, reported to his colleagues in 1880: "On a business of half a million copies in 1859, as a two-cent paper, the *Tribune* made a net profit of $86,000. At the beginning of 1879 we found that a business of nearly three-quarters of a million copies, as a four-cent paper, it had made $85,588."[14] In North's *History of Newspapers* he points to a diminishing influence of well-known "personalities" among editors and publishers and a tendency toward more impersonal editorial product. By the end of the nineteenth century, independent papers were better at gathering and reporting the news, and the readers preferred papers with no political alliances. As to other areas of the country, Boston in 1846 had fourteen daily newspapers. By 1880 there were only eleven daily newspapers, but their circulation was five times greater than all fourteen in 1846. The history of newspapers in most major cities follows the same pattern. Those that could endure seemed to hold on to the loyalty and support of their readers. The growth of technology, the advent of wire services, and even more intense competition were waiting in the wings.

Some of the young people who went to work at urban publications came from college newspapers. Dartmouth is given credit for having the first campus newspaper—in 1800. The oldest surviving college paper, called the *Yale Literary Magazine* in 1836, became the *Yale Daily News*. The *Harvard Daily Echo* began at Harvard in 1879. It will surprise some contemporary college administrators that, according to S.N.D. North, nineteenth-century college newspapers were purveyors of "articles, for the most part, the fruit of careful reading, earnest thought, and careful revision." One extraordinarily generous (or addled) Ivy League professor called the campus newspaper "the outstanding member of the faculty."[15]

During the Civil War many states exempted newspaper men from military duty because of the importance of gathering and disseminating information about the conflict. General Irvin McDowell of the Union army was quoted by the fabled British military correspondent William Howard Russell as saying, "I have made arrangements for the correspondents to take the field . . . and I have suggested to them that they should wear a white uniform to indicate the purity of their character."[16] The greatest period of development in the newspaper world began in the post–Civil War era. By 1880 there were 812 million copies of newspapers mailed in the United States and 40 million magazines. The *New York Sun* management reported that 14,443 copies of its newspaper were delivered by rail each day to out-of-town destinations; 5,221 were mailed; 12,237 were sold by newsboys shouting at street corners or outside railroad stations; and 101,000 were sold by local news agents from booths and kiosks. Newspaper earnings in that era represented a large proportion of the wealth generated in the United States. In summarizing the importance of newspapers at the end of the nineteenth century, North reports both "eulogy" and "condemnation" but sees newspapers as "a factor in our civilization which is unsurpassed by any other in the energy, the enterprise, and the success of those who are engaged in its conduct." The advent of radio and television was a long way off, and for the time being, the swiftness and the relative accuracy with which newspapers could supply individual citizens with the "information that was essential to their private concerns" was indisputable. There was an equally valuable role for the newspapers as conservators of historical material. Preachers, teachers, politicians, and philanthropists agreed that newspapers offered the only methodology for a widespread "intercommunication" among all the resources of what was considered civilization. Without any reservation, North looked forward to "the glorious opportunities" of the future.[17]

Much of the controversy over the "rights of the people"—a free press among them—flowed from differing expectations in each of the states. Madison had signaled that development and lamented afterward his failure to achieve one uniform national bill of rights with no deviations state by state. Because he failed to win that contest, the primary protectors of individual freedoms were, at the end of the day, the states themselves. Each had its constitution and each had a view of basic rights—some more emphatic or extensive than others. It was not until the twentieth century—and then only by reinterpreting the Fourteenth Amendment—that the Supreme Court began to use the national Bill of Rights as an assurance for *all* citizens abiding in any state. Various decisions of the Court inexorably expanded the Bill of Rights, applying the "due process" clause of the Fourteenth Amendment, passed in 1868: "nor shall any state deprive any person of life, liberty, or property, without due process of law; nor deny to any person within its jurisdiction the equal protection of the laws." The problem Madison had anticipated was not the absence but the inconsistency of rights among the states. In recent years, legal scholars have revisited constitutional law at the state level so far as individual rights are concerned—especially where state constitutions provided "stronger and broader" rights definitions. The contemporary abortion issue may well revive a competition in rights protection at the local level.[18]

On the national level, amendments to the Constitution have been a potential alternative to Court opinions. Amendments, however, require public debate and a political process of considerable complexity. Those who find that extended process preferable see in it the "consent of the governed" and therefore measurable support from "We the People." Those who do not, fear manipulation, demagoguery, and the tyranny of an "ignorant majority." For the believers in judicial review, the judges represent the best of both worlds. In the long run they believe the judges can be the most reliable and thoughtful defenders of the nation's conscience.

Whatever the future holds for greater political participation at the state and local levels—and for the contributions of the press to an *informed discussion*—the historical record indicates that there was, from the very beginning of the republic, a high rate of turnover in both the state legislatures and in the Congress. That revolving door was not set in motion primarily because the voters were dissatisfied. It was the *elected* members who complained the most; the selfless duties of public life were not so appealing as some had assumed. For one thing, the workload was greater than they had expected, and many representatives served only the minimum term before getting out. They wanted to get back to private ambitions sooner than the Federalist ideals prescribed. The concept of a "filtration of talent," which was meant to attract the most distinguished and highly motivated men into government, could protect the nation from the undisciplined democracy Madison and his colleagues had witnessed with horror in the state legislatures. But the Federalist faith in a spontaneous emergence of a leadership class was not answered. The same voters who elected the "rabble" to the state bodies would choose their congressmen. Neither the Federalist vision of new talent brimming with desire for "disinterested" public service nor the attractions of prestige and influence were able to lure many of the most qualified men away from private careers, wealth, and contentment.

Madison had deliberately avoided any significant change in the *powers* defined in the Constitution by concentrating on a list of rights that would connect themselves to those already written into state documents but would *not*, at the same time, increase state powers. Such a strategy would satisfy the "individualists," he believed, as well as the Federalists. But it did not produce, in the end, the kind of stability of tenure in Congress that the Framers had desired. "The interest of the man," Madison had written of officeholders, "must be related to the Constitutional rights of the place." Private interests had to be abandoned or at least suspended. That sacrifice was not a common occurrence. For nearly fifty years the Congress attracted numerous candidates but retained few. The record was no better at the state level, where legislators rarely endured.[19]

That pattern began to change toward the end of the nineteenth century, though senators were still appointed rather than elected. Representatives, in particular, were to find reasons for pursuing a career in politics, which meant seeking to stay in office for longer periods. (At the end of the twentieth century the pattern may be changing again.) Without any missionary fervor the newspapers and pamphlets had produced public access to the views of major political groups and the agendas of individual public figures—first in the form of letters, speeches, and essays, later in the evolution of discriminate reporting, editorial opinion, caricature, and denunciation. What was not visible to the readers of such material was the frequent tumult and self-serving in the state legislative meetings.

Unfortunately the distinctions of the men who served in the first Congress were not to be matched for more than a century, and by then the game was played on a far different field dominated by the industrial revolution and technological changes, which permitted news and opinion to be transmitted—sometimes stridently, always influentially—to very large audiences each day. There was, however, never to be another group of men in office who had been involved with the American Revolution or the ratification of a constitution. The first Congress included twenty members of the federal Constitutional Convention—among them James Madison, Elbridge Gerry, Rufus King, Roger Sherman, William Samuel Johnson, Oliver Elsworth, William Paterson, and Robert Morris. Most of the members saw their role as defenders of the Constitution. Not all had inherited social status. Many members had earned their place by risking all they had during the Revolution.

For the "great men" of the first Congress, politics, almost by definition, was a duty. Patronage was not a political mechanism on the massive scale known to modern practitioners, though it had become part of the process long before the 1790s. What was surprisingly new was the widespread, almost spontaneous, aptitude for *using* the press. This disposition was so commonly found among the "people's representatives," that the vision of a dispassionate, deliberative body protected from the incursions of special interest and influential constituents had nearly vanished by the first election.

10

THE BLOODIEST WAR

There are natural tensions built in between the press and the military, and the same natural tension is built in between the press and the Congress, or the press and business. It is just the role of the press. It's part of the checks and balances system in this country. It's very, very important, by its very nature, and the role that it plays is basically being intrusive in a free society—as opposed to being a mouthpiece, as it is in a totalitarian society.

—General Bernard Trainor,
former military correspondent, *New York Times;*
retired director, National Security Program,
Kennedy School of Government, Harvard

The Civil War propelled expansion in the newspaper business, but it did not inspire much, if any, growth in the sense of responsibility or the ethical awareness of publishers, editors, or reporters. For them the contest would be won by gains in circulation; accuracy, fairness, and compassion were neither necessary nor particularly desirable. The few correspondents who tried to understand the cosmic issues of preserving a nation, freeing slaves, and reviving the constitutional vision were disheartened, repelled, and outraged by the quality of the men who had so inadequately and mendaciously reported on the brutal aspects of the Civil War. The inhumanity of tactics that led to senseless slaughter; the overcrowded, undersupplied prisoner-of-war "death camps"; the too frequently incompetent and egomaniacal leadership; and the cynical profiteering among suppliers were scarcely touched. Years later on the floor of the Senate, Hiram Johnson intoned, "The first casualty of war is truth."[1]

British author Phillip Knightley borrowed Johnson's phrase for the title of a searing study of war coverage, from the Crimea to Vietnam, called *The First Casualty*.[2] In a carefully documented chapter on the Civil War, Knightley concludes that there were a paltry number of brilliant and authentic accounts filed by a handful of courageous and thorough journalists, but these were conspicuous exceptions. There were, however, many re-

markable artists who, in the absence of the technology that could have produced photographic half-tones, managed to draw authentic pictures of battles, individual soldiers, and the realities of military life. "Illustrated weeklies, such as *Harpers* and *Frank Leslie's Illustrated Week*," Knightley
reports, "flourished, the latter alone employing some eighty artists and
publishing in four years more than three thousand sketches and drawings"[3]

There were, in addition, about 50,000 miles of telegraph lines in the eastern states, which made it possible for newspapers to provide the most extensive and timely reporting the world had seen to date—though much of it
was worthless. The larger papers each sent dozens of reporters into the
field. Many European papers devoted as much space to the Civil War as
their American counterparts. France's Georges Clemenceau came to America for *Le Temps*. The *Times* of London sent the premier war correspondent then writing, William Howard Russell, whom Lincoln received with
respectful politesse, telling him that his paper was "one of the greatest powers in the world—in fact, I don't know anything which has more power—
except perhaps the Mississippi. I am glad to know you as its minister."[4]

Gary Wills believes Lincoln had set out to change the very concept of his
nation and the view of it held by foreign countries. He wanted the world to
understand that the Union was preeminent over the separate states. "Up to
the Civil War," Wills writes, "'the United States' was invariably a plural
noun: 'the United States *are* a free country.' After Gettysburg it became a
singular; 'the United States *is* a free country'"[5] (emphasis added).

Lincoln had used his war powers to issue the Emancipation Proclamation
during the first month of 1863, but in November of that year, at Gettysburg,
he did not mention emancipation or, for that matter, the Union he was determined to save. Invoking the concept of *equality for all*, he moved closer
to the Thirteenth Amendment, which ultimately ended slavery, and in Gary
Wills's interpretation he installed the Declaration of Independence as the
"founding document." The very opening words, "Four score and seven
years ago," carried his listeners back to 1776 (not 1788 or 1791), but that
calculation did not elicit a single known comment in the newspaper coverage. Slavery survived for so many years because nothing in the Constitution
could cast it out. Lincoln may well have aspired in his careful selection of
words and the rhythm of their arrangement to change the Constitution
"from within, by appeal from its letter to the spirit." That change, however,
even with the constitutional amendments, was far from complete.[6]

Journalism did not earn itself many honors during the Civil War. The
majority of northern correspondents were "ignorant, dishonest, and uneth-
ical." More often than not their stories were inaccurate at best, fictional at
worst, and nearly always partisan. J. Cutler Andrews, who wrote a comprehensive critique of newspaper coverage during the conflict, *The North
Reports the Civil War*, laments that "sensationalism and exaggeration, out-

right lies, puffery, slander, faked eye-witness accounts, and conjectures built on pure imagination cheapen much that passed in the North for news."[7] The correspondents who covered the dedication of the national cemetery at Gettysburg paid little or no attention to the president's "brief remarks." Some didn't mention him at all. One wrote: "The President also spoke."

Henry Adams wrote from London, "People have become so accustomed to the idea of disbelieving everything that is stated in the American papers that all confidence in us is destroyed."[8] He may not have known how much government censorship affected the quality of the reporting on which he commented. Censorship was, in fact, rampant, capricious, and, as is so often the case, counterproductive. The hundreds of American reporters who were sent to the battle areas were, by and large, young and inexperienced. The Associated Press, which might have provided a broader range of information, was in the early stages of development, and most of its reporters were hired because of their ability to use a telegraph key. The work was, if pursued with any sense of duty, exhausting, and the pay was low. The larger papers in New York and Philadelphia, Chicago and Boston, could sell many thousands of additional copies when the alleged details of a major battle were printed. Scoops were far more important to frantic editors than mere factual material. One Chicago editor ordered "all the news you can get and when there is no news, send rumors."[9] The correspondents were not only underpaid but found it difficult to recover expenses. Many accepted cash for promising to mention certain officers in their dispatches or for sending tips to stock speculators who gambled on the effect of military procurement. The *New York Tribune* estimated that at least half the mail dispatches from battle areas never reached the paper. Reporters learned to write quickly and then race for a telegraph office or a rail junction if they could.

The southern press was even less capable of securing and communicating accurate information. Nearly every paper in the South was a weekly—partisan and propagandistic. With little general appeal, these papers earned meager incomes and were never able to compete with the extensiveness or speed of northern reporting. Many of these struggling southern enterprises were forced to close altogether as the Union army moved into their territories. A few retreated with the southern forces, taking their equipment and printing in different towns along the way. Paper and ink supplies were diminishing rapidly, and this forced the handful of surviving papers in the South to print on "wrapping paper, writing paper, paper bags, and even the blank side of wallpaper."[10] What was produced by southern editors was so unreliably romantic and distorted, if not ludicrously false, that their contributions to history were minimal. Accounts of southern victories were likely to begin, "Glory to God in the highest," and the Union soldiers were described as always going into battle "drunken with wine, blood and fury" or by some similar hyperbole.

The northern press was not so easily co-opted. More than twenty newspapers that were not afraid to report incompetence or losses were suppressed or closed down by government orders. And accurate reporting that was not censored by the government eventually succumbed to competitive zeal. The battle of Bull Run—the first major clash of the war—was a victory for the South, but General Winfield Scott seized the telegraph office in New York, where accounts in great detail of a defeated North had been sent by the Associated Press. The New York papers consequently ran stories of an imagined Union triumph. The misinformation and propaganda that coursed through the overall coverage did not cease. Casualty figures, in particular, were misstated deliberately on both sides. Secretary of War Edwin Stanton practiced censorship, withholding news, arresting editors, and banning correspondents. Nothing worked to his satisfaction. In 1864 he took to issuing his own dispatches through the Associated Press. Such daily bulletins were meant to set the record straight, but they could also set it crooked. Nevertheless, Stanton's device became a standard procedure in subsequent wars throughout the world.

No one regarded the press with greater disdain than the feared General William Tecumseh Sherman, who took every possible step to keep correspondents far away from his command. He saw reporters as a menace "filling up our transports, swelling our trains, reporting on our progress, guessing at places, picking up dropped expressions, inciting jealousy and discontent, and doing infinite mischief."[11] So few correspondents followed Sherman's capture of Atlanta and the march through Georgia that the full meaning of his tactics went virtually unnoticed. The *New York Times* did not have a reporter on the scene, and the *New York Evening Post* ran a story written by Major George Nichols, one of Sherman's staff officers. The Nichols file was later enlarged as a book called *The Story of the Great March—From the Diary of a Staff Officer*. The volume sold well after the war and was praised for its authenticity.

One correspondent who did succeed in filing eyewitness accounts of the highest quality was David P. Conyngham of the *New York Herald*. His reporting required physical courage and the balancing of compassion with the ultimate responsibility to render the truth as well as he could determine it. There was in his writing a connectedness to both subject and reader that was wise beyond his years. A young man in his early twenties, he accompanied General Sherman's army on its fabled march through Georgia. One of his stories included the following passage:

A battle-field, when the carnage of the day is over; when the angry passions of men have subsided; when the death silence follows the din and roar of battle; when the victors have returned triumphant to their camps to celebrate their victory, regardless of the many comrades they have left behind; when the conquered sullenly fall back to a new position, awaiting to renew the struggle—is a sad sight. It is hard to listen to the hushed groans and cries of the dying, and to witness the lacerated bodies of your fellow-soldiers strewn around, some with broken limbs, torn and mangled bodies, writhing in agony. How often has some poor fellow besought me to shoot him, and put him out of pain. It would be a mercy to do so, yet I dared not.[12]

The *New York Times* did a good job of covering the riots in its community in 1863. For three days and nights in July, New York City went out of control. The "reign of rabble" attacked the government draft offices and turned on African Americans as well. Troops had to be sent up from Gettysburg to restore order. The draft, in fact, was suspended. New Yorkers had learned much about the military from the press. The penalty for desertion was death. Capture meant slow death, so appalling were conditions in the camps on both sides. There was friction between officers and volunteers. Slaves, former slaves, and blacks born free were not wanted in the military until commanders were forced to accept them into segregated units because white men were not volunteering in large enough numbers. Deserters were often lined up and shot in groups with reporters and artists deliberately invited to watch the massacre in the hope that their depiction of mass execution would discourage further desertion. One reporter wrote that a military band played a dirge before the shooting and the popular song "The Girl I Left Behind Me" afterward.[13]

Mary Boykin Chesnut's *A Diary from Dixie* described the April 1864 storming of Fort Pillow, where a Union force was routed. The southern troops found that there were "two-hundred-sixty-two negroes" at the fort. Their commanding officer, General Bedford Forrest, gave orders to shoot all of them "after resistance had ceased."[14] That story, ultimately confirmed by a congressional investigation, and many others like it were largely ignored. Racism in the Union army, which habitually sang a song called "Sambo's Right to be Kilt," was not reported or was buried by the censors. Prisoner camps were not written about by either side in a tacit agreement to avoid equal guilt. The *New York Times* did expose some medical mismanagement, but no reports revealed the vast corruption in the Quarter Master Corp or in the letting of contracts to suppliers. Isolated accounts reflected the plight of the wounded—the endless amputations (some performed by inebriated surgeons), the slaughter of young men unprepared for battle, and the suffering of soldiers without shoes or adequate food.

Lincoln feared that the South might persuade Britain to support its cause. Both the North and the South sent agents to England to mount propaganda campaigns. The *New York Herald* correspondent George Train made twenty-three speeches in England in two months. Others wrote secretly for the British press, and Lincoln sent public letters to the working men of Manchester and London, to be published in British newspapers. The South provided one agent with large amounts of cash. He was to co-opt British journalists, and he did so with ease. Seven London newspapermen placed stories and editorials slanted favorably to the South in return for "boxes of cigars ... whiskey ... and other articles" or, of course, folding money. C. Vann Woodward, in *American Counterpoint*, writes: "The backlash to emancipation was frightening. Lincoln thought his Proclamation had 'done about as much harm as good.' The Illinois legislature adopted a resolution denouncing it and debated enforcement of the State Exclusion Law with 'thirty-nine lashes on the bare back.'"[15] There were anti-Negro riots in Toledo, Chicago, Peoria, and Cincinnati. Republican politicians insisted that there would be no Negro migration into their territories. In any event, the English, who had already rejected slavery, were politically in favor of emancipation, and the temptation to recognize the Confederate government in return for favorable trade agreements was never quite strong enough.

Full equality for African Americans was not even a peripheral goal of the leadership in the struggle to preserve the Union. There were voices heard in abolition organizations, and there were sermons preached (though the clergy as a group was not in the forefront of the movement to free slaves—let alone help them achieve equality in an open society); and the newspapers, which were the only means of mass communication, provided sporadic essays and letters deploring the enslavement of human beings. There was widespread animosity, fear, suspicion, and contempt toward Africans. The lives of African Americans who were freed from slavery by the Civil War did not improve measurably.[16]

Lincoln had heard his Illinois constituents angrily demanding resistance to any migration of Africans into their state, and he had heard the same deep-seated prejudice almost everywhere he traveled as lawyer, politician, and president of the United States. He was aware of an irrevocable, ugly racism that pervaded a large segment of American society. If he was to win his war, he had to accept the support of racists. There is much evidence that he was saddened by this political reality, but he was not unmindful of the virtuous Americans who demanded a cleansing of the "stain upon the Constitution."

The Civil War and the Thirteenth Amendment, which stated that "neither slavery nor involuntary servitude ... shall exist within the United States," finally extracted from the American "experiment" the legitimacy of a disenfranchised, enslaved, and degraded segment of the population that was limited to menial tasks. But self-serving economic advantage had been the progenitor of slavery, and the underlying racism wrapped its tendrils around any organized effort to question the status quo. In southern states, it was conventional wisdom to ban the dissemination of newspapers or pamphlets in which the remotest suggestion of abolitionist sentiment appeared. The clergy in those same states found convenient references in the Bible to control any sympathy for the slaves. Biblical admonitions that all men must obey their masters and all wives must obey their husbands were solemnly applauded in local publications. Lincoln's presidency threatened the closed southern society with the power of appointing Republican postmasters who could and did lift the ban on abolitionist newspapers—indeed, on any northern newspaper opposed to slavery or willing to print differing views on the subject. Presbyterians, Congregationalists, Baptists, Methodists, Episcopalians, Lutherans, Unitarians, and Catholics all took positions at one time or another "that placed the majority of their clerical leaders in opposition to the anti-slavery movement." The most frequently used explanation by churchmen was that abolition would disrupt their congregations by dividing the members.[17]

Whatever sustenance the antislavery conviction in the South might have received—and eventually did receive—from abolitionists in other regions of the country was a matter of communication by mail. Articles from northern newspapers and pamphlets were reprinted frequently by papers in distant cities. If the ban on mail delivery of newspapers containing antislavery views was lifted by a Republican postmaster, a steady flow of moral outrage and shared values could reach the antislavery forces in the South. Pamphlets and newspapers remained the sole mechanism for disseminating political opinions, religious concern, or broad philosophical principles, which were the major resources of reform or change or, for that matter, the obdurate defense of existing policies. In 1852 the antislavery newspapers in the North reported a statement by the renowned black abolitionist Frederick Douglass that "the only way to make the Fugitive Slave Law a dead letter [is] to make a half dozen or more dead kidnappers." Such remarks, when printed, were not expected to make it past southern postmasters; nor was Douglass's own newspaper, the *North Star*, which took its name from the celestial body followed by slaves who escaped in the darkness of night, heading for the better dawn that very few of them found.[18]

The contradictory attitudes and the depth of hostility toward African slaves and their descendants in the New England, central Atlantic, and northwestern states astonished foreign visitors. Alexis de Tocqueville is the most often quoted observer, but there were many others who reported for European publications or corresponded with their government officials regarding the racism in the North, even among those who were antislavery. Publication of material friendly to the African American, although rarely advocating more than minimal civil rights, could become dangerous, particularly in the middle years of the nineteenth century. In 1833 Elijah Lovejoy published the vigorously abolitionist *St. Louis Observer*. His office was stormed and his press burned down several times. He moved to Alton, Illinois, and published an abolitionist newspaper there until 1837, when he was shot and killed by an unidentified gunman who was part of a mob seeking to destroy all of Lovejoy's possessions. Lovejoy tried to protect his printing press and was known thereafter as the "martyred abolitionist."

William Lloyd Garrison, born in Massachusetts in 1805, worked as a printer's apprentice and soon began writing essays for newspapers in the region. With his first written words, he became an ardent abolitionist. At twenty-one, he became the editor of the Newburyport *Free Press* in his hometown. Five years later he founded his trademark journal, the *Liberator*, in Boston. It became the foremost publication of the antislavery movement. At first, Garrison alone wrote the *Liberator*'s articles and did the typesetting, printing, and distribution of his small paper. In 1835 he was attacked by a mob in the Boston streets because of his abolitionist views. He had called the Constitution's tolerance of slavery "a covenant with death and an agreement with Hell." In 1854 he publicly set a copy of the Constitution on fire and watched it burn. Garrison also served for many years as president of the American Anti-Slavery Society. Characteristically, after the Thirteenth Amendment was passed and slavery outlawed, he agitated for women's suffrage and fair treatment for American Indians.[19]

The early journals and gazettes, as Franklin so clearly understood, could reach distant places by mail and could then see some of their important partisan articles issued by like-minded publishers in other parts of the colonies. The reprinting process permitted larger reach providing the postmasters were faithful to their obligations. Thus the opinions of key politicians could be repeated in widely dispersed communities across what was then America. The number of significant property owners who could vote and hold office was in each location not much larger than the circulation of newspapers that reflected or illuminated their views. The censorship of the mail to prevent the import of abolitionist opinions into the southern states operated effectively for many decades. Meanwhile, the southern press censored itself, joining the clergy and the politicians in prohibiting criticism of slavery.

11

THE BOTTOM LINES

The press has been talking for years and years and years about getting more minorities in the news room. So they're up to 7%. Big deal! Until you get minorities to some adequate degree reflecting the society at large, I don't think we can report black America or Hispanic America or Asian America. So that's number one. And I guess I just simply agree, as I did twenty odd years ago when the Kerner Commission brought out its report, that we are still doing a lousy job in covering these problems.

—Osborn Elliott, former dean,
Graduate School of Journalism, Columbia University;
editor in chief, *Newsweek*

The Civil War had, among its side effects, enhanced the idea of "war correspondence." Large newspapers in Europe and the United States would never again neglect the appeal of stories "from the front" wherever military conflict took place. The ingredients were death and heroism, strategy and resistance, patriots and villains. War stories increased circulation, making the presses run overtime. Blood and thunder enhanced profits. The potential for enormous daily sales had been analyzed by opportunistic publishers in urban areas. The elements of mass appeal were still easily measured. In addition to war, there was crime and corruption, violence and scandal. Such ingredients sold well and always would. Another lesson had been learned, perhaps too well. Inaccuracy and fabrication required neither apology nor redress unless a victim could afford a good lawyer, and libel or slander could be convincingly demonstrated. To say that all major papers were irresponsible would, of course, overstate the case. What became clear was that the standards of the expansive newspaper industry were uneven, ill-defined, and too frequently dominated by competitive venality. For the thoughtful, educated segment of the public that was willing to look for and read a higher level of editorial product, the small, "quality" magazines began to appear and, inevitably, over the last two decades of the nineteenth century included among their concerns a critical examination of the mass press. The transgressions of the high-circulation daily press had multiplied in the heat of competition and a deadline atmosphere. A daily newspaper was, by nature, evanescent. Yesterday's paper was for wrapping fish.

The most significant structural transition was the passing of the small owner-operated papers, usually edited by the proprietor. These gave way to emerging corporate enterprises. Profits were realized first from the numbers of copies sold and then, increasingly, from advertising. Advertising agencies, market studies, and the process of determining space rates were at a primitive stage, but the driving business principle—once the single proprietor's allegiance to a specific political party was eclipsed by the independent publishing companies—was to engender the support of business itself. News coverage was increasingly shaped by advertiser attitudes. Vigorous monitoring of government or corporation actions diminished, and editorials were written so as to avoid offending those who might be able to retaliate in any way that would threaten profitability. Print advertising presented dazzling possibilities for selling goods and services to the burgeoning marketplaces of the cities.[1]

The process had begun out of necessity in the colonial years. The engine was immigration and self-sufficiency. The limited advertising was linked to fundamental and local economic concerns—cargoes arriving from abroad, farm equipment, tools, cloth, building supplies, and slaves. Importing slaves became illegal in 1808, but slavery continued as a source of free labor and the slave population in America multiplied. An ad offering a healthy slave woman "suitable for work on the farm or in the city" was no different from those for plowshares or patent medicines—same size, same typeface, indifferently listed one after the other in neat columns that were often on the front pages.[2]

American ingenuity and innovation had been encouraged by the economic philosophy of Alexander Hamilton, who had envisioned the strength of a central government as a means of inspiring a sense of nation more compelling than exclusive loyalty to local communities and state legislatures. Many years before the Civil War, "curious tinkerers," borrowing and adapting existing products as Thomas Jefferson had done at Monticello, created their own machines—screw-cutters, turret lathes, circular saws, the typewriter, the McCormick reaper, vulcanized rubber (a process devised by a man named Goodyear in New Haven, Connecticut), the safety pin, and Eli Whitney's "interchangeable parts" (also conceived in New Haven), which presaged the assembly line. Whitney had earlier invented the cotton gin but received no benefits from his idea, even though it was patented, because southern plantation owners copied it shamelessly without paying fees or royalties. The patent office was created in 1790 under a constitutional provision, and one of its first administrators was the multitalented Thomas Jefferson. Hamilton, in his *Report on Manufactures*, had recommended tariff laws to protect American inventions against foreign imports, but tariffs between the states were banned. During the Civil War, landowning southern politicians feared that northern industrialists would use the central government's subsidies to develop large business interests in the North and penetrate the new western states as well.[3] It did not work that way. The northern environment was receptive to investment and entrepreneurship. Individual inventors could count on growing markets nourished by the "national political economy." Inventors and their backers were more interested in sales and distribution than in localized concerns. People who thought of themselves as part of a nation with national commercial possibilities uninhibited by state regulations moved rapidly into an industrial strategy.

Industrial growth dramatically enlarged the profits of newspapers, whose ads were the only means of attracting buyers in great numbers. The advertisements, too, began to assume national characteristics. If the distribution was available, the pitch in one city would usually work as well in another. Product emulation and competition followed, but without diminishing the need for advertising.

The South was reluctant to see localism eroded. The other great and persistent fear in the South was the abolitionist movement and the seepage of religious and philosophical opposition to slavery into the political debates at the national level. Southern postmasters could not forever suppress abolitionist publications. Some made their way into southern homes, and a small but fervent antislavery movement—part of it had sprouted from moralistic seeds among southern idealists and clerics—was fed by the convictions and tenacity of abolitionist newspapers in the North.[4]

Abolitionist papers were never able to build large circulations, let alone attract much advertising. Overwhelmingly, Southerners, accustomed to obvious economic advantage, clung to their rationale and defied antislavery sentiments. Many Northerners, including "liberals," were content to see slavery disappearing in their own states without forcing similar trends on the South that might rock the boat economically, politically, and constitutionally. The fear of mass migration of freed slaves into northern states had stirred racist paranoia. Some editors of northern newspapers felt compelled out of conscience to examine the institution of slavery and the intractable contradiction it flaunted at the principles of the Declaration of Independence and the federal Constitution (including the Bill of Rights). And beyond those documents, slavery mocked the character of the freewheeling, entrepreneurial republic that a new class of manufacturers and businessmen celebrated.

William Lloyd Garrison had stubbornly campaigned in favor of disobeying the fugitive slave laws and denounced court rulings allowing slaveowners to reclaim runaways. The "pursuit of happiness" was an inconceivable goal for slaves, but liberty might be possible. James Madison had written that property "in its largest and more just meaning embraces everything to which a man may attach a value and have a right; and which leaves to everyone else the like advantage." For Madison, a man had property in his opinions, his religious beliefs, and in the "safety and liberty of his person . . . the free use of his faculties and free choice of the objects on which to employ them. . . . As a man is said to have a right to his property, he may equally be said to have a property in his rights."[5]

Such concepts were part of the essence of the American Revolution and the "great experiment" in democracy. To accept at the same time a view of Africans as so inferior and uneducable that they could be regarded as less than human was an immoral and self-corrupting aspect of American political life from the Declaration onward. The highest cost—which decent citizens understood but did not seem to know (or want to know) how to change—was the poisoning of American self-esteem, vision, and leadership in a world where America was once thought of as the virtuous shining city on the hill. The psychologist C. G. Jung wrote early in the twentieth century: "Every Roman was surrounded by slaves. The slave and his psychology flooded ancient Italy, and every Roman became inwardly, and of course unwittingly, a slave. Because living constantly in the atmosphere of slaves, he became infected through the unconscious with their psychology. No one can shield himself from such an influence."[6]

In 1864, Lincoln had not fully defined his own attitudes toward slavery. He appeared to be ambivalent. The Union was his preoccupation. "If I could save the Union," he wrote to Horace Greeley, the editor of the *New York Tribune*, "without freeing any slave, I would do it; and if I could save it by freeing all the slaves, I would do it; and if I could save it by freeing some and leaving others alone, I would do that."[7] The issue of race in America was combustible and bedeviling, but it was not totally ignored. There were many voices of conscience, many more that were viciously racist. A large number of voices, however, remained silent—at least in public and therefore in the press. The backlash C. Vann Woodward describes in *American Counterpoint* should not surprise students of the one communication system available to those who *wanted* to speak out—the newspapers. Though every point of view on race was expressed in some journal or another, few papers considered—let alone risked—defying perceived public opinion among their constituents. Church publications, abolitionist papers and pamphlets, and those rare and courageous editors who dared to incite public disapproval gave eloquent but scattered testimony to antislavery and antiracist values. The record, unhappily, provides hard evidence of deep-running, innately hostile attitudes toward Negroes and widespread reflection of those attitudes in the newspapers long before the Civil War and the Emancipation Proclamation.[8]

The doctrine of white supremacy flourished throughout the states. The blacks living in the North were a despised part of an antebellum segregated society. Most northern states denied voting rights to Negroes; Indiana, Illinois, and later Oregon (among others) imposed severe penalties on any Negro who tried to settle within their borders, and everywhere the Negroes went they encountered barriers to jobs and little or no protection of life, liberty, or property—if they had any of the latter. Senator Lyman Trumbull of Illinois told the press in 1858: "We are for free white men and for making white labor respectable and honorable, which it can never be when Negro slave labor is brought into competition with it." Thus, Trumbull (like so many others outside the South) reconciled antislavery with anti-Negro bias.[9]

Horace Greeley, a Republican editor, lamented that some of his political colleagues wanted "to prove themselves the 'white man's party' or else all the mean, low, ignorant, drunken, brutish whites will go against them from horror of 'Negro equality.'" Senator Henry Wilson of Massachusetts unabashedly insisted that he did not believe "in the mental or the intellectual equality of the African race with this proud and domineering white race of ours."[10] Trumbull, Wilson, and other top Republican leaders were echoing the widely held opinions of voters in the Midwest, the mid-Atlantic states, and New England. The black historian W.E.B. DuBois said: "At the beginning of the Civil War, probably not one white American in one-hundred believed that Negroes would become an integral part of American democracy."[11]

All of the foregoing makes it more remarkable that there actually existed a black press in the United States during the first half of the nineteenth century. In 1827, Reverend Samuel Cornish and John Russworm, two black activists (the total number was pitifully small), visited the editor of the *New York Sun* and asked for some coverage of the organization they represented. They reported later that the editor told them: "The *Sun* shines bright for all white men, but never for the black man."[12] Cornish and Russworm responded by founding their own paper, *Freedom's Journal*—the first of at least twenty-four black papers published before the Civil War. Few of them survived for long; Frederick Douglass's *North Star* was an exception. There were, what is more, some free black women who worked as volunteers in abolitionist groups. Black women were usually confined to employment as laundresses, scrubwomen, seamstresses, and household servants. A few became teachers. One notable exception was Mary Ann Shadd Cary, a writer and lawyer who was the first black woman to edit her own newspaper. These women formed abolitionist societies, and many joined white women in the Female Anti-Slavery Societies of Boston, Philadelphia, and other cities during the middle decades of the century. Their work achieved little political resonance, and the newspapers did not repeat their message with any greater enthusiasm than they gave other abolitionist organizations. Slavery and racism were not pervasive national issues before the Civil War. They were part of a virtual anti-Negro consensus.[13]

Politicians of every shading and stripe in nineteenth-century America wanted to keep slavery out of their debates. They knew that open discussion of Negro rights in the press could break up political parties and their subgroups—could, as it turned out, even threaten the Union. Banking, tariffs, and commerce were more manageable issues. But the subject of slavery intruded with gradually increasing persistence not merely because of moralistic agitation but because of basic national and international concerns. By 1835, slavery had been abolished in Haiti, Argentina, Chile, Colombia, Central America, Mexico, Bolivia, and the British West Indies. In America, an admixture of political reformism and religious revivalism was spreading across the northern and midwestern states. Historians have produced a variety of explanations for this general ferment. Some see it as the natural product of egalitarianism that was nourished in a unique manner in the United States beginning with the language of the Declaration. There is also a body of opinion that connects revivalism with the hardships of frontier life. Another view is that reform—call it a strengthening of the virtuous life—was advocated by establishment Americans who feared the competition of the growing "commercial class." Reform could protect the control, they believed, of the elite over social and political life in the new nation. Finally, there is the theory that ethnic groups—immigrants from Europe, England, Wales—were attracted to "militant Protestant revivalism." According to Cushing Strout, a Cornell professor of American studies, post-Calvinist Protestantism, "the seed-bed of the missionary, philanthropic, and humane societies of the ante-bellum period, was also the background of abolitionist crusaders." These men and women had added "individualistic volunteerism" to their religious piety. They believed "a holy life" could be "made manifest by social action." For religious abolitionists sin was a form of slavery and, as Strout observes, "slavery was a form of sin, voluntarily engaged in by slave-holders and their defenders."[14]

After decades of publishing pamphlets, editing newspapers, and occasionally preaching from the pulpit, abolitionists began, toward the middle of the nineteenth century, to recognize the "need for political action." They had earlier helped to persuade Congress that the slave trade should be outlawed, and they used their publications to campaign against slavery in the new states admitted to the Union. Political power, however, was not achieved by the abolitionists. They were, in Strout's words "much too uncompromising in their moral and religious zeal to be at home in any major political party."[15]

The movement lacked cohesion in national terms, and though it finally found some satisfaction in the Emancipation Proclamation, it was never able to counteract the destructive racism in the northern and midwestern states and, in a sense, among many of its own advocates who opposed *slavery* but could not embrace *equality*. Revivalists and reformers were not able to utilize the mass media for their appeals as they might today. They were confined to newspapers with narrow circulations—if not in numbers, which did gradually grow, certainly in terms of geographic reach, which remained unattainable until the telegraph system improved after the Civil War.[16]

The amalgam of Yankee conservatism, revivalism, and social unrest had spawned regional abolitionist organizations. There were even a few antislavery groups in the upper South. An editor named Benjamin Lundy had been a catalyst among them, but he moved out of Tennessee to Baltimore, where he hired William Lloyd Garrison to assist him in publishing a paper in 1829. Two years later, Garrison was back in Boston producing his *Liberator* and calling for "immediate emancipation." Nat Turner's slave rebellion took place in 1831, and a massive slave revolt erupted in British Jamaica. News of these events appeared in some, but not all, urban newspapers, reflecting diverse views and many inaccurate accounts. New England's abolitionist leader, Theodore Dwight Weld, organized the American Anti-Slavery Society and sought to engage national interest by founding auxiliaries in every state. (There were 250,000 members in fifteen states by 1840.) He told any editors who would listen that the abolitionist cause "not only overshadows all others but absorbs them into itself." The cry for immediate action ignited young reformers who had been discouraged by "gradualism." They campaigned for emancipation that was "immediate, unconditional and uncompensated"—rejecting any claims of "property rights." Garrison's editorials promised, "Make the slave free and every inducement to revolt is taken away."[17]

Meanwhile, political party loyalties meant the continuing suppression or neglect of any broad discussion of slavery, and the partisan press bent its knees to party dictum. For reformers, slavery was the ultimate sin, the cause of all "moral collapse." In their fervor and dedication, the abolitionists published their pamphlets and newspapers, tried to persuade postmasters to carry such publications by rail to distant communities—particularly to the South—and dreamed of all Americans repenting the "sin of slavery." In this effort (as in others) they failed, and the most serious reason for their failure was their misjudgment of northern racism and the intransigence of the southern rationale.

The fervor, however, was not entirely wasted. It planted many seeds and brought unease to many who had tried to look the other way. Very effective in this regard were the illustrations appearing in the *Anti-Slavery Record*. So-called pictographs appeared regularly on the *Record*'s front page, providing images of "women being whipped or separated from their children, and of men being beaten," which became persuasive kindling for the antislavery brushfire. It was not a sudden conflagration, but the embers were still hot when Lincoln, belatedly in the eyes of the faithful, realized he had to begin the federal process of emancipation or lose the Union. Newspapers published by antislavery groups or individuals dedicated to freedom for slaves persisted despite violent opposition, but these enterprises were unable to grow. One story that *was* widely read and aroused the conscience of many Americans was *Uncle Tom's Cabin*. This novel by Harriet Beecher Stowe (Lincoln described her as "the little woman who wrote the book that made this great war necessary") was first serialized in 1851 and 1852 in a paper called the *National Era*. Later produced as a book, it sold more copies than any other in American history to that date. It was the story of Uncle Tom, an old slave who is sold when his master goes broke. His new master is a kind man, but Tom is sold again, this time to the cruel Simon Legree, who brutalizes him and, in a burst of fury, flogs the old man to death. The novel became an enduring part of American folklore. Famous passages described Eliza, a fugitive slave, escaping the pursuit of bloodhounds and the death of Little Eva, daughter of one of Tom's masters. The story was adapted for the stage and was performed all across the country for many years. Its influence in the ultimate marshaling of a larger segment of public opinion against slavery was considered significant, but no way of precisely measuring that kind of persuasion had yet been devised. The very large sales figures were remarkable in themselves, and on the basis of that calculation, *Uncle Tom's Cabin* may well rank as the most important American novel of the nineteenth century. Nonetheless, outrage about slavery was unable to coalesce and engage a wider share of the American imagination. One reason was the paucity of major columnists and public intellectuals, writers whose moral fervor (and national distribution) could overcome the perception that it was acceptable to be repelled by Negroes and to regard them as degraded, unintelligent, and dangerous—even if slaves had never been seen or talked to by the citizen who harbored such animosity. Those writers who might have achieved enlightened powers of persuasion had no means of syndication, no way of reaching many audiences at the same time, no way of gathering momentum.

The laws adopted by the new western states duplicated those passed by the midwestern legislatures. Oregon was admitted into the Union in 1859, and it had already excluded Negroes from the militia and prohibited voting by blacks even though slavery itself was rejected in a state referendum. The *Oregon Weekly Times* editorialized: "Oregon is a land for the white man. Refusing the toleration of Negroes in our midst as slaves, we rightly and for yet stronger reasons, prohibit them from coming among us as free Negro vagabonds."[18] In Utah, the Mormons announced that the black race was inferior even "in the next world." The same sentiments of anti-Negro bias appeared, even among antislavery groups, in the newspapers of Colorado, New Mexico, and Nebraska.[19]

The inexorable approach of the Civil War was, ironically and enduringly, accompanied by the hardening of racist passions into political realities. There were no party reforms, no political splinter groups, dedicated to erasing the "stain" on the Constitution. Slavery had been countenanced in 1788 by those who might have wished it could be renounced, because the South threatened to leave the Union. The economic advantage of free labor had become so important to the southern way of life that any thought of revisiting the issue in 1791 when the Bill of Rights was being drafted seemed futile, and so began what historians regard as an inescapable spiral toward a war between the states. That inexorable event was measured in terms of economic competition, constitutional interpretations, and what sociologist Kai Erikson calls the "moral contours" of American society.[20]

Within two years after the war began, the Union would become committed to freeing the slaves. What started out as preserving the Union by military action and preventing secession was to be, in many ways, "a war of ideologies, a moral crusade with divinely sanctioned ends." So it was for some, and so it is rendered in many histories. But for contemporary politicians it was other things as well. Congressmen and their supporting newspapers worried out loud about "free Negroism" and "Africanization." These men were loath to "mix up four millions of blacks with their sons and daughters." The never timid *Chicago Times* described the nightmare of the North invaded by "two or three million semi-savages." Indiana politician George Julian told the newspapers in his state, "The real trouble is that we hate the Negro. It is not his ignorance that offends us, but his color."[21] Lincoln was keenly aware of the demonizing prejudice against slaves and former slaves. It was a factor he could easily hear and observe. His early intellectual preparation for such passions had been very limited. Growing up in a poor family, he had little access to books. He kept notes of his early readings, as had his hero, Thomas Jefferson, but the two presidents had come from opposite ends of the social and economic spectrum. John F. Kennedy once told a gathering of Nobel laureates at the White House that never had so much accumulated knowledge been in that place except when Jefferson dined there alone.

Jefferson had been provided with a superb education, including formal training from the age of five, college, and a legal apprenticeship. He had been able to study the large numbers of books in his father's library and he himself later accumulated what was probably the best private library in America at the time. It became the basic collection of the Library of Congress when it was rebuilt after the British burned it down in 1814. Jefferson's 6,700-book library was twice the size of the collection that existed before the fire.[22]

Lincoln, as a House member in the 1840s, was known to spend as much time as possible in the Library of Congress. His stepmother remembered that as a boy he became an "avid reader of newspapers." Partisan papers may well have stimulated his interest in politics. A friend recalled that he gave young Lincoln one of many newspaper stories about Jefferson's death on July 4, 1826. The Bible, English poetry, and the works of Shakespeare (which he often read aloud) influenced Lincoln's prose and speeches, but newspapers were the text for his self-education as a politician. The newspapers of the late 1820s and early 1830s were the source of Lincoln's perceptions regarding Andrew Jackson, and his decision to finally turn against Jackson. What kind of reporting helped to shape a devotion to the bonds of the Union— ("the mystic chords of memory" he so poetically summons in his first inaugural address) may not be possible to determine, but there is no doubt that he was attentive to the sentiments expressed by the political leaders of his time in the only form available outside legislative halls—the free and fractious press.

For fifty of the first seventy-two years of the American republic, slaveowners had occupied the White House. When Lincoln was elected, the "lower South" rejected the will of the electorate. It believed the new president was committed to the "ultimate extinction" of slavery. The Republican Party owed nothing to the South. The Republicans had not even been on the ballot in the southern states. Lincoln received little more than 26,000 votes from slaveholding states and 1.8 million from "free" states. The lower South chose secession, and after shots were fired at Fort Sumter on April 12, 1861, the other southern states followed. Few people expected a long or bloody war. They were, of course, wrong beyond imagining. The War of 1812 had cost the United States 7,000 lives. The Mexican War cost the nation 2,000 lives on the battlefield and 11,000 from diseases. By the time the Civil War ended, more than 600,000 men were dead, and thousands of survivors had lost limbs or were maimed. The deaths were calculated as 1,967 per 100,000 of the population. World War II, in comparison, took 318,000 American lives—241 per 100,000 of the population.[23]

"A house divided against itself cannot stand," Lincoln had declared. The agony, the destruction, and the grotesque, rag-doll corpses crowded on each battlefield of the struggle to save the house were so obscene that Matthew Brady and other photographers such as Alexander Gardner and T. H. O'Sullivan could repudiate romantic notions about the Civil War without using a printed word. The best known and most eloquent photographs were made by Brady, who followed the Union army with his cumbersome box camera and tripod. He became one of America's first photojournalists, though he could not make candid pictures. The images were recorded on collodion-coated glass plates that had to be sensitized in a chemical bath before exposure and developed quickly in another chemical almost at once after exposure. No other testimony regarding Lincoln's determination and anguish could match the visual evidence produced by

Brady. Less than three-quarters of a century later the picture magazines were publishing photographs of news events, world leaders, violence, and war from all over the world—within days, sometimes overnight, and, as printing technology progressed, in color. Not even the most talented photographers (such as those employed by *Life* magazine) using handheld thirty-five millimeter cameras, risking their lives (and sometimes losing them) to get in close, to be enveloped by action, could provide more enduringly the melancholy, sobering effect of wartime scenes stilled by Matthew Brady's laboriously created glass negatives. During the war Brady organized about twenty photographers and several wagon darkrooms for processing. They became known as Brady's Photographic Corps.[24]

Brady's 1860 portrait of Lincoln in Springfield reveals a somber, hollow-cheeked, youngish man with a prominent nose, deep-set eyes, and thick black hair. After four years of war, another portrait made in April 1865 revealed a worn, wretched face with a beard that had not been there in the earlier pictures—its white hairs bristling—and eyes peering over the lines and folds of worry and care. In this second photograph, Brady recorded not only the accelerated aging but the philosophical resignation of a fallible man who can permit a rueful smile that seems to be directed inward to the thought that no matter how relative the validity of his convictions, to hold on to them unfalteringly with no guarantee of their corroboration is the best he can do.

Post–Civil War developments in journalism should be instructional for contemporary purveyors of news and public affairs. The newspapers of the 1870s and the 1880s became less partisan politically but more lightweight editorially. Between 1880 and 1890 the number of newspapers grew more rapidly than ever before or since, and subscribers increased by nearly 40 million. The slide toward "entertainment" and "the new journalism" brought an emphasis on scandal, crime, gossip, and distortion. Concurrently, the first meaningful criticism of the press itself began to appear in the small, intellectual magazines. More entertainment meant *less* watchdog surveillance over governments and corporations, which could account for the minimal movement toward regulation or limitation by statute initiated by politicians. Self-criticism, as it could be construed in the highbrow magazines, could also account for the channeling of antipress contempt and anger festering in the minds of academicians, moral leaders, and advocates of responsible journalism away from pseudocensorship or boycotts that might have been supported on a local basis. The withholding of advertising was then, as it is now, a subtle form of pressure frequently applied, but only the most blatant cases were publicized. Common *self-censorship* by editors, all too aware of advertiser sensitivity, is a subject for further discussion. No matter how important these factors were in the growth of press standards (press ethics were for a long time sarcastically dismissed), there were eloquent and influential spokesmen for responsible reporting long before the twentieth century.

The first significant challenge to the mass press was Reconstruction. Could reportorial justice be given *all* Americans after the Civil War? Though Reconstruction became an issue on the national agenda, widely covered by newspapers finally able to use the wire services, the editorial bias was no less reflective of public opinion than it had been before the war. Northern, midwestern, and western politicians were, of course, primarily concerned with the migration of freed slaves who could take jobs away from poor whites employed in the proliferating industrial centers. Nonetheless, if former slaves were allowed to vote in the South, the rebel states could *gain* at least twelve new seats in the House. If no ex-slave was given the right to vote in the South, the rebel states might *lose* as many as eighteen seats (based on the elimination of the prewar formula of counting every fifty adult slaves as thirty members of the local "population" to be represented in Congress).

There was no disposition on the part of those who had supported the Union to reward in any way those who had rebelled against it, but there were mixed emotions on how to handle the former slaves, the role of political leaders of the rebellion, and the federal debts attributable to the crushing of secession. "It may be," the Charleston *Mercury* speculated in 1867, "that Congress but represents the feelings of its constituents, that it is but the moderate mouthpiece of incensed Northern opinion. It may be that measures harsher than any . . . confiscation, incarceration, banishment, may brood over us in turn! But all these things will not change our earnest belief—that there will be a revulsion of popular feeling in the North."[25]

A few months later elections took place in Connecticut and the Democrats won in nearly every district. The *Independent*, a "radical" Connecticut paper, acidly accused the North of hypocrisy: "In Congress they are for impartial suffrage [for Negro voting rights]; at home they are against it. . . . It ought to bring a blush to every white cheek in the loyal North to reflect that the political equality of American citizens is likely to be sooner achieved in Mississippi than in Illinois—sooner on the plantation of Jefferson Davis than around the grave of Abraham Lincoln."[26] After the war, in only six states outside the South were Negroes allowed to vote (after considerable artful dodging by the local authorities), and the states with large Negro populations did *not* permit them to vote. Horace Greeley wrote in his Republican paper, "The Negro question is at the bottom of our reverses. . . . Thousands have turned against us because we propose to enfranchise the Blacks. . . . We have lost votes in the Free States by daring to be just to the Negro."[27] The *New York Times* was less certain. Its editors thought that "the Southern people seem to have become quite beside themselves in consequence of the *quasi* Democratic victories" in the North, and there was "neither sense nor sanity in their exultations."[28] The Raleigh (North Carolina) *Daily Sentinel* needled the Pennsylvania legislature, which had voted 29–13 against Negro enfranchisement: "This is a direct confession," said the *Sentinel*, "by Northern radicals that they refuse to grant in Pennsylvania the 'justice' they would enforce on the South . . . and this is Radical meanness and hypocrisy. . . . This their love for the negro."[29]

Reconstruction, despite all that had gone before it, gave short-lived comfort to the Negroes. In 1868, the Republicans decided to take some action on Negro suffrage. The Fifteenth Amendment was one consequence. As noted earlier, Congress had ratified the Thirteenth Amendment in 1864, which declared that "neither slavery, nor voluntary servitude . . . shall exist within the United States." In 1868, it became necessary to add the Fourteenth Amendment, which in section 1 guaranteed the rights of citizenship and the *equal protection of the laws for all Americans*. But neither of these amendments had addressed the issue of voting rights. The Republican press continued to equivocate. Frederick Douglass editorialized: "Slavery is not abolished until the black man has the ballot." Reformers warned that even if the vote was assured to all by the Fifteenth Amendment, resistance at the state level—in the North *and* the South—would turn nasty. Rhode Island required all citizens to be property owners if they were to vote. Massachusetts required a literacy test. In the South there were "grandfather clauses" and poll taxes and the usual bureaucratic runaround whenever a Negro tried to register. Even before the Fifteenth Amendment the Negroes in the South had been fully franchised as part of the agreements that readmitted the Southern States to the Union. For a while Negroes had actually voted in great numbers with little difficulty. It was assumed that in any state the Negro vote would be overwhelmingly Republican. Much of what appeared in the newspapers during that period skirted the central issue of close elections. In Indiana, Ohio, Connecticut, New York, and Pennsylvania the whites were divided nearly evenly between the two major parties. The addition of a Negro voting bloc would tilt many elections. All the same, the Fifteenth Amendment was ratified—with considerable help from the South. The readmission of Virginia and other southern states depended on their approval of the amendment in 1870.

C. Vann Woodward sees that passage as the prologue to terrorism and intimidation of Southern Republicans—and, not long thereafter, in the midwestern states as well. The Ku Klux Klan and other groups "used violence of all kinds, including murder by mob, by drowning, by torch; they whipped, they tortured, they maimed, they mutilated." No cruelty was too great, it became clear, if it resulted in a denial of the vote to the Negro. Congress passed the Enforcement Act in May of 1870, followed by the second Enforcement Act, and the Ku Klux Klan Act of 1871. Federal authorities tried to combat the violence in the South against Negro voters, but the intimidation of witnesses, the brutal local punishment of people who assisted federal officials, and the lack of funds doomed the good intentions. Congress provided so little money for the southern courts that "due process" became a myth. Too many marshals and district attorneys, what is more, were southern-born and tended to be sympathetic to local views.[30]

To prevent the secession of the southern states, Lincoln had to abandon his political agnosticism—widely shared in the North—on slavery. He was confronted with that inevitable conflict between public will, and personal responsibility. That conflict had been at the center of debates that roiled the Constitutional Conventions and defined the meaning of self-government. If the United States was to be a nation where individual freedom would be enlarged to its fullest potential, there had to be a sense of responsibility for restraining those freedoms for some that denied freedom to others. In a country that had been founded on the importance of individual freedom, the concepts of justice, accountability, and personal responsibility were not paramount.

In one fateful year, Lincoln had tried to achieve a balance between unbridled freedom and the burdens of responsibility. Freeing the slaves in the rebel states was a first step, and reviving the promise of equality and self-government, at Gettysburg, was the second. Neither aspiration was fully realized in 1863 or in the period of Reconstruction or, for that matter, a century later, in 1963, when the rumbles of the civil rights movement began to shake the ground beneath the Fourteenth Amendment. By the year of the emancipation, the 427,000 slaves imported by Americans before and after independence had become a population of well over 4 million. There were fears of how such a large segment of society, suddenly empowered, might behave. The newspapers in the North offered a range of uneasy speculations. Would there be overnight migration away from the scenes of enslavement? Would there be armed acts of vengeance? Could "uneducated," "inferior," black men be entrusted with the right to vote and to serve in public office? If the freed slave had no property, and therefore no stake in the community, was he not a likely target for manipulation by unscrupulous politicians? Even the abolitionists could not decide on a united front in their private counsels, let alone in their newspapers. They were emphatically against slavery, but their views on suffrage, social equality, and the pace of empowerment remained varied and often paternalistic.

Editor Horace Greeley, reflecting public sentiment, had insisted that the unoccupied West "shall be reserved for the benefit of the white Caucasian race."[31] Where could the African Americans go without encountering racial hostility and violence? Deportation to Africa was discussed in many states and in many publications but without much resolve. There were those who believed that, once freed, the slaves would stay put and northern blacks would migrate back to the South, away from the racism inflicted on them by reason of color alone. Against that uncertain background, the Fourteenth Amendment was passed and revealed the ambivalence of what was believed to be the majority of white Americans. It rejected, in effect, the impassioned pleas for meaningful reforms embraced by a handful of well-intentioned politicians in the North and the South, along with a few preachers and writers. Senator Charles Sumner of Massachusetts had urged a guarantee of Negro suffrage—but that was left to each of the states by Congress. Northern legislators could actually disenfranchise Negroes living among them in presumed freedom. The southern politicians soon perceived that their representation in Congress was to be determined by the number of eligible voters and not by any formula regarding the number of nonvoting ex-slaves.

There were still individuals who spoke out for greater integration of Negroes in the South. Louisiana novelist George Cable wrote fiction and nonfiction and lectured tirelessly about the unjust treatment of the Negro. The conservative Charleston *News and Courier* printed editorials lamenting the petty, demeaning cry for more and more Jim Crow regulations. A Richmond, Virginia, merchant-aristocrat named Lewis Harvie Blair wrote a series of articles for the New York *Independent* in summer 1887, vilifying the "brag and strut and bluster" of the "boosters" and the prosperity propaganda of such papers as the Baltimore *Manufacturers' Record*. Blair laughed at the notion that the South was in a "happy Arcadia." He wanted the truth to be known about "the real South—that is to say, of 95% thereof." Blair's "real South" was a wretched, backward region where unspeakable poverty was the fate of the "six millions of Negroes who are in the depths of indigence" and 90 percent of the whites, who had "nothing beyond the commonest necessaries of life." Blair listed many reasons for the South's poverty and deterioration, but he suggested that all of them combined were not so damaging as "the degradation of the Negro." The attitude toward the Negro's civil rights and sanctity of life undermined the sanctity of life and civil rights for all.[32]

Blair's remarkable solution was a recommendation that found little support in 1887, but it resonates in every survey, every inner-city riot, and every civil rights bill that has been proposed in the past fifty years. "Man's life is now too short to wait for the natural process of time," Blair wrote. The Negro "must economically, morally, and socially be born again, and self-respect, hope and intelligence are the trinity that will work out his elevation, and they are also the rule of three to work out our own material regeneration." New York *Independent* readers with considerable discomfort encountered Blair's scathing view of white supremacy, a condition few of them had found hard to accept. He declared that "our remote ancestors were as scurvy a lot as ever scourged the earth . . . a raving set of pirates and free booters, whose lives were spent in ravishing and in murdering women, in slaying infants and old men, and in reducing to slavery all able-bodied men who escaped the edge of the sword." White supremacists were, wrote Blair, "the descendants of these monsters."[33]

Blair went on to deride fears of Negro political power, the iniquity of segregated schools, the humiliation of cultured blacks who were intellectually superior to their white neighbors, and the damage done to young whites who were taught arrogance and false pride by assigning inferiority to black children. These views and others related to them were offered just as Jim Crowism was about to intensify into an "era of reactionary racism." Blair warned the North that it needed the South, and the North had not helped to elevate the Negro, a neglect that was a great "impediment" to southern redemption.[34]

Though Blair apparently retreated from these views privately near the end of his life, the articles in the *Independent* were an extraordinary act of editorial courage on his part. The inconsistency of policy and practice in race relations throughout the South in the last two decades of the nineteenth century was matched by the newspapers. Editorials echoed the narrow range of views that conventional wisdom produced. The Carnegie steel interests and John D. Rockefeller's oil business were at that time growing rapidly, and the enormous profits generated by largely unregulated and untaxed major industries were attracting the attention of bankers, corporate managers, and ambitious young men who saw an era of unlimited economic opportunity shimmering before them. These same men, as they accumulated wealth and power, were rarely, if ever, aware of the press as a potential barrier, as a watchdog or muckraker. The fact that a large laboring class was living near the factories and refineries and railyards in ramshackle deprivation was not an issue profit-oriented publishers were about to illuminate. Only the small magazines would produce the warning voices of social critics.

In Louisiana, where lynchings were numerous—ranking third among all the states—education was at the very bottom. In 1887, the state had allowed the sugar industry to use private police forces in crushing a strike. More than thirty workers were killed. Vigilante actions against black workers were ignored by law enforcement agencies. When racial segregation became the cry, the New Orleans *Times-Democrat* and other leading newspapers seconded the motion. Despite the obvious overturning of Civil War resolutions and the defiance of amendments to the Constitution, the large newspapers shrank from any expression of indignation—moral or political. The exceptions were Negro newspapers such as the New Orleans *Crusader* and a few commentators writing for the northern press—notably Albion W. Tourgée, who had been an officer in the Union army, a lawyer in North Carolina, and a leader of the Republican Party. In an increasing effort to fight segregation and other injustices inflicted upon Negro citizens, Tourgée gave speeches, wrote articles and books, and provided a weekly column in the Chicago newspaper *Inter Ocean*. He was described as the "Garrison of a new struggle." He organized the biracial National Citizen Rights Association for the defense of Negro rights and claimed over 100,000 members— including many southerners.[35]

There were several influential newspapers founded and published by Negroes during the years between the war and the end of the century, including the *Washington Bee*, 1881; the *New York Globe* (later called the *Age*), 1887; and the Norfolk, Virginia, *Journal and Guide*, 1901. These papers reported lynchings, Ku Klux Klan activity, and the deteriorating conditions facing freedmen in the South. But Tourgée, born in Ohio of French Huguenot descent and an indefatigable campaigner, probably wrote in defense of American Negroes more persistently than any other journalist. The Tourgée crusade was conducted by a man who Edmund Wilson, in his book on the literature of the Civil War, described as "a Northerner who resembled Southerners: in his insolence, his independence, his readiness to accept a challenge, his recklessness and ineptitude in practical matters, his romantic and chivalrous view of the world in which he was living."[36] It was not unlikely that such a man would be asked to represent African Americans in their first major legal struggle against Jim Crow laws. (The name Jim Crow, as applied to Negroes, has murky origins. Thomas D. Rice wrote a song-and-dance piece called "Jim Crow" in 1832. Why it became a pervasive social adjective subsequently is unknown.)

In June 1892, a man named Homer Adolph Plessy got on a train at New Orleans going to Covington, Louisiana. Though Plessy was "seven-eighths Caucasian and one-eighth African blood" and would not normally be identified as a Negro, he was told to move from a "white" car to the Jim Crow car. Few people doubted that the railroad officials had been informed in advance of Plessy's deliberate actions. When he refused to move he was arrested and charged with violating Louisiana's Jim Crow laws. Tourgée had agreed to be Plessy's counsel along with another white lawyer named James C. Walker. They entered a plea before Judge John H. Ferguson of the Criminal District Court for the Parish of New Orleans. Their claim would be that the Jim Crow law was in conflict with the Constitution of the United States. Judge Ferguson rejected the claim. The lawyers then applied to the state supreme court for a writ of prohibition and "certiorari" (to be made more certain). They secured a hearing in November 1892. The case would be known as *Plessy v. Ferguson*, the New Orleans *Times-Democrat* solemnly reported. The state supreme court, in a decision handed down by Justice Charles E. Fenner on December 19, 1892, held that the sole question was whether a law requiring "separate but equal accommodations" violated the Fourteenth Amendment. The court stated that accommodations did not have to be identical to be equal, listed many confirmations of that supposition by lower courts, and in effect upheld the law of Jim Crow pertaining to seats on railroad trains.

Most newspapers in the northern cities followed the Jim Crow saga with cursory, subordinated accounts or neglected the subject altogether. The enormous profits of the Rockefeller interests and the family squabble over Commodore Vanderbilt's will had received daily attention, but except for the isolated fulminations of a Tourgée or the reporting of the black press, the slowly festering infection of race issues—despite the 600,000 Civil War deaths that had scarred so many American families only three decades earlier—received meager attention in the popular press.

The Louisiana chief justice in 1892 was Francis Tillon Nicholls; he had been governor of the state in 1890 when the Jim Crow act was signed. A decade before that, Nicholls had been known for his "conservative paternalism," which, the New Orleans *Daily Picayune* reported, advocated a policy of fairness and justice for "colored men." By 1892 the "conservatives" (not to be confused with civil rights advocates seventy years later who were called "liberals") allowed their views to be swept away by fears of labor unrest and the racism of poor whites. Tourgée and Walker were denied a second hearing but did manage to get a "writ of error" accepted by the U.S. Supreme Court in January 1893. It took three years for the case to be scheduled. Tourgée welcomed the delay. He believed time was on his side, allowing him more opportunities to galvanize public opinion. The brief he finally filed in 1895 emphasized the meaning of equality and scored few points with a court moving in the opposite direction.[37]

One ploy Tourgée had decided upon—after deliberation and planning—was to assert that Plessy had been deprived of "property" without "due process of law." The "property" referred to (reminding us of Madison's assertion that each man has "property in his rights") was the "reputation of being white." It was "the most valuable sort of property, being the masterkey that unlocks the golden door of opportunity." Tourgée presented whiteness as almost fundamental to getting ahead. "Probably most white persons," he stated, "if given the choice, would prefer death to life in the United States as colored persons."

Tourgée's other arguments were more closely linked to the amendments. Here the press, to the extent that it paid any attention at all, had sporadically informed its readers on the issues, not always because editors understood the potential expansion of rights for all Americans, but most often because of immediate political impact. Supreme Court decisions could and did ignite widespread editorials—for and against—as in the aftermath of the 1883 Civil Rights cases. The focus on timeliness and localism was not unlikely. A few publishers had begun to think about overarching responsibilities—to the electoral process; to the independence of citizens, communities, or regions; or perhaps in the long run to the nourishing of liberty *and* justice for all in a rapidly changing, industrialized society. Tourgée's newspaper columns had inveighed against segregation and all its implications. Segregation was, he accused, merely another way of sustaining servility, bondage, subjection. The "separate but equal" doctrine was a fraud. "The object of such a law," Tourgée wrote, "is simply to debase and distinguish against the inferior race. Its purpose has been properly interpreted by the general designation of 'Jim Crow car law.'" Tourgée called the segregation apparatus, including its sanctimonious repetition of "separate but equal," little more than the "gratification and recognition of the sentiment of white superiority and white supremacy of right and power."

In May of 1896, the Supreme Court declared its opinion on *Plessy v. Ferguson*. The justices to a man—with the exception of Justice Brewer who was not a participant, and Justice Harlan who dissented in a memorable fashion—agreed that "separate but equal" was sound and acceptable. The opinion reflected the prevailing views of the public, and those of the regional courts, North and South. Many lower court decisions had already affirmed similar views, and no federal court had ever gone against them.

The core of the *Plessy v. Ferguson* opinion upholding Jim Crow was expressed by Justice Henry Billings Brown who was a Northerner, born in Massachusetts where some would say human rights in America had found its earliest proponents. Said Justice Brown: "If the civil and political rights of both races be equal, one cannot be inferior to the other civilly or politically. If one race be inferior to the other socially, the Constitution of the United States cannot put them upon the same plane."

The remarkable opinion crafted by Justice Harlan, a southern gentleman and a one-time slaveholder, was given vastly less comment in the nation's newspapers than the majority decision, but it took on a long life of its own among legal scholars, historians, and those people with moral concern who were eventually able to find the full text in libraries. He had first dissented in 1883 in what was known as the *Civil Rights Cases*, when he spoke out against the insidious encroachments of racism to which the "substance and spirit of the recent Amendments of the Constitution have been sacrificed." Said Harlan, the "Great Dissenter," in 1896: . . . "In the eye of the law, there is in this country no superior, dominant, ruling class of citizens. There is no caste here. Our Constitution is color blind, and neither knows nor tolerates classes among citizens. In respect of civil rights all citizens are equal before the law. The humblest is the peer of the most powerful. . . . The thin disguise of 'equal' accommodations for passengers in railroad coaches will not mislead anyone, nor atone for the wrong this day done." Justice Harlan added this prediction: "The present decision [*Plessy v. Ferguson*], it may well be apprehended, will not only stimulate aggressions, more or less brutal and irritating upon the admitted rights of colored citizens, but will encourage the belief that it is possible, by means of State enactments, to defeat the beneficent purposes which the people of the United States had in view when they adopted the recent Amendments of the Constitution."[38]

According to Otto H. Olsen, author of *The Thin Disguise* (Harlan's words), a book about segregation and also a biography of Tourgée, the national reaction to the Supreme Court's decision on "separate but equal" accommodations was much less heated than it had been in the civil rights cases of 1883, but there was disappointment and anger, and not only in the Negro press. There were profound differences of opinion in the United States regarding segregation. Nonetheless, most newspaper accounts agreed that the Court was echoing the "dominant mood of the country." The "aggressions" Justice Harlan feared were soon unleashed, and the fate of most American Negroes was sealed for at least half a century. They would find so few level playing fields that any will to improve their lot from *Plessy* on seemed doomed. On January 12, 1900, the editor of the *Richmond Times*, a paper that had resisted popular bigotry during Reconstruction, editorialized: "It is necessary that this principle be applied in every relation of Southern life. God Almighty drew the color line and it cannot be obliterated. The Negro must stay on his side of the line and the white man must stay on his side, and the sooner both races recognize this fact and accept it, the better it will be for both."[39]

12

TURNING AWAY

Between the idea
And the reality
Between the motion
And the act
Falls the shadow.
—T. S. Eliot, *What the Thunder Said*

It is a matter of record—often observed in the newspapers of that time—
that the conservative white leaders in the South shared and even supported
the fearful views of black politicians and officeholders regarding the advent
of Jim Crow. The patrician whites were not advocating true equality for
their former slaves, but they were apprehensive of fanaticism among poor
whites and rabble-rousing racists. When the first segregation railroad law
was passed, in 1887, a conservative southern newspaper confessed that it
was a reluctant gesture "to please the Crackers."[1]

Conservative southern gentlemen wanted to preserve what was called
"the traditional harmony." They were alarmed by the white "lower class"
and its surge toward Jim Crowism. Black protests against Jim Crow were
led by the most successful blacks, the professional people, and these men
looked to their white counterparts for assistance. The sympathy of white
conservatives was all too briefly available. The voting right—in significant
form—survived in the South for nearly thirty years. But by 1905 Jim
Crow's triumph was complete. Suffrage was either prohibited by statute or
by custom, with all its subtle if not violent methods of intimidation. Paternalism and rising Jim Crow barriers bound the black man to the past, to
dependence and withdrawal, to "his place." Could the press and the intellectual magazines have put a light on these developments in any manner
strong enough to arouse thoughtful, pragmatic concerns about the future of
democracy? The answer would seem to be no. It had been no when news-

paper circulations, editorial cohesion, and distribution were limited by inadequate technology. But it was still no after improved machinery and widespread telegraphy made information accessible to larger segments of the population and provided a forum for national policies. Progress in a practical sense did not presage progress philosophically or ethically; nor did technology produce farsightedness. Stories in newspapers were ephemeral. Contemplation and analysis were not part of their purpose. Some of the small magazines looked to higher ground—to analysis and reform. But they preached to the converted—not a large group statistically. Meanwhile, the industrial revolution was luring talented Americans into free enterprise and the "gospel of wealth."[2]

For editors and publishers, the story of America's clamorous, glittering economic future was—along with the entertainment provided by tabloid common denominators—far more profitable and appealing than revisiting the controversial past. Very few newspapers were interested in probing the nerve ends of slavery and what they thought might best be left under the carpet rather than on it—racism. The post-Reconstruction travesty that permitted slavery in America to be exchanged for harsh segregation took place without much organized resistance. The thunder in the distance was the destructive force of resentment and violence that erupted in the early part of the twentieth century as open season on blacks—no longer enslaved but increasingly exploited and impoverished—and reappeared later in the century as race riots, crime, and political corruption. If men are so poor, so uneducated, and so powerless that they cannot exercise the rights given to them constitutionally, such rights become meaningless. The society that does not provide adequate education, justice, and economic opportunity for a segment of the population may still claim that liberty and justice for all is written into its system. But between the rights and the ability to use them, between the idea and the reality, the shadow of hypocrisy falls.[3]

The newspapers and magazines of the late nineteenth and early twentieth centuries did provide a forum for the discussion of what value, if any, the people of the United States were willing to place on the promise of life, liberty and the pursuit of happiness for all citizens. Before the United States became a reality, very few men had thought of freedom as worthwhile in itself. In the Old World, nearly all men preferred being ruled because the ruler gave them food and shelter. The concept of self-government in a free society was for the European masses an incomprehensible idea. But out of the wilderness that the Pilgrims found in New England there emerged over a century of religious order and the experience of building a community, a defining belief in a "commonwealth of laws and not men." The Massachusetts Body of Liberties, adopted in 1641, not only inspired many of the liberties ultimately written into the Bill of Rights of 1791 but contained protections for "life, liberty and property" in language derived from section 39 of the Magna Carta. It also guaranteed that every person "shall enjoy the same justice and law"—a vision that reappeared in the first section of the Fourteenth Amendment as "due process of law" and "the equal protection of the laws."[4]

The sporadic discussions appearing in the press on the plight of ex-slaves who for a brief period after the Civil War finally tasted the fruits of liberty, political participation, and the equal protection of the laws were, as always, muted. Publishers emphasized news rather than views. From the first arrival of slave ships in America and up to the Civil War, the journalistic debate regarding slavery—except in abolitionist newspapers—was never widespread or persistent.

After the Declaration of Independence and during the Constitutional Conventions, slaves were generally regarded as property. With few exceptions news reports in the border states approved of the measures taken by southern slaveholders to recapture runaway slaves. In 1804, Andrew Jackson ran an ad in the Tennessee *Gazette & Mero District Advertiser* (Nashville) concerning a "mulatto man slave, about thirty years old." Jackson, who was to become the seventh president of the United States and served two terms (1829–1837), stipulated in his ad that if the slave was "taken out of the state, the above reward (fifty dollars) will be given, and all reasonable expenses paid—and ten dollars extra for every hundred lashes any person will give him to the amount of three-hundred." Such ads were numerous and routine in newspapers located near the southern state borders. Examples:

"Ranaway, a Negro woman and two children; a few days before she went off, I *burnt her with a hot iron,* on the left side of her face, I *tried to make the letter* M."

"Ranaway a Negro man named Henry, *his left eye out,* some scars from a *dirk* on and under his left arm, and *much scarred* with the whip."

"One hundred dollars reward for a Negro fellow Pompey, 40 years old, he is *branded* on the *left jaw.*"

"Ranaway a Negro named Hambleton, limps, on his left foot where he was shot a few weeks ago, while running away."[5]

There was, however, a very significant difference between the forums provided by eighteenth-century newspapers with a circulation of 200 subscribers and those in an urban daily in the late nineteenth century with a circulation of a half-million copies. A provocative story in the larger papers could produce public reactions, sometimes violence. Abolitionist publishers had for over a century risked hostility and suffered attacks on their printing presses or assaults upon themselves, but the ugliest mobs in American history were those who were soon to be galvanized by political opportunism, white supremacists, and racial hatred into a kind of savagery most Americans think of as happening in far-off places among primitive peoples. The brutality in southern communities seeking to overturn Reconstruction was far worse than the antebellum treatment of slaves in those same areas.

The newspapers of the South followed the events of Reconstruction closely, and those papers that represented the "conservatives" were for a time benevolent in their comments on black citizens as a voting bloc, as political officeholders, and as a community sharing public services such as trains and trolleys, parks, and gathering places. Even South Carolina resisted Jim Crow segregation until 1898. That year, the conservative Charleston *News and Courier* maintained a policy of tolerance it had followed for more than two decades. The editor wrote: "We have got on fairly well for a third of a century including a long period of reconstruction, without such a measure [Jim Crow]. We can probably get on as well hereafter without it, and certainly so extreme a measure should not be adopted and enforced without added and urgent cause."[6] He went on to suggest the absurdities to which Jim Crow might well lead—separate waiting rooms, separate lunch counters, Jim Crow sections "in county auditors' and treasurers' offices" for Negro tax payers, and so on. Nearly every possibility he ridiculed became a fact of life within a few years. The same paper, in 1906, supported a policy of deportation. Segregation was not a sufficient remedy, it had decided. "There is no room for them here."[7]

For twenty-five years after the war, southern Negroes voted in large numbers. White candidates solicited black support. Blacks took part in public life, nearly always in secondary positions, but they held office and served on juries and were elected to state legislatures and to the federal Congress. Every Congress but one from 1869 through 1901 had at least one Negro member from the South. Jim Crow laws began with separate railway cars, but between 1900 and 1905 the vigilant, demeaning enforcement of segregation was introduced at every level of human existence in southern states. Drinking fountains, lavatories, waiting rooms, hospitals, prisons, even separate entrances and exits to circus tents, were included.

In 1913, the *Progressive Farmer*, an influential newspaper for the agricultural sector, campaigned successfully to get the North Carolina Farmers Union to endorse segregation in "rural districts." In a short time there were Jim Crow Bibles for Negro witnesses in courtrooms and textbooks in segregated schools were themselves segregated so that no small white hand might touch the pages turned by Negro children. By the second decade of the twentieth century, the white supremacy doctrine was not only firmly in place throughout the South, but it was creatively seeking more and different ways of "pushing the Negro further down." Historian Edgar Gardner Murphy, in 1911, described an aggressive, destructive Jim Crow compulsion in the South. "The new mood makes few professions of conservatism. It does not claim to be necessary to the State's existence. . . . These new antipathies are not defensive but assertive and combative. . . . Its spirit is that of an all-absorbing autocracy of race, an animus of aggrandizement which makes in the imagination of the white man an absolute identification of the stronger race with the very being of the State."[8]

There had been a series of civil rights acts passed by Congress in 1866, 1870, and 1875 that outlawed racial discrimination in public transportation, hotels, theaters, and parks. These were the first antidiscrimination laws ever passed by Congress. There were to be no more for over 100 years. The acts opened the voting process to Negroes (though not yet to women of any color). In 1867 there were 735,000 blacks and 635,000 whites registered to vote in the ten states of the Old South. The black vote became a serious, frightening prospect for white politicians.[9]

By the 1890s, to control the poor, uneducated whites in the South, the political establishment invoked Negrophobia as a tool to take the vote— and therefore any semblance of power—away from the black man. In Louisiana, in 1896, there were 130,334 registered Negro voters. In 1904 there were 1,342. If the poll tax didn't drive the Negro voter out, the converting of primary elections to a whites-only process finished the job. Speaking to the 1876 Republican National Convention, Frederick Douglass, still a figure of courageous black defiance, asked: "What does it all amount to if the black man, after having been made free by the letter of your law, is to be subject to the slave holder's shot gun? The real question is whether you mean to make good to us the promises of your Constitution."

Where was the respected Northern press while this "new mood" took its toll? For one thing, it was absorbed in United States imperialism abroad. In the Philippines, Hawaii, and Cuba, among other adventures, the Americans were carrying the "White Man's Burden." Millions of people who were called "colored" were coming under the control of American power. The *Nation*, a magazine for intellectuals of a sort, reported on these colored subjects as "a varied assortment of inferior races, which, of course, cannot be allowed to vote." The editor of the *Atlantic Monthly*, another magazine for educated readers, made the ultimate connection: "If the stronger and cleverer race is free to impose its will upon 'new-caught, sullen peoples' on the other side of the globe, why not in South Carolina and Mississippi?" An editorial in the *New York Times* on May 10, 1900, confessed that "Northern men . . . no longer denounce the suppression of the Negro vote as it used to be denounced in the Reconstruction days. The necessity of it under the supreme law of self preservation is candidly recognized."[10]

Meanwhile, the Spanish-American War in 1898 had given William Randolph Hearst's *New York Journal* a chance to build circulation in its competition with Joseph Pulitzer's *World*. Richard Harding Davis, an internationally renowned foreign correspondent, had been covering the Cuban insurgency against Spain for two years. Hearst wanted the United States to enter the conflict on the side of the rebels and Davis not only shared that aspiration but had become an eyewitness advocate, filing memorable stories that celebrated the underdog heroism of the rebels. To further assure a triumph in the circulation war, Hearst sent a prominent artist, Frederick Remington, to provide the drawings that would enhance Davis's coverage. Remington, early on, became the central figure in one of "yellow" journalism's best known myths. There is evidence to support the truth of the Remington-Hearst legend, but no firsthand or physical proof. When he got to Cuba and found few signs of a struggle going on, Remington reportedly cabled his employer: "Everything is quiet. There is no trouble here. There will be no war. I wish to return." Hearst—though there is no known copy of his telegram—is said to have replied: "Please remain. You furnish picture. I will furnish war."[11]

Not long thereafter, on February 15, 1898, the American battleship U.S.S. *Maine* blew up in the Havana harbor, killing 266 Americans. The Spanish government said it was an accident and not their doing. Hearst headlined the incident and blamed it on "an enemy's secret infernal machine." With most newspapers joining the fervor, the cry of "Remember the *Maine!*" impelled the United States to declare war. Two hundred correspondents headed for Cuba twenty-five from Hearst's *Journal* alone. The Associated Press chartered a flotilla of boats, which scooted in and out of the line of fire during the naval engagements. Newspaper circulation soared and the size of headlines expanded. Some typefaces were four inches high and were printed in red ink. Correspondents, hounded by their editors, wired stories so filled with exaggerations that a New York *Herald* reporter disgustedly wrote that there was a "factory out there for faking war news."[12] Stephen Crane, the novelist who had written *The Red Badge of Courage* about the Civil War, but never witnessed military actions, was hired by Hearst. After failing to reach the Cuban insurgence, Crane went to Greece to cover a conflict between Greeks and Turks. He then changed employers and covered the charge up San Juan Hill by Theodore Roosevelt and his "Rough Riders" for the New York *World*. When the American forces moved into Puerto Rico, the inhabitants welcomed them with wine and flowers. Crane was traveling with Richard Harding Davis, and he declared he would capture a town all by himself. He promised to take Davis along but, instead, left him sleeping and during the night headed for Juana Diaz "wearing a khaki suit, a slouched hat and leggings." The villagers, seeing his outfit, surrendered to him on sight, and Crane organized them into two groups—according to an account amusingly filed by Davis a few days later—the "good fellows" and the "suspects." The "suspects" were sent to their homes having been so castigated by Crane purely on the basis of appearance. The "good fellows" then joined Crane in a celebratory feast.

The following morning a unit of American soldiers arrived at Juana Diaz led by a colonel. The colonel was delighted to meet the author of *The Red*

Badge of Courage and assumed his own fame would now be assured. "Have you been marching with my men?" the officer asked the novelist.

"I'm really very sorry, Colonel," said Crane, "but I took this town myself before breakfast yesterday morning."[13]

Before the Spanish-American War was over, publisher Hearst himself visited the battlefield, with a gun in his waistband, clutching a notebook and pencil. He found that one of his best correspondents, James Creelman, had gotten carried away by excitement and helped lead a bayonet charge. The charge ended in triumph, but a bullet had struck Creelman's left arm, and when he was found lying on the ground in some pain, it did not surprise him that Hearst insisted on taking notes at once. The wounded correspondent recounted the facts as best he could remember them. "We must beat every paper in the world," said Hearst.[14]

In the face of such competition, the fate of black Americans in the southern states was given little thought by northern editors and publishers. Extremist racism in the South had been impeded for a few years by scathing reports in a few northern papers, by the courts, by prestigious southern conservatives, and by the so-called "southern radicals" who had supported rapid movement toward equality. At the end of the century, liberals and former abolitionists were shamelessly writing, not only in the *Nation* but in *Harper's Weekly*, the *North American Review*, and *Atlantic Monthly*, in defense of the less extreme views of southerners on matters of race. It was racism nonetheless, and as C. Vann Woodward comments, "Such expressions doubtless did much to add to the reconciliation of North and South, but they did so at expense of the Negro. Just as the Negro gained his emancipation and new rights through a falling out between white men, he now stood to lose his rights through the reconciliation of white men." American imperialism abroad and accelerating racism at home coincided. Both ideas were accepted by many respectable American scholars. At home and abroad, biologists, sociologists, anthropologists, and historians as well as journalists and novelists, gave support to the doctrine that races were discreet entities and that the Anglo-Saxon or Caucasian was the superior of them all. That so few white leaders in government and the press confronted the possible consequences of putting a distinct segment of the population "outside the system" seems astonishing. Innate bigotry, indifference, complacency—do not fully explain the fateful self-deception.[15]

There were so many licenses to hate, so much approval of oppression, that even the Ku Klux Klan was idealized. Unsurprisingly, the southern press was a partner in the frenzy of aggression against Negroes. Hoke Smith, the editor of the *Atlanta Journal*, who ran for governor of Georgia on a "disenfranchisement" platform, brazenly assisted his own campaign with an outpouring of Negro atrocity stories. When he won the election, white mobs roamed the Atlanta streets, looting and lynching for four days with impunity. The year was 1906. The same wanton violence had taken place in New Orleans after disenfranchisement. For several days black Americans were fair game for assaults, torchings, and murder. One lonely dissenting voice came from ex-Governor Oates of Alabama, who was quoted in 1901 as being shocked at "the change in public opinion in regard to the status of the Negro." He asked the press, "Why is the sentiment altogether different now, when the Negro is doing no harm? Why do the people want to kill him and wipe him from the face of the earth?"[16]

The highly esteemed North Carolina newspaper editor Josephus Daniels wrote an editorial one month before the election of Woodrow Wilson as president of the United States, stating that the South would never feel secure until the North and the West had embraced the disenfranchisement and segregation policies against Negroes. Daniels shortly thereafter accepted an appointment to Wilson's cabinet. By 1915 the entire South was in the thrall of the Jim Crow codes. The central moral questions remained unanswered—and largely neglected.

More than 360,000 Negroes served in the armed forces during the First World War—a great many of them in Europe. They came home with a glimmer of hope. The war was to have made democracy safe. Their modest expectations were exploded, however, by more than twenty race riots in American cities during 1919. When blacks tried to defend themselves, the violence escalated—Longview, Texas; Tulsa, Oklahoma; Elaine, Arkansas; Knoxville, Tennessee. But it wasn't all in the South. Many atrocities took place in the North, the worst in Chicago. Overall, more than seventy Negroes were lynched, some of them veterans still in uniform. The Ku Klux Klan was recruiting thousands, more outside the South than inside, reaching a reported membership of five million. Jim Crow and its hate-filled companions in the Klan flourished through the '20s and the '30s. Now and then, people "of the better sort" would gather at symposia, or academic conferences, and discuss agonizingly the "race problem." Generally speaking, such dialogues concluded with pessimistic assessments of the Negro as given to crime, capable of only limited education, and probably doomed to menial labor. These sentiments were the underpinnings of William Graham Sumner's conclusion that the mores of the American people cannot be changed by law, nor could legislation make new mores. As late as 1944, the Virginia legislature, where once Madison and Mason had sat, ratified regulations for separate waiting rooms and toilets at airports in the state. That same year the Nobel prize–winning sociologist Gunnar Myrdal published his epic study called *An American Dilemma*, describing in exhaustive, statistical detail, the racism that he considered "the most glaring conflict in the American conscience and the greatest unsolved task for American democracy."[17]

Well-known southern journalists like Virginius Dabney and Mark Ethridge had scoffed at any suggestion of alteration in the "way of the

South." Dabney wrote (in 1943): ... "Negro agitators and another small group of white rabble rousers are pushing this country closer and closer into an inter-racial explosion which may make the race riots of the First World War and its aftermath seem mild by comparison."[18] Publisher Ethridge declared in his own paper: "There is no power in the world—not even in all the mechanized armies of the earth, Allied and Axis—which could now force Southern white people to the abandonment of the principle of social segregation."[19] But the determined and seemingly immutable patterns of behavior in the South were not nearly so rigid as advertised. In terms of public facilities, and the "quality" press, more humane and flexible policies, gradually, became acceptable. The Atlanta *Constitution*'s Ralph McGill was a nationally recognized editor who advocated equitable treatment for all citizens without regard to race or creed. Extreme discrimination was very slowly rolled back and the "distant intimacy" that had been the accommodation of the Reconstruction conservatives drifted again into the body politic during the 1940s and 1950s. The concerns of large urban newspapers were shifting unevenly toward enlightened public policy, but segregated schools and housing, and a largely segregated military establishment, were issues still to be confronted.

13

THE FIRST AND THE FOURTEENTH

If human nature is utterly corrupted, no government is possible. If we are, as Rousseau would have it, natively good, no government is necessary. It's the middle ground where human nature is a damaged piece of goods and where you say, "I can know the good but not do it," that calls for the restraints of government, either by imposition or by contract.

—S. J. Timothy Healy,
former president, Georgetown University;
president, New York Public Library

The significance of the Fourteenth Amendment, enacted in 1868, so far as freedom of the press is concerned found its roots in the Zenger trial of 1735 and had to evolve (as already described) through a number of Supreme Court cases in the twentieth century to become full grown. The most commonly held view was and is that the Fourteenth Amendment rectified the flaw in the Bill of Rights that had been imposed by the Senate's rejection of Madison's separate proposal giving supremacy to the federal Bill of Rights over any action by state legislatures affecting the rights of individual citizens. Some scholars, however, feel that the evidence for such a view is inconclusive.

There was little doubt, however, that interpretation of the Constitution and the amendments reached its apogee before the Supreme Court. Whatever the Court decided became the law—unless, as Lincoln vowed, it was changed by the people through their representatives or by amendment. During the 1920s and 1930s the decisions of the Supreme Court began the movement toward "incorporating" the First Amendment rights—speech, press, petition, and assembly—into the "privileges and immunities" and the "equal protection of the laws" described in the Fourteenth Amendment. The abolitionist leaders, including the clergy, had seen freedom of speech and press as inseparable from the issue of slavery. Early in the nineteenth century, slaveowner states were more sharply aware than ever of the danger free expression represented. The publications of the abolitionist societies, the editorials of key northern newspapers, the petitions of activist antislavery groups (a few of them in the South), were a threat to the preservation of the slave system, and all were harshly resisted.

The Philadelphia *North American and U.S. Gazette* proclaimed in September 1866 that freedom of speech, press, and assembly were paramount "privileges or immunities." (Similar language appeared in the Fourteenth Amendment.) Various political campaigns of individual congressmen and some party conventions limited the amendment to freedom of discussion and emphasized that the "importance of speech, press, petition, assembly rights" were central to its purpose. The possessors of combined First and Fourteenth rights were not a few public figures or lawyers—they were the "People." In *Federalist 51* Madison saw free speech and free press as vital in confronting two afflictions—an "unrepresentative" (or self-dealing) central government and the tyranny of the majority over the minority. Reformists, dissenters, preachers, publishers, and other sentinels of liberty were mindful in the Reconstruction period of the religious roots of the antislavery movement. Religious speech was part of the equation, and reference was frequently made to the right of speaking one's conscience. The Fourteenth Amendment would, it seemed, outlaw the state law (as in Georgia) that could imprison a minister for teaching the Bible—presumably when antislavery interpretations were used. Freedom to teach and to preach entered the list because southern states had prohibited free Negroes and mulattos from being "a minister of the Gospel." The Bill of Rights had placed freedom of religion at the top of the First Amendment enumeration. Not one of the earlier state constitutions had put religion together with speech, press, petition, or assembly. It was, however, neither illogical nor unproductive to link them. The connectedness, in Akhil Reed Amar's words, "helped reinforce a libertarian theory of freedom of all expression—political, religious, and even artistic. (*Uncle Tom's Cabin* was, of course, all three.)"[1]

The stipulations regarding free speech and press in the First Amendment and due process in the Fourteenth produced, over time, for most lawyers and ultimately for the Supreme Court a single, overriding protection of free speech and press against any limiting action by either the federal or the state governments. They also brought under the umbrella freedom of speech and of the press in the religious, artistic (novels, cartoons, theater, etc.), and minority context. Contemporary Americans take all of that for granted, but it was less than eighty years ago that free speech and press— particularly in the South—were being denied to certain individuals and groups on a local basis by citing Court interpretations of the Fourteenth Amendment that allowed a gray area between the First Amendment's prohibition of congressional action in regard to speech, press, assembly, and petition and the Fourteenth Amendment's assurance of due process and equal protection for all citizens no matter what state they called home. The gray area was the shading of difference in the language used in each of the amendments. A melding of the two amendments seemed logical—even in terms of original intent. The process began in the 1920s, but it was not until *Sullivan v. New York Times* in 1964, almost a century after the Civil War, that the theory, the logic, and the practice were emphatically unified by the Court.

Suffrage for women, nonetheless, came at a swifter pace even though it was long overdue. Women were granted voting rights in 1920 by the Nineteenth Amendment. The language of the amendment was unambiguous and has been subjected to no Court interpretations. Even those male politicians who were reluctant to permit women the political right of voting or holding public office just after the Civil War generously (in their view) allowed that *civil rights* could not be denied on the basis of gender. The Republican New York *Evening Post* had declared in 1866 that the Civil Rights Act (the precursor to the Fourteenth Amendment) must include women. Free speech, press, assembly, and petition, the *Post* stated, were provided by the act (though not enumerated) for both sexes, but voting, jury service, and holding office were not. If women and blacks could assemble and petition, let alone publish newspapers and give public speeches, their *political rights* seemed imminent. Newspapers, until the middle of the nineteenth century, were viewed largely as a function of the political process. Conceptually, the Founders had envisioned the press—free and unfettered—to be the only means of informing the electorate on the issues and on the men in political life. William Cushing, chief justice of Massachusetts, had exclaimed rhetorically to John Adams in 1789, "Without this liberty of the press, could we have supported our liberties against British administration, or could our Revolution have taken place?"[2]

The private ownership of newspapers was essential, according to conventional wisdom, because the only alternative was government control. The evils of prior restraint, censorship, and the requirement that all printed matter—books, treatises, pamphlets, broadsides—must suffer the advanced approval of a ruling authority, church or state, were still fresh in the minds of the early citizens of the United States. What could not have been accurately predicted was the depth of partisanship among the proprietors of newspapers. Voter support for one or another of the political parties depended to a considerable extent on the eloquence of the materials produced in the local newspaper. With few exceptions, however, by the middle of the nineteenth century, the press was gathering news as a *commodity* to be valued more for its profits than for its importance in keeping the voters well informed. It was during those years just preceding the Civil War, and then during the war years themselves, that the news (or information) itself became a significantly marketable product on a multicity, regional, and, ultimately, national and international level. Samuel F.B. Morse's electromagnetic telegraph, developed in 1837, could transmit only *five words per minute*. Technical improvements, the proliferation of transmission systems, and the hunger for news of the Civil War battles created the opportunities to collect news and stimulated the public appetite for more information swiftly delivered to communities scattered across an expanding democratic nation. If news was vital to the public interest, was the means of its dissemination a public utility? Not quite, said the lords of the press. They would share in wire services, but those organizations had to be owned and administered by the private sector.[3]

Without the continuing prosperity of the independent press in the face of frequent challenges to its practices (and to the validity of its constitutional protection), the rise of cooperative associations whose purpose it was to gather the news from all parts of the country—from Washington in particular but also from other cities at home and abroad—would have had a brief ascent, if not a crash on takeoff. As has already been established, the freedom of the American press was almost universally accepted; the federal Bill of Rights prohibited Congress from abridging that freedom, and eight of the original state constitutions specifically protected the press. All of these, it should be understood, singled out prior restraint as the prime evil, and many of them allowed, to one degree or another, penalties for sedition, obscenity, and material "unacceptable to law"—that is, to local law—most especially libel. It was the collaborative essays of those two Englishmen who used the pseudonym Cato that suggested libel should not be determined without convincing evidence of intent, and even so, libel should be seen as an "occasional evil rising out of a much greater good."[4]

The centrality of newspapers to political life was still manifest even after the focus shifted to profits. Politicians and newspaper proprietors became more sophisticated in the use of information. Some publishers were enjoying the power of their editorials over public affairs and political candidates. Legislative actions on a state or federal level were never going to be hermetically negotiated if the press was vigilant, but the rising influence of special interests required something more. There were those who called for standards, codes of ethics, press councils, and the monitoring of press performance in such a way as to provide some kind of licensing process. There was no consensus among critics or practitioners, but the need for a set of core principles that would protect the independence of the press while encouraging accountability was widely agreed upon. What was articulated in various ways by the justices in the key opinions on freedom of the press handed down in the twentieth century was the conviction that the press should serve the governed, not the government. Out of that supposition flowed the concepts of condoning "falsity"—in the form of unintentional, nonmalicious error that resulted from seeking the truth—and the emphasis on protection of the truth when it exposed government lies, deception, or illegality.

One other aspect of the judicial dialogue worth noting in regard to First Amendment rights—particularly those affecting the press—was the movement toward federal judges rather than juries as guardians of freedom. Juries, it seemed obvious to many, could too easily reflect or be influenced by local opinion and practice. This suspicion of juries was not significant in the first hundred years of the republic, but during and after Reconstruction, it became a major factor in the conduct of First Amendment cases. Twentieth-century libel cases found juries increasingly prepared to recommend enormous financial penalties against the press. Even though outrageous or crippling fines were overturned most of the time by federal judges, the chilling effect was significant. News organizations without large financial resources dared not risk bankrupting penalties.

The judicial thinking about the language and precedence of the First Amendment and the Fourteenth Amendment opinions led to a "unitary theory of freedom of speech [and press] against both State and Federal governments." That theory seems to call for the more dispassionate consideration of a judge rather than the "unconstrained" findings of a jury.[5] Sir William Blackstone, the English jurist whose book on the common law had been the basic text for many early American lawyers, crafted the theory that dominated American judgments on the press for more than two centuries and probably still does:

> The liberty of the press is indeed essential to the nature of a free state; but this consists in laying no previous restraint upon publication, and not in freedom from censure for criminal matter when published. Every freeman has an undoubted right to lay what sentiments he pleases before the public; to forbid this is to destroy the freedom of the press; but if he publishes what is improper, mischievous, or illegal, he must take the consequences of his own temerity.[6]

What is improper (obscene) or mischievous (reckless disregard for the truth) or illegal (injurious to the national security) is a matter that recurs and is reexamined on a continuing basis. These considerations are, Alexander Meiklejohn wrote, "as are all principles—never finally decided."[7] Robert Hutchins, once a very young dean of the Yale Law School, later president of Chicago University and the chair of the Commission on Freedom of the Press (1942–1947), stated in a 1964 debate: "We *must* regard the Constitution as a charter of learning. . . . I don't mean that it is a blank check to spend our national resources, intellectual or other, in any way; but the Constitution cannot bind to specific forms of action that in the nature of the case were unforeseen at the time the Constitution was adopted."[8]

14

THE NEWS BUSINESS

The question is, how do you carry out the fiduciary responsibility? What does that mean? In the case of the media, it means an ethical or social responsibility, not a legally enforceable one. But there are lots of obligations in life that are not legal. I don't understand why we think only of legal obligations.

—Geoffrey Hazard, University of Pennsylvania Law School

Not many learned commentators would agree that the Framers always said clearly and fully what they meant. The absolutist interpretation of the words "Congress shall make no law . . . abridging the freedom of speech or of the press" may suffer no exceptions. The nonabsolutists observe that such language cannot be reconciled with the law relating to libel, slander, misrepresentation, obscenity, perjury, false advertising, solicitation of crime, complicity by encouragement, conspiracy, and so on.

Alexander Meiklejohn, defending the absolutist view, does not see it as inflexible. "To think without facts," he says, "is as ineffectual as to think without principles." The Constitution, he reminds us, provides for its own amendment and, through the courts, for its reinterpretation. If we accept the premise that the Constitution and the Bill of Rights protect the freedom of thought and communication that are vital to our ability to *govern*, we would be confining First Amendment protection to information on which we might base our vote for a political candidate. If we accept Meiklejohn's interpretation of self-government, however, voters must acquire "the intelligence, integrity, sensitivity and generous devotion to the general welfare that in theory casting a vote is assumed to express."[1]

For the first century of the "experiment" in self-government, the casting of a vote was not a meaningful exercise for most Americans. Many were not permitted to vote; others were so impoverished that the franchise was ignored in the struggle for survival. But for those who participated, the concerns were primarily local, often self-serving, and not likely to involve a philosophical overview except among the very few whose education and moral awareness gave them reason to look at the future of the nation as a whole. The great majority of voters in the nation's first century heard little of the world outside their own regions, and what they were able to learn was, more often than not, printed in their local papers as brief "letters" from abroad.

The *unforeseen* change in the availability of news from distant places, nationally and internationally, was brought about by the wire services. If the enlarged voting population at the beginning of the nation's second century was to understand the issues facing the United States as a nation, formulate judgments, and help make the decisions of the government effective—or change them—more comprehensive and sophisticated information was needed. News became, with extraordinary swiftness, a social institution and a cultural force in the United States—all this as it was simultaneously becoming a commodity. As American institutions began to understand their essential need for various kinds of information promptly collected and distributed to a large and geographically scattered society, the news as such moved upward on the list of national priorities.[2]

In its role as a sentinel over all our liberties, the press, at least in the minds of many educators and social thinkers, was becoming a public utility. After the Civil War, the wire services faced a task far different from mere transmission of personalized reporting. Even that process had been frequently aborted during the Civil War by government intervention. When reporting from the field was censored, the fledgling Associated Press settled for the dissemination of official handouts. The postwar task was to provide a far greater reach than individual editors could have imagined possible with existing staff and funding. The newsbrokers could produce coverage of events and political actions in distant places on a constant basis. The editors who subscribed to their services had only to select what they thought their readers wanted to or should know. Even though the capacity was limited and the romantic qualities—the color and pungency—were the first to be sacrificed, brief, factual accounts were the precursor of what became known several decades later as objective reporting. The U.S. census, in its *Historical Statistics*, asserts that only 29.1 percent of the total urban population in 1860 was reading daily newspapers and only a little more than 5 percent of the nonurban population received daily newspapers. About 11.5 percent of the white population and 79.9 percent of Negroes and other nonwhites were illiterate.

Education, at least to the level of literacy, grew steadily, and one consequence was the growth in newspaper circulations. Publishers had also added the common-denominator components of entertainment—gossip, trivia, illustrations, and comic strips. Charles Dudley Warner, who had been Mark Twain's coauthor of *The Gilded Age* and was an editor of a daily newspaper, was dismayed by the deterioration of editorial standards in the big-city press. He found the popularity-seeking mix of printed matter inadequate for "the public's understanding of events and issues." In 1897, Warner wrote a piece for *Harper's Monthly*, observing, "The solemn truth is, that the printed matter of some of our metropolitan dailies has now for a dozen years been making it impossible for the people of this city to read anything, long or short, on any serious subject." The average American of the time received about five years of formal education. On this point Warner mused, "The young people who leave the public schools with reading and little else, make the newspaper their only literature."[3]

The evolution of press criticism—within its own ranks and among the highbrow magazines and educators—is a subject examined more fully in later chapters. It was, in any event, a concomitant development as the daily newspapers gained in size, profitability, and influence both politically and culturally. "All I know," Will Rogers would say, "is just what I read in the newspapers." The papers in the latter part of the nineteenth century were printed more swiftly and efficiently. The cost of this advance and its refinement were borne by the newspaper proprietors, and inevitably, they became part of the entrepreneurial calculation that in many ways positioned the business aspect of journalism far above any ethical responsibility to the public or the political process.

The telegraph was, on its own, an attractively profitable enterprise. Western Union became a monopoly for a great many years, and the Associated Press (AP) protected established member newspapers from the competition of new dailies that appeared all over the country during the 1860s and 1870s. Regional AP organizations were formed and applied for affiliation with the powerful eastern AP, which became more exclusive as time went on. The competitors, such as the United Press, did not become significant until 1882. Over 200 papers were served by the AP in 1872. By 1880 there were 357. New members were not admitted unless the nearest older members agreed. During that period, a membership added measurably to the value of any newspaper. In 1884 each AP franchise held by the New York City partners was worth at least a quarter of a million dollars.[4] There was an actual market (largely among insiders) for the sale and transfer of AP franchises. The Western Union Company and the AP conducted a long and profitable love affair that was not always platonic. In 1874 the *New York Graphic*—not admitted to membership in the AP—reported that Western Union "finds in the New York Associated Press its best customer and natural ally. The success of each depends mainly upon the aid of the other. The one collects, the other transmits the news of the world. The president of the telegraph company is a trustee of the *New York Tribune* and the publisher of the *New York Times* is a director of the telegraph company."[5]

The obvious conclusion drawn by the *Graphic* was that no "despot or censor" had such power over the press as a whole any time in history. By

1870, the New York AP controlled transatlantic cable news; most of the key stories came out of Washington, the financial news emanated from New York City, and the dispatches went to eight auxiliary AP groups in the hinterlands. It also made exclusive contractual agreements with Reuters, France's Agence Havas, and Germany's Wolff News Agency. One of the top AP executives told a Senate committee in 1884: "We are not in the newspaper business as missionaries or philanthropists, but in pursuit of bread."[6]

The butter on the bread was to be spread evenly for a while—perhaps a decade—after a joint executive committee was formed with Whitelaw Reid representing the newspaper proprietors, William Henry Smith, the AP, and Jay Gould speaking for Western Union. Their management of the AP's development permitted considerable expansion of news coverage and greatly improved technology. What did not grow during that period (1880–1890) was independent journalistic judgments and reporting by member newspapers. For the time being, the major papers and their proprietors controlled the nature and substance of the wire services despite Western Union's continuing leverage.[7]

By 1901 Whitelaw Reid was writing and speaking disparagingly of "prolix" journalism, that is, journalism that covered too much too thinly. He and other serious editors were aware of the vast amount of miscellaneous printed information chattering out of the AP machines and quickly deposited each night in wastebaskets. In 1890, the AP announced an extension of its leased wire system to over 40,000 words per day. Demand for baseball scores and statistics along with other sports news grew rapidly. Close to 6,000 words of sports news were filed each night. Political bias and skewed reports of campaigns were charges frequently hurled at the AP, prompting Smith's retort: "The violence of the attacks on the Associated Press in partisan newspapers has been equaled only by the untruthfulness."[8] The charges, which were not entirely unfounded, provided the struggling United Press (UP) wire service with an opening. UP encouraged the assaults on the monopolistic AP. A trade weekly, the *Journalist*, in 1884 thundered that the AP's election coverage was "weak, vacillating and uncertain." It described the preeminent wire service as "a gibbering, tottering old wreck. Like a superannuated old virgin, it is fit for nothing but to gossip idly about its neighbors."[9]

The most important subscribers to the UP services in the 1880s were the *Boston Globe* and the *Chicago Herald*. The *Globe* had been denied membership by the AP when it was taken over by Charles Taylor (whose descendants are still centrally involved) in 1872. Over the next two decades, several major changes in the technical aspects of American journalism took place. When we look back at that era, the trends seem predictable, but for the managers of newspapers in the 1880s and 1890s, the competition, the profits, and the personalities created a heated atmosphere in which the significance of news as a vital element of the political process was not paramount. The racism that was becoming more deeply embedded in American social and commercial life may have been commented on in a learned journal now and then, but as an editorial focus for any large urban newspaper, the subject was not apt to come up even in the memoirs of the more enlightened editors.

AP and UP executives were increasingly mindful of their dependence on Western Union and smaller telegraph companies. They were also interested in developing their own stature as national resources and not merely allowing their services to be manipulated by combative proprietors seeking exclusive contracts to shut out upstart competition. The wire services, despite a period of preoccupation with deal-making and "stock pools," turned eventually to the service of leased wires and the employment of competent editorial staff.[10] The product they turned out became more sophisticated, rapidly delivered, and innovative. "Bulletins" were introduced, and lead paragraphs were updated. Breaking news came clamorously into subscriber offices, shaped by the external managers and writers. The same material went to all. Was this egalitarian product of high quality? Was it analytical, stylish, insightful? Not very likely, and not very often. It was bound to be superficial and rarely better than local reporting, but it came in steadily and swiftly, usually arousing interest if only because of the remote locations of many stories—disasters, small wars, sports events, even garish crimes committed in some distant place. Though nearly always lacking depth or subtlety, such reporting forced itself onto the pages of large-circulation newspapers and thus into hundreds of thousands of homes, providing what has been called a "shared national news experience, a daily common public knowledge of selected events and personalities."[11]

All of this change contributed, perhaps positively, to a limiting effect, a kind of netting thrown over the national economy and the political awareness that heightened a sense of nationhood. It also stimulated the appetite of newspaper editors for seemingly endless shreds of new developments, sudden twists and turns, and additional information on dramatic stories. Americans were becoming addicted to news, but some observers such as publisher Whitelaw Reid wondered how useful this plethora of so-called facts and "particulars" might be. The feeling of participation and discussion that had characterized American newspapers little more than half a century earlier was virtually gone. Nonetheless, by 1921 there were six news associations feeding Negro newspapers. One of them, the Associated Negro Press, described its function as a "news gathering organization that scours the world for race news and thereby makes it possible for our publications to present to their readers an authoritative and uniform accounting of matters of genuine interest from every corner of the globe."[12]

For more than sixty years following the Civil War, the AP had maneuvered to maintain its preeminence and, to a certain extent, its exclusivity.

The United Press became a serious competitor—after earlier attempts by different managements—just before World War I under the leadership of Roy Howard. UP's member papers went from 491 in 1912 to 745 in 1919. In the 1920s the AP and UP developed a number of similar characteristics, using byline reporters, producing special features, and improving the quality of the writing. When INS (International News Service) joined the competition, it marketed itself as a source of "supplemental news and commentary" that could complement either AP or UP. The AP continued to focus on cooperative and exclusive membership; UP pursued a role of producing news for profit and selling to anyone who wanted to buy. At its peak in 1948, INS could claim only about 20 percent of America's daily newspapers as subscribers—most of them, as was INS, owned by Hearst.

By the early 1900s, many prominent social critics—men Walter Lippmann would describe as public intellectuals—began to harshly question the value of fragmented, undifferentiated bursts of strident news from abroad. Harvard's president James Russell Lowell was quoted in an *Atlantic Monthly* piece written in 1900 by journalist Rollo Ogden: "Great events are perhaps not more common than they used to be, but a vastly greater number of trivial incidents are now recorded." Lowell believed that "the telegraph strips history of everything down to the bare fact but it does not observe the true proportion of things." Two decades later Walter Lippmann would formulate his enduring theory of the "pictures in our heads," those images all curious human beings who could read a newspaper created to deal with the distant realities, complex ideas, and events that entered their consciousness. Lippmann reminded thoughtful people that "the news is not a mirror of social conditions, but the report of an aspect that has obtruded itself."[13]

The pictures in the minds of Americans were becoming substantially similar because of the wire services and their virtually standardized, but fragmentary and brief, accounts. Correspondents, pushed to meet deadlines and concoct "bulletins," were rarely given time to dig deep into context or even determine whether alleged facts were accurate. Perspectives, followups, balanced views, and other qualities of reporting that enhanced accuracy were diminished, if not eliminated, by the competitive pursuit of the next day's news and the compulsion to keep the wires choked with bits and pieces of information. By the 1920s, teletype machines were proliferating and replacing the men and women who had received and translated Morse-coded materials. After that, radiotelegraphy superseded cable telegraphy, and by the 1950s teletypesetters delivered printed, or "punched tape," stories structured for standard column width. News photos were being delivered electronically from the mid-1930s on, and in the 1970s satellite transmission replaced wired systems in most urban newsrooms. In the 1990s another technological leap made it possible for the wire service terminal-computer-satellite systems to produce teletext news for cable TV operators.

Clearly, packaging the news was very big business and seemed always to be getting bigger. In 1835, with $500 in hand, James Gordon Bennett started the *New York Herald* in a basement office "furnished with a few packing cases covered with planks." Charles A. Dana, editor of the *New York Sun*, estimated that the start-up of a daily newspaper in 1840 would cost between $5,000 and $10,000. After the Civil War, the costs were almost $1 million to launch a big-city newspaper.[14]

The 1850 U.S. census estimated that more than 80 percent of America's newspapers were distinctly, unashamedly partisan in their political coverage. They might do some crime and violence stories, even cultural reports, but politics dominated, and a great many editors were themselves politically active in a direct and visible fashion as campaigners, platform drafters, and general organizers. In Gerald J. Baldasty's *The Commercialization of News in the Nineteenth Century*, statistical studies of major urban newspapers—and those in a few smaller communities—illustrate a consistent pattern of editorial copy during 1831–1832. Politics accounted across the board for half or more of the stories published, though many papers devoted nearly 70 percent of their editorial space to political writings.

Figures in a survey of eight city papers in 1897 contrasted sharply with those of the 1830s. In Pittsburgh, New York, Boston, Chicago, Charleston, and San Francisco—among other cities—political coverage was between 10 and 20 percent of the content. These percentages in the same group of papers were either matched or surpassed by the coverage given to business and labor. All other subjects, such as crime, religion, science, and society, were in each case less than 10 percent. In smaller cities and large towns during the 1890s, politics was given the largest amount of space, though less than 50 percent—in the smallest towns, about 20 percent. Business and labor, even before the Civil War, claimed the second-largest proportion of editorial coverage, and that share grew rapidly after the war. The transition from politics to profitability was driven by circulation growth and the lower cost per reader. In America's early years it cost so little to start a newspaper—even taking inflation into account—that many politicians owned all or part of a newspaper that vigorously supported their views. The major change in the late nineteenth century was the marked independence of the press from government influence. Unhappily this autonomy did not often stimulate high-quality reporting, and not many publishers spent much time thinking about the electorate, the democratic process, or any other higher-altar aspect of responsible journalism. The preoccupation was keeping the circulation high and steady. That meant, inevitably, entertainment and common-denominator materials, which soon became more important than serious, competent news reporting whether local or from staff correspondents in other locations. The brief—call it staccato—rattle of news coming in by way of the wire services was used by editors subjectively and without elaboration.

In the years following the Civil War, interest in foreign news was neither intense nor systematically measured. It didn't seem to count for much. Ironically, the phenomenon of finding news from all over the world in the local paper had helped build circulations. The demographics and intellectual appetites of hundreds of thousands of people reading the same newspaper presented a challenge to the editors; either they would attempt to raise the reader's level of consciousness about political and world events or they could develop whatever divertissements might be targeted at the various segments of the audience—women, businessmen, factory workers, religious groups, sports fans, and so on. In earlier times, party politics, the selection of candidates, and planning election strategies were part of the job. Once that integration was ended, largely by mutual consent, the editorial concern shifted to business—in the world at large and internally as well. In a sense, the advertiser replaced the politicians. Newspapers had become the single most important marketing instrument for American products by the end of the century.

Advertisements had, of course, been part of newspaper publishing even in the colonial years. The availability of goods and services were important, often essential, information everywhere in the colonies. When circulations were small, the ads were regarded as business news in themselves, but the power of advertising grew with the circulation, and the value of circulation was measured by subscriptions, sales, and advertising revenue. In the larger cities, the key advertisers were department stores. In the 1890s a single New York City department store would spend $100,000 or more on newspaper advertising each year. John Wanamaker, a successful Philadelphia merchant, acknowledged: "I owe my success to newspapers." He spent approximately $400,000 annually for advertisements in Philadelphia papers.[15]

In *The Daily Newspaper in America: The Evolution of a Social Instrument*, Alfred McClung Lee reports that by the end of the 1890s about 55 percent of newspaper revenues came from advertising and 45 percent from subscriptions and sales. For the first time, the advertisers became the propelling force. It was not unexpected that they would make demands. Most papers, over time, accepted the influence of ad agencies and their clients as part of the business. A few editors tried to resist the notion that advertisers could dictate the page and position for each of their ads or, even more perniciously, insist that their ad copy be surrounded by specifically supportive editorial materials. Many advertisers demanded "puff pieces" to accompany their ads and warned editors that a competitor's ad should never be printed near their own. Often both conditions were stipulated.

Printers' Ink, a trade journal for magazine and newspaper publishers, actually recommended, in 1894, that advertisers pay reporters a few extra dollars to "look after their interests." That familiar phrase could mean promotional plugs in news stories or the suppressing of negative stories about the advertisers' products. Powerful ad agencies suggested that newspapers shape the news so as to avoid politics or the denigration of public officials, which might discomfort some readers and turn them away from the persuasive influence of that particular paper and, therefore, its advertisements. The agencies recommended "pleasant news" that would appeal to women in particular. The assumptions of business interests, which provided large amounts of money for advertisements in newspapers, were widespread, and many editors gave in to pressure from their major patrons.

The pervasive pressures on newspapers at the turn of the century from advertisers who openly claimed they were subsidizing the press spawned numerous nonjournalistic gimmicks designed to boost or sustain circulation—contests and premiums, most notably. Prizes were offered for everything from solving mysteries to the best loaf of homemade bread. Coupons were printed in each paper and were required with each entry to a contest. When cash prizes were involved, the incentive to enter a contest more than once with numerous approaches or answers invited the seizing of newspapers on their way to subscribers or newsstands. Coupons were torn out and the papers thrown away or left in damaged condition for disgruntled customers. Despite the distortions, contests and coupons were a staple of circulation promotion for many years—more so in urban areas than in the less populated regions—but advertising remained a controlling factor anywhere newspapers were published as the nineteenth century came to a close. The gimmickry employed to increase circulation and the characterization of newspapers as "the agent and servant of the advertising spirit" did not receive the support of all editors and publishers, but few could afford to fight back. In an 1896 edition of the trade journal *Newspaper Maker*, the editor of a Boston newspaper wrote caustically, "What are the financial questions, what are presidential elections, what is the silver issue, in comparison with the delicious joy of getting paper dolls in the Sunday newspaper?"[16]

Thoughtful, serious publishers and editors of the time, though not great in number, were eloquent in their concern and outrage. Whitelaw Reid condemned excessive preoccupation with profitability, "which sacrifices principles and morality to the cash drawer and makes the newspaper not the exponent of principle but the coiner of money."[17] The trend was so deep running that proprietors and editors actually became voices for business interests—including their own. Not only was editorial coverage tilted sharply toward industry and business with specific emphasis on the advertiser interests but editors campaigned in print, directly and indirectly, against any threat to the commercial advantages of their own newspapers. Pressure was exerted on and against competition such as billboards, streetcar displays, or any other device that might take revenue away from the printed press.

There were some papers, it should be acknowledged, that managed to report important political news—local, national, and international—along with the puffery and the gimmicks. They argued that the one (trivial) paid for the other (significant). Over time, radio and television would force a reconstitution of print news, but at the beginning of the twentieth century, such dramatic and inescapable competition had not been imagined. The technology newspapers confronted in 1900 was their own and that of their fitful bedfellows, the wire services. Despite larger circulations and massive advertising revenue, the operating costs were growing so rapidly that newspapers cut back on editorial costs by limiting news space, hiring fewer reporters, and paying them less. Convenient, easily anticipated stories were more commonly covered than those that required research and time-consuming investigation. Deep-seated sociological problems like racism were avoided as unpleasant and complex. The unpleasant stories irritated the advertising community, and the complex issues discomforted the bean counters.

Though the more responsible editors slowed the momentum away from the public interest and the political process, their primary concern had to be demographic—the purchasing power of the consumer-reader. The poor could vote, but they could not spend. News gathering responded to the need for stimulation, entertainment, and profitability. What suffered was the depiction of social reality, of ideas, of context. In addition, many reporters, low on self-esteem and underpaid, were vulnerable to bribes and easily co-opted by business interests seeking promotional stories. Others who were paid according to the number of words they submitted turned to fabrication and stunts in which they themselves occasionally participated, thus producing first-person accounts. The concept of journalism as a responsible craft—if not a noble calling—was little heard of in the management offices of the big newspapers. Many of these were now beginning to merge or to be sold as the new century began. Groups of papers with a single owner came to be known as chains. At one point William Randolph Hearst owned forty-two newspapers.

Among the more than 2,000 newspapers in the United States in the early 1900s, very few indicated any strong obligation to public interest. Some, proprietors, such as Joseph Pulitzer, tried to have it both ways. He purchased the *New York World* with the intention that he would attract readers by publishing lively news but also by entertaining them with comic strips, puzzles, short stories, and illustrations. He told his associates that he would deal with serious public matters on the editorial page and support humanitarian causes whenever possible. In its first year under Pulitzer's direction, the circulation of the *New York World* rose from 15,000 to 100,000. By 1900 the circulation was over a quarter-million (out of a population of little over 1 million). The editorial material had exposed corruption in the city government, revealed bribery, exhorted aid for the needy, and even solicited contributions from the readers to pay for a base upon which the Statue of Liberty could be mounted.

It was during this period that the voices of the critics were heard for the first time on a regular basis. The "new journalism"—high circulation, vulgar, trivial—was attacked by the editors of small, quality magazines. Most of the critics were intellectuals, graduates of leading universities, and were what one historian called "missionaries in the cause of culture." They defended a literary tradition grounded in the values of serious reading and reflection. In *Harper's* and *Atlantic Monthly*, *Scribner's* and *Dial*, indignant, sometimes sanctimonious essays were published excoriating the shallowness and sensationalism of contemporary journalism. One English editor who had visited his American colleagues observed that American reporters turned in "bright, racy, trivial, contemptible stuff which should interest no one of any intellectual capacity, but which does interest ninety-nine out of one hundred people."[18]

The twentieth century would witness the contest between the large profits and power of mass communication on the one hand and the survival of the Founders' vision of an informed electorate on the other. It would be the mission of the critics and ethicists to demand, in one way or another, some moral payment for the First Amendment protection given to the nation's press.

15

TOWARD PROFESSIONALISM

I see my job as trying to understand what is going on and then trying to explain it to people as best I can and as fairly as I can. But I don't have any sort of calling to do that. I think that elevates the press to a higher role than I would give it. I don't think it's as worthy a calling as public service, for instance.

—Cokie Roberts, commentator,
National Public Radio and ABC television news

Because freedom of the press was envisioned by the Framers as the only means of informing the citizenry on public issues and signaling governmental abuse of power, there were those who believed the proprietors of news organizations had a responsibility to the people. The press had to be privately owned and exempt from any prior restraint if that responsibility was to be honored. Absent from that concept, at least in the formative early years, was any remedy for *irresponsibility* unless libel, slander, or other statutes were violated—in which event the legal remedy would have to pursue the offender after the fact. There were, of course, instances of *public* offenses against news organizations, as when unruly mobs burned down the premises of a publication that espoused unpopular views or committed personal acts of violence against the publisher, including murder. The abolitionist newspapers could testify to frequent attacks of both kinds.

Once retaining the subscriptions, if not the loyalty, of large numbers of readers became less essential, the mass circulation papers turned their attention to the bright promise of advertising revenue. The determination of differences between good and evil in public life was left to the pulpit, and the ethical quandaries were, by and large, left to the small, highbrow magazines and the academies where philosophy was taught and discussed. Those were the arenas where criticism of the press and moral remonstrance first found voice. When he was seventy-three and out of politics, Thomas Jefferson observed that "laws and institutions must go hand in hand with the progress of the human mind. . . . As new discoveries are made, new truths disclosed, and manners and opinions change with the change of circumstances, institutions must advance also, and keep pace with the times."[1] By the time the nineteenth century neared its end, the institution called the press was keeping pace less with the human mind than with the tumultuous growth of American commerce.

The concept of "new journalism" had introduced the separation of news and editorial comment in the 1880s, and the idea caught on. It served publishers' interests well because one political party or individual politicians could be supported in editorials while the rest of the paper pandered to popular tastes, even when the tone or emphasis contrasted sharply with the moral view of the recommended candidates or officeholders. Using entertainment values as the basis of appeal was obviously attracting enormous audiences, and some commentators wondered when that vast reach of circulation might be harnessed to political power. No politician, local or national, including the man in the White House, had at his command such a potentially powerful amplifier.

There were many voices raised in answering such apprehensions, some of them distinguished, most of them passionate, a few enduringly influential. The cumulative effect of the early criticism, which rarely had more than minimal circulation, is difficult to measure. During the first half of the twentieth century the names of incisive, provocative surveyors of the press became widely known, at least among the intelligentsia—Will Irvin, George Seldes, Walter Lippmann, and later A. J. Liebling and Ben Bagdikian. They were followed by media columnists at the major newspapers, sharp-edged writers at the news magazines, and the editors of journalism reviews and think-tank reports. Concerned and caustic commentary, however, began to appear regularly at least as early as the 1880s. A few scattered jeremiads were recorded in the so-called Reconstruction period when cities and newspaper circulations grew concomitantly and demanded more extensive telegraph services and faster presses. The indifference to widespread American racism even in the best of the papers had been veiled by some support for the Thirteenth, Fourteenth, and Fifteenth Amendments, which were perceived as breakthroughs for Negro equality. By and large, the white press, first in the South and then in the North, with a few laudable exceptions, drifted away from indignation or even curiosity about the evasive actions employed systematically in the South (and with scarcely less vigor elsewhere), pontificating instead on the problems of absorbing freed slaves into a white society. It was intimated that former slaves and their descendants lacked the levels of intelligence, skill, and urbanity required of politically active citizens.

The black press, which tried to expose Jim Crow, was underfunded, and few of its newspapers lived long. Frederick Douglass had launched the *North Star* in 1847, in Rochester, New York. He kept it afloat until 1860, though its name was changed to *Frederick Douglass' Paper*.[2] In a book called *Black Journalists in Paradox,* Clint C. Wilson II, an associate dean of Howard University, describes the legislation rushed through southern state legislatures after the 1831 Nat Turner rebellion. Slaveholders were anxious to keep slaves illiterate as a defense against insurrection, and southerners also believed that "excluding African-Americans from the press would make the issues they represented disappear."[3] No such draconian actions were necessary to make the northern white press back away from covering such stories. Business interests had triumphed.

The new highbrow magazines sprouting in the 1880s published the concerns of the intellectuals—many of them editors and writers themselves. The *Arena, Forum,* and the *North American Review* were explicitly interested in the role of journalism in American life. Responsible efforts to report important events and issues on the one hand and the profit-oriented dynamic of seeking mass circulation on the other were widely conflicting objectives. Newspapers and magazines experienced the same kind of division that afflicted literature, the arts, and the tastes of society at large. European visitors were somewhat shocked by the vulgarity of most large American papers. They could not understand the appeal of a single publication to so many people of different social classes. European newspapers of that period were edited almost exclusively for the educated and the comfortable.

Anthony Trollope's fourth novel, *The Warden,* was published in England in 1855. It was a gently satirical story of village life and concerned itself with a number of dilemmas encountered by the family of an Anglican clergyman. The fear of and the effect of comments in the press are central to the plot. In one passage, Trollope describes the power of a political journalist whose adversarial reporting on Church of England affairs painfully disrupts and alters the lives of Trollope's main characters. Of Tom Towers, editor of the imaginary *Jupiter*, Trollope reports:[4]

> He loved to watch the great men of whom he daily wrote, and flatter himself that he was greater than any of them. Each of them was responsible to his country, each of them must answer if inquired into, each of them must endure abuse with good humour, and insolence without anger. But to whom was he, Tom Towers, responsible? No one could insult him; no one could inquire into him. He could speak out with withering words, and no one could answer him. Ministers courted him, though perhaps they knew not his name; bishops feared him; judges doubted their own verdicts unless he confirmed them; and generals, in their councils of war, did not consider more deeply what the enemy would do, than what the *Jupiter* would say. . . . It is probable that Tom Towers considered himself the most powerful man in Europe; and so he walked on from day to day, studiously striving to look a man, but knowing within his breast that he was a god.

With this sardonic portrait Trollope prophetically indicted powerful and unaccountable journalists. In mid-nineteenth-century England, the press was devoted to the ruling class, and mass circulation had not yet reared its fin de siècle head. In this the British trailed behind America's brash and boisterous urban newspapers for many years before they, too, discovered the profitability of tabloids, vulgarity, and entertainment. By the middle of the twentieth century, there were critics who felt the English press had caught up with the competition in scandal, gossip, lurid crime stories, and entertainment at the lowest level—perhaps taking the lead.

Meanwhile, in the lost colonies of the New World, the American intellectual class (never rulers) looked upon developments in the daily press with a mixture of dismay and disgust. Among the most respected voices raised against the lowered standards of successful newspapers was that of E. L. Godkin, editor of the *Nation*, a conservative weekly in the 1890s. Godkin criticized the large newspapers rigorously. He disliked the "new journalism" style that accented sensationalism and distorted the news by neglecting serious issues. He was convinced that newspapers would be able to distort "the social and political world of the Twentieth Century" because so many young Americans were reading newspapers and little else.[5]

Godkin saw the newspapers of the 1890s in much the same light that many modern critics see television—as the opiate of the young. Each newspaper, Godkin observed, "furnishes a complete change of scene."[6] Young readers did not have to concentrate or to analyze. The appetite for books, for exploring ideas, was so diminished by addiction to abbreviated, undifferentiated news reports—along with garish crime stories and tales of scandalous behavior among the rich and powerful—that Godkin feared great numbers of Americans would leave school without any further interest in reading books or the ability to understand them.

Richard Watson Gilder, editor of the *Century* from 1880 to 1909, deplored the faking of news and the loss of character among reporters who produced what their editors wanted, true or not. Gilder was willing, however, to admire the effectiveness of vast publicity provided by the big-city newspapers, particularly when that publicity assisted charitable community projects. He also saw the advantage in "the search light it throws on dark places." But he was distressed that "members of the more intelligent portion of the community will buy the very papers they abuse and despise." Gilder urged his readers not to support the sensational press in any manner.[7]

The Sunday newspapers were also proliferating in the 1890s, and their characteristics were attacked for the same reasons as the daily press but with particular distaste by the clergy and the devout. Most of the Sunday editions were owned by the dailies, though a few were independent. They published the kind of features and illustrations that required more time to prepare, and they competed with the weekly magazines for talent and ideas. In 1886, an article in the *Forum* warned that the Sunday newspapers were matching the influence of the pulpit in regard to lifestyles and public opinion on social and political matters. The corrective suggestions inevitably included some attention to "professionalizing" journalism. The first weekly trade paper devoted to the press was the *Journalist*, founded in 1883. It recommended that bylines be used to make reporters more conscious of personal responsibility and generally advocated programs of self-improvement among editors and publishers. The *Forum* in one issue asked three experienced journalists to discuss their working habits. One of them was J. W. Keller, a New York City reporter who described journalism as being in its "essential qualifications a learned profession" but in actuality a trade or craft with low pay, no job security, and a lack of public recognition. He accused publishers of hiring the best brains and turning them into hacks who wrote what the publisher wanted to hear.[8]

The big-city newsroom was frequently portrayed as a destructive place, whereas the smaller papers—some of them weeklies—in the hinterlands could be refuges for kindred spirits and aspiring idealists. It was in that context, and because of it, that codes of ethics were contemplated. "The liberty of the press," W. S. Lilly said in a *Forum* article, "like all liberty, means action within the great principles of ethics, not emancipation from them."[9] Lilly conceived of newspapers as educators and philosophers who could teach masses of people by making them think. He wanted newspapermen to identify abuses of power, advocate reforms, and offer supporting arguments based on what the facts and the individual conscience identified as the truth.

Dial magazine, in 1893, offered an ethical guideline for responsible newspapers:

1. Collect news scientifically with accuracy as the primary consideration.
2. Select and present news based on sound judgment of significance to the public, not on sensational qualities.
3. Express the views of the publication based on well-defined principles and honest convictions.

The *Dial* editors stated: "If journalism is to be considered a form of business and nothing more, then the only proper tests of sources are the daily circulation, the number of advertisements, and the annual balance sheet."[10] In what was no doubt regarded by many newspaper proprietors as unrealistic righteousness, *Dial* insisted that *ethical standards* were the only measure of service to society. There were two prominent publishers who in large part agreed with such assessments—Charles A. Dana of the *New York Sun* and Whitelaw Reid of the *New York Tribune*.

Dana was acutely aware of the power the press could have over the minds and opinions of uninformed and uneducated readers. He wanted his paper to be alert to the misuse of governmental authority, primarily in the executive branch, and act as a countervailing force against despotism of any kind. Toward these ends, Dana hired college graduates with a liberal arts education and trained them on the job. Whitelaw Reid was quoted in an *Atlantic Monthly* article by George Alger about sensationalism: "I only insist that whether you consider the common school or the free press, faulty as each may be, it is a necessary concomitant of our civilization and our government; that it has been steadily growing better, and that the best way to remedy the evil it works is to make it better still."[11] Reid considered the popular press and public schools as "twin brothers"; both needed criticism and both would be only as good as the community demanded. A newspaper could not, he insisted, sustain higher standards than the community wanted and accepted. A good paper would always "tell the truth and be fair," and over time the community would support a good paper. If it wanted something less, that's what it would get.[12]

The commentary on newspaper standards increased in the 1890s and the first decade of the twentieth century. By 1911 more than thirty substantial articles were being published each year in serious monthly magazines. There were three trade magazines that also published critiques—*Newspaperdom* (1882–1925), the *Journalist* (1883–1904), and the *Fourth Estate* (1894–1927). The audience was, however, made up of a small constituency—those among the intelligentsia who were interested and those editors, publishers, and reporters who cared. The critics dolefully witnessed the continuing growth and financial success of the sensationalist papers they considered trashy and irresponsible. Charles Dudley Warner summarized the predicament: "This is the penalty of cultivating the ability to read in advance of the taste to discriminate."[13]

Writing in the *Arena*, W.H.H. Murray suggested that if newspapers were endowed, the bended knee would not be necessary. Neither political nor commercial concerns would interfere with what Murray called "honorable and right thinking journalism." The power behind the big newspapers, Murray asserted bitingly, was money: "Money has no conscience, no honor, no patriotism, no sympathy with truth, right, and decency, and never has had."[14]

The *Dial* editorialized, in 1893, in favor of an endowed press because it saw the press as a teacher in the public interest and therefore not merely a business. The *Dial*, along with many academics and a few publishers, envisioned the press with the same fiduciary and ethical obligations as medicine or the law or the academy—in other words, as a true profession. The recognized graduate programs in journalism had frequently proposed curriculums of common purpose and substance that could provide the kind of training (intellectual rather than vocational), and graduate degrees, that would create a pool of professionals. The self-appointed or management-manipulated reporters, even with the best of intentions and in some cases with high-quality undergraduate credentials, were soon molded by the kind of journalism that placed a higher value on circulation than on the search for truth and the fair discussion of vital public issues. A small group of men and women who believed in professionalism and credibility argued in one way or another—some within their own newspaper or magazine organizations, others from the outside—that there was a significant constituency that would welcome and support newspapers published for the primary purpose of accurately and fairly reporting the news of the day. That ambition would have to be expressed in language and format dramatically different from what came to be called yellow journalism. The need for a public commitment to responsible discourse, education, ethical principles, and intellectual distinction remained an idea whose time had not yet come.

16

TRASH AND FLASH

I once proposed that philosophy departments be disbanded and that every faculty of the university have its own philosophy department, that there be one in the law school and in the medical school and in the school of journalism and the rest, to raise these questions of presuppositions, methodology and implication which philosophers are professionally prepared to raise in special ways. And I think, in part at least, it's that lacuna that's now taking its revenge on us.

—Jaroslav Pelikan,
former president, American Academy of Arts and Sciences;
Sterling Professor of History Emeritus,
Yale University

The color-me-yellow momentum might have been given other pigments, but its editorial characteristics grew out of the intense competition among mass circulation papers in America's big cities. Best known among those contests was the race between Hearst and Pulitzer in New York City at the turn of the century. William Randolph Hearst, born in California, had inherited money, property, and a newspaper from his father. The *San Francisco Examiner* was the first in a chain of papers the young and ambitious Hearst put together while creating a press empire with national influence. In 1895, he bought the *New York Journal* and went east, taking some of his staff with him. Pulitzer's new journalism had impressed Hearst, who had already adapted the breezy, aggressive style of the *New York World* for the *Examiner*'s readers with considerable success. As would often be the case in the shrill, ceaseless scramble for circulation, Hearst raided his opponent's talent roster, brandishing higher salaries. Some reporters and editors switched and the battle was on. The *World* had to lower its newsstand price to match the *Journal*'s penny. Each paper pumped up its Sunday editions with color printing, comics, sports, and splashy illustrations. Circulations climbed to 600,000—about the same for both papers. It was then that the inevitable pressure for faster and more versatile printing presses quite accidentally produced the symbolism for the sensationalist press.[1]

On Sundays, the *World* ran a half-page cartoon drawn by a man named Outcault and called "Hogan's Alley." The most prominent figure in the "Alley" was a small, smart boy in a nightshirt who tossed off one-liners about life in the big-city slums. He was known as the "yellow kid" because the paper's art department had suggested his nightshirt be printed in bright yellow. "Hogan's Alley" and the yellow kid became so popular that Hearst bought its creator, leaving Pulitzer with the problem of finding a replacement. Pulitzer, never one to accept defeat, hired a new cartoonist named George B. Luks, who provided his own version of the yellow kid. Newspaper historians generally agree that these cartoons elicited the most enduring opprobrium in the annals of press criticism. Ervin Wardman, the editor of the *New York Press*, was the first to put the term *yellow journalism* in play when he used it to refer to the editorial style of both the *World* and the *Journal*. Charles A. Dana was among the earliest and most prominent publishers to amplify that imagery, frequently citing yellow journalism as a synonym for the worst press practices. Over time the label became associated with extremes of fabrication, brutality in crime stories, gossip, and titillation. Such criticism did not, however, change many minds in the newspaper business. The profits that flowed from soaring sales figures—circulation and advertising—were, as always, the controlling factors. What was apparently not broken required no fixing.[2]

Sociologist Max Weber commented on two distinct political ethics. One was the ethic of ultimate goals, which directed statesmen to pursue an ideal system not unlike Plato's "Ideal State" described in the *Republic*. The other was the ethic of responsibility that owed much to Plato's pupil, Aristotle, who decided some 2,300 years ago that the ideal state was not possible and that political structures must aspire to something less, perhaps the best attainable in each time and place. Democracy in America had to settle for the second ethic, and nineteenth-century politicians used newspapers to communicate policy choices that could never be ideal for everyone. The themes of responsible journalism in America began with the portrayal of these choices. An inner dialogue regarding responsibility had begun in the colonial years. Benjamin Franklin wrote about the issues long before he helped Jefferson draft the Declaration of Independence.

To bring all this fast forward to the mass circulation newspapers of the early twentieth century and to their ethical standards, the point need only be made that the First Amendment protection of the press has nothing to say about truth or the right to publish it; nor does it grant the right to pillory public officials. It merely allows the press to say what it pleases, when it pleases, without seeking *in advance* the permission of the government. The laws of the land are not suspended by this protection. They are only limited to being used after the fact. The press, if it violated the law, could be held accountable *after* it published. And what of accountability for material that did not violate any law? Lurid, fabricated stories shocked the arbiters of taste, repelled the intelligentsia, and enraged the guardians of patriotic beliefs. But what accountability was there when the press abandoned its role as a sentinel for the public interest and occupied itself with prurience for the public's entertainment? It was to this concept of voluntary accountability that the critics of the press directed their most passionate essays and lectures in the 1920s. Critics would return, forty odd years later, to the importance of the press as a watchdog for crucial, evolving liberties—and return as well to the Zengarian notion of truth as a defense—but critics of the press in the decade after World War I were, it seems, more concerned with the press as teacher.

The teacher role marks the enlargement of First Amendment meaning, the importance attached to a more widely informed electorate. It was not enough that the people be informed on political matters, but they must, in Alexander Meiklejohn's words, "so far as possible understand the issues which bear upon our common life."[3] That kind of understanding required a larger scope for the nation's press. Information on foreign affairs, business, the arts, science, the environment, and more was needed if the people were to judge the longer-range effects of actions taken by public officials or of regulations put in place thoughtlessly or left in place beyond their usefulness, and if people were to judge how public lands should be used, how children should be educated, and how great music and theater and art could be nurtured. The press was seen as the only means of educating the masses so that they might best decide what was the common good. This vision of responsibility—years later H. L. Mencken called it "the swamp of uplift"[4]—was not exclusively assigned to the press. But the critics called for far greater awareness of the widened public interest and the influence of mass circulation newspapers, which were described as uniquely capable of conveying information to the largest audiences.

These considerations were a far cry from the press the Framers had known. They had advocated a press free of any prior restraints, but not above the law. The Framers knew only a highly partisan, sometimes scurrilous press, frequently a kept press in that it printed what the owner or the backers wanted it to print. Truth—albeit desirable and defendable—was not relevant to press freedom. Truth, however, was as much in the mind of the reader as beauty was in the eye of the beholder. Truth, what is more, was rarely the goal of partisan publishers. Other aspirations usually prevailed. As to accuracy and fairness, the presumed fundamental virtues of ethical reporting, there was no assumption among the Framers that the free press could be bound by such standards. Perhaps the Miltonian marketplace would examine conflicting views and, in due course, virtue would triumph, but there is no evidence that the Framers expected such commendable results. The legal system was the best safeguard, government regulation the worst. The intuition seemed to be that responsible journalism would finally be defined by what a significant segment of the citizenry regarded as a proper and appropriate performance. Entertainment features and as much advertising as the market could produce were components of newspaper-making from the earliest and smallest colonial papers to the twentieth-century behemoths. How fared the citizens?

Hearst had, in 1898, almost single-handedly created the Spanish-American War. He advertised his New York paper with the question, "How do you like the *Journal's* war?" The public seemed to like it very much, but men such as Charles Dudley Warner and E. L. Godkin did not. Said Godkin in the *Nation*: "This is an absolutely new state of things. . . . A blackguard boy with several millions of dollars at his disposal has more influence on the use a great nation may make of its credit, of its army and navy, its name and traditions than all the statesmen and philosophers and professors in the country. If this does not supply food for reflection about the future of the nation to thoughtful men, it must be because the practice of reflection has ceased."⁵

When some public figures asked for censorship of the press following the assassination of President McKinley in 1901, Godkin defended freedom of expression and rejected censorship as a remedy, but he editorialized: "The real offense of yellow journalism is . . . that it steadily violates the canons alike of good taste and sound morals, that it cultivates false standards of life, and demoralizes its readers; that it recklessly uses language which may incite the crack brained to lawlessness, that its net influence makes the world worse."⁶

Not all commentators turned on the yellow press. Allan Forman, editor of the *Journalist,* had credited the *World* and the *Journal* for "sending thousands of sick children to the seashore every summer, exposing fraud, fighting corruption."⁷ He believed able writers and compassion for the downtrodden, not the fake stories and the disregard for privacy, had attracted the multitudes. But editorials written in the same period by *Dial* saw the compassion as hypocrisy. The yellow press, said *Dial*, was "preaching virtue in such a manner that it nowise interferes with the practice of vice." The vice was, in its view, column after column of stories dealing with crime and brutality—not much of it factual.⁸ *Dial* praised the public libraries and the private clubs that had banned both the *Journal* and the *World,* and it urged readers to treat both papers as "moral outcasts." A judge writing in *Arena* called yellow journalism a tyrant with too much power that the libel laws of the time could not check. He did not advocate censorship, but he believed that providing strong, principled alternatives would attract public support.⁹

In 1900, Dr. Delos F. Wilcox, a social psychologist, analyzed 147 major newspapers in twenty-one metropolitan areas. He found 47 to be "yellow," 45 "conservative," and the rest somewhere in between. The ideal newspaper, he concluded, would be independent of private or factional interests. "Newspapers," Wilcox said, "should be responsible to society just as teachers must be."[10] George W. Alger, a prominent lawyer who wrote about journalism and the law for the *Atlantic Monthly*, stated that the yellow press was a "pernicious influence" on the courts of justice. Among other damage done, people were being "tried by newspapers" long before an actual trial, and unprejudiced juries were therefore difficult to find.[11]

According to Don Seitz, who wrote *Training for the Newspaper Trade* in 1916, Joseph Pulitzer (for whom Seitz had worked) proposed a truce. He suggested to Hearst in 1903 that both papers would raise their price to two cents, as papers in Chicago had done. Hearst wouldn't play. He continued his strident yellow tactics in every city where he had a paper and made no apology for building "an empire."[12] Pulitzer responded with alterations in his own policy. He told his editors to raise their sights. "We cannot do—may not do—what the *Journal* does in recklessness and disregard of good taste and public opinion." He ordered an end to faked reporting and a restraint on "divorce, murder, and salacious stories." He wanted to woo the kind of readers who subscribed to the *New York Times* and the *Herald,* but he wanted to hold on to the mass circulation as well. It was not an easy task and it was not ultimately successful, but Pulitzer did regain much of his reputation as a serious, responsible publisher. Those who admired him thought the man of integrity was the real Joseph Pulitzer. They were not surprised when Pulitzer established an endowment for a new school of journalism at Columbia University.[13] The groundbreaking ceremony took place in 1904, but the school was not officially opened until 1912. It was preceded by the founding of the College of Journalism at the University of Missouri in 1908. Journalism courses were at the same time being offered as part of undergraduate education in at least a dozen universities and colleges.

Nicholas Murray Butler, Columbia's president, was restrained in his expectations. He believed a journalism school could train competent newspapermen "if they have the root of the matter in them." There were then, as there have always been, journalists and academics who believed that a high-quality liberal arts degree was the best preparation for a career in journalism. The technical requirements could be learned on the job. Henry Luce, founder and publisher of *Time, Life, Fortune*, and *Sports Illustrated*, was one of several leaders in the field who preferred bright young generalists from undergraduate colleges. The most important preparation, such men agreed, was broad exposure to the humanities, some science, and a sense of the diversity of cultures a journalist might encounter in his career. Writing skills and experience in producing undergraduate newspapers were obviously helpful distinctions, but the essential intelligence, curiosity, and judgment did not spring up spontaneously when students entered professional schools—they were qualities already demonstrated by the kind of undergraduates the top newspapers and magazines wanted to hire. This view was bound to work against the success of journalism schools, but Joseph Pulitzer had offered another opinion in a lengthy analysis published by the *North American Review* in May 1904. He objected to the notion that a journalist had to depend upon "natural aptitude . . . that he must be born not made."[14] Pulitzer's educational program eschewed business management. The business office, he argued, should be kept separate from the editorial functions. He proposed a curriculum at the graduate level to include courses in law, ethics, literature, history, economics, statistics, languages, and physical sciences, along with the practical study of style, accuracy, basic journalistic principles, and the definition of news. He wanted ethical perceptions to pervade all the courses, and he hoped to see graduates who would become more distinguished for moral standards, education, and character than for moneymaking.

Harvard's president Charles W. Eliot suggested a course of study for undergraduates who wanted to go into journalism that included the intellectual disciplines Pulitzer had advocated, but he added newspaper administration and production. His was the traditional liberal arts preparation in most respects, and he thought the undergraduate newspaper was the best training ground. Oddly, Pulitzer's disagreement with Eliot was over the matter of including business instruction, and Eliot's quarrel with Pulitzer was over the need for a "professional school." As it turned out, neither Yale nor Harvard has recognized journalism as a scholarly discipline, though Harvard did establish the Nieman fellowships in 1937, which provided journalists with an opportunity to go back to college and enhance their understanding of particular areas of scholarship. Yale, in the 1970s, began a program supported by the Ford Foundation that gave talented journalists on leave a year's study at the Law School and a degree called master in the study of law. The coverage of Supreme Court cases and other judicial matters has, in the view of many lawyers and scholars, markedly improved because of this program.

George Harvey, editor of *Harper's Weekly*, offered a series of lectures at Yale in 1908 in which he defined the accomplished journalist as "the guardian of all, the vigilant watchman on the tower, ever ready to sound the alarm of danger, from whatever source, to the liberties and the laws of this great union of free individuals." For Harvey, the best journalism training required character and the dispassionate atmosphere of university life. He saw that life as not only the most suitable place in which to develop character but also the place to find the "breadth of knowledge to conduct the daily teaching of our millions."[15]

One of the crystallizing assessments of the state of the press was written in 1911 by Will Irwin in a series of articles that appeared in *Collier's*. Irwin had been a reporter for Charles Dana's *New York Sun* and then an editor of *McClure's Magazine* before joining *Collier's*. He went about his task like a modern-day investigative reporter. He spent a year traveling around the country, interviewing reporters and editors, community leaders and politicians. His assignment had been envisioned as an exposé, but what he wrote was called "American journalism's first social history." He discussed and documented the shift of power from the editorial page to the newsroom. He noted the absence of any formal code of ethics. Above all, he illustrated the gatekeeping power exercised by editors and reporters even within the borders of the owner-publishers' predilections. The editors selected, by and large, which stories would be covered, how much space each would be given, what kind of pictures, if any, and what position on what page the story would run. Reporters in the field, even when under close surveillance by editors, could exercise considerable discretion as to how and what they chose to collect as raw material for the finished product. In a historical overview Irwin observed:

> During a half century in which the press grew from a humbler, professional enterprise to a great business, turning out its millions in profits every year, there was nothing to restrain the baser members of the craft except public disgust as expressed by the withdrawal of public patronage, or the opposition and exposure of better contemporaries. This force surprised civilization; it was born without the law, its power kept it above the law.[16]

Irwin was kinder to yellow journalism than most critics. He accorded to that genre of the newspaper business the ability to improve the quality of writing, attract college graduates to its staffs, and create more newspaper readers. Between 1880 and 1921 newspaper circulation increased from 3.6 million to 33.8 million. Nonetheless, Irwin believed yellow journalism had peaked. It was declining partially because of Hearst's excesses and his personal attempt to get into politics and, more significantly, because the readers of yellow journalism grew tired of it and moved on—especially immigrants and women. Circulation records indicated that the entire yellow-journalism readership turned over every six years.[17] Irwin offered a great many insights regarding the newspaper business. Among them were these: The publisher-owner gives each paper its moral tone; reporting is part craft, part art, and good reporters have the qualities of mind and heart that help them to observe and report; the romance of reporting and the individual inspiration to express a thought in words should not be replaced by mechanical uniformity—a possible side effect of wire-service distribution.

On the brighter side, Irwin detected a kind of informal ethical consensus among good reporters and editors—for example, not publishing information picked up at a friend's house, getting permission from informants before publishing their material, and respecting privacy. He believed that the improved standards of education and training had enhanced the quality of the press in America and diminished corruption. Irwin warned against the influence of advertisers and recommended that publishers avoid close association with business or social organizations. Finally, Irwin was encouraged by the recognition among a great many journalists that there was a need to continue raising standards because journalism was achieving respectable status—if not as a profession, surely as a calling.

17

THE IS AND THE OUGHT

I think the popular impression would be that the bottom line guy, the guy in the green eye shade, comes down from some business floor and says to the editor, "You'd better not run *this* story, or you'd better run *that* story to please advertisers."

—Jonathan Alter, *Newsweek* editor,
columnist, and media critic

The attributes of a *calling* are difficult to define; even more so are its requirements. The word itself has evangelical, mystical undertones. Some journalism teachers describe journalism as a *craft* with professional responsibilities. Because the publishers, editors, and reporters who earned their living on newspapers in the preelectronic era of the media had no defined qualifications, no entrance exams or organized scholarly training, the designation as a *profession* was never formalized. It was and is impossible to define by consensus a body of knowledge aspiring journalists should study as an entrance qualification. Medicine, law, engineering, and theology have such qualifications, rightfully claim professional status, and, more often than not, require a license to practice.

For the first century and a half of U.S. history, anyone could be a newspaper publisher, editor, or reporter. It was a condition achieved by self-appointment. Compensation admittedly was more likely to depend on others, including the readers, but the regulatory aspect commonly experienced by the traditional professions was not an issue. The restraints imposed by libel actions, public opinion (violent or not), or even the ill-conceived sedition laws were not directed to the press exclusively, as were specific regulations affecting the behavior of lawyers, doctors, and engineers. Because no prior restraints were allowed by the Constitution, the opportunity and need for self-regulation became a concern of the press and more certainly of its critics. In one sense the achievement of a state of grace seemed more alluring for journalists who might choose to pursue it than for the licensed professionals coerced by the fear of suspension. In reality, the temptation toward what Madison had called "licentiousness" was apt to be far more common in the newspaper world than the glorious exercise of restraint and responsibility on a voluntary basis. That being the case, the volume of critical remonstrance in the 1920s and thereafter should not surprise.

There was, to begin with, great skepticism that the newspaper proprietors were motivated by, let alone capable of, self-restraint. Some observers—not always for unselfish reasons—advocated stiffer laws to protect privacy. Postal regulations were passed requiring a certain amount of financial information about owners and directors of newspaper and magazine companies. The idea of an endowed press, frequently put on the table, had finally received some practical attention in 1912 when Andrew Carnegie offered to support the concept, but it never developed a significant constituency and soon lost its place on the list of potential reforms.[1] The Congress, in that same year, passed the Bourne Act, which prohibited the mailing of false advertising. The dean of the College of Journalism at the University of Kansas, Merle Thorpe, observed that in 1913 alone twenty states had considered some form of newspaper regulation. Thorpe identified the four major concerns the most thoughtful critics had expressed: carelessness and inaccuracy in reporting the news; suppressing information to protect special interests; conspiring with advertisers to mislead consumers; and the excesses of yellow journalism.[2]

Although any attempt to create a licensing procedure for journalists was bound to excite fierce resistance, attempts were actually made in Illinois and Connecticut. They failed on two counts: Constitutional protection would not let such statutes stand, and there was widespread belief that the vital independence of the press should not be jeopardized. These were the surface pontifications, but despite the sanctimony, most proprietors were simply defending their turf and their profits against outside interference of any kind. Not so easily rejected was the alternative suggestion put forward by Joseph Pulitzer's son Ralph, who had become president of the *New York World*—namely, a bureau of accuracy and fairness at each paper. The younger Pulitzer had first introduced the project in a lecture at Columbia's School of Journalism, where he extolled his father's dedication to accuracy as being virtually "a religion." He told his student audience that "truth telling is the sole reason for the existence of a press at all."[3]

The Bureau of Accuracy and Fairness at the *World* published in a newsletter its ethical standards and recommended penalties for wrongdoing. Faking and chronic inaccuracy would result in dismissal of reporters. Carelessness and unfairness would receive a strong reprimand, in some cases suspension. The administration of these standards would be carried out by editors, not the bureau. The bureau's first director was Isaac D. White, a former police reporter who had previously run the legal department at the *World*. White assiduously traced libel actions to their origins and kept records that included the names of reporters and editors who had been involved. He also urged the publication of corrections and retractions in the offending newspaper as soon as possible. The consequences of such efforts were demonstrably beneficial. The process helped managing editors to evaluate staff performance, reduced libel costs dramatically by encouraging out-of-court settlements, and soothed the indignation of alleged victims by acknowledging their grievances with courteous correspondence, published corrections, or both.

The Kansas State Press Association had issued the first known journalistic code of ethics in 1910. That same year the director of New York University's School of Journalism, Professor James Melvin Lee, spoke out in favor of written codes of ethics to include monitoring of circulation claims and the prohibition of "immoral" and fraudulent ads, particularly for patent medicines. Professor Lee claimed that a written code was essential even if "we don't always live up to it."[4] One of the most eloquent exhortations for carefully wrought codes of ethics came from Oswald Garrison Villard, editor of the *New York Post*, who warned that people did not trust what they read in newspapers because the press did not put things right when they printed inaccuracies or falsehoods; nor had the press been able to break loose of Wall Street control or prevent the distortion of news, the violation of privacy, or deliberate fabrication.[5] Villard urged that a monitoring body be formed like those functioning in the law and medical associations. Without such remedies, Villard warned his colleagues, they would have to function under "baleful supervision and control" by government. Said Villard: "No achievement of huge circulations can compensate for the lack or loss of public respect."[6]

Such ideas and the texts of supporting authors were embraced by America's expanding journalism schools. By 1916 there were fifty-five schools and 3,500 students. The perception that journalism had to pursue higher goals was intrinsic to the curriculums, whatever other variables might be found. The issues, the boundaries, and the sporadically proposed ethical standards remained remarkably similar from the eighteenth century to the mid-twentieth. The advent of radio and television news did not materially alter the basic conflict between profit making and public service. Because of FCC regulations, electronic news was under the restraining necessity of meeting licensing and renewal requirements. The anomaly presented by government licensing of radio and television operations and the freedom of expression that First Amendment law had seemingly cast in bronze is a subject for a later chapter. Samuel Warren and Louis D. Brandeis (before he became a towering figure on the Supreme Court) wrote persuasively in an 1890 *Harvard Law Review* article about the paucity of "propriety and decency" in the nation's press. They suggested that the law must soon encompass a protection of "the right to privacy."[7] In an elegant phrase, the two authors observed that humankind, "under the refining influence of culture, has become more sensitive to publicity, so that solitude and privacy have become more essential to the individual."[8]

Though privacy is not mentioned in the Constitution or the Bill of Rights, Warren and Brandeis speculated that privacy would become a factor in common law and was already inherent in property law. It was inevitable, they believed, that in contrast to public life, the private life of American citizens would be protected. A century later the same concerns persist, though the line between public and private has been blurred. In many instances, honest people have disagreed on where the line should be drawn. In many others, the convenience of invoking the First Amendment or the "public's right to know" or the specter of private habits shaping public behavior wiggled the line into a corkscrew.

When Gary Hart chose to be a presidential candidate in 1983, his private life became a clamorously public matter because, the press argued, morality in the conduct of personal affairs signals the kind of political leadership the public can expect. The same rationale had permitted scathing newspaper stories about George Washington, Alexander Hamilton, Thomas Jefferson, Abraham Lincoln, and others to follow. What obviously differed in the more recent media environment was the nearly instantaneous notoriety provided by television and, conversely, the near impossibility of correcting mistakes or distortions effectively. A sordid headline in a tabloid, the lead item on the evening news, and the cackling irreverence of talk radio can and have indelibly proclaimed that which is not true—or that which is true with so many ramifications that the allegation should never have been made. Whatever the recourse—the law suit, the apology, or the correction—undeserved damage has rarely if ever been repaired. Even the best of amends can only cling to the backside of media transgressions like a tick-bird on a hippopotamus.

In 1920, Upton Sinclair financed the publication of his own book, *The Brass Check*, and later claimed it sold more than 100,000 copies. It was a rancorous attack on the press for being the toady of big business and indifferent to the rights of labor.[9] Frederick L. Allen, writing for the *Atlantic Monthly*, reviewed Sinclair's book as an "extraordinary diatribe." He rejected the author's conspiracy theory but recognized that newspaper owners, editors, and reporters too frequently saw "on which side their bread is buttered" and used "illegitimate means" to undermine whatever they disliked.[10] The irascible Baltimore curmudgeon H. L. Mencken weighed in with his predictable and justly famed acidity concerning the limitations of "*homo boobus*." Said Mencken: "What ails the newspapers of the United States is the fact that their gigantic commercial development compels them to appeal to larger and larger masses of undifferentiated men, and that truth is a commodity that the masses of undifferentiated men cannot be induced to buy."[11]

One truth the masses apparently weren't buying was the cancer of racism, despite its ugly side effects—the Ku Klux Klan, Jim Crow, the sanctimonious indifference of middle-class white America, and the depredations of urban ghettos. By and large, the mass circulation newspapers confined their coverage of such matters to crime or antisocial behavior in the Negro or "colored" neighborhoods. Racism had not yet become an economic problem, which seemed to be the only force that would move newspaper proprietors. The reformers continued to advocate better training and preparation, higher intellectual standards, and the expansion of press associations as the means of professionalizing journalism. Curtice N. Hitchcock of the University of Chicago concluded that freedom of opinion was not the issue so much as "free access to all the important facts on which opinion is to be based."[12]

Nelson A. Crawford, who wrote the first text on journalism ethics in 1924 and urged journalism schools to include the subject in their curricula, cited Walter Lippmann's concept of a "pseudo-environment." Lippmann had warned that the ideas, the prejudices, the sense of things produced in the limited self-created "pseudo-environment" must be acted upon in the *real* environment, where truth often contradicts the pictures in our heads. Crawford advocated a journalism, armed by education and high standards, that would help discover truth. He also recommended a national study of the press, privately endowed, and conducted by "a representative committee of fair-minded analysts who were familiar with the journalistic practices and would cover various sections of the country and types of newspapers."[13] It was a suggestion that may have been considered before Crawford, but his formulation would be revisited many times in the years that followed—most notably by the Hutchins Commission on Freedom of the Press, organized at the University of Chicago in 1942, about which more in Chapters 19 and 20.

The faith in voluntary and internal vigilance to control excesses, irresponsibility, inaccuracy, and fabrication seemed to evolve in the 1920s and was attributable to the growth of journalism schools, the insistent criticism published in the small magazines, and the enhanced status of journalism as a vocation. Nonetheless, reform—when it was prescribed—did not sink deep roots. That, said some pundits, was because the public demanded and got what it wanted—no more, no less. In 1928 renowned lawyer Clarence Darrow told a gathering of the American Society of Newspaper Editors that newspapermen were "lacking in high ideals in a business filled with temptations but, as such, were in tune with the spirit of the age."[14]

Silas Bent, a journalist who wrote a celebrated book about the news business called *Ballyhoo*, told the same gathering that "there is no visible evidence that editors are getting out the kind of newspapers people want." He expressed dismay that many of his former colleagues were engaged in the "selling of news like hooch." Summing up the prevailing critical views, and indeed the feelings of many critical consumers ever since, Bent railed at the big, profitable papers demanding that "they must become responsible."[15] The ASNE's (American Society of Newspaper Editors) response was defensive, but it did not reject all the charges hurled at its members. The editors vowed to work with the American Bar Association on crime coverage that would protect the innocent, provide balanced reporting, and avoid false charges. They also called for more stringent and standardized requirements at journalism schools and in undergraduate courses dealing with journalism. Mencken, writing in the *American Mercury*, had accused the journalism schools of being "too easy."[16] Other critics continued to repeat the view that journalism schools were inconsequential centers for *vocational training* far inferior to a high-quality liberal arts undergraduate education.

The themes taken up by critics were strikingly consistent. The priority given to profits was incompatible with serving the public interest. The editorial staffs were underpaid, undereducated, and unable to comprehend science, finance, international affairs, ethical perceptions, and more. The influence of the advertisers was demeaning and ultimately corrupting. Finally, said the critics, the published materials in the mass circulation press were too frequently trivial, inaccurate, incomplete, and biased to the extent that the flow of information necessary for informed decisionmaking by the citizenry was stifled, if not subverted. Hyperbole was not always absent from such critical essays, but there was also some recognition of useful achievements by the mass press—among them the dissemination of wire-service news from around the world, the marshaling of community support for charitable causes, and the provision of minimal literature for people who would otherwise have nothing at all to read.

The year 1859 had marked the death of Europe's preeminent defenders of individual liberty and freedom of expression—Alexis de Tocqueville and Lord Macaulay. In that same year Darwin published *On the Origin of Species*, one of the most significant works of science in the nineteenth century. Almost simultaneously an "obscure economist" named Karl Marx wrote his essay *The Critique of Political Economy*. In it he expounded on the materialist interpretation of history, what the world came to know as Marxism.[17] None of these writers, the British philosopher Isaiah Berlin declared, had an impact "more immediate and no less permanent" than John Stuart Mill's 1859 treatise called *Essay on Liberty*. Mill was a journalist and a politician who tirelessly and eloquently devoted his life to the expansion of individual freedom—most especially freedom of expression. Mill believed no approximation of truth could be realized without freedom of expression and particularly the expression of dissenting views. The most unpopular notions, the most eccentric, the most revolutionary, should be heard and published and examined because truth is never final, Mill said. It must be constantly disputed, enlarged by new discoveries, or altered by corrective vision.

To leave conventional wisdom untested by different or opposing ideas was to give in to a "collective mediocrity," to fall victim to "the deep slumber of decided opinion."[18] For Mill, the American concept of self-government was a fundamental right. He detested people and ideas that sought to limit the liberties of other persons by imposing their power or because they wanted conformity of thought and action or because they were convinced that how human beings should live their lives can be determined by one true standard and only one—and any deviation from it could justify legislative or regulatory action. Mill was not prophetic about the issues of nationhood, social upheaval, patriotism, and law and order that would afflict the twentieth century. His passionate but narrow focus on individual rights and his fear of spiritual obstacles to those rights left little room to consider poverty, disease, moral decay, and the other issues that confronted communities and required political consensus. For his critics, Mill left too many large questions unsettled.

The mass circulation newspapers taking shape in America in the late nineteenth century demonstrated a belief in individual freedom, but primarily in terms of the proprietors. Faceless readers were seen in gray tones, easily manipulated by the format that entertained them and appealed to their lowest level of imagination. The great issues of free expression within an ordered society were not the editorial grist for yellow journalism or for the big advertisers who regarded themselves as sponsors and underwriters of the newspapers in which they advertised. Their purpose was to sell goods and services to large numbers of consumers. Social responsibility and social problems such as racism were largely irrelevant except when the plight of the underprivileged could be dramatized sympathetically to enhance the popularity of the paper.

Pulitzer substantially broke with this pattern—first by separating the editorial page from local news, wire-service coverage, and entertainment features such as comics, crossword puzzles, and sports and then by treating the news with greater respect, accuracy, and flair. Hearst continued marketing sensationalism. The *New York Times* meanwhile maintained its standard of seriousness and the reporting of news "fit to print." Its circulation grew slowly. In Alexander Meiklejohn's view, "human interests are in constant conflict with one another, they cannot all be realized. We cannot make the common good by simply adding them together. To give play to one of them means often to deny play to others. And for this reason, the public interest cannot be merely the totality of the private interests. It is, of necessity, an organization of them, a selection and arrangement, based upon judgment of relative values and mutual implications."[19] Though Meiklejohn was describing constitutional principles in the second half of the twentieth century, his words and their meaning have always been particularly relevant to the concept of responsible journalism—descriptively and prescriptively. The function of choice in the day-to-day editing of a newspaper reaching hundreds of thousands of readers with each edition clearly involved value judgments, competing interests, and the gatekeeping power of selection.

It was in the 1920s and 1930s that critics of the press produced the analytical and sophisticated essays that took into account the rise of journalism as an industrial entity that employed many thousands and supported ancillary enterprises. The papers had become absolutely essential to the retail business in America's cities. The critics who demanded that editors ignore the concerns of advertisers may have been on the moral high ground, but they were not able to offer viable alternatives to the advertising revenue that paid most of the overhead and permitted the gradual upgrading of salaries and working conditions. What did emerge from critical discourse, journalism schools, and sporadic public revulsion—for example, to the raucous circus that descended on the Lindbergh kidnapping case[20]—was more far-reaching self-awareness in the ranks.

To attract talented, educated writers and editors, the press could not resist self-improvement. Progress in quality and standards of reporting achieved a level of prestige and status that were not easily abandoned. Lawyers and doctors were able to accumulate wealth without loss of reputation or public rebuke. It was widely assumed that professional excellence engendered well-earned rewards. The journalist had neither the license nor the record of personal service to enhance his career, and even among the most talented practitioners, the financial rewards were rarely grand. If there were no sense of mission and no public recognition, the news business could not attract competent, motivated people. The critics either neglected the effect of such economic realities or expected journalists to settle for sacrifice. The vow of poverty, however, was not openly recommended; nor were reasonable men persuaded to think of the newsroom as monastic. There were many ironies and contradictions when moral remonstrance confronted the profitable power of the press in a nation not yet two centuries old but already the citadel of democratic capitalism. What kind of appeal would move the purveyors of news toward understanding how much the still-fragile freedoms of the New World depended upon them?

18

THE CRITICS

One of the problems is that when the founders arranged freedom of the press, it was a really vile press—lying, vituperative. On the other hand, they were not all on the same side. Every faction had its press. And now the press has a monolithic quality to its opinions that I think is troublesome in a way the old press was not. All the same, I don't know what to do about that because if you start censoring for bias, you're probably in a much worse situation than you are putting up with the bias.

—Judge Robert Bork,
former circuit judge for District of Columbia Court of Appeals;
John M. Olin Scholar in Legal Studies,
American Enterprise Institute

The recognition of crucial public roles to be performed by the press and the responsibilities that evolved from this understanding had been developing in the minds of serious editors and publishers for many years. Self-awareness grew in part because of the rapidly rising industrial prosperity following World War I, but more urgently because of the depression in the early 1930s, the demagogic voices of fascism rumbling out of Europe, and the first signals of Japanese expansionism in the Far East. The news weeklies, picture magazines, wire services, and radio were coalescing into a mass communications ethos that was not yet prepared for television. News reached the marketplace of ideas primarily in the form of printed words. Despite the absence of the instantaneous "real time" coverage that the networks and CNN would bring to the world in the latter part of the century, the influence of mass communications was already being blamed for immorality, election results, violent crime, and political corruption.

It is said that when Tallyrand was told that the Russian ambassador to Paris had died, the renowned French diplomat mused, "I wonder what his motive could have been?"[1] Politicians have long wondered in the same skeptical fashion about the media wherever it has been independent and about its manipulation wherever it has not. For the citizens of a free society, the media, whatever else it could do and despite its hubris and its mistakes, became central to that "delicate balance" between government authority and individual liberty.

The critics saw themselves as the answer to those who asked: "If the press is our watchdog, who watches the watchdog?" There have been, as this chapter suggests, many savants who took on the task of watching the watchdog. A few among them, however, contributed more enduringly than others to the literature and substance of useful media criticism. It was logical that the important theoretical work would appear in the 1920s and 1930s because it was in those decades that the power of the printed press— for better or worse—was reaching its peak. The abuse of that power seemed palpable. Scholars noted the judgment Jefferson and Madison made regarding religion. The only safeguard for freedom of religion, the two Virginians agreed, was pluralism, and that condition could be achieved only if the state and religion were independent of each other. Just so, it appeared, was the case for a free press—many voices, no prior restraint. Though the Bill of Rights had not originally linked the religion clauses with free expression, it was not illogical that they be combined. Free speech in the pulpit had ranged far beyond ecclesiastical matters. The churches were, in fact, a primary source of public education in the early decades of the United States. In any event, the diverse media and its capacity to enlarge public information was bound to inspire equally diverse critics.

Among the most notable in the first half of the twentieth century was George Seldes, who began his career as a critic in 1929 with an indictment of the European press for its distortion of the news after World War I.[2] In 1935, Seldes produced *Freedom of the Press*, a study of the pernicious influence advertising and business management were exerting on the independence of news operations. One remedial measure he advocated was adding courses in journalistic ethics to the required training for newspaper reporters. *Freedom of the Press* was a widely admired work and sold well, but Seldes's next book, *Lords of the Press*, established his gift for outrage and muckraking and made him famous. Retrospective scholarship credits Seldes with making critical analysis of press performance "popular and important."[3] He accused specific newspapers of publishing stories that were inaccurate, craven, or deliberately slanted—a practice he continued in his newsletter about press iniquities called *In Fact*, which was published from 1940 to 1950. Journalism scholar Edmund Lambeth asserts that "despite a twenty year fall from grace as the result of a brief period of Communist infiltration of his newsletter, Seldes's contributions have had lasting significance." Seldes was given special (and rare) recognition by the Association for Education in Journalism (1980) and a citation from the George Polk Awards (1982) for excellence in media criticism. Though his books made the best-seller lists, Seldes did not receive a uniformly laudatory reception. Some reviewers objected to his hyperbole, others found his research imprecise, and newspaper proprietors accused him of turning on the business that had given him his start. He had covered World War I in Europe for the *Chicago Tribune*, becoming chief correspondent, but predictably, he quarreled with Colonel McCormick over matters of policy and quit to write his books.

Everette E. Dennis and Claude-Jean Bertrand, in their 1981 article "Seldes at Ninety: They Don't Give Pulitzers for That Kind of Criticism,"[4] reported that the *New York Times* and the *New York Herald Tribune* had refused to run ads for *Lords of the Press*, but it sold 150,000 copies nonetheless. Seldes wrote eighteen books in all, scores of articles, and edited his newsletter for ten years. At its peak *In Fact* attracted 100,000 subscribers. When Seldes learned that an associate had accepted a small amount of funding from the Communist Party, he vigorously denied that he was ever influenced by the party in his opinions or his writing, and there was no evidence to the contrary. The charge of venality, nonetheless, became a blemish on a crusading career. He had pioneered press criticism of the highest levels, naming owners and publishers who were selling out to advertising and financial interests while neglecting public issues and reasonable standards of responsibility. He used specific examples to demonstrate the influence on the press of powerful corporate groups such as the utilities and oil producers, and he documented the control that a few families had over major papers. Seldes shaped many of the ideas critics, in subsequent years, would embrace. Ferdinand Lundberg, for example, enlarged on several Seldes themes—among them the concentration of media power in the hands of a few. He maintained that the possibility of a real threat to a free press "from the right" was more serious than interference from the government.[5] Despite the flaws in his work, Seldes was the first major critic to be read by a large audience over an extended period. His exhortations for better-educated, higher-paid reporters and editors and for a greater emphasis on institutional responsibility in the public interest became increasingly credible to the people who cared about the integrity of the news and more respected by those who controlled the means of providing it.

Though many other writers subsequently examined the morality or the effectiveness—adverse or positive—of the large-circulation newspapers and magazines, there were two who left particularly influential bodies of work—A. J. Liebling and Walter Lippmann. Liebling wrote elegant, acerbic pieces (most of them for the *New Yorker*) that were gathered into book form and given a second life. Lippmann, who was a distinguished newspaper editor and columnist, wrote several profound books that analyzed political thought and the organization of public opinion. Lippmann's concern for the press and its importance to democratic governance earned him the highest regard of scholars and journalists—even when some of his political predictions went wrong. In his understanding and description of the dynamics that shape public opinion, and therefore politics, he provided insights that were instructive in their time and that have gained in value despite the vast growth and change in the nature of the press. Lippmann laid out his most provocative theoretical ideas in the context of printed information, but his knowledge of historical and psychological factors and the standards he advocated apply to electronic reporting with equal force.

Liebling, in contrast, rarely attended to cosmic issues, overarching principles, or psychological aspects. In eighty-two of his ninety-six contributions to the *New Yorker* called "The Wayward Press"—appearing from May 19, 1945, through April 13, 1963—his preoccupation was the skill of talented reporters and their need for independence from managerial bias. The perceived antilabor views of the establishment press was a condition Liebling decried, along with concentrated ownership and an unqualified desire for profits. He was a roving public editor sensitive to excess in style or language. Many of his columns were literary tour de forces—pithy, erudite, mordant, and unforgiving when he encountered irresponsible or sloppy reporting. Liebling alerted intelligent readers to the inadequacies of day-to-day journalism and urged his newsroom constituency to include more context and interpretation in their writing. He was an uncompromising exemplar of his most persistent recommendation—more intramural criticism—but in his time there was very little, if any, reporting on the press by the press. When Liebling died in 1963, the *New York Times* commented editorially: "He was, by his own description, a chronic, incurable, recidivist reporter and his admiration for skill in reporting was boundless. His death stills a pen that could inspire as well as wound. The press will be duller for the loss of his barbs."[6]

Strangely, Liebling had little love for columnists and apparently did not wish to include the news magazines in his purview. When William Randolph Hearst's obituaries were published in August 1951, Liebling ruminated on how the press covered the departure of one of its most flamboyant and controversial titans. His *New Yorker* account neglected any mention of *Time* and *Life* despite the fact that a *Life* magazine reporter[7] was the only press witness at Marion Davies's home in Beverly Hills when Hearst's body was rushed out to a small delivery truck and taken to a mortuary. That same reporter, later in the day, conducted an exclusive interview with the former film star who had been Hearst's companion for nearly a third of a century. "He was mine for thirty-two years," Marion Davies told him tearfully, "and whoosh—they took him away from me."

She had been sedated by her doctor when Hearst died that morning, and while she slept the publisher and all his clothes and personal possessions were removed. The Associated Press reportedly held a meeting not long thereafter to determine how two weekly magazines could hold on to a story the daily press was unable to fully report. The official news release from the Hearst Corporation made no reference to Marion Davies. *Time* was the first to report the facts, and *Life* ran a cover story and a substantial photo essay on Hearst's career. The closing shot was a full-page photograph of the bed on which Hearst had died, now neatly made with a white silk spread on which a sharp-eyed dachshund sat staring at the camera's lens. Dachshunds had always been Hearst's favorite breed, and he had once owned dozens. The dog on the bed, named Helena, was the last of them. Next to the bed, on a small table, was a photograph in a mother-of-pearl frame of Marion Davies. Scrawled across one corner of the picture was an inscription—"My love is as boundless as the sea." The words were from *Romeo and Juliet,* and the three-letter signature at the bottom was well known in the newspaper business—W.R.H. When Liebling was asked how he could have omitted such colorful information from his magazine report, he grunted, "I was only interested in newspapers."[8]

Liebling would mourn the collapse of any newspaper and fretted caustically about one-newspaper towns where the absence of competition crimped news coverage and denied reporters the option of an alternative job if they resisted editorial censorship. Any alien incursion into the reporter's territory aroused Liebling—even nomenclature. As a case in point, he was openly suspicious of academic courses that used the word *communication.* In one of his columns Liebling wrote,

> Communication means simply getting any idea across and has no intrinsic relation to the truth. It is neutral. It can be a peddler's tool or the weapon of a political knave, or the medium of a new religion . . .
> Q: What do you do for a living?
> A: I am a communicator.
> Q: What do you communicate? Scarlet fever? Apprehension?[9]

Walter Lippmann's interests were not limited to newspapers, but his free-ranging curiosity about the relationship between news and politics produced a great many perceptions and judgments that became important resources for media criticism—internal and external. Lippmann's concerns were less topical than Liebling's, and less parochial. The tidal movements in public affairs engaged his curiosity. He had studied philosophy at Harvard, helped start the *New Republic*, and written the books that made him a permanent voice in the intellectual examination of the press of twentieth-century America. In that process he formulated a core concept regarding the consent of the governed in a viable democracy. The people, he postulated, could cope with complex issues provided they were given the facts clearly and objectively by the only independent method of mass communication—the press. The converse of objectivity was a dishonest use of the press to propagandize. Lippmann recognized the necessary inclination during a war to shape the news, but the distortion of truth-telling in time of peace, he warned, would be self-defeating. "All that the sharpest critics of democracy have alleged is true," he wrote in *Liberty and the News*, "if there is no steady supply of trustworthy and relevant news. Incompetence and aimlessness, corruption and disloyalty, panic and ultimate disaster, must come to any people which is denied an assured access to the facts."[10]

Lippmann spoke of the "higher law" and of the "truly sacred and priestly offices in a democracy, the careful, accurate "ordering of news." Such theological language was not an affectation. There was an almost holy writ in Lippmann's view of the role newspapers (today he might say media) must play: "For the newspaper is in all literalness, the bible of democracy, the book out of which a people determines its conduct. It is the only serious book most people read. It is the only book they read every day."[11]

The limitations of the press were not ignored in Lippmann's canon. He realized that editors were not omniscient, not even knowledgeable on a firsthand basis regarding events and issues taking place beyond their own experience, and often in distant, unfamiliar territories. Censorship, propaganda, even patriotism, could mislead, confuse, and prevent "realistic thinking." The most formidable enemy in Lippmann's universe was ignorance. Freedom, liberty, democracy, however they were defined and sustained, required a well-informed, consenting citizenry. These were not new ideas. Lippmann appropriately used an excerpt from Plato's *Republic* as a frontispiece for his book *Public Opinion*. The excerpt was from Book 7, describing those enigmatic prisoners in an underground den who can see little more than shadows "which the fire throws on the opposite wall of the cave." It was the play of those shadows taken for reality that Lippmann feared. Suppositions, rumors, gossip, deliberate fabrication, jingoism—such were the shadows in journalism that could obscure the truth. Only independently gathered and factual information could serve the public interest. For that task, Lippmann urged the recruitment of the brightest and the best. He wanted to "bring into journalism a generation of men who will, by sheer superiority, drive the incompetents out of business."[12]

The vision of intelligent, motivated journalists pursuing truth with scientific thoroughness led Lippmann to the writing of *Public Opinion*—probably his best-known book—in 1922. The notion that masses of people could read raw information and decide what was wise had not materialized. In *Public Opinion*, Lippmann emphasized the importance of "publicists" and political scientists as organizers of reliable information that reporters and editors could turn to for help. He thought of political scientists as informed insiders who could frame the issues for the people; the press could then report those positions objectively so that the people could make a final judgment. That, too, was a flawed idealism, as time would teach. Objective reporting of official or public utterances made it possible for demagogues and charlatans—more so than dispassionate, informed insiders—to get their views amplified and disseminated until they so poisoned the atmosphere that reason and discourse could not hold their ground. It was a bitter but inescapable truth that the modern sophists, the zealots, and the hatemongers, given objective coverage (i.e., simple replication of what they said in public or shouted at rallies or insinuated at press conferences), were able to falsify the democratic process.

Despite the dampening of his belief in "the power to determine each day what shall seem important and what shall be neglected . . . a power unlike any that has been exercised since the Pope lost his hold on the secular mind," Lippmann had articulated and continued to analyze the elements of journalistic practice that would best serve the body politic in a democracy. He opted, early on, for the use of bylines and mastheads to indicate who was responsible for what. He recommended corrections and retractions when errors were made, and he conceived of open forums where readers could question editors and reporters regarding selection of facts, inaccuracy, or misrepresentation. He dwelt on the power of words taken separately or in phrases as the tools of both truthful eloquence and deceptive innuendo or falsehood. Above all, he stressed the vital importance of reliable reporting to serve the common good.[13]

In *Public Opinion* several of Lippmann's most sophisticated formulations were expressed in terms that were to be examined often and admiringly wherever journalism was studied or reflected upon thereafter. He began with his essay "The World Outside and the Pictures in Our Heads" (mentioned earlier). He argued that because the "real environment" is too big and diverse or too fleeting and bewildering, we have to make a simpler rendering of it that we can understand: "The analyst of public opinion must begin then, by recognizing the triangular relationship between the scene of action, the human picture of the scene, and the human response to that picture working itself out upon the scene of action. It is like a play suggested to the actors by their own experience, in which the plot is transacted in the real lives of the actors, not merely in their stage parts."[14]

Lippmann perceived that the world we have to deal with politically is for most people "out of reach, out of sight, out of mind." Someone else must explore it and report on it, so that we can focus a picture in our head. If that information is provided by the press, truthfully and comprehensibly, then we might actually create a "trustworthy picture" inside our heads and, in due course, act upon that image.

Lippmann came to the conclusion that the enormous complexity of gathering reliable news and the economic concerns of private newspapers required that the press have considerable outside help. No one newspaper—or a chain of them, for that matter—could afford the staff (assuming qualified people could be found) to deal with all the issues and all the debatable positions taken by public figures. In this regard he identified the most reliable sources of outside assistance: first, the political scientists; second, and perhaps less favored, the "publicists" or "press agents." It should be noted that even so learned and experienced a scholar-journalist as Walter Lippmann had not envisioned the development of the fine arts of "lobbying" and "spin" that soon made so murky the clear, factual waters in which the political scientists and nonpartisan publicist-experts were meant to swim.

The pictures in our heads are inevitably the source of stereotypes, and to this subject Lippmann gave a great deal of attention. The "good stereotype" is based upon enough accurate, truthful data to allow what is reasonably typical to stand in for what might be a more complex truth that neither time nor resources permit us to pursue. In this the press has the responsibility of providing those useful generalities that come close to the truth, that give us a basis for making decisions, if not wisely at least not self-destructively. If experience overturns our stereotypes, our stability may be damaged or we may become ostriches with portable holes or, dare we hope, we may alter our concept of truth to accommodate the correction. John Stuart Mill, we will recall, insisted that the truth is never final. It must be disputed and tested constantly. If it stands up, we can take some comfort in our stereotypes. If it is enlarged or diminished we can exult in our ability to learn and to change. If we hide or deny or simply reject demonstrable evidence that we have the wrong stereotypes, then we will suffer the remorseless erosion of our society until truth no longer triumphs and freedom withers.

Lippmann offers the thesis of good and bad stereotypes by using vivid historical examples. Though he no less than other distinguished commentators did not confront racism directly as a deep-rooted malignancy nourished stubbornly by stereotypical assumptions, Lippmann did take an unblinking look at one of history's most spurious rationales—Aristotle's defense of slavery in *Politics*, written in the fourth century B.C. Lippmann states that Aristotle begins by "erecting a great barrier between himself and the facts." The most important characteristic of an unreliable stereotype is that "it precedes the use of reason; is a form of perception, imposes a certain character on the data of our senses before the data reach the intelligence."[15] Aristotle suggested that those men who are slaves must have been intended by nature to be slaves. He avoided entirely the fatal question of whether those particular men who happened to become slaves were the particular men intended to be slaves. Slaveholders were taught to see their "chattels as natural slaves" and to observe "as confirmation of their servile character the fact that they performed servile work, and that they had the muscles to do servile work."[16] It was not Aristotle's finest hour.

The perfect stereotype, Lippmann deduces, is validated when what we see corresponds with what we expect. The problems arise quickly when that confluence is not evident. The larger problems will arise more slowly when we have been so conditioned to see only what confirms our stereotypes that we cannot acknowledge a flaw even when it is fatal. The press, in Lippmann's cosmic view, had to take into account the fact that the images it brings to the minds of individual reader-citizens must confront the "stored up images, the preconceptions and prejudices" that have been formed in these stereotypes. Early American democracy, born in a far simpler time and in almost self-contained communities where private initiative meant survival, never "seriously faced the problem which arises because the pictures inside people's heads do not automatically correspond with the world outside." Some critics of the press, Lippmann charged, expected the newspapers "to make up for all that was not foreseen in the theory of democracy" by providing the data necessary for each reader to "acquire a competent opinion about all public affairs."[17]

In Lippmann's analysis, a large segment of the press was merely reflecting, and therefore intensifying, the ignorance and confusion that shaped public opinion. This was the case because the press was not equipped to do more. The remedy he offers is to be found in its collective form among trained, disciplined, orderly practitioners of political science. In its particularized form, the remedy must depend upon brighter, better-educated reporters, experienced editors, and organized information produced by what James Madison called the "disinterested practitioners of public service." Said Lippmann nearly seventy-five years ago:

> The methods of social science are so little perfected that in many of the serious decisions and most of the casual ones, there is yet no choice but to gamble with fate as intuition prompts. . . . But we can make a belief in reason one of those intuitions. We can use our wit and our force to make footholds for reason. Behind our pictures of the world, we can try to see the vista of a larger duration of events, and wherever it is possible to escape from the urgent present, allow this longer time to control our decisions.[18]

The truth is not what journalism can report. News and truth are not the same thing; nor are facts and truth one and the same. This Lippmann recognized, but that the press should not join in the *search* was contrary to everything he believed. H. L. Mencken concurred in what was, for him, a rare and sentimental incantation: "It is a fine thing to face machine guns for immortality and a medal, but isn't it a fine thing, too, to face calumny, injustice and loneliness for the truth which makes men free?"[19]

19

FEAR AND LOATHING

The idea of objective truth is very problematical. Yes, it works at certain levels and the newspapers are accurate when they give you the ball scores. They're not so accurate when they give you the prediction of the next day's weather. You can't write history based on this—ask any historian that and they'll say they give you a sense of the temper of the times, but when you put them up against the documents and the journals and what was really taking place at the time, they're quite far off.

—Lewis Lapham,
Harper's magazine editor and columnist

In *Ballyhoo*, Silas Bent's 1927 book about the sensationalist press, the failings of the yellow newspapers were vividly revealed. *Ballyhoo* was the descriptive term Bent attached to the editorial products of Hearst and his fellow tabloid publishers. The distortions began, in Bent's view, with the Spanish-American War, but during World War I the cynicism of the mass circulation papers accelerated to the point that they sounded like "the circus broker" selling entertainment, sex, crime, sports, and polemics. Bent called for the increasingly familiar reforms most critics had agreed were necessary: more qualified editors and reporters, vigorous self-criticism, and published corrections. If the press didn't accept greater responsibility for keeping government in line and the citizenry alert, Bent warned, "regulation and inspection" would soon intervene. The public, he believed, would not defend the press against supervision, because people had little respect for the casual invasion of privacy so common in yellow journalism and the generally low level of its moral standards. Looking for a villain, Bent singled out advertising as the agent of deterioration. Advertising had made independent newspapers retreat into conformity, gutless reporting, and an emphasis on amusement.[1]

Indignation gave way by the 1930s to a more compelling campaign for higher standards. Yellow journalism was not winning the day, and though the tabloids were surviving at one end of the market, it was the "quality" press that attracted the attention of critics in the years leading up to World War II. The American Society of Newspaper Editors had, in the 1920s, tried to compose an ethical code that could apply nationally to all newspapers. The familiar excesses were rounded up, and the noble aspirations were listed. Accuracy and fairness would be the guardians of truth. There was little to argue about. All were in favor of virtue and conscience, but when the canons of approved journalism smiled, there were no teeth. "Lacking teeth," said Bayard Swope of the *New York World*, "it is a beautiful gesture that is perfectly meaningless."[2]

The toothless canons have appeared and reappeared all through the twentieth century. Many lyrical, high-minded codes have been circulated by newspapers, magazines, and television stations. They have, on occasion, reminded reporters of the nature and purpose of their craft, but they have very rarely been useful to the individual journalist under the pressure of competition, deadline, career advancement, and demanding supervisors. Above all, there is no evidence that violators were punished, editors reprimanded, publishers censured. The codes had no bite. Ethics, most journalists soon learned, begin at the top. If the proprietor articulated ethical principles and demonstrated their importance by the manner and substance of his decisions, the organization would follow. This was the conventional wisdom, and the critics, teachers, and writers of codes have tended to agree upon that point ever since. Those with any working experience in the press would also agree that young reporters starting out were "initiated into a world of moral and intellectual confusion"[3] in which it was seldom possible to find specific guidelines for any higher purpose than pleasing the editor. Filing a story that would get public attention seemed the surest route toward the editor's good disposition.

During the 1930s one standard did begin to rise out of the elevated prose of the codes and find general support in the newspaper business. It was called *objectivity*. The abstract qualities of fairness and accuracy and the apparent neutrality of reporting could link arms beneath the banner of objectivity. The criterion was single-minded, not high-minded, and the name given to it was *fact*. Somehow, a fact could stand on its own no matter what opinion or prejudice, enthusiasm or fury, might rage around it. Facts existed in reality, and truth could be constructed out of them without additives. In theory a newspaper's editorial views could be confined to one page and reporting could be separate, factual, unbiased. When Franklin Roosevelt's New Deal was introduced in 1932, the press was largely opposed to it. Newspapers were overwhelmingly conservative and their proprietors considered themselves part of America's business community. More than 80 percent had urged their readers not to vote for Roosevelt. The voters disregarded the advice—a fact that might have been used as an argument in defense of newspaper objectivity had the lords of the press cared. Surveys of newspaper readers in the 1930s consistently found the editorial page to be the least read and the comics, the most. Reporters, by and large, were instructed to operate as tabula rasa, writing first the facts, then getting opinions from people involved on both sides of an issue. The readers would, presumably, make their own judgment. (Fifty years later the *MacNeil-Lehrer News Hour* would use a similar but more informed theory for television.)

William Rivers puts a precise date on the loss of faith in objective reporting. In his book about the Washington press corps, *The Opinion Makers*, Rivers wryly reports, "Some correspondents say they can fix on the exact time when 'the old journalism' failed: the day in 1933 when the United States went off the Gold Standard. Vainly trying to report that cataclysmic and baffling change, they appealed to the White House, and a government economist was sent over to help."[4] Objectivity, measured in the statistical sense, may not have died with the gold standard, but the cry for more interpretative reporting was being heard insistently in the journalism schools and in the newsrooms. The news magazines were well into it. *Time* was a self-designated journal of opinion and offered analysis of the weekly news along with the facts. Signed columns were also emerging—particularly on political matters.

Pulitzer's commitment to accuracy and his redemptive vow in the aftermath of his war with Hearst to publish "straight, clean reporting" had helped to launch the objectivity standard. Walter Lippmann had supported the concept and was among the first to use the term *objective reporting*—in the 1920s. He brought to it, however, an intellectual dimension—the dispassionate, scientific inquiry that would search for the truth. He saw the real strength of such objectivity as flowing from an independent "trained intelligence." Lippmann wrote, in a 1931 magazine article, a valentine to the "old journalism—a romantic art dependent on the virtuosity of men like Bennett, Hearst and Pulitzer."[5] He anticipated a new form characterized by greater professionalism, a product of culture that comes only with the knowledge of the past and acute awareness of how deceptive is our normal observation and how wishful is our thinking. Frank Gannett, during the same period, urged his own editors and his fellow publishers to "go beyond the local stories and provide background and interpretation on topics of major interest and consequence to the whole country."[6] The *New York Times* emphasized the particular need for interpretation in foreign news, and *Los Angeles Times* proprietor Harry Chandler stated: "These are times when the conduct of a daily newspaper ceases to be a commercial enterprise. It becomes a stewardship that often involves great self-sacrifice and great courage."[7]

It was inescapably clear to newspaper people that radio commentators and news magazines were offering their audience more than just the facts—

they were providing explanation. The public was leaning toward supporting such an approach, and surveys indicated they were not satisfied with
their newspapers. Men such as Herbert Brucker of Columbia University
and Lester Markel, who had been the editor of the *New York Times* and
then Sunday editor, wrote and spoke—along with others across the country—about the shortfall in daily newspaper coverage. Brucker echoed Lippmann in prescribing a press policy that would seek to link two worlds—the
pictures in our heads and the reality on the ground. The first world is what
we know from experience—as with the practice of self-government that
colonial Americans had learned long before the Framers wrote that ideal
into the Constitution of the United States—and the second world, beyond
experience, is one the mass of citizens know nothing or very little about.
Brucker charged the press with the responsibility of providing information
on unfamiliar realities that could be reliably reported and nonpartisan.[8]

The distrust of the press, many modern critics believe, was engendered
by the size and power and self-interest of the large newspapers. They
seemed indifferent to the concerns of the average American. Brucker did
suggest that despite widespread editorial opposition to Roosevelt, the
newspapers helped elect FDR by their objectivity in their news columns.
Objectivity, he imagined, would ensure open debate and many voices.
Markel, who had conceived "The Week in Review" in the Sunday *Times*,
favored the educational mission. The voters were not well informed, not
educated, and therefore vulnerable to manipulation. Such ignorance was a
danger to democracy, and only more interpretive journalism could lift
public awareness and bring enlightenment into America's homes.[9] Theologian Reinhold Niebuhr, who in 1942 became one of the commissioners
gathered in Chicago to report on a "free and responsible press," later wrote
an essay "The Role of the Newspapers in America's Function as the Greatest World Power." He challenged journalism to present the facts even when
they ran "counter to our presuppositions." To place facts in the right setting would, he said, require a "moral and political imagination."[10]

No other political phenomenon brought so much disillusionment to the
followers of objectivity than the rise and fall of Wisconsin senator Joseph
McCarthy. Speaking in his relentless, droning voice, McCarthy launched an
evangelical mission to stimulate apprehensions of a Red menace threatening America's freedoms and attacking a naive society on every level with secret agents, duped liberals, and false prophets. Because the press merely repeated McCarthy's apocalyptic warnings verbatim in print and on the air,
the journalistic atmosphere became so highly charged with Cold War
rhetoric, patriotic litmus tests, and black-listing paranoia that objective reporting was inseparable from demagogic hyperbole. Congressional committees were like kangaroo courts. Newspapers and magazines headlined
accusations that could end careers, sully reputations, and injure the inno-

cent without significant recourse. Congressional immunity and First Amendment rights protected the accusers, who could hurl a vast web of suspicion over writers, teachers, entertainers, and politicians in a search for "Communist sympathizers," "pinkos," "liberal dupes," "traitors," and "spies." Those in the press and public life who dared to remonstrate, to defend themselves, to demand evidence, were few in number and became even fewer as the accusers turned on any opposition with shrill counterattacks that invoked guilt by association. Said one writer for the *New Republic,* "Under this technique, a public official can use totalitarian methods— knowing his utterances will be reported straight and that the truth will never catch up with his falsehoods."[11]

The "big lie" was bedeviling editors and broadcasters who knew better. Men like McCarthy could save their heavy charges, and did so with calculation, until very close to deadlines so that reporters had little time to check the facts. Charges of all kinds, innuendo, suspicions, and malicious personal opinions were easily mixed with accurate information. Reporters would inscribe the innuendos between quotation marks in traditional objective fashion and theoretically absolve themselves of doing any injury to the innocent or aiding the wrongdoers. Editors either held the story until some facts could be checked and thereby risked losing ground to the competition, or they ran with the story, adding mild disclaimers or using the word *alleged,* and risked their own careers. Even those who were uncomfortable with what seemed to be hysteria muted their distress. Fissures appeared in the normally level ground of American intellectual life. Angry quarrels about McCarthy's crusade took place among members of government committees, among the staffs of newspapers, and at the wire services.

At the dinner parties of the intelligentsia, fistfights had to be broken up and friendships were dissolved. The divisiveness and paranoia troubled intelligent people in the media, but even the principled and courageous hesitated before they began to ask the tough questions. The most celebrated voice, finally heard in March 1954 on CBS television, belonged to Edward R. Murrow, the chain-smoking reporter who had described firsthand on radio the horror of Hitler's blitz over London during World War II. He had moved into television in the postwar years. His clipped, calm delivery conveyed dispassionate, trustworthy integrity. His convictions and intellectual involvement created context for isolated facts. Murrow's characterization of Senator McCarthy's roundhouse accusatory swings ("I have here in my briefcase the names of two-hundred Communists in the . . . ") was disciplined, moderate, and precise. It was laudably free of angry, unreasoned indictments, but it seemed to some insiders that considerably more reservation had been brought to the famed half-hour report under the rubric of "See It Now" than was necessary. Murrow and his colleagues, subsequent articles, memoirs, and interviews confirmed, were sharply aware of the possibly harmful reverberations such a broadcast might have in Washington and among certain advertisers. CBS News needed money to do its job, and the money came primarily from management. Commercials covered only a small part of production costs for news and public affairs programs in the 1950s. But the network's fortunes overall depended upon advertisers, and upon public opinion expressed in the form of so-called ratings.

At Time, Inc. and in other media companies, similar calculations were being made—sometimes fearfully—concerning advertiser reactions to news stories, postal rates, government licensing of broadcast stations, and the power of a few zealous columnists who could fire off broadsides or roil the muddy bottom of Madison Avenue dealmaking with insinuations about left-leaning sympathies. Before truth or principle, it was said, came the bottom line. The higher purposes of the press and the truth-telling responsibility to the readers and viewers needed leaders in press management who were prepared to take risks, to gamble on the long-term support of the public once reason and balance had triumphed. That was too large a gamble for most media executives. Ironically and fittingly, the McCarthy hysteria was hoisted on the same two petards that had provided its original power of intimidation—the government and the press. Ultimately, congressional hearings were conducted on a number of the senator's accusations about public officials. He was confronted, finally, by some of his victims and in particular by an able, disarmingly civilized Boston lawyer named Joseph Welch who had the temerity to ask the senator about unambiguous evidence and raise the question of basic decency—a quality Welch seemed to virtually embody in his client's defense.

The junior senator from Wisconsin had dominated front pages and been at the top of the network newscasts of the 1950s, but he was fatally revealed by the live television coverage of congressional hearings—a form of journalism not nearly so common then as it is now. The effect of those exchanges on public opinion was profound, but the demise of the "witch hunt" did not take place quickly. The guardians of American patriotism were reluctant to yield the tocsins they had sounded against the Red menace to the tedious deliberations of due process. But the decline of strident, punitive anticommunism and vindictive prosecution by publicity that clouded First Amendment rights was inexorable. McCarthy's career sputtered. He spent his last days in Walter Reed Hospital, where he died in 1957 at the age of forty-eight ravaged by drink and emotional tension. His search for communism under domestic beds was discredited. The Cold War engaged America's resolve and billions of its dollars, but the dangers were now reported in distant lands—Eastern Europe, Africa, the Middle East, Southeast Asia—not inside the American government.

The press learned much from the McCarthy experience. Mere repetitions of statements by public figures, while safe, were no longer considered accurate if accuracy was meant to find truth. Interpretation was more widely and openly embraced, and the goal required looking behind the facts. The late, great radio commentator Elmer Davis, often quoted in the literature of press ethics, observed in 1952,

> The good newspaper, the good news broadcaster, must walk a tight rope between two great gulfs—on one side the false objectivity that takes everything at face value and lets the public be imposed on by the charlatan with the most brazen front; on the other, the 'interpretative' reporting which fails to draw the line between objective and subjective, between a reasonably established fact and what the reporter and editor wishes were the fact. To say that is easy; to do it is hard.[12]

For example, Soviet intelligence records released since the advent of *glasnost* have cast new and corroborative light on some of McCarthy's allegations.

Among the highbrow newspapers and magazines, interpretation of the news became a common undertaking. Interpretation had as many shadings as there were writers and editors who were determined to impose a perspective or bias on each major story. The conventional facts were not to be neglected, but background was added, arcane terms employed by economists and scientists were explained, and when possible, the context in which a story had evolved was provided. Experienced editors kept the door open for changes and updates. The theoretical aspect of reporting what appeared to be the truth on any particular day wisely allowed for subsequent additions or deletions. The advantages of just-the-unvarnished-facts journalism had once been broadly accepted, and as strict objectivity was discarded, the need for some other kind of consensus arose. The notion that cold, flat facts without elaboration was good journalism became "socially complacent."[13] The standards that began to emerge out of interpretation were based on the importance of the story to society as a whole and on the depth of research and preparation. Such standards amounted to "social responsibility" in one way or another, and the academics, the critics, and the spokespersons for the more prominent media groups refined the discussion, which had begun in the 1890s, in terms of what *definition* of responsible journalism would be accepted by most publishers. Aristotle's golden mean was somewhere between objective detachment and subjective interpretation.

Could journalists write responsible, interpretative news accounts that went beyond the simplistic who-when-what-and-where in a way that illuminated political and social complexity? For many, this was the appropriate challenge. Ben Bagdikian, whose experience as a reporter, ombudsman, and educator made him a credible witness, observed that journalism is "essentially subjective" and "value laden." In his view, the widespread adoption of so-called objectivity had created a journalism that was superficial, "official and establishmentarian."[14] The critics of this institutional bended-knee reporting pointed out that the media's first decision on any assignment involves choices—what will be reported and what will not—the gatekeeper role. The editors will decide how the material will be handled—the tone, the pictures, the headlines. These choices are clearly laden with values, Bagdikian insisted. And when important public issues are covered, objectivity demanded that all attributable sources be identified. Since the sources were primarily government officials, the press became, in the words of one *Washington Post* editor, "more conduit than critic of government."[15] I. F. Stone, who produced for many years his own independent commentary on politics and social issues in a well-known newsletter, said, "Objectivity is fine if it's real. . . . Every society has its dogmas and a genuinely objective approach can break through them. But most of the time objectivity is just the rationale for regurgitating the conventional wisdom of the day."[16]

Statistical research confirmed in the 1980s that the great preponderance of sources cited in front-page stories of the *New York Times* and the *Washington Post* were the same groups—U.S. government officers, foreign officials, public figures. Less than one of five sources were "typical citizens, scholars, labor leaders, political activists, environmentalists, etc."[17] At the end of the day—if the press was given its special constitutional protection to encourage public discussion, debate, and exchange in the interest of a healthy democracy—objectivity had failed. For the Commission on Freedom of the Press, which began its investigation in 1942 and published its report in 1947, the heart of the matter was recognizing the solemn *obligations* of a constitutionally protected press.

The commission was not an academic enterprise, though most of the commissioners were distinguished academicians. It was a carefully planned, highly promising response to widespread criticism within and outside the world of journalism. The Roosevelt years created social ferment and political partisanship that the United States had not experienced before on such a scale. Within the tumult of public policies introduced by an activist government, the American press encountered its own crisis atmosphere. The New Deal legislation frightened publishers of newspapers and magazines. On editorial pages and at corporate meetings, the proprietors spoke out against Roosevelt almost uniformly. If legislation to improve working conditions was passed, the newspapers would have to pay higher wages, provide better working conditions, and face the potential invasion of union organizers. Reporters and editors were increasingly conscious of their tenuous job security. The attempt to report fairly on events and issues the employers had already decided to oppose or support could mean dismissal. Without professional status, reporters and editors were hired and fired as if they were laborers. However eloquent their ethical codes of operation, very few newspapers provided appeal mechanisms for employees, and there was little or no enforcement of editorial standards.

Newspaper chains were growing larger, but the number of newspapers overall in America was diminishing. By 1935 there were sixty-three chains that owned 328 papers—about 40 percent of total national circulation.[18] Local reporting suffered wherever chains took over because more wire-service material and canned editorials replaced knowledgeable reporting on local matters by journalists with working experience in the community. Chains also tended to increase the number of one-newspaper towns because they could push the smaller or less affluent competing papers to the wall. The identity crisis among newspapers was agitated by the critics. Some threatened the long arm of government interference; others accused the press of a monolithic opposition to social programs. The more attentive public constituencies were left to wonder whether their newspapers were vigilantly watching for abuse of power or merely protecting their own. One certain casualty was the movement toward greater professionalism and common standards, which was virtually halted. The perception was widely shared that newspapers—once the combative, partisan voice of one or another segment of voters, later the objective purveyor of raw facts the reader could judge in his or her own good time—were now becoming large, aloof business interests managed by corporations with faceless boards of directors. The failure of every attempt to establish some criteria for the practice of journalism—licensing, entrance examinations, press councils with enforcement authority—and the impracticality of ethical codes that were inadequate to day-to-day newsroom pressures placed the press in the center of a troubling dilemma. Marlen Pew, of *Editor and Publisher*, found that the press was "reeking with doubt and insecurity." Dean Carl W. Ackerman of Columbia's Journalism School made a list of nineteen charges he had heard from what he called an "intelligent minority." The complaints were directed at individual papers but also at the press in general. They provided a litany of familiar fault lines—sensationalism, bowing to special interests, glorifying crime, invasion of privacy, incomplete or false accounts, and so on. Said Ackerman philosophically, "What our critics desire is a superhuman institution."[19]

The responses of the proprietors by the end of Roosevelt's first term were angry and alarmed. They feared the loss of autonomy, but they feared more the deterioration of modern capitalism. Newspapers were privately owned businesses. Their survival and prosperity depended upon a free enterprise system they were certain Roosevelt was out to destroy. *Chicago Tribune* publisher McCormick wisely counseled restraint, which did not come to him easily. As chair of the American Newspaper Publishers Association's Freedom of the Press Committee, he advised his colleagues not to use the First Amendment to excuse meager wages, excessive hours, and child labor. The inclination to ignore employee rights had opened the door to Newspaper Guild organizers. The guild argued that because reporters were not professionals, they could and should be organized as skilled craftspeople.[20] Publishers fought Roosevelt on the suspicion that he wanted to control the press, and they fought the guild on the ground that guild members would become biased in favor of labor. Critics of the "press lords" accused them of using such arguments as a smoke screen for their own economic interests.

There was, unquestionably, a growing disconnectedness between the body politic of readers and the newspapers they once depended on for a sense of security, particularly for the exposure of corruption in government. Gerald W. Johnson of the *Baltimore Evening Sun* wondered whether the public would care "when freedom of the press is actually threatened with invasion."[21] If the public was disenchanted with the press, the political powers might hack away at the First Amendment with impunity. That view and similar alarms resonated in the executive offices of the media, and the concern intensified when Roosevelt was reelected with nearly 61 percent of the vote. The *New Republic* conducted a study of voting patterns and newspaper coverage. It concluded that the press was "unrepresentative of its readers" because its management was too far removed. Radio, according to the study, was an inconsequential factor. Furthermore, the only remedy for the lack of rapport between the public and newspapers was a revolt by the subscribers. This was not an unlikely suggestion, coming as it did from the *New Republic*, but it was also not without substance as a market reaction—provided the public could find alternatives.[22]

During Roosevelt's second term a number of important judicial decisions went against the press (e.g., *Associated Press v. Walker*). The president himself spoke out on numerous occasions about press bias and incompetence. He advocated the strictest objectivity as a goal for reporters and disapproved of subjective journalism. His jubilant supporters spoke of the "waning power" of newspapers, and the chair of the FCC, James Lawrence Fly, ridiculed radio news. At the annual meeting of the National Association of Broadcasters, Fly told a press conference that radio reminded him of "a dead mackerel in the moonlight—it both shines and stinks." Meanwhile, a well-known Republican editor, William Allen White, who was serving as president of the American Society of Newspaper Editors, told the members they had better take a look at their own policies and performance instead of putting the blame on government.[23]

It seemed to Henry Luce that it was high time the press reviewed the events that had so lowered the reputation of news organizations in the public opinion polls. He wished to see an independently organized evaluation of the media that would recast the importance of a free press in a democracy. It was then that he asked Robert Hutchins to head a commission on the freedom of the press. He donated $200,000 from Time, Inc. to the undertaking. Hutchins, who had been dean of the Yale Law School at twenty-eight and president of the University of Chicago at thirty, was now serving the university as chancellor. Literary critic and writer George Steiner, who came to America from Europe to study at Chicago as an undergraduate, believed Hutchins had made the university the best institution of its kind. He was, said Steiner, a leader suffering from an "inebriation with excellence" that "set ablaze every aspect of an undergraduate's day."[24]

Hutchins and philosopher Mortimer Adler had formulated a core curriculum for students and adults alike. The core was made up of classic texts and was called the Great Books program. Hutchins said, "This is more than a set of great books, and more than a liberal education. Great Books of the Western World is an act of piety. Here are the sources of our being. Here is the West. This is its meaning for mankind. Here is the faith of the West, for here before everybody willing to look at it is that dialogue by way of which Western man has believed that he can approach the truth."[25] There must have been in Henry Luce's selection of Robert Hutchins to conduct a study of the free press some sense of the quest for truth in journalism that parallels the quest of great universities. Hutchins recalled the offer in a dispassionate opening paragraph in his foreword to the final report: "In December, 1942, Henry R. Luce of *Time, Inc.* suggested to me an inquiry into the present state and future prospects of the freedom of the press. A year later this commission, whose members were selected by me, began its deliberations."[26]

The disinterested pursuit of truth about the state of the press—a term the commission used to cover all existing media—was carried out by a group of scholarly men. That there were no women and no black or Hispanic Americans among them does not diminish the quality or the luster of Hutchins's appointments, though one suspects the composition would be more inclusive if Hutchins were beginning today. The vice-chair was Zechariah Chafee Jr., professor of law, Harvard University. The eleven commissioners were John M. Clark, professor of economics, Columbia University; John Dickinson, professor of law, University of Pennsylvania; William E. Hocking, professor of philosophy emeritus, Harvard University; Harold D. Lasswell, professor of law, Yale University; Archibald MacLeish, former assistant secretary of state, librarian of Congress, poet and playwright; Charles E. Merriam, professor of political science emeritus, University of Chicago; Reinhold Niebuhr, professor of ethics and philosophy, Union Theological Seminary; Robert Redfield, professor of anthropology, University of Chicago; Beardsly Ruml, chair, Federal Reserve Bank of New York; Arthur M. Schlesinger, professor of history, Harvard University; George N. Shuster, president, Hunter College.

From 1943 through most of 1946 the Commission on Freedom of the Press, in full session or in smaller committees, heard in depth the comments and suggestions of fifty-eight men and women connected with the press. The commission's staff of four (including one woman) recorded interviews with 225 members of industry, government, and private agencies concerned with the press. Finally, the commissioners held seventeen two- or three-day conferences among themselves and reviewed 176 documents prepared by staff members or one of the commissioners. Hutchins suggested they confine their report "to the role of the agencies of mass communication in the education of the people in public affairs." He advised that a similar study might well be made of the "inter-relationship between the American press and American culture," which would further illuminate how mass communication has become a part of the "American environment."[27]

There were several references to race relations, though not with emphasis, in the commission's final report. The fact that it recommended "the projection of a representative picture of the constituent groups in society" as a basic principle for modern journalism was the nearest it came to a serious focus on racism. Hutchins, during the press conference following publication, included race relations among the important topics to be considered. What emerged from all the discussions and position papers, and indeed from a good many drafts and rewrites designed to achieve a text on which all the commissioners could sign off, was a remarkable document that seemed to please no one. The six "special studies" written by commissioners and staff members, including Chafee's highly respected *Government and Mass Communications*, amplified certain points of view, but the general report, compiled from analysis and recommendations gathered in large part during World War II, was described twenty years later by James Boylan in the *Columbia Journalism Review* (summer 1967) as "in a sense a post-war charter for the press."

Chairman Hutchins acknowledged the report's limitations: "The Commission's recommendations are not startling. The most surprising thing about them is that nothing more surprising could be proposed. The Commission finds that these things are all that properly can be done and that the neglect of them, which now imperils the freedom of the press, should be replaced by a serious and continuing concern for the moral relation of the press to society."[28]

20

THE WEIGHT OF OBLIGATIONS

Going back to the First Amendment, it's a right *and* a responsibility, as I'm sure everybody agrees. With our rights to be free come some responsibilities to use those rights. And I think some of the responsibilities include being a son-of-a-bitch at times, to the local bank in town or the local polluter in town, or whatever.

—Ed Diamond, former *Newsweek* editor;
professor of journalism, MIT and NYU

The "moral relation of the press to society" has been the grist of dialogue—and diatribe—in the United States for as long as the nation has existed. When the University of Chicago published in 1947 the general report of the Commission on Freedom of the Press, it printed on the title page a remark made by John Adams in 1815: "If there is ever to be an amelioration of the condition of mankind, philosophers, theologians, legislators, politicians, and moralists will find that the regulation of the press is the most difficult, dangerous and important problem they have to resolve. Mankind cannot now be governed without it, nor at present with it."[1]

Henry Luce, whose editors had helped to make Robert Hutchins famous, was not thought to be philosophically attuned to the outspoken university president's views, but he nonetheless selected Hutchins to organize a comprehensive study of the press as an institution, hoping—perhaps expecting—that a ringing reaffirmation of first principles would emerge. The founder and publisher of *Time* and *Life* not only provided most of the funding but agreed to keep hands off. He waited for an invitation to speak to the esteemed group of intellectual paladins Hutchins had assembled and, after that, kept his distance as promised.[2]

During his one meeting with the commissioners, Luce discussed his view of their ruminations. "It is important to produce a broader understanding," he said, "in the democratic society as to the agreed standards and the responsibilities of the press." He declined to suggest any specific agenda, expressed his confidence in the commissioners, and reminded them—and in effect his colleagues everywhere—that "you can't talk about freedom without postulating a theory of responsibility."[3]

Not surprisingly, it was responsibility that resonated throughout the ultimate report, but it was the commission's suggestions as to how press responsibility could be ensured that aroused the greatest resistance. Hutchins set out to determine what forces were limiting freedom of expression in the media—by which he meant printed press, radio, and documentary or news film. Nearly fourteen years earlier, the "boy wonder of higher education" had been asked to speak at a convention of the American Society of Newspaper Editors as part of an effort by the society to consult with cultural leaders. Hutchins had made his disdainful opinion of journalism quite clear on a number of earlier occasions, but at the 1930 convention he spared no one. As a preface to his prepared remarks, he scolded his hosts for not introducing him as a lawyer and for giving him an incorrect middle initial in the printed program. He then went on to describe the members of the collective press as "individuals weak in mind and low in character" who were "totally defective in that scientific spirit, which should be the principal trait of all great men." As for the notion that journalists could be in some sense teachers, Hutchins growled with contempt. If Americans relied on the press to educate people," he said, "it would take a long time."[4]

Hutchins's sentiments were not unknown among the proprietors of the American media, but there does not appear to have been any defensiveness or suspicion in the testimony of those dozens of practitioners who were interviewed by the commission. If senior figures in the business recalled Hutchins's 1930 critique with any residual resentment, there was no evidence of it. There was, however, a chill in the air from the very moment the Hutchins report went public. Henry Luce made no official comment, but his associates confirmed that he was disappointed.[5] A. J. Liebling's review of the report found it to be too tepid. Very few newspapers reported on its substance. Editorials did not appear. Columnists neither fulminated nor commended. The small magazines described the report's major exhortations with little fervor one way or the other. Why? Possible answers will follow. Revisiting the report should come first.

The language is scholarly, faintly legalistic, philosophical, and rooted in intellectual history. Those characteristics were to be expected considering the backgrounds of the commissioners. The ideas unfold in an orderly fashion and, taken in layers, fit into each other like a Matryoshka doll. The first layer describes the problems and deals with large principles born out of the American experience. In the colonial years, as discussed earlier, freedom of the press and speech were closely linked. Small newspapers served small communities, and for those who did not read there was always the talk at the tavern or at the church or on the street. The opportunity for politicians to get their views printed involved either acquiring a printing press or engaging a publisher's support. More than a century later, A. J. Liebling would say, however ironically, "Freedom of the press is guaranteed only to those who own one."[6]

To explain the need for its disquisition, the commission pronounced three ground-level reasons the press of 1947 was in trouble: First, the organs of mass communication were *increasingly* important to the people in a democracy, but access to their facilities was *decreasingly* available to those who were not in the mainstream; second, those who owned and controlled the facilities were not adequately serving the people; third, in their use of facilities, those in control had practiced many kinds of distorted journalism "the society condemns." Society, the commission warned, would take steps—politically or legally—to wrest control if changes were not made by the press establishment.

The commission attributed the vulnerability of a free press to profit-seeking economics, the "industrial organization of modern society," and the failure of proprietors to understand the role of the press and its closely related *responsibilities*. The remedy, the commissioners agreed, was not government. Freedom of expression is always in jeopardy because those in power will want to suppress views contrary to their own. If mass communication is harnessed by those with hidden agendas, the media can "spread lies faster and further than our forefathers dreamed." Hitler and Stalin may not have studied the media manipulation utilized by American demagogues in the twentieth century—Father Coughlin, Senator McCarthy, and Alabama governor George Wallace among them—but the Big Lie is useful to all who would censor, intimidate, or take over and all too frequently to those who employ press agentry, photo ops, and political lobbying in shaping opinion to the left or to the right for money. Wallace, in particular, reveled in conflict with the press, using his microphone at political rallies to goad and ridicule: "The national press, now anything that's bad about yo guvnah, oh yes, they gonna run that."[7]

Echoing Walter Lippmann, the commission observed that the masses get their "picture of one another" through the press. If society must live by "self-restraint, moderation and mutual understanding" (or die by the opposite), the press is crucial to the creation of a "world community" by helping to provide both knowledge and context for a free society at home and abroad.[8] In the former Soviet Union, such cosmic notions are now debated by journalists who are suddenly and bewilderingly unfettered. The Russians have not had the advantage of America's colonial experience that included a largely independent press, but they have seen since glasnost in the 1980s a proliferation of newspapers and magazines ranging over a colorful spectrum of political views and polemics. Because the government still owns much of the printing and paper industries and subsidizes the major newspapers and television networks, there is always a self-censoring fear of allowing too vigorous criticism of official actions. In the 1996 elections the press, by and large, supported candidate Yeltsin not merely because of government controls but because many mainstream editors and commentators, including those who did not regard Yeltsin with much respect, opted to support him so as to prevent a possible return of communism and extreme nationalism. Writers and commentators who have enjoyed a large measure of independence were certain that their own careers—and perhaps personal safety—would be threatened by a resurgence of communist authority. Some of those journalists made plans to leave the country if necessary. The effect of nearly unanimous support for Yeltsin in the press was apparent in the polls. The money contributed by private banks and companies flowed more readily to the Yeltsin campaign than to his opponents—though there was some early hedging by these same organizations. It should be noted as well that campaign commercials and media events created by Yeltsin's advisers studiously borrowed the techniques used by American political consultants, who were secretly closeted in a Moscow hotel.

A case could be made that Russia and the so-called republics that have broken away from the Soviet Union have, in the 1990s, entered a period of experiment and adjustment not unlike that which faced the United States a little more than 200 years ago. Regional interests, political self-dealing, and a fear of central authority nearly prevented the formation of union in America. Many of the political issues inherent to federalism, and the importance of private property in a concept of self-government, are stirring passions in Eastern Europe and Russia that are not unlike the partisan politics in America following independence. It was reported in the early 1990s that Russian translations of the *Federalist Papers* sold out in St. Petersburg—known under the Communist regime as Leningrad. The once thoroughly controlled and slavish Soviet newspapers and magazines, and the television newscasts, are at the center of the effort to give the Russian people an understanding of their new power as citizens and how to use it against those who cling to authoritarianism.

The ultimate function of a responsible press is to act as sentinel over abuses of power, public or private. The sentinel that stands guard for the freedom of press, speech, and expression—artistic, religious, or political—protects not only liberty in the form of knowledge but all our other liberties as well. The government, said the commission, supports the process through the administration of the laws. The commissioners invited controversy of many kinds when it described the terms of government involvement. The government belongs to the people, they said, and it must limit its interference to those forces and actions that *prevent* freedom of expression. The temptation to "manage the ideas and images entering public debate" is always great, not least because those in power wish to keep their jobs.

The thoughts of James Madison and Alexander Meiklejohn enter the commission's elegy to principle. Freedom of expression is vital on three

counts: first, to support the political process, which requires a well-informed electorate; second, to permit the airing of ideas that for many citizens is an *obligation* to the community, to truth, and to their consciences;
third, to encourage *public discussion,* which is absolutely necessary to a
free society, and *freedom of expression,* which is absolutely necessary to
public discussion. The commission describes "the duty of the individual
thinker to his thought" and the cumulative nourishment diverse expression
brings to public discussion, to education, "to a mentally robust public,"
and finally to the participation of individual citizens as a sovereign people.

The commission observed, "To protect the press is no longer automatically to protect the citizen or the community. The freedom of the press can
remain a right of those who publish only if it incorporates into itself the
right of the citizen and the public interest. . . . The press must be *free from*
the menace of external compulsions from whatever source. . . . The press
must be *free for* the development of its own conceptions of service and
achievement. It must know that its faults and errors have ceased to be *private vagaries* and have become *public dangers*" (emphasis added).

In 1975, Justice Potter Stewart, speaking at the Sesquicentennial Convo-
cation of the Yale Law School, stated that the Framers intended the press
clause to guarantee "the institutional autonomy of the press." Stewart believed the First Amendment clause was a "structural provision" that provided for a "fourth institution outside the government to check the potential excesses of the other three branches." The separate entity had been
given its name by Edmund Burke in the nineteenth century when he told his
colleagues that there were three estates in parliament: commons, lords, and
the Crown. "But in the Reporters' gallery yonder, there sat a *Fourth Estate*
more important than they all."[9]

It was this autonomous Fourth Estate that the commission was examining in the light of what seemed to them in 1947 a defining period for the
free press. Certain principles, the commission agreed, were timeless, but
freedom of the press was "not a fixed and isolated value, the same in every
society and in all times." It could vary with the conditions of society and
public opinion. Jefferson's homage to free expression spanned the years but
did not and could not anticipate the changes in access to "the marketplace
of ideas." He wrote: "The basis of our government's being the opinion of
the people, the very first object should be to keep that right; and were it left
to me to decide whether we should have a government without newspapers
or newspapers without a government, I should not hesitate a moment to
prefer the latter. But I should mean that every man should receive those papers and be capable of reading them."[10]

Because of the growth in population, technology, and the profitability of
the press, the right of free expression, in the commission's view, had lost its
"earlier reality." Constitutional protection no longer ensured "that a man
who has something to say shall have a chance to say it." The proprietors of

the press "determine which person, which facts, which versions of the facts, and which ideas shall reach the public." A responsible press, the commission declared, must be *accountable* to society, to public needs, and to "the almost forgotten rights of speakers who have no press." It may have been a neologism to some publishers, discomforting at the least, to read the commission's judgment that the press must reckon "its moral right will be conditioned on its acceptance of this accountability. Its legal right will stand unaltered as its moral duty is performed." With that in mind and having enumerated the abiding principles of responsible journalism, the commission proceeded to lay down five fundamental requirements "of a free, self-governing society." These requirements became the most enduring legacy of the commission's study:

1. A truthful, comprehensive and intelligent account of the day's events in a context that gives them meaning.
2. A forum for the exchange of comment and criticism.
3. A projection of a representative picture of the constituent groups in the society.
4. The presentation and clarification of the goals and values of the society.
5. Full access to the day's intelligence—diverse opinions and wide distribution.

The commission emphasized its belief that the ideals represented were not easily fulfilled; nor was it likely they ever would be. No single newspaper or magazine or broadcaster alone could achieve all five standards. It was noted, however, that the ideals were drawn largely from practices and goals submitted by contemporary press managers.[11]

The commission's prescription was a tough challenge. If taken in the context of private enterprise, the medicine could price most of the media right out of the market. For those managers who saw duty as a straight line to profit and public service as a luxury, not an obligation, the report of the commission was unrealistic and ominous. Fear of government intervention was the proffered explanation for the chilly response the report received at management level. The less influential editors and writers who believed the press had to raise its sights commended the spirit, if not all the details, of the report, but the public found little news of it, either pro or con, in the mass media. In the years since—half a century—the commission's recommendations have been revisited in journalism schools and at a few think tanks to little effect.

The trade paper *Editor and Publisher* complained early on about the commission's secrecy. The commission defended confidentiality as necessary "to insure frank discussion," as did the Framers in 1788. Privacy was sustained, and it was not until 1946 that part of the commission's summation went public. A separate study called *Peoples Speaking to Peoples*, assembled by Llewellyn White and Robert D. Leigh (respectively assistant director and director of the staff) called for an international agency to be formed by the newborn United Nations for the purpose of reporting violations of peace treaties and keeping an eye on media that were "fulminating discord." John S. Knight, then president of the ASNE, joined other media officials in warning that such a body would have censorship proclivities and would subject American reporters to the judgment of foreign reporters. The agency, he feared, would be in a position to say what was acceptable and what was not, thus threatening the independence and responsibility of individual reporters. The AP, UP, and INS (International News Service) considered their own reporters more than competent enough and surely not inferior to those an international agency might select. As to the general observations of *Peoples Talking to Peoples* regarding equal access to news and distribution, the ASNE insisted it had already taken the same stands in its own campaign for world press freedom begun in 1945.[12]

When the comprehensive report *A Free and Responsible Press* was published in March 1947, an advance press release gave away enough to set media teeth on edge. It seemed clear to a great many editors that the commission was going to recommend a national monitoring organization to watch the watchdog and that the government would be urged to intervene if the press did not clean its own house. The perception of many executives was that no matter how high-minded the intentions, the result would be regulation. Even before a full examination of the text was made and the commission's disclaimers regarding government intercession were heard, the media was mobilizing opposition.

In its conversations with practitioners, the commission had concluded that government was *not* the remedy, but it also concluded that merely revealing government secrets or propaganda was not the measure of responsible press performance. The two major shortcomings in press operations that prevented professionalism, said the commissioners, were the lack of defined and accepted standards and the ability to enforce them. The report was meant to be purposefully directed at the *proprietors* and *managers* of the press, not at working editors and reporters. Chairman Hutchins publicly stated the commission's support for private ownership, but he reiterated the concern for improvement in many areas, including more rigorous criticism (and self-criticism) of the press. Race relations, labor relations, and overarching national and world issues were not adequately covered, according to the commissioners. The targeted audience was less than enchanted by such commentary. They were irritated, justifiably, by the omission of material about existing ethical codes and the consensus in the news business about the importance of accuracy. There were mutterings that leftist groups, conspiring to stimulate government regulation of the press, had been given too much voice in the report. A *Chicago Tribune* writer, Frank Hughes, produced a book called *Prejudice and the Press* that suggested the commission was so inclined to the left that its findings were Communistic.[13] The records show that there was considerable internal debate in the preparation of the commission's final version of *A Free and Responsible Press*, but fair-minded readers would agree that its tone was liberal by the standards of the day. The published version had been shorn of many contentious passages so as to achieve unanimity with, Hutchins added, "the inevitable caveat that, if each [commissioner] were to employ his own language instead of speaking with a common voice, the tone and emphasis at this or that point might be somewhat different."

There is no doubt that Archibald MacLeish would have liked to have seen more emphasis placed on *accountability*. He believed the bosses needed to be accountable to their readers and not merely to the business world. MacLeish joined his fellow commissioners in recommending a citizens' council of some sort to monitor press performance nationally. This was one of the two most sensitive points—the other being the implication that government might have to intervene. The commission advocated a triangular partnership of the press, the people, and the government in the effort to preserve free expression. The people would be represented by the citizens' council—a totally independent body that would be funded by private foundations and would locate its offices at a major university. The council would help the press "define workable standards of performance," ensure press service in every community, work toward securing access for minority groups, cooperate with international agencies, investigate deliberate distortion and inaccuracy, monitor all government actions "affecting communications," help establish centers of study and research, promote and publicize all the actions taken in regard to these purposes.

The reaction to the proposed council was wary and largely negative. As has so often been the case, the powers that be rejected outside interference. They could do their own reforming and surveillance internally. Anything else would be censorship. What is more, cried the naysayers, they would not give up editorial judgment or the right to choose the stories they wanted to run. In their view, the commission threatened basic rights with its notion of "common carrier" status. What the commission actually said was as follows:

> The growth of the press acts together with the growth of the nation to make more remote the idea that every voice shall have the hearing it deserves. Concentration of power substitutes one controlling policy for many independent policies, lessens the number of major competitors, and renders less operative the claims of potential issuers who have no press. For this clash there is no perfect remedy. There is relief, to the extent that the wider press, *somewhat as a*

common carrier, assumes responsibility for representing variant facets of opinion. (emphasis added)[14]

The commission completed its report as the Roosevelt era was drawing to an end, as optimism was pervading America following triumph in World War II, and as the Iron Curtain was descending in Europe. These factors had their effect on attitudes in the press and toward the commission, but no amount of euphoria, commercial opportunity, or jingoistic patriotism could fully explain the cold dismissal of the commission's manifesto. Its thoughtful conclusions, carefully rendered after several years spent listening, discussing and composing, were generally ignored or given short shrift by the few in the press who took any notice at all.

Surely the responsibilities of the media are a reality, for if they are not, the press is merely another private business with no greater right to constitutional protection than the maker of widgets. What the commission provided that rejection or indifference could not erase was a concept of social responsibility. That idea has not always been welcomed by the press, but it can no longer be neglected.

21

THE PARADOX OF SELF-GOVERNMENT

I think that there is, in most journalists I know, however cynical and however hardened they are about politics or public life in this country, or however discouraged about problems that never really get resolved or situations that never improve, there remains a very strong streak of idealism. They do think they are part of an important calling that is vital to the democracy. They really do.

—Robert MacNeil, television journalist,
Canadian Broadcasting, NBC,
MacNeil-Lehrer News Hour

James Madison contemplated the possibility that newspaper publishers who printed inaccurate or unpalatable criticisms of political figures would be fined or thrown in jail—or both—because of sedition laws. "It would seem a mockery," he said, "to say that no laws shall be passed preventing publications from being made, but that laws *might be passed for punishing them in case they should be made*" (emphasis added).[1]

The Zenger case in 1735 had introduced the principle that truth was a defense. Criticism, no matter how harsh, damaging, or satirical, appeared to be protected if a jury found the substance of the writing to be true. The judgment, however, was not scientific or statutory and, as discussed earlier, it could cut in both directions. What was true in the view of the publisher and his readers might be called false, libelous, malicious, by a jury that was sympathetic to the plaintiff. If the speaker or publisher had to prove that what had been said was true in every respect, the cost alone of that process could be forbidding. The cost of failure could be prison. The fear of sedition charges, no matter how undeserved, could and did chill the open discussion of public issues. The word *licentious* was commonly used in the early nineteenth century to describe seditious materials, that is, materials that criticized or disparaged the government. Laws made to prevent licentious expression could be manipulated by those in power who wished "nobody to enjoy the Liberty of the Press but such as were of their own opinion."[2]

The issue that began to emerge grew out of the widely accepted provision that no censorship in advance did not mean no punishment for false accusations, lies, or misrepresentation *after* publication. Jefferson had insisted that libel was not permissible and could be prosecuted in the courts. Madison disagreed. In regard to the actions of government officials—the people's servants—there was no criticism so vicious or damaging that it could justify legal action. That kind of criticism, he insisted, ought to be borne by the man in the political arena because in the houses of government the public official had the same unfettered freedom to express his opinions, attack, and defend as did his critics. The public official was immunized against libel no matter what he said when on duty, and so, Madison believed, should be the press when holding public officials to account. Therefore, libel suits brought by public officials against the press for criticism of their official performance would not be possible under the First Amendment.

In 1798, when there was fear of imminent war with France, President John Adams opposed the visit to America of a delegation of French scientists. He declared that a delegation of Frenchmen was "incompatible with social order." There were already numerous refugees from France in the United States, and the view that they would become subversive was gaining momentum. The French were made targets of suspicion and hostility. Congress passed several laws in reaction to near hysteria. One law increased the residence requirement for citizenship from five to fourteen years. Another law permitted the president of the United States to order the deportation of any alien considered a threat to security. And a third law authorized the jailing or deportation of aliens during wartime.[3]

The most troublesome law passed by Congress, however, was the Sedition Act. The statute made it a crime to publish "false, scandalous, and malicious" criticism of the government, Congress, or the president. It was this imprudent rationale for censorship that threatened the greatest harm to the concept of liberty articulated by the Constitution and the Bill of Rights. There was, in fact, no war with France. No French aliens were tossed out or incarcerated. And after a few years had passed, the citizenship residence requirement reverted to its original five years. But there were victims, all of them American citizens. The Sedition Act passed the Senate 18–6 and the House 44–41. As stated earlier, editors, scientists, publishers (and even one congressman), were fined and imprisoned. Every one of them was a Republican and unfriendly to President Adams. Judges and juries, hearing the clamor of public opinion in a highly charged atmosphere, ignored the Bill of Rights. And despite Jefferson's pardons in 1801, the freed Republicans waited vainly for restitution of money they had paid in fines.

The Sedition Act as a federal instrument was discredited, but achieving the full effect of the Fourteenth Amendment required Supreme Court reinterpretation, particularly if state laws were to become subordinate to constitutional laws. Jefferson, when he succeeded Adams in the White House, believed he could alter the purpose of the Sedition Act so as to permit prosecution of the press only *after* false material about public officials was published. He set out to make truth once more a fair defense. The charges would be dismissed if a publisher could prove that what had been written and printed was true. It didn't work out that way. Truth was chimerical, subjective. Sedition laws permitted government the power to prosecute free speech and a free press in general. The claim that the facts or opinions presented were truthful was an unreliable defense. To criticize government was to risk a costly trial, heavy fines, even jail. Pardoning the Republicans who were locked up in 1798 and 1799 had not ended the matter. If government could punish editors and publishers *after* publication by simply branding alleged truth as falsity or maliciousness, then censorship by fear was tantamount to prior restraint.

The Republicans in the early nineteenth century had supported a concept of forbidding government prosecution of political comment regardless of its ferocity or callousness because it served their own aspirations and limited the power of the Federalists—the power of central government. Such a limitation, however, would apply, it evolved, to any and all political parties, and in that sense partisan passions began to serve the common good. If a sovereign, self-governing people were to make sensible judgments, they would need all the facts available on public issues—and all the competing views that followed. The Sedition Act was repealed, in effect, before it could be tested in the Supreme Court. All the same, because the repeal did not apply to state laws, a free press was still not able to function in many states—most notably in the South. The abolitionist press and other critics of slavery were not the only victims but were certainly at the top of the casualty list.[4]

The long journey of the First Amendment free-press clause from 1798 to *New York Times v. Sullivan* in 1964 was given fresh impetus by the Civil War but slowed again when World War I began its carnage. Immigrants from France had been convenient targets in 1798, German American citizens were to be vilified in 1917, and twenty-five years after that Japanese Americans would be herded into detention camps following the Pearl Harbor attack. In the World War I years the Supreme Court replaced the Sedition Act with the Espionage Act. Eugene Debs, a well-known Socialist leader, was convicted of encouraging insubordination, disloyalty, and mutiny because he gave speeches criticizing the U.S. government for entering the war. Said he to a workers' rally in Ohio, "You need to know that you are fit for something better than slavery and cannon fodder."[5] He was sentenced to ten years, and the Supreme Court upheld his conviction with the same reasoning it had constructed for an earlier opinion that jailed a Socialist pamphleteer named Charles Schenck because he published a leaflet urging Americans to oppose the military draft.

Schenck had mailed his leaflet to men accepted for military duty, telling them the draft violated the Thirteenth Amendment, which prohibited "involuntary service"—a definition of slavery. In a third case closely related to those of Schenck and Debs, two German immigrants, Jacob Frohwerk and Carl Gleeser, were charged with conspiring to violate the Espionage Act by publishing in late 1917 a series of articles in a paper called the *Missouri Staats Zeitung*. One article stated: "We cannot possibly believe it to be the intention of our administration to continue the sending of American boys to the blood-soaked trenches of France." A common theme in the legal defenses of Schenck, Debs, and Frohwerk was the characterization of World War I as a rich man's war, but a poor man's fight, designed to benefit Wall Street and the monopoly industries.[6]

The "clear and present danger" test survived for several decades after World War I. It was enhanced by different wordings that added emphasis and urgency to the perception of danger. Holmes himself employed "a clear and *imminent* danger" as one variation. His colleague and friend Justice Louis Brandeis added "incitement" to the theme and the likelihood of "immediate, serious violence." The factors that remain undefined are *how specific* and *how criminal* are the actions that might result from *verbal incitement*—in print, at a rally, on television. And should the seriousness of the action to which the incitement might lead determine the severity of the penalty?

The dramatic history of First Amendment jurisprudence in the twentieth century provides a convincing portrait of the American Constitution as a "living document" subject to growth and interpretation, to amendment and reinterpretation, and to the wonderfully algebraic query put by Judge Learned Hand, "whether the gravity of the evil, discounted by its probability, justifies the invasion of free speech as is necessary to avoid the danger."[7]

As the press grew from its scruffy, partisan beginnings to its mass circulation power and as communications technology burgeoned in a manner the Framers could not have envisioned, the laws of the land had to keep pace. Judicial decisions in the early twentieth century and during World War I were more inclined to protect the government than its critics. Free expression was not widely seen as a bulwark of a healthy democracy. Some public figures who became renowned civil libertarians in the 1920s were willing to support restrictions of free press and speech among labor leaders and socialist organizations during the war. Roger Baldwin, a New England patrician and one of the founders of the ACLU in 1920, was able to countenance some limitations on free expression even though he himself was jailed briefly in 1918 as a conscientious objector. But as David Rabban of the University of Texas Law School observes, men like Baldwin and Zechariah Chafee, Judge Learned Hand of the Court of Appeals, Justice Holmes and Justice Brandeis, "believed in a harmonious society based on scientific principles. . . . Abuses of economic power loomed much larger to most of them than threats to civil liberties. . . . They felt no reason to anticipate dissent in Paradise."[8]

The Espionage Act of 1917 was passed by Congress a little over two months after America entered the war. In the debate before passage, a provision was considered that would have given the president the right to censor the press. That suggestion died in committee, as did an ill-conceived effort to give the postmaster general sweeping power regarding mailing privileges—presumably to be used against subversive printed matter. Many congressmen defended "legitimate public criticism," but the law that was finally enacted was made more stringent a year later by a *new* sedition act.

The combined force of these two acts was more than adequate to squelch nearly all criticism of the government in print or in public speech. Words that could be characterized as damaging to government, to the American flag, or even to military uniforms were forbidden. Conviction could bring as much as twenty years in prison and a $10,000 fine. Over 2,000 federal prosecutions were undertaken, and about 1,000 convictions were obtained. Most of the charges were directed at criticism of the war effort. The individual states also prosecuted many alleged offenders. One man was sentenced to fifteen years in prison for reading the Declaration of Independence in public, and a minister went to jail for a similar term because he had said the war was un-Christian. Editors and publishers who questioned any aspect of the draft or of military policy were prosecuted. The surveillance was widespread and relentless for the remainder of the war, which was a blessedly short time. The new Sedition Act was passed in May 1918, and the war ended that November, but during those months harsh treatment was the fate of a great many Americans who dared to speak or write in opposition to the nation's wartime policies.

For the first time in American history, free expression could be called espionage—for which severe punishment was inevitable. Nine cases reached the Supreme Court, and the government's charges were upheld in all nine. Ira Glasser, the executive director of the American Civil Liberties Union, observed in his 1991 book *Visions of Liberty*, commemorating the two-hundredth anniversary of the Bill of Rights: "By today's standards the Court was much too deferential to Congress and to the desire of the government to eliminate dissent during war time. And by the standards of the Republican libertarians of the early Nineteenth Century, the Court cut the heart out of the freedom of expression, leaving it vulnerable to government power."[9]

Public opinion, or the will of the community, could mean the will of the most numerous or powerful part of the community. The tyranny of the majority (or the powerful) frequently operated through the acts of public officials. Such power misused had the capacity to destroy the liberty of a few people or many, and unchecked it could bring about the end of liberty for a whole society. The only defense against corrupt or tyrannical government was the press. We may and must assume our opinion to be true for the guidance of our own conduct, but we cannot forbid the expression of other opinions even though we may regard those opinions as false and pernicious. In John Stuart Mill's words, "There is the greatest difference between *presuming* an opinion to be true because, with every opportunity for contesting it, it has not been refuted, *and assuming its truth for the purpose of not permitting its refutation*" (emphasis added).[10]

Justice Holmes not only listened to disputation in solving public issues but considered dissenting views in his own internal dialogue, reflected in his correspondence. In a letter to Zechariah Chafee written in 1922 and referring to his earlier (and casual) acceptance of no "prior restraint" as the heart of press freedom, Holmes confessed: "I simply was ignorant."[11] He had changed his views over time, and he openly acknowledged that process. Judge Learned Hand had written a letter to his friend Holmes in 1918, commenting, "Opinions are at best provisional hypothesis, incompletely tested. The more they are tested, after the tests are well scrutinized, the more assurance we may assume, but they are never absolutes."[12] John Stuart Mill would have nodded.

Justice Felix Frankfurter, in a 1949 opinion, said about Holmes: "Since he also realized that the progress of civilization is, to a considerable extent, the displacement of error which once held sway as official truth by beliefs which in turn have yielded to other beliefs, for him the right to search for truth was of a different order than some transient economic dogma. And without freedom of expression, thought becomes checked and atrophied."[13]

In the Schenck case, Holmes propounded an example that has been frequently quoted and often misunderstood in discussions of just how free freedom of speech and press can be. The Schenck antidraft leaflets, Holmes said, were comparable to "falsely shouting fire in a theater and causing panic." By that analogy Schenck's words were equated with actually obstructing the recruitment of troops. In wartime, any publication or utterance of dissent that could or might work against government policies was to be suppressed. Woodrow Wilson had, in fact, asked for the censorship of newspapers by suggesting that the president should have control over defense information—a step that was allegedly necessary for the protection of the nation. Wilson didn't doubt the "patriotic reticence" of most newspapers, but a few would not abide by self-imposed restraint; and the president thought he needed the power to suppress them. He didn't get that power, nor has any president since. But the Court, for a while, imposed "patriotic reticence" by asserting "clear and present danger."

Schenck and Debs and Frohwerk did not walk free, because the public was overwhelmingly on the government's side. In addition, the postal rate created a subsidized press that would be, by definition, a tame press. Chafee abhorred the World War I Espionage Act for ignoring such social interests as the search for truth and the value of free speech for its own sake. He did not believe that freedom of speech and of the press was "merely an individual interest which must readily give way like other personal desires the moment it interferes with the social interest in national security." He believed quite the opposite—that the Framers intended to erase the British common law of sedition and exempt all citizen criticism of the government from prosecution unless there was a demonstrable incitement to lawbreaking action. He wrote: "We can with certitude declare that the First Amendment forbids the punishment of words merely for their injurious tendencies." In his view, the Sedition Act of 1798 was clearly unconstitutional because "it surely defeated the fundamental policy of the First Amendment, the open discussion of public affairs."[14]

In putting Eugene Debs in jail, the Court acted on its belief that a speech Debs gave "had a *tendency* to bring about resistance," but it did not see a clear and present danger of overt acts. Chafee was prepared to accept a "clear and present danger" formula, but "bad tendency" was, in his view, an inadequate argument. By 1920 Holmes and Brandeis (who had both closely read Professor Chafee's essays) moved toward a more liberal position on free speech and press. Of "bad tendency" Holmes wrote, "A deed is not done with intent to produce a consequence unless that consequence is the aim of the deed." He came to believe that *possible* or *potential danger*, as opposed to *clear, imminent danger*, was not a basis for conviction. "Only the emergency that makes it immediately dangerous to leave the correction of evil counsels to time, warrants making any exception to the sweeping command, 'Congress shall make no law . . . abridging freedom of speech, or of the press.'"[15]

Holmes and Brandeis collaborated on dissents in virtually every First Amendment case after 1920. (Holmes was already sixty-one when Theodore Roosevelt appointed him to the Court in 1902.) In *Gitlow v. New York* (1925), they insisted that a certain publication expressed ideas "too remote from possible consequences" to be prosecutable. In 1929 they wrote in *U.S. v. Schwimmer* that a woman who was a pacifist could *not* be refused citizenship because she would oppose war as declared by Congress. The dissent stated that the Constitution defends freedom of thought, "not free thought for those who agree with us but freedom for the thought we hate."[16] Most of the time the two dissenters stood against the rest of the

Court, but the elegance and vision of their ruminations became the foundation for future decisions of great significance to all Americans—no less so now as a rapidly changing society approaches a new century. Louis Brandeis, as a private lawyer, had set himself against what he saw as the "curse of bigness"—big banks, big oil trusts, big corruption. He was called the people's lawyer, but he believed fervently in capitalism and free enterprise with the emphasis on "free." For Brandeis, capitalism had more "moral worth" than financial opportunism. He believed in free enterprise as the expression of character, individuality, self-reliance, and personal responsibility. He was, says David Rabban, devoted to "individual dignity" and the connection "between economic and political liberty." A Supreme Court clerk of that time is said to have observed, "Brandeis feels sympathy for the oppressed, Holmes contempt for the oppressor."[17] It was a good match.

Brandeis first brought to the developing discourse on free speech and free press a focus on direct "incitement." Said he: "Fear of serious injury cannot alone justify suppression of free speech and assembly. . . . Men feared witches and burnt women." He wrote many dissents, usually concurring with Holmes that "freedom to *think* as you will and to *speak* as you *think* are means indispensable to the discovery and spread of political truth" (emphasis added).[18] Justice Brandeis often provided insights on free expression that were uniquely his own. He believed the Framers had written the First Amendment "to preserve the right of free speech, both from suppression by tyrannous, well-meaning majorities, and from abuse by irresponsible, fanatical minorities." He was, as he had to be, concerned with *competing* interests and *just* laws. He saw that "the path of safety lies in the opportunity to discuss freely supposed grievances and proposed remedies; and that the fitting remedy for evil counsels is good ones."[19]

Holmes and Brandeis agreed nearly always on the cosmic issues. Supported by Chafee's esteemed academic writings, the two justices had tried to make the various forms of "clear and present danger" a constitutional standard. They had differing views on free speech and press in regard to specific issues, but they seemed to join seamlessly in dissenting against the reactionary majority opinions. Finally, in the Gitlow case, the majority opinion appeared to have been influenced by the arguments Brandeis and Holmes had crafted. The majority opinion was written by Justice Sanford who had not, until *Gitlow*, indicated that he saw in the Fourteenth Amendment any obligation of the individual states to recognize the First Amendment protection of speech and press for *all* citizens. Justice Sanford wrote: "For present purposes we may and do assume that freedom of speech and of the press—which are protected by Congress—*are among the fundamental personal rights and 'liberties' protected by the due process clause of the Fourteenth Amendment from impairment by the States*" (emphasis added).[20]

Gitlow was found guilty, nonetheless, for his part in writing a socialist manifesto in New York, thus violating a state law against "the criminal anarchy doctrine." He was not convicted of incitement or of encouraging immediate action to overthrow the U.S. government. He was, in a sense, found guilty of believing in a cause. Holmes's dissent produced—as was so often the case in his written opinions (and Brandeis's as well)—splendid prose:

> Every idea is an incitement. It offers itself for belief and, if believed, it is acted on unless some other belief outweighs it or some failure of energy stifles the movement at its birth. . . . Eloquence may set fire to reason. . . . If in the long run the beliefs expressed in proletarian dictatorship are destined to be accepted by the dominant forces of the community, the only meaning of free speech is that they should be given their chance and have their way.[21]

This was heady stuff for those who accepted the people as sovereign but not necessarily for those who feared manipulated mass hysteria. It was, they were certain, the "Red scare," international communism, that lay behind Socialist manifestos, not the will of the people—and most assuredly not the *informed* will of the people. The so-called Red scare of the early 1920s was a prologue to extremist witch-hunts that continued for nearly seventy years. Communist espionage and the massive bloodletting of Stalinism have not been, nor should they be, forgotten, but for Americans born in the 1960s and 1970s, the fear of left-wing plots, of a sinister conspiracy to infest the West with disruption and Marxism, seems now best suited to old Cold War movies and high-tech spy novels. Contemporary law students must find it incomprehensible that conservative Harvard Law School alumni nearly succeeded in having Zechariah Chafee removed from the faculty for such views on free speech and press as "All discussion opposed to the government is bound to have some effect in delaying the progress of the war, however slight. . . . The First Amendment was designed to insure that risk is taken."[22]

One Brandeis opinion that ought to be cited in any chronicle of free-press doctrine—perhaps in any study of American democracy itself—was inspired by *Whitney v. California*. This was an organized labor case on the surface, but it wound itself like bindweed around property issues, workers' rights, communism, and class warfare. The defendant was Anita Whitney, who came from an affluent upper-class family but participated in the founding of an organization called the Communist Labor Party of California. This group aligned itself with the Industrial Workers of the World, known as the Wobblies by friend and foe—mostly foe. Anita Whitney was convicted of being a member of the Communist Labor Party and advocating a revolutionary movement composed of workers, Wobblies, and presumably subversive Communists seeking to use force and violence for the purpose of achieving "a change in industrial ownership," along with political upheaval. The conspiracy was called "criminal syndicalism" by the prosecutor, and for harboring such treachery in her patrician bosom, Anita Whitney was sent to San Quentin for one to fourteen years. In 1927, Justice Sanford and most of his colleagues on the Supreme Court upheld the incarceration of Whitney. Brandeis wrote a separate opinion for Justice Holmes and himself, accusing the defense lawyers of not having asked the right questions. It was in this treatise that Brandeis not only recommended that the case against Whitney be dismissed but also, as Anthony Lewis writes in *Make No Law*, offered "the most profound statement ever made about the promises of the First Amendment in protecting the freedom of speech."[23]

The statement, often cited by teachers, lawyers, and editorial writers for more than sixty years, said in part, "that without free speech and assembly, discussion would be futile; that with them discussion affords ordinarily adequate protection against the dissemination of noxious doctrine; that the greatest menace to freedom is an inert people; that public discussion is a political duty; and that this should be a fundamental principle of the American government." Further on in the same opinion, Brandeis devised the formula, mentioned earlier, that would shape judicial language regarding free expression for decades, just as he had reshaped the "clear and present danger" dictum of previous decisions. He said, "To justify suppression of free speech, there must be reasonable ground to fear that *serious evil* will result if free speech is practiced. There must be reasonable ground to believe that *the danger apprehended is imminent* . . . that it may befall before there is opportunity for full discussion" (emphasis added).[24]

There was also in the *Whitney* opinion a prophetic admonition: "Only an emergency can justify repression. Such must be the rule if authority is to be reconciled with freedom. . . . It is, therefore, always open to Americans to *challenge a law* abridging free speech and assembly by showing that there was no emergency justifying it" (emphasis added). Brandeis, in anticipating the right of challenge in the future, such as the *Pentagon Papers*, studied timeless signals from the past. The role of responsible citizens in ancient Athens was the model he admired, and in the opening of the *Whitney* opinion, he borrowed from Pericles when he stated that the Founders "believed liberty to be the secret of happiness and courage to be the secret of liberty."[25] This and other Holmes-Brandeis dissents were sometimes specifically instrumental, as when California governor C. C. Young pardoned Anita Whitney a short time after the Supreme Court turned down her appeal. The dissenting opinion written by Brandeis, in which Holmes concurred, was extensively quoted in the governor's pardon.[26]

The Fourteenth Amendment (1868) clearly expanded the scope of the Bill of Rights, but that dramatic enlargement went unnoticed by many jurists—or perhaps it was willfully neglected.

For nearly twenty years after his appointment to the Court, Justice Holmes was willing to rely on the common-law view of a free press—no interference in *advance* of publication. This was (to say it again), in the words of the First Amendment, a prohibition upon Congress only. The Fourteenth Amendment was not yet viewed as "incorporating" the Bill of Rights against unconstitutional laws proposed by *state legislatures*. In the 1920s, Holmes, who had passed his eightieth birthday and was still exploring, moved toward acceptance of that view. Law professor Akhil Reed Amar proposes a basis for understanding the effect of the Fourteenth on the first ten amendments. He calls it "refined incorporation." Amar notes that the Fourteenth provides to *all* citizens *all* the "privileges and immunities" recognized in the Bill of Rights. "But," he adds, "not all of the provisions of the original Bill of Rights were indeed rights of citizens." Some were rights—at least in part—of states, most obviously the Tenth Amendment: "The powers not delegated to the United States by the Constitution, nor prohibited to the States, are reserved to the States, respectively, or to the people." The question that might be asked, suggests Amar, is whether any given provision of the Bill of Rights guarantees a "privilege" or "immunity" of "individual citizens rather than a right of States, or the public at large." By examining the Bill of Rights clause by clause, we can determine how some of them change when they are "incorporated" by the Fourteenth Amendment, which says in part, "No *State shall make or enforce any law* which shall abridge the privileges or immunities of citizens of the United States; *nor shall any State deprive any person* of life, liberty, or property, without *due process of law*; nor deny any person within its jurisdiction the *equal protection* of the laws" (emphasis added).[27]

Such language seems to be aimed (at least in part) at racism. The amendment was passed after the Civil War to enforce the elimination of slavery. Two years later the Fifteenth Amendment was passed to ensure that the right to vote could not be "denied or abridged *by the United States or by any State* on account of race, color, or previous condition of servitude" (emphasis added). What was not perfectly clear—in the language of the Fourteenth—was the meaning of the words *privileges and immunities* relative to free speech and press.

The First Amendment rights were originally submitted by the House to the Senate in two separate amendments—the first one on freedom of religion, the second on free speech, press, assembly, and petition. The Senate merged the two House amendments on fundamental rights into one statement now called the First Amendment, and the long-standing assumption is that it did so to protect states' rights. Why the Fourteenth Amendment did not make a simple statement to the effect that those rights given to the individual American citizen by the Constitution would henceforth be recognized and protected by each of the *states* as well as by Congress is not explained in the transcript or the minutes of the debate in the House or by any known private correspondence.

When a lawyer named Wilkes defended Philadelphia newspaper publisher Eleazer Oswald against sedition charges in 1782, the argument was offered that "government officials, as servants of the people could not be libeled by criticism of their performance, even by false sentiments."[28] That was not the first time such a perception had been declaimed; nor was it the last. It was a recurring theme and it resonated from a time when kings and queens were above criticism, superior by definition. How the *people* became superior, in practice as well as principle, is the story here. In historian Gordon Wood's words, "The rulers had become the ruled and the ruled the rulers." The American colonial experience had inspired the constitutional transfer of sovereignty from Parliament to the *people*, a process that required "continuous assent"—elections, debate, decision. Continuous assent meant continuous scrutiny. The press was the chief scrutinizer.[29]

Long before independence, the American settlers had learned that a free press was a sentinel over all their other liberties. For several years the intelligentsia had been passing *Cato's Letters* around, those outspoken essays counseling vigorous support for a free press and written by two British "intellectual middlemen," John Trenchard and Thomas Gordon. The *Boston Gazette* reprinted Cato's essay on free speech seven times between 1755 and 1780. When the states began drafting their separate constitutions, nearly all included strong expressions of freedom for the press. For a while in the early 1700s, the colonial governments were able to substantially control the press by subsidizing the printers with government contracts. The temerity required of a printer who published criticisms of official figures could result in the fatal loss of such contracts, but once the sources of financial support widened and tensions between Britain and the colonies intensified, the courage of the critics stiffened. The relationship between colonial governors and the printers was not all one way, however. The government needed to print and distribute laws, journals, and proclamations. Even during the War for Independence, the very papers that were vilifying their colonial masters printed the official documents and regulations issued by those same officials. The British law of seditious libel was violated ceaselessly by American newspaper editors, but little or no action was taken against the publication of criticism, caricature, or even calumny concerning officials and their public duties. There was, to put it another way, a kind of conventional wisdom that charges of sedition were unlikely and ineffectual in America. Cato had written, "I would rather many libels should escape, than the Liberty of the Press should be infringed."[30]

All the same, *Cato's Letters* did not go so far as to preclude *personal* libel suits. To one extent or another, most American scholars and public intellectuals have shared that reservation in a general sense ever since. It is drawing the line that troubles. Where does comment of any kind on public officials end and unacceptable personal abuse and defamation begin? Can there be such a thing as libel inflicted by the people through their free press upon public officials in regard to their performance as servants of the public interest?

Zechariah Chafee and others who followed in this century look back at the First Amendment enactment as a deliberate rejection of seditious libel. This prohibition was explicitly aimed at the Congress. All other considerations of the scope of a free press seemed to be left to the states. The Framers believed that the press had to be free to criticize the government. The Framers also believed, as many official records and much private correspondence attests, that malicious, false criticism could be (and should be) punishable. The depth of the divide between public and private has been measured by those few important First Amendment cases brought before the Supreme Court—most of them since 1925. The Framers could know the press only as it was in their own time. They therefore guaranteed—perhaps with the premonition of vast changes in mind—what has been called "the *practice* of freedom of the press." It is a practice that has never been totally unlimited.

The fiercest exponents of an unfettered right to publish political views were the anti-Federalists, who became the Republican Party. Their motives were not entirely unselfish. First, they wanted to defend themselves against any abuse of power by the more elitist Federalists, who became the Democratic Party. The tradition Madison called "disinterested public service" encouraged many Federalists to condemn the unruly voices of more ordinary men who were just beginning to acquire wealth and property and who were often characterized as greedy merchants and craftsmen motivated only by self-interest. Many Federalists believed the government ought to retain substantial independence from public opinion. Many people still do.

Jefferson wrote to Abigail Adams in 1804 explaining why, as president, he had "discharged every person under punishment or prosecution under the Sedition Law. . . . I considered . . . that law to be a nullity, as absolute and as palpable as if Congress had ordered us to fall down and worship a golden image."[31] It is worth noting that Mrs. Adams's husband, when he was president, had not included the vice president of the United States among those officials to be protected by the Sedition Law in 1798. His vice president was Thomas Jefferson. Though their friendship was sorely tested, it later resumed a closeness that lasted until their almost simultaneous deaths on July 4, 1826.

There are three philosophical foundations for the extraordinary consideration freedom of expression—speech and press—has been given since the early part of the twentieth century. The first is the Madisonian view that a sovereign people cannot rule without the knowledge produced by all the relevant information available and by open discussion. The second is the value-laden concept of the marketplace of ideas, where truth will triumph in any dispute with falsity. This notion broadens the political base so as to include the wider interests of a democratic society. And finally there is the "checking theory," the case for free expression as a countervailing power against the abuses of big government. Government, in the context of the checking theory, is all too fallibly inclined toward protecting its power by fiat rather than by votes or reason.

As to the political purpose of free expression, no modern advocate has been more eloquent than Alexander Meiklejohn, the philosophy professor and university president who believed self-government to be the unique and essential engine of American democracy. Meiklejohn stated that the First Amendment is an *absolute*, but he scoffed at the critics of absolutism who equated the word *absolute* with "an unlimited license to talk." Not only was the familiar litany of *unprotected speech*—obscenity, perjury, false advertising, solicitation of crime, and so on—fully accepted by absolutists but Meiklejohn brushes away "unlimited license" as not worthy of serious consideration because "no competent person accepts it."[32]

In 1953, Meiklejohn told the Senate Committee on the Judiciary, "Speech as a form of human action, is subject to regulation in the same sense as is walking, or lighting a fire, or shooting a gun. To interpret the First Amendment as forbidding such regulation is to so misconceive its meaning as to reduce it to nonsense." The point, to which Meiklejohn persistently and logically returns, is this: "The freedom that the First Amendment protects is not, then, an *absence of regulation*. It is the *presence of self-government*" (emphasis added).[33] The press in its serious role as purveyor, analyst, and interpreter of news and information becomes an instrument of *self-government*. Said that simply, the concept seems unarguable. But when we add to the mix the economic factors (profit from circulation and advertising) and the social factors (editing the product for a perceived market) we bring the instrument full circle to the point where it must examine itself. In the pragmatic, ethical universe Meiklejohn advocates, how does the press define its *own* self-government?

Zechariah Chafee wrote in 1942, "There are individual interests and social interests, which must be balanced against each other if they conflict, in order to determine which interests shall be sacrificed under the circumstances and which shall be protected and become the foundation of a legal right."[34] Chafee had also searched for some "rational principle" that could "mark the limits of Constitutional protection." For absolutists like Meiklejohn, the issue was to formulate a First Amendment rational principle that would be *absolute* in that it would not be "open to exceptions" but at the same time would be "subject to interpretation, to change, or to abolition, as the necessities of a precarious world may require."[35]

That sounds like a formula that would force a multitude of separate, perhaps unique, voices to sing in the same choir. But Meiklejohn keeps moving logically toward his summation. First, he reminds us of connections between the First Amendment and other components of the Constitution—that is, the preamble ("We, the *People*"); the Tenth Amendment ("The powers not delegated . . . are reserved to the States respectively, or to the *people*"); and section 2 of Article 1 (representatives shall be chosen every second year "by the *People* of the several States"). Constitutional authority to govern the *people* of the United States "belongs to the *people* themselves, acting as members of a corporate body politic." They are the *governed*, and they are the *governors*. The people have the authority to structure "subordinate agencies"—the legislature, the executive, the judiciary—and delegate to those agencies *specific* and *limited* powers. The people do not give away all their sovereign powers by any means. Finally, the people can *vote*. They can choose their representatives. They can participate in government—governing *themselves* by obeying the laws made by their representatives and governing their *representatives* by voting them in or out of office. With this preparation Meiklejohn returns to the First Amendment and interprets its *intent* as being "to deny to all subordinate agencies authority to abridge the freedom of the electoral power of the people" (emphasis added).[36]

Self-government must involve the act of voting, but voting wisely and well requires that we "understand the issues," that we pass judgment on the decisions our representatives have made, and that we share in the process of making government decisions work or of getting them changed. These activities, says Meiklejohn, are the "scope of the First Amendment." The language of the First Amendment—the mere forty-five words—does not by any means say all these things. Meiklejohn surmises that the Framers found it so difficult to agree upon a description of the operative relationship between free men and their delegates that they settled for a list of basic freedoms that expressed the revolutionary idea of the American experiment in self-government.

No other nation in the history of mankind, it is worth repeating, had constructed a government from the bottom up—from the people, of the people, for the people. Carrying these ideas into practice meant that the freedom to vote (with no need to say for whom or why) was to be "absolutely protected." All the forms of communication from which the voter derives the knowledge to make judgments must "suffer no abridgement." By extension, this need to understand, in Meiklejohn's view, involves freedom of education, literature, and artistic expression. But above all, public discussion and the dissemination of news and opinion on public issues must remain unfettered. To those who ask what fiction, poetry, painting, music, or drama have to do with voting rights, Meiklejohn argues that these forms of expression also educate and reveal. They are vital to the examination of new ideas, says he, because "our dominant mood is not the courage of people who dare to think. It is the timidity of those who fear and hate whenever conventions are questioned."[37]

The tough question remains on the table. How do the people's representatives regulate the "activities by which the citizens govern the nation?" Here Meiklejohn narrows his focus. There is, he explains, a great difference between *belief* and *communication*. We can be told by the authorities *when* we can meet in a public hall or a park because of competing schedules or safety factors. We cannot be told, however, what we will *say* or what we must *believe*. Like Socrates, we support the Constitution and obey the laws of the land, but we do not have to believe in them. "Loyalty does not imply conformity of opinion," Meiklejohn states.[38] The people must obey the enactments of the government to whom they have delegated power in order to be *governed*. The same people, as *governors*, may disapprove or seek change.

The libel laws have been enacted by legislators and upheld by the courts. The First Amendment does not protect a speaker or a writer who defames or slanders another individual in the private sector. The victim may sue, and the violator may suffer. Meiklejohn sees such private issues as completely unrelated to the "business of governing." The same or similar attacks, if spoken or printed to show "the unfitness of a candidate for governmental office," have the protection of the First Amendment because such expression is "properly regarded as a citizen's participation in government."[39]

Meiklejohn believes that the people have not delegated to any of the "subordinate branches of government" the authority to tell them what they may write or read or see. Such authority is "reserved to the people"—each deciding what "he finds worthy of his attention." The arts, in this view, are of "social importance"; therefore, they are of "governing" importance. The arts help people understand the human condition, and that understanding is at the core of governance. The Framers borrowed much from English law, but the American "experiment" moved in a new direction that separated it fundamentally from the British system. In England the power that had for centuries emanated from the Crown gave way in the eighteenth century to the Parliament. It was Parliament that determined the administration of the colonies. The Founders, who rebelled against Parliament's oppressions, decided that power must rise upward from the people, not downward from a legislature. The Constitution is the authority. How it is interpreted and how the interpretations build upon each other must reflect the understanding and the will of the people. The people have the power to stop the government from infringing on individual liberties, but that power can't be limited to periodic elections. A free press openly criticizing the governors between and during elections could help alert the people. In the early years, the only independent reflector of the people's will was the press. Not then, and not today, has a better instrument for that purpose been found.

22

LIBEL AND LIABILITY

I think it's important to give judges more power than they now have to impose costs on the loser. I wouldn't make it a rule the way it is in England, but I would move it away from what is known as the American rule which is that each side pays its own costs, including all legal costs, and at least give judges more power to conclude that a position taken by one side or the other, particularly in a First Amendment context, was so frivolous that what was really involved was an effort to suppress speech. And if the judge makes that finding, I think it's important that he have the power to make the party that has misbehaved pay.

—Floyd Abrams, First Amendment authority;
partner, Cahill, Gordon & Reindel, New York

The First Amendment issues regarding freedom of expression multiplied dramatically in the twentieth century; but serious unfinished business remains, and many new issues are forming in the regions of high technology. The always-uncertain line between public and private information—indeed the very nature of privacy itself in a modern society—could bring the subject of libel into the media arena more frequently as time goes by, and at greater cost until some basic changes are codified. The technologies of fax, computers, satellites, and fiber optics—among others—will demand the attention of constitutional lawyers and lawmakers in determining where free expression ends and private business commences. What kind of information, conveyed by what kind of device, should have the protection of the First Amendment? By what means can offenders be held accountable for misinformation deliberately and maliciously communicated, and by what means can such misinformation be corrected?

If the information necessary to informed political discourse, and therefore to the "self-government" Alexander Meiklejohn has so eloquently canonized, is to include art and fiction, drama and "docudrama," *and* the normally private data made public because the electorate *needs to know* about the *character* of those who may or do govern, by what criteria do society and the courts decide when and where to stop? Obscenity can poison community standards and do demonstrable harm to children. Hate speech and organized bigotry utilizing high-tech communication can injure old and new victims (no less than, perhaps more than, physical assault), but can also undermine the fundamental comity necessary to the survival of democracy.

Finally, there is the vexatious question of profits versus ethics. The importance of advertising revenue to newspapers, magazines, television, and perhaps in due course to the more specialized digital forms of communication has been examined, lamented, criticized, and defended for as long as advertising has paid the bills for paper, printing, distribution, and salaries. Advertising has also provided information essential to commerce. It has assisted the consumer. It is a vital component of the free enterprise system. It is also capable of—and has been guilty of—wielding unaccountable power by acting as both censor and manipulator.

Ethics are collectively an abstraction (some say a chimera). After all the philosophers and reformers have had their say, ethics—particularly in terms of a free *and* responsible press—are principles defined by what we *ought* to do rather than what we think we can get away with. There is unarguably no way of policing the press without destroying its freedom. The Framers recognized that fact early on and were themselves not spared from scurrilous attacks. The "noxious doctrines" promulgated in the name of free expression were and are presumably vulnerable to correction by "nicer doctrines." Justice Brandeis did not live to see how pervasively noxious some doctrines could become or how long it takes for the truth to recover (if ever). Ed Murrow once said, "Lies can go around the world while truth is getting its pants on." Still, there has been no better remedy discovered than voluntary, determined effort on the part of the Fourth Estate—in all its formulations—to set high standards and vigilantly enforce them within its own precincts. A responsible, free press, very much like political liberty, does not mean doing what pleases or profits. It means doing what *ought* to be done, saying what *ought* to be said, by combining conscience with reason. Having said that much, we might hasten to add that ever since Plato gave up on finding philosopher kings, we have accepted—as he did and as his student Aristotle so vigorously articulated—the importance of laws. "Where there is no law there is no freedom," John Locke wrote. "Laws hedge us from bogs and precipices."[1]

Among the bogs and precipices cited at the start of this book, the first to be considered is libel. *New York Times v. Sullivan* built a fence around public officials—a fence that would soon surround "public figures" such as movie stars and basketball players and columnists—and provided a "keep-out" sign for libel, though it left open that small gate called malice. Some public personae, political and otherwise, have tried to squeeze through that gate, and some have succeeded in proving malice or reckless disregard for the truth. Public opinion has, for several generations, overwhelmingly supported a larger gate. But the problematical aspect of libel actions is the cost to the alleged media offender and therefore the chilling effect it has on robust reporting. If newspapers and magazines are afraid that legal fees will be perilously high even when truth is proven, they may and probably will censor themselves.

Studies made by the Iowa Libel Research Project and other scholarly groups, in addition to considerable anecdotal evidence, clearly indicate that most libel suits against the media could be avoided if the newspapers in particular, but news magazines and television stations as well, were more responsive to complaints. Rudeness, dismissal, indifference, arrogance, are all kindling for the fires of litigation. Few people who feel they have been wronged by the press want to pay a lawyer and go to court. It is a time-consuming, costly exercise for the alleged victim, and even the corporations or organizations with deep pockets would prefer more reasonable correctives—an acknowledgment of error with a correction or the publication of a clarifying letter—to a libel suit.

Libel cases rarely provide cause for jubilation on either side. Everyone loses most of the time, according to the surveys made by law schools and press organizations. Money is the lubricant libel squeezes out of plaintiff *and* defendant. Money is what the lawyers seek to repair damage to reputation, and when malice is found—"actual malice" is the phrase of choice—punitive damages follow like gulls behind a fishing boat. "Libel suits have become a growth industry," wrote Nat Hentoff in 1985. The search for malice is therefore crucial and, as Lucas Powe Jr. observes, that search

> turned the libel trial away from what the defendant said about the plaintiff to a scrutiny of how the press put the story together, what reservations the reporters and editors may have had about parts of the story, and why they chose to say one thing rather than another. . . . It is now the *defendant's conduct*, rather than the *plaintiff's reputation* that is on trial. (emphasis added)[2]

There has been in recent years no more confounding example of that phenomenon than the notorious and virtually simultaneous libel trials in which Israel's General Ariel Sharon sued Time, Inc. in 1984 and America's General William Westmoreland sued CBS. The two hearings were held a floor apart in the same New York City courthouse. Both plaintiffs had, in one way or another, to convince a jury that actual malice and/or reckless disregard for the truth had been practiced by two of America's most distinguished news organizations.

In the end, the American general chose not to see the legal ordeal through to a courtroom conclusion. The other general, the Israeli, had political ambitions that his days in court (and in the media) would enhance, and a triumphant verdict might have even galvanized his chances. There were deep-seated issues involved in both cases that might have been constructively aired and examined by both the trial procedure and the media coverage. Instead, the media itself became the story—with an emphasis on accountability. Neither CBS nor Time were willing to frankly and unequivocally acknowledge mistakes. Nor would either openly apologize for the damage done by errors in fact or judgment. Richard Clurman, onetime chief of correspondents at Time, analyzed the two generals and their lawsuits in *Beyond Malice*. Clurman is critical of Time's defensive attitude—as he is of CBS's smoothly orchestrated legal maneuvers. "Once committed in print or on the television screen," Clurman writes, "news people—more than other humans—hate to admit they were wrong. That feeling is so strong that even in the face of arguable contrary evidence, they tend to convince themselves their story was right and hold their ground."[3]

The shadows cast by the Sharon and Westmoreland libel trials fell upon the reputation of the media. The jury in the Sharon case could not declare that actual malice was evident. Sharon lost on that technicality, but Time, in the minds of many readers, lost part of something far more important— its journalistic standing and its reputation for truth-telling. A year later, in Israel, Time settled the case out of court, publicly announced its regrets for "this erroneous report," and paid Sharon's legal costs. If it had done the same in the first place, there would have been no *multimillion* dollar legal fee (largely paid for by an insurance company that shortly thereafter went out of business).

As to the spectacle of CBS defending itself by very nearly charging a retired military hero with treason, the court became a setting for the rerun of the Vietnam War. Why did America lose? That is probably a question no one will ever answer convincingly. Why did General Westmoreland settle his case for unfavorable terms? Because there was not enough money coming in to go all the way. (CBS recovered more than $7 million from the same company that had insured Time.) This was an ideological libel suit, Lucas Powe Jr. writes, and "if a case like his, carrying great (if speculative) gain as a hope, nevertheless flounders on financing, then few cases driven solely by ideology and the desire for vengeance are likely to succeed."[4]

In 1986, the Supreme Court ruled that "clear and convincing" evidence had to meet a high standard even before a trial. Judges had to review the evidence in pretrial proceedings as stipulated. In that directive, the Court overruled a lower court decision made by Antonin Scalia even though he was about to join the Supreme Court himself. Had the higher standard been established before the Westmoreland-CBS trial, Richard Clurman surmises, "Judge Laval could have been more likely to dismiss the suit without trial."[5] No one walked away from the actions brought by the two generals with much, if anything, to cheer about. The media was, however, the biggest loser. In the April 1988 *Harvard Law Review*, Judge Pierre Laval (who in 1993 was promoted to the Court of Appeals) advocated that someone who sued for libel but did not seek money damages should not have to prove actual malice. Laval believes that common sense would shift the process away from how a story was prepared to the more significant element of truth or falsity.

Major surveys of public opinion on the press—print or electronic—as already reflected upon in this book show low levels of general esteem but considerable respect for specific practitioners who satisfy the consumer because they maintain certain standards perceived to be acceptable. Among First Amendment scholars, lawyers, and leading members of the press itself, it is widely agreed that the press *must* remain free and unfettered but also *must* be more responsible. If the cherished right to be, as Justice Brandeis so neatly put it, "left alone"—to have one's reputation protected from defamation or blemish by an irresponsible newspaper or television station—is to be balanced against the unquestioned value of free expression, the laws of libel need to work better than they do. Libel law somehow should restrain the violation of individual rights without chilling the courage and energy of the press in its role as sentinel—as the voice that reveals government abuse of power, holds public servants' feet to the fire, and sustains the widest and most robust form of political discourse on which democracy feeds. How can libel be harnessed to such high purpose?

Some remedies have been explored by task forces at distinguished law schools and by individual scholars such as Marc Franklin of Stanford, Rodney Smolla of Virginia, David Anderson of Texas, Gilbert Cranberg and John Soloski of the Iowa Libel Research Project, and Randall Bezanson of Washington and Lee. They report, to one degree or another but generally with consensus, that most libel suits need not go to court. A courteous response to complaints, reasonable published corrections, or an opportunity to reply (op-ed, letters column, or on the air) will in most cases solve the problem. There is, however, a prevailing pattern of defiance by the press— that bedeviling clenched fist called "we stand by our story." Admittedly, there are gray areas, there are complaints that deserve no redress, and there is the fear on the part of the press that if it appears to be weak and irresolute, it will attract nuisance lawsuits. But more important, the press has learned since *New York Times v. Sullivan* that it is more likely the press can win "on issues of legal privilege" than by demonstrating truth. If the so-called victim does get to court but can't prove actual malice, he or she will lose the case and the cost of it without a declaration that the alleged offensive material was true or false. All the same, one large verdict that sticks can destroy underfinanced newspapers and severely hurt any news organization. If malice is perceived, juries inevitably award large money penalties on punitive grounds. As noted earlier, when made by juries (notoriously hostile to the press in this century), most of these awards are overturned by more dispassionate judges.

Law professor Fred Schauer, a libel specialist, believes that legal costs are an integral part of doing journalistic business. He makes the point that if a pharmaceutical company carelessly markets a harmful drug, it has to pay the victims. Why, he asks, should the press get away with not paying for the harm it inflicts?[6] There are answers to that question. Drug companies have a financial incentive to develop and market new products. There are no such incentives for media organizations to take risks. Second, the questionable drug may harm many people; libel usually harms an individual. A hostile jury awards higher damages to the libel plaintiff for damages to "reputation" than to the victim of a harmful drug product for damage to his body.

So what to do? Truth is not the issue. Lawyers' fees are nearly always the issue. Why not have losers in libel cases pay all the costs, as they do in England? One reason to do so: Such an arrangement helps to discourage litigation. One reason not to do so: It probably overprotects the press and penalizes the victim who has a legitimate case but won't risk the double cost. That leaves the possibility of "caps." If there is a cap on damages, both sides know where the line has to be drawn and whether the game is worth the ante. That would be helpful. As to so-called punitive damages, there is little disagreement that unlimited punishment of a monetary nature not only has a serious chilling effect on the press but "cannot be squared with the premises of the Constitution."[7]

What has evolved, however, and may be the best direction to go, is called "declaratory judgment" action. Such judgments declare "what the facts and the rights are" but make no damage awards. The assumption of the Iowa Program and the Annenberg Washington Libel Reform Project is that most plaintiffs want the truth to be pronounced, presumably repairing their reputations. Declaring the truth (or at least the facts) without any money involved will, it is further presumed, take the chill off the press, and the best interests of the parties (and the public) will be served. Without money the remedy becomes retraction or the right of reply by the plaintiff. There is, in addition, an expectation that if the citizen-victim agrees not to go to trial and accepts the option of receiving a "declaratory judgment," he or she cannot then sue for damages. What is more, if he or she (under the terms of this particular suggestion) then is found to have no legitimate complaint in the declaratory judgment, he or she must pay the newspaper or television station's legal fees.

There are several wrinkles left even if the no-money declaratory judgment concept eventually prevails. For one thing, the media may resist such a reform because *New York Times v. Sullivan* provides a haven in law to be wrong and still win. Why, to repeat an earlier reference, fix the successful mechanism that isn't broken? For another thing, what about the victim who has been hurt economically and can prove it? She or he will want restitution and will sue to achieve that end. It may be that libel laws in the fu-

ture will make room for many of the suggestions covered here—including
the right to sue when demonstrable economic loss has been caused by the
media. What seems inevitable is that some measure of truth will become
more important than trying to prove actual malice. That way, the positive
aspect of setting the record straight prevails over the arcane and elusive
pursuit of "state of mind" of the reporters and the process of putting a
news story together. Professor Powe, writing in favor of a "declaratory
judgment remedy," observes that the "dilemma" created by the *New York
Times v. Sullivan* opinion is that it centered on "not a lack of actual malice
by the defendant [the *Times*], but rather an excess of money damages to a
wholly uninjured plaintiff [Sullivan]."[8]

The major change in access to news has less to do with *understanding* the
news than with *impressions* that come no closer to knowledge than largely
undifferentiated facts permit. The change is called television. No other
technology has been so pervasive, but its relationship to First Amendment
protection was preshaped by radio. A sales slogan used in the early days of
television anticipated the logical evolution: "Stop *staring* at your radio."[9]
The intellectual community in the 1930s hoped people would stop *listening*
to radio as well. There were a few extraordinary radio voices "fighting
against the main current," among them Elmer Davis, Edward R. Murrow,
H. V. Kaltenborn, and David Shoenbrun. Nonetheless, radio was widely
considered to be "outside the sphere of the press." Radio could and did reveal the headlines in a timely fashion, using the wire services and frequently
reaching the public hours before the newspapers were available. On Sunday, December 7, 1941, those Americans who were listening to a Toscanini
concert on NBC Radio heard a voice interrupting the music to announce
that the Japanese had bombed Pearl Harbor. Very few of the listeners had
ever heard of Pearl Harbor, but most of them wondered how soon war
would be declared. The Monday morning newspapers would begin to answer that question. Years later, National Public Radio would enter the universe of mass communications with solid, dispassionate news, and in the
1980s Rush Limbaugh and his diverse colleagues discovered the power of
anger, discontent, hate, and faceless populism delivered by microphone and
telephone.

In the salad days of commercial radio (before television), the owners of
stations (and ultimately networks) were described as the "lineal descendants of operators of music halls and peep shows." It was show biz, not
First Amendment biz. Harry Kalven once suggested that the broadcasters
needed their own "Zenger case"—at least in terms of news and information. The broadcasters did not pursue that goal, and the door was thus left
ajar for licensing—the evil that John Milton had railed against in the middle of the seventeenth century when he wrote his *Areopagitica* ("Whoever
knew Truth put to the worse in a free and open encounter?"). English li-

censing of the press was the touchstone for early American aversion to *any* prior restraint, but in the twentieth century the new media settled for licensing by the Federal Communications Commission. That body, presumably, would be nonpartisan and would have no authority to censor content. Congress not only guarded against censorship when it passed the Communications Act in 1934, but it made provisions for appeals to the federal courts if broadcasters felt they had been subjected to unfair regulation.

By the 1970s, legal scholars were examining the validity of differentiating between electronic and print journalism. Some wanted to regulate newspapers and magazines in the same manner as radio—and certainly the rapidly developing intruder called television. Others would end all distinction and leave the press (in any form) to the First Amendment, the bright line between public and private affairs, and the recourse of libel. A third group kept to the regulation of only radio and television on the grounds of scarcity and/or pervasiveness. Scarcity could be construed as the limited number of broadcast signals available to those who wanted to own a station, or it could be given a second interpretation—one that is currently more intensely argued—that the cost of most radio and television facilities is so high that only people (or corporations) of great wealth can afford them. Scarcity defined by economic reality becomes exclusivity, which denies dissenting or nonmainstream views a hearing. In 1974 the Supreme Court in *Miami Herald v. Tornillo* found that newspapers had a constitutional right to print whatever editorial opinions they liked. This was not a bad arrangement despite the argument that in many locations "news corporations"—through acquisition of newspapers and television stations—exercised monopolistic privileges. Electronic communications, in contrast, were so far-reaching and instantaneous, so expensive, so mesmeric and corrupting, that they needed at least limited regulation. Furthermore, it was reasoned, the existence of an unregulated print press would encourage broadcasters to be more fearless when reporting on *public* matters. Lee Bollinger in his 1976 *Michigan Law Review* article, "Freedom of the Press and Public Access," supported the duality theory. The very free print press could act as a check on any abuse of the regulatory power over the nearly free broadcast press. It was a notion easily transferable to cable television, fax, satellite, computers, and so on in the technologically Brave New World of the next century. Randall Tobias, of American Telephone and Telegraph, said, "It has long been recognized that the pen is mightier than the sword. The modern version of that is 'the fax machine is mightier than the rifle.' It is impossible for a society that has more open telecommunications to continue to be repressive."[10]

Repression was not the rationale the FCC would accept, even if it was acting *against* evil. The doctrine of the FCC was allegedly "in the public interest." The termination of a license could be legally decided when the commissioners determined that the licensee's programming did not serve that elusive condition called public interest. This was not an issue in the early days of radio. Nearly all programming was entertainment then, and most of that was selected by a handful of advertisers. But the rise of networking raised concerns about local affiliates and their right to produce independent programming. The major radio networks—NBC, CBS, and ABC—resolved to take on the commission, arguing that the FCC was not in the antitrust ballgame and had no authority to interfere with how the networks managed their affairs. As to programming, the radio networks asked for First Amendment protection. This was a new development, and the argument would take on weight over time. But in 1943 the Supreme Court found little merit in it. Said the Court: "The licensing system established by Congress in the Communications Act of 1934 was a proper exercise of its power *over commerce*. The standard it provided for the licensing of stations was 'the public interest, convenience, or necessity.' Denial of a station license on that ground is valid under the Act, is not a denial of free speech" (emphasis added).[11] The bottom line was scarcity; the need to allocate broadcast frequencies was a government's job, or so it would appear.

It was logical that the protection of public interest would expand into reportorial areas. News coverage, the FCC said, must be "fair in that it accurately reflects the opposing views." The powerful commercial and propaganda advantages the broadcasters secured *under* government regulation could be restrained *by* government regulation. Regulators assumed that the right of the viewers and listeners, not the right of the broadcasters, is paramount. An interesting twist on the First Amendment began to formulate around the government's role in broadcasting. Power had been predictably enlarged by the "chains" in the print media and was now enhanced by the "networks" in the electronic media. There was fear of a chilling effect, the tendency toward self-censorship, among broadcasters because of the government's licensing authority. Justice Arthur Goldberg is credited with the coining of "chilling" as a First Amendment concern, but no one came up with a better metaphor than the head of President Richard Nixon's Office of Telecommunications Policy, T. Clay Whitehead: "The value of the sword of Damocles," said he, "is that it hangs, not falls."[12]

Justice Byron White, however, believed the government had the responsibility of preventing chill (call it timidity or self-censorship) by lifting the license of the fearful or lazy broadcaster. Another aspect of the problem has been searchingly explored by Owen Fiss, the Alexander M. Bickel Professor of Public Law at Yale. "For me," says Fiss, "the First Amendment is really a protection of public discourse. Its purpose is to enable collectivities to make up their minds in public debate. It is not 'freedom to *speak*' but 'freedom of *speech*.'" Fiss is concerned about who speaks and when. Most of those decisions, he says, are being made by the market, and the market is not unbiased. In recent years the FCC repudiated the fairness doctrine—a policy that had required radio and television stations to provide outsiders and dissenters with airtime to reply or to debate previously broadcast viewpoints. "Control of the market," Fiss insists, "belongs to those who have the wealth and the advertising budget. . . . The state should create access for those who are dissidents."[13]

That argument finds its origins—though few solutions, as is so often the case—in early American history. Newspapers at the end of the eighteenth century, as described earlier, had very small circulations, were only locally available (though publishers frequently sent copies to other publishers throughout the nation), were relatively easy to produce, and were a major source of political discourse. If an educated man (aka white landowner) wanted to disseminate his views on public issues and could not find a suitable newspaper to publish those views, he could buy into a paper or start one of his own. Over time, however, the opportunities to get one's views heard and read became scarcer and more complex. Once the mass media took over, scarcity was the rule, not the exception, in terms of pluralistic public discussion.

The legal minds who agree with the Fiss assessment are ready to argue that the government (federal or state) shall make no law *abridging* free speech or press—but that is not to say government shall take no action to *enlarge* that freedom or to put its own case forward on public policies. This was the rationale, at least in part, for public radio and public television. Money collected by the state is public money, and those who are not entirely comfortable with the market as the dominant force in First Amendment thinking believe that state revenues can be constitutionally used to preserve democracy by ensuring that a variety of viewpoints the market might ignore are given voice. Subsidies—to art, education, or political discourse—could not, says Professor Fiss, be used to "reinforce the prevailing orthodoxy." Editor Lewis Lapham puts it the other way around: "Believing everything and nothing, the media composes the advertisements for preferred reality."[14]

23

FREE AS THE AIR

It will be a long day before broadcast news gets rid of all government controls. Some of the most powerful members of Congress favored the Fairness Doctrine and still favor it. There are special interest groups and academics in the private sector that would like to have the Fairness Doctrine back again. The Fairness Doctrine was anything but fair. William Paley once said, "It is like the Holy Roman Empire, neither holy, nor Roman, nor an empire."

—Emerson Stone,
former vice president, CBS News;
columnist on ethics in broadcasting news,
Communicator Magazine

The electronic press will always be vulnerable to the charge that it is a public utility in private hands. In that "corporate world" morality does not rise to the top, borne by internal principles. It is formed by all kinds of changing relationships, economic and political, and in that context, managerial moralities are always situational, always contingent. Does it follow that government regulation will ensure enduring principles? The Supreme Court, in 1969, upheld the notion of a "new" First Amendment, "one befitting this 'new' method of communication."[1]

The "new" First Amendment said, and still seems to say, that TV anchorpeople—hair blown and calculatingly garbed, sitting in what looks like a theatrical set surrounded by flickering monitors and the nimbus of overhead spotlights—do not have quite the same constitutional protections available to their cousins in the print media. The assumption continues to be that entertainment is not a contributor to the "public debate" envisioned by the First Amendment. The lively fly in that ointment is the statistical evidence that most Americans get the greatest proportion of their "news" from the television set. If news is going to be delivered primarily by television—not thrown on the front steps by a youngster on a bicycle—attitudes concerning the electronic medium might change, and government policy might adjust.

A half-hour evening news program on a television network contains about twenty-two minutes of information and/or opinion in the form of words spoken by a "talking head" and pictures conveyed live, filmed, or on videotape. The other eight minutes go to commercials, promotion, station identification, special effects, titles, credits, and so on. Theme music has been deemed essential by those who worry about ratings and the loyalty of viewers. The personality and trustworthiness of anchors and key reporters of either gender are significant, calibrated factors in the presentation of news.

There is not enough time to develop context and background. The implication is that the leading newspapers and news magazines, and the special interest journals, provide the deeper exploration; the collecting of more extensive data; the analysis, the editorializing, and the fuller account (if not the complete text) of a speech; a portentous announcement, a manifesto, a legal statement; an angry reply, a felicitous endorsement, a paragraph or two for the record; or any other communicated components of events that have marked (illuminated or darkened) the day, the week, the month. Whether they also provide opportunity for the voices and ideas that are displeasing to the vested interests but potentially useful to public debate—if only to validate conventional wisdom—is a question both the citizen-critic and responsible media have to ponder.

Not yet, however, has the duality of First Amendment protection for the printed word and the flickering amalgam of words and images that come out of "the tube" struck American lawmakers as illogical. For the time being there is the First Amendment as it was written for speech and press, and there is the "new" First Amendment for the "new mediums" that the Framers could not have anticipated. Mass communication of any kind was not part of the world they knew. What would the Founders have thought public opinion might favor in regard to almost instantaneous, compressed news enacted somehow upon a rectangular window in the corner of every citizen's humble (or grand) sitting room? The Congress and the Supreme Court may not have set about determining how the Founding Fathers might have answered that question, but constitutional determinations were made, nonetheless, and upheld. There had to be a First Amendment adjustment for new, undreamed of means of communication. It was thus for the telegraph, the wire services, radio, and, ultimately, television. In 1991, Alfred Sikes, the chair of the FCC, wrote in *Newsweek*:

> And this year the FCC will hold public hearings on the "Networks of the Future." The hearings will cover the full range of issues relating to the new technologies. We intend to examine the outmoded Federal and State rules that now restrict the market. We want to identify which regulatory policies are helpful and which ones risk jeopardizing the future of communication in this country. . . . The challenge in the 1990s is for *the public to become involved so that the stakes will be understood by more than just the stakeholders.* (emphasis added)[2]

There was something in that formulation for Jefferson, Hamilton, *and* Owen Fiss (see Chapter 22). Government regulation of broadcasting seems to be saying that listeners and viewers are the equal of owners and operators. Perhaps only the government can protect the public on the question of fairness and balance in programming concerned with public issues. The regulatory aspect of broadcasting has been in place for more than half a century not only in terms of the granting of licenses but just as meaningfully in the renewal or nonrenewal (a very rare occurrence) of those same licenses. Meanwhile, the scarcity concept has seen considerable alteration. The once plentiful array of daily newspapers in America—several thousand at one time—had shrunk to less than 1,800 in the 1980s, along with approximately 7,600 weeklies. In contrast, television and radio stations, the presumably scarcer entities, were growing in number and variety. In 1985 there were more than 1,220 television stations, 654 of them VHF (very high frequency), which covered the larger market areas, and the rest UHF (ultrahigh frequency), which had a smaller reach. In most ways, scarcity had shifted from radio and television to newspapers. The exception was VHF, still limited in number and by cost. FM radio stations proliferated, as did UHF-TV and cable channels open to "public access."

Against the argument for equivalency, there is the argument for greater democratization by government fiat—assurance through some form of positive action that the views heard, seen, and read in the media do not exclude nonmainstream, eccentric, oppositional, radical ideas on which democracy depends for both innovation and the kind of dispute that validates, enhances, subtracts from, or adds to the nation's perception of truth and virtue. As for free enterprise, the licensee may sell his station for enormous profit, and the approval of the FCC has been virtually pro forma unless the new owners are foreigners or known criminals. In the year 1984 (with or without the advent of Big Brother) more than 782 radio stations and 82 television stations were sold in the marketplace. How many players can afford to enter such a market is a legitimate question if society needs (or wants) to allow all that is worth hearing or seeing on public issues a fair opportunity. It is true, nonetheless, that what is in the public interest does not always interest the public.

Local television-station owners usually regard their local evening news as a matter of recording public statements by public officials, covering fires and accidents and crime scenes, and then reviewing sports scores and weather. Analysis or discussion, sophisticated interviews, opposing or contradictory opinions, and background data are too costly, time consuming, or beyond the capacity of a small news department. It was the network news reports and public television that were expected to offer those ingredients. But when it came to controversial stories like Vietnam and Watergate, the networks discovered just how vulnerable their news divisions were even when there was determination and funding to discover the facts. The late Richard Salant, a lawyer-president of CBS News, remarked during his tenure, "We have two very soft underbellies; one is the affiliates, who have the perfect right under the law, and the obligation, to turn down everything from the network that they don't want. They can put us in news completely out of business by simply turning off the faucet. Our second soft underbelly is our licensing. There is no solution to either problem."[3]

The political party that has its leader in the White House can appoint a majority of the FCC members. That majority may reflect the views of the party or have some ideas of its own, but its political influence by action or innuendo is probable—and no doubt so is self-censorship by proprietors who want to avoid licensing renewal problems, advertiser discontent, or pressure from special interests. Nonetheless, the prevailing view, supported by the courts, is that broadcasting is fundamentally different from printing so far as First Amendment interpretation is concerned. Critics of this position scoff: "The government owns the radio [and television] frequencies because it has power to regulate their use, and the government has power to regulate their use because it owns them. A nifty circle, and it does not break."[4]

That circle is still drawn by scarcity. Many people want broadcasting licenses, but the government has only a few to give away. The Supreme Court, to date, has accepted that rationale. Cable television was a horse of a different color, and it soon became many horses and finally a stampede. In the late 1970s and through the 1980s, cable television proliferated because the FCC relaxed its regulatory power, but Congress passed the Cable Communications Policy Act of 1984, which, in effect, denied to cable the First Amendment protections every newspaper and news magazine took for granted. Local authorities, in the meantime, consolidated power to supervise cable companies, and the 1984 act gave the municipalities a certain number of access channels for public *and* private purposes. The rule of thumb for leased access channels was 10 percent of capacity in a system with thirty-six to fifty-four channels and up to 15 percent of the channels in larger systems.[5]

The law covering such allocations also treats obscenity. Cable operators must provide, by sale or lease, a lockbox (soon to be the V-chip) for parents who wish to control what their children watch. Language that is "obscene or otherwise unprotected by the Constitution" may *not* be transmitted by a cable system. No examples are cited, no definitions attempted, and the result is at best an imprecise content regulation at the federal level, a franchise-granting regulation at the local level, and the increasing complexity of issues regarding the use of access channels that are locally mandated but whose content may trigger First Amendment issues surrounding hate speech, indecency, and political slander.

A letter in the *New Haven Register* commending a high-ranking military officer for his publicly expressed vilification of his commander in chief (a blatant defiance of military regulations) is protected by the Constitution because the letter appears in a newspaper. That same letter read aloud by its author on an access cable channel could inspire, politically or philosophically, a legal action against the cable operator based on slander or obscenity or some other offense not sheltered by First Amendment protection. When a case is made for constitutional rights by a cable company, the courts will have to confront several troubling issues. First, is there any point in continuing to call cable a scarcity when its very nature is abundance? Second, is there a convincing argument that the enormous cost of creating and operating a cable company amounts to "economic scarcity"—that is, prohibitively high stakes on which only a very few can afford to gamble? Third, is each cable company, in essence, a monopoly because only one service could survive in each community and therefore only one is given a franchise? If the monopoly status holds, then the government can insist—as it usually has—on some form of regulation. Finally, there is the constitutionality of enforcing access. The government cannot force a newspaper to run an op-ed page. Why should it have the right to force a cable operator to provide the electronic equivalent of op-ed? The municipal authorities, however, do have justifiable jurisdiction over streets and telephone poles and wires into homes that may be unsafe and over repair trucks and digging equipment that cause traffic snarls. Then there is the "common carrier" comparison, cable defined as a public utility. All the same, program content and access regulation could be beyond the acceptable grasp of government. The regulations could be seen as unconstitutional in the future.

The judges who are appointed over the next few decades will have experienced the new technologies in full form. How much can the First Amendment's forty-five words accommodate? The same cable company that provides a hundred or more channels also will be monitoring the viewing habits of each subscriber. For $4,000 (at 1995 prices) anybody will be able to buy a personal computer more powerful than a $4 million mainframe purchased a decade ago. The ability to collect and analyze information about private individuals, to say nothing of public figures, will explode. "The cumulative effect," says the *Economist*, "will cast a shadow over personal privacy. Is it really acceptable for most of your actions, even the most mundane, to be recorded and then sold to the highest bidder or made available to governments?"[6]

Some experts here and abroad applaud the Freedom of Information Act as the best safeguard. Any citizen has the right to obtain from the government or from some private organization all the information that those institutions hold about that individual. What restrictions can the law place on the use of collected data about individuals? One group of legal scholars supports "a lean and mean First Amendment"—protecting the demonstrably important matters rather than dealing with all the "issues of communication and communicators." Another group holds that the press should not be bifurcated—one kind of press protected, the other regulated. The risks of confusion and abuse of power are too great.

Professor Stephen Carter, writing in the *Yale Law Journal,* says the fears "of the power of the media are not wholly irrational. Left unregulated, the modern media could present serious threats to democracy." Echoing the 200-year-old admonition of James Madison, offered in a time unafflicted by technology, Carter declares, "We are moving into a world . . . in which the information is controlled increasingly by those who are not totally disinterested in the outcomes produced by the system."[7] For Carter the danger lies in the concentration of opinion-shaping communications conglomerates in fewer hands and the limiting effect that trend has on open, robust debate. He is preceded in this view by the late Judge J. Skelly Wright of the Washington, D.C., Circuit Court, who wrote trenchantly about the economic aspect of communications. Wright's concern was that money will vanquish ideas as the central force. The big media companies, the large advertisers, and the financial interests could dominate the airwaves. For Professor Carter and Judge Wright, and many critics of television news, there is a monolithic sameness about network news that reflects specific background textures—gender, education, economics, and corporate hierarchies. It may be said (irreverently) that taking on the trinity of faith, hope, and money, the media will find the greatest of these is money.

To summarize, the Supreme Court has sustained regulation of the electronic press on a single ground—scarcity. The *economic theory* has been used by advocates of regulation as a new form of scarcity (cost), replacing the early imbalance between demand and supply regarding broadcast signals. There are those scholars who just as vigorously argue—in the Justice Douglas tradition—that the First Amendment in its original form and intent told the government to "keep its hands off the press," and that's the way it should be unless a "new First Amendment is adopted."[8]

The economic argument is, of course, not merely centered on corporate ownership of media conglomerates. The source of revenue is advertising. As noted earlier, the press has always kept two sets of books—editorial (including "infotainment") and business (circulation and advertising revenue). There is a strong—if not totally persuasive—case to be made for the notion that the greatest threat to a free press in America comes, with and without design, from the private interests. The most significant source of revenue for media proprietors is advertising. Print ads and broadcast commercials underwrite the high cost of wide-ranging news coverage. The same contracts empower large corporate interests with a capacity for censorship. Some of that censorship, as already cited, is self-inflicted by media reporters and editors all too aware of the advertiser's predilections.

A comprehensive study of advertising influence on media content, and possible remedies, has been made at the University of Pennsylvania Law School under the direction of Professor C. Edwin Baker. A report of the study's findings was published in June 1992.[9] The notion that advertising subsidizes the press (discussed in an earlier chapter) is regarded as plausible. In Germany the Constitutional Court reaffirmed in 1991 that broadcasting companies must be prevented from cutting into the critical advertising revenue needed by the print media—considered in German law as the "real" press and therefore the kind of communication most deserving of constitutional protection. The question of advertising content is a separate issue, as is the argument for any constitutional protection that might pertain to *commercial* speech, expression, or publication. Meiklejohn would not equivocate—*commercial* interests including advertising are *private* interests with no place under the First Amendment umbrella.

The issue, then, is to determine the character of the contribution advertising makes to the essential function of the media as a servant of democracy. The use of political advertising, the seductiveness of false claims, the pernicious effects some ads may have (deliberately or not) on children, and the serious medical damage caused by cigarettes and patent medicines are issues still on the table. Some products have been voluntarily banned from television commercials, others prohibited by regulation of one sort or another. The advertising of products with a direct impact on public health (e.g., tobacco) is, it would reasonably seem, more apt to be forbidden on television, which must deal with licensing agreements, than in print.

The prevailing view is that advertising revenue does help—to a substantial extent—underwrite editorial expenses in print and on the air. From a commercial aspect, advertisers may need the audience more than the media need the advertisers. There is a difference between print and broadcasting in that subscription or single-copy costs are borne in large part by the readers of magazines and newspapers. Cable TV fees do not relate closely to advertising—indeed may discourage advertising on pay channels.

The history of newspapers indicates that competition created better coverage of news events and the publication of varied viewpoints because the individual newspaper could differentiate itself and increase its appeal to certain constituencies by enhancing the delivery of both news and opinion. Where one paper takes over a market by garnering the major share of advertising, the tendency—no matter how much greater the expenditure on news and discussion—has been to become centrist, often bland and noncontroversial. In theory this is not in the interest of a democratic society.

In a study of American magazines published in 1991, John Tebble and Mary Ellen Zuckerman report that for most of the twentieth century, advertising covered about two-thirds of publication costs, but during the 1980s the figure sank to 48 percent. Paid circulation, however, increased by 35 percent between 1979 and 1989.[10] Meanwhile, in the same period, newspapers continued to be among the most profitable business enterprises in the United States—far ahead of the median Fortune 500 companies. Why then did newspaper competition shrink—as it has steadily in the

American urban markets? Ben Bagdikian attributes the drop in competitive publishing to mass advertising. Large regional and national corporations purchase newspaper space so as to reach large audiences on a widespread basis. The process creates monopolies by driving the lower-circulation papers out of business. What follows is the pursuit of advertising rather than the pursuit of reader interest. What suffers the most, serious critics and researchers insist, is the coverage of diverse and strongly held political and social ideas. Partisanship, fervor, provocative intellectual fiber, have been—and still can be—profitable for some publications, but the reader pays the freight in most of those cases, not the advertiser. In that universe, partisanship and passion become paramount. Not so when mass advertising takes over. The inclination and the incentives for mass advertisers are to swim in midstream and to keep the waters calm.

One significant effect of blandness and lack of competitive partisanship in the press, measured by a number of scholarly studies published in the late 1980s, is the alarming decline in American voter turnout. In the 1980 American presidential election, of the *eligible* voters, only 55 percent voted. In European elections at about the same time, the figures contrast sharply: 90.7 percent in Sweden; 90.4 percent in West Germany; 85.9 percent in France; and 75.9 percent in Great Britain. Ronald Reagan went to the White House with the votes of 28 percent of the *potential* electorate.[11] While many scholars document the relationship between partisan, competitive newspapers and voting habits, there is a view held by some that the voters would have become less motivated anyway because of the changes in American political culture, skepticism, and consequential apathy.

Advertising, whatever its influence on editorial decisions and self-censorship, currently takes up about 65 percent of newspaper space (somewhat less than magazines) and 22 percent of television time. The argument can be made that overwhelmingly the content of advertising reflects market forces and not social values or ethical principles. Corporate advertising, commonly if not predominantly, seeks to persuade the public on political and ideological issues—not necessarily a bad thing in the face of the vanishing debate on public matters in the press but certainly likely to be tilted to one side. As for network documentaries, writer Erik Barnouw's research produced the conclusion that the prime evil was self-censorship: "Its monuments are proposals not budgeted, ideas never proposed." Why? It is assumed that the sponsor wouldn't approve. The producers and writers, like most editors and publishers, are usually aware of "what might not be acceptable."[12]

Professor Baker and his Pennsylvania colleagues, providing meticulous documentation, find four basic damage areas advertising can and has created: coddling of advertisers; softness on social issues that advertisers believe to be inimical to a "buying mood"; avoidance of strong positions on public issues so as to offend no one; and emphasis on the needs and interests of the affluent buyer-reader to the near exclusion of the poorer or marginal non-buyer-reader.

If the democratic and free press is seen as an institution that must respond equally to the needs and concerns of all people, that must help to educate diverse groups about important issues, and that must take courageous stands and lead crusades for the good of society as a whole, the four damage areas mentioned can render the media ineffectual, if not counterproductive, in the nurturing of democracy. That condition, it follows, can initiate a reexamination of First Amendment protections. In many Supreme Court opinions, a leap backward in time to the vision of the Framers has suggested that the press clause of the First Amendment was deliberately terse and unencumbered with exceptions. Exceptions have been proposed by Congress over the years with virtually all of them appearing in the twentieth century. The rationale of Supreme Court justices in these matters has not always produced a predictable pattern or a reluctance to interpret "Congress shall make no law . . . abridging the freedom of speech or of the press" in language invested with shadings and outright contradictions. Alexander Bickel observed:

> The Court, an independent body of men, not responsible or responsive after the fashion of democratic institutions, but answerable only, as Chief Justice Warren pointed out in his farewell remarks, *each to his conscience*, is not only an effective instrument for ensuring fairness and justice in the government's dealings with the individual, but a splendid instrument for forcing the society's attention to issues of principle, particularly issues of moral principle that often are submerged in the welter of affairs. (emphasis added)[13]

Among the "welter of affairs," restraints on extreme obscenity, the protection of children from "adult" television, and the uses of advertising are elements of a continuing dialogue in Congress, in the academy, and in the courts. Of these three complex areas, the most statistically measurable is advertising because the subject is a commercial enterprise. Page rates, broadcast-time charges, circulation, ratings, are quantifiable. Such numbers have inescapable significance for the media—directly in regard to profits, indirectly in regard to budgets for news coverage. The hidden agenda, however, was and is the influence of advertiser support on content and the conundrum of money spent on space (print) and time (air) to move goods and services. Thus advertising becomes the primary resource for the underwriting of news and public discussion, fundamentally necessary to a democratic society but without commercial characteristics.

Professor Baker's study examines a number of possible measures aimed at safeguarding news and information on public issues from advertiser pressure, either overt or subtle—including the subtlety that leads to self-censorship. Legislative action could forbid, either by criminal or civil law, any attempt to use "economic relationships with a media enterprise" to influence the content of reportage, editorials, broadcast news, or documentaries. Some scholars would construe what they call "economic censorship" as, in effect, preventing public access to information and opinions. In theory, advertisers and media companies could be denied by law the buying and selling of advertising space or broadcast commercial time based on "positioning"—exact placement in a publication or within a given television program. The purchasers would have to choose demographic characteristics in circulation or viewing habits without specific conditions or knowledge of content. Such legislation is unlikely, but Justice Hugo Black's comment, made in 1945, still resonates: "Freedom of the press from governmental interference under the First Amendment does not sanction repression of that freedom by private interest."[14] The role of the government is not entirely neutral as things stand. Very substantive subsidies are provided to newspapers and magazines through second-class mailing privileges and some government advertising. And newspaper owners are barred from owning a broadcast facility in the same market in which they publish.

The concept of a special tax on advertising in newspapers goes back to the stamp tax imposed by the British, which led many small colonial newspapers to go out of business and was a major factor in the uprising that became the War of Independence. Nonetheless, taxation aimed solely at advertising has been seriously considered by legal scholars for many decades. Sweden, thought to be the most newspaper-reading country in the world, in 1971 implemented a "production subsidy" supported by a tax on advertising. The purpose was to encourage competition and subscription. The subsidy is keyed to the amount of space devoted to news and public affairs. Other subsidies, or taxes, could be utilized to encourage more editorial diversity and more sophisticated coverage and diminish the enormous power of advertising. A tax on commercial broadcasting could provide some, if not all, of the funding for public broadcasting. Britain has long had a licensing fee collected annually for radio and television sets privately used. Until the 1960s, the BBC virtually dominated broadcasting in England and still receives substantial government funding for its operations. In the 1970s and 1980s the competition provided by several privately owned channels and the advent of cable and satellite television has altered program strategies and marketing. Competition stimulated noncommercial collaboration between the BBC (and in America the Public Broadcasting System) and corporations—a development that was not envisioned when the British government went into the broadcast business on the assumption that radio was a public utility or when public broadcasting was first funded in America.

The technological scene has radically changed, but the demonstrable dangers of government regulation have not. The problems of bureaucracy, political ax grinding, and restraint of trade make any discussion of the commercial aspect of the free press delicate at best. Those who believe that advertising produces its own form of censorship, limits content, creates inequalities, and dampens competition readily acknowledge the positive contributions of advertising but see the negative effects as outweighing the benefits. One expressed fear is that "newspapers would eventually sink under the weight of . . . 'Revenue Related Reading Matter.'" The same could be said of viewing matter—even in and among the news-related "shows" currently proliferating.

The qualities of a free democratic press that are threatened by blandness, avoidance of controversy and social problems, and a need to reach a reasonably affluent marketplace are the very qualities that gave the press its place in the Constitution in the first place and, before that, its place in the hearts and minds of colonial Americans who were becoming politically alert and entrepreneurial. The question, as yet unanswered, is, Can the negative consequences of having the media so dependent on advertising revenue be changed without inhibiting or stifling the positive effects of advertising? The debate, if any, surrounding that question will have to determine and deal with its linkage to the First Amendment, which is read by some scholars as protection for autonomy, by others as primarily a bulwark of the broadest possible public debate. The autonomy concept focuses on individual free expression—including the individual who owns a newspaper or a television station. When and if the individual's right to speak or write what he or she wishes limits the rights of others, the issue becomes a question of which form of expression serves the public best. Autonomy has become, through adjudication in twentieth-century cases, an instrumental method for keeping government at bay, but the instrument is meant to serve the larger purpose, articulated by Justice Brennan as "uninhibited, robust and wide open" public debate.

The government as a regulator (i.e., the FCC) and the corporations as selectors of news (networks, newspaper publishers, and others) are each presumably serving the public interest, but both have the power to distort or censor information. Self-government, call it self-determination by the people, is dependent on the free flow of information and news. If the media are too controlled by the market (advertising and circulation revenue), what is the countervailing power that can balance the public account? Owen Fiss believes: "The State must put on the agenda issues that are systematically ignored and slighted, and allow us to hear voices and viewpoints that would otherwise be silenced or muffled."[15]

Alexander Bickel, in contrast, saw the *press* as the countervailing power to the state. He also saw the relationship between the two as a contest not unlike the "collision between prosecutor and defense to produce the just result."[16] Bickel's concern, in this context, was the conflict between privacy (or secrecy) in government actions and the process of informing the electorate by press actions. Fiss fears the "distorting influence of the market" on both politicians *and* the press. The state has the power, he says, and the obligation, to intervene when necessary to keep the public debate open. Bickel, having observed a press confronting the government and the establishment in the Vietnam and Watergate years, stated: "So we are content in the contest between press and government, with the pulling and hauling, because in it lies the optimal assurance of both privacy and freedom of information. Not full assurance of either, but maximum assurance of both."[17]

24

TRAINING THE WATCHDOGS

I sort of drew up the specifications for the job [ombudsman] back in 1970. And I thought that what the paper needed out of this character was firstly a person who would monitor the paper every day for fairness and balance and whatever professional standards we were trying to uphold. Secondly, that this character should be available to the public to deal with complaints about the news columns or the editorial page.

—Richard Harwood,
Washington Post editor, ombudsman, columnist

Assurance of the broadest freedom of information, whether assisted by the government, discovered by the journalist, or validated by the judiciary—a kind of separation and balance of powers in itself—requires a comity on all sides, an acceptance of common principles, and the knowledge that those who are involved in the communications of a democracy play a major role in its governance. That mandate introduces the last component—at least in this rendering—of unfinished First Amendment business: the ethical responsibility of the press. In previous chapters the subject of ethical codes, press criticism, and public disenchantment has been examined. The point to make now concerns the pragmatically beneficial fallout from a policy of responsible, accountable journalism. Virtue in this regard has not been its own reward—not, that is, in the minds of bottom-line managers, cynical editors, and careerist reporters. For them the rewards must be more immediate in the highly charged mass media universe, although awareness of the long-term benefits has been growing substantially since the late 1980s. Seminars and symposia are organized more frequently at universities and among the large number of journalistic associations. Ombudsmen are functioning more visibly and effectively at more than thirty important newspapers. There is even one surviving news council that was formed in Minnesota and that has carried out, since 1971, statewide monitoring of the press. Most papers, daily or weekly, are learning to use letters from readers, op-ed pages, and other kinds of forums for ventilating disagreement with editorial positions, acknowledging bias, or providing alternative opinions.

More and better courses in ethics at journalism schools, internal discussions of ethical dilemmas, and workshops are taking place voluntarily among a variety of press groups. The literature of ethics and communication is gaining a permanent place in education and in trade magazines. The *Nieman Reports* and the *Columbia Journalism Review* are maintaining their traditional high standards, and they are not alone in the field of media criticism. Nearly every major newspaper and news magazine has at least one media reporter, and some television news departments have conducted sporadically televised forums on their own performance. Public television stations regularly present discussions of news coverage triumphs and shortfalls against the background of ethical obligations. A variety of books are published every year by trade houses and university presses on the technology, the jurisprudence, the achievements, and the failures of modern journalism.

Intramural criticism and accountability have engaged finally the most serious publishers and television news producers. Who is watching the watchdog is still a riddle. There is no definitive solution, and probably there never will be a satisfactory all-encompassing response. Ethical behavior cannot be codified or designed by committee. It may have to begin at the top, but it will inevitably depend on the individual conscience at every level. What can be accomplished by more education and understanding of the origins of ethical principles and the reading of a moral compass seems to be self-evident. Osborn Elliott, once editor in chief of *Newsweek*, later dean of Columbia University's Journalism School, said in 1985: "I don't think there's any industry in the country that has done as much soul searching over the past ten years."[1]

The various methods of self-criticism can be gathered together over time and become a strong force in the practice of journalism. Many experienced and distinguished reporters and editors have concluded that the sensitized individuals who write news stories for print and broadcast will examine their own work more conscientiously because they have been made *aware* of the casualties caused by indifference to strict accuracy and the care required to produce a fair and balanced account. Richard Clurman suggested for the news media "two immediate and effective reforms to deal with their worst faults and the public's greatest frustration with them." His reforms, he admonished, will require no laws or internal upheaval, "just a change in attitude."[2] First, the media must report honestly and candidly on themselves and on each other, in effect demanding the same standards of rectitude of the press that the press demands of public officials. Second, the media must allow prompt and adequate reply from their victims—or those who reasonably *think* they are victims.

These two reforms have not been entirely neglected in the past. As already noted, many papers and magazines assign reporters to media stories on a regular basis. Public television examines news coverage in discussion and documentary programs, and network news anchors have been known to apologize for errors and do so on the air. Major newspapers have acknowledged mistakes and printed corrections on a daily basis. There is movement in the area of "sorry about that" publicly expressed, but access is a less-developed country. The most commonly used avenue of reply or corrective addendum is the letters columns. These are not long on space or amenable to comprehensiveness. Now and then a letter to the editor is enlarged or polished and becomes an op-ed piece. Sometimes a phone call gets through to the appropriate editor and the caller receives an apology of sorts or perhaps finds a correction published the next day.

The *New York Times* introduced, in recent years, a correction box and occasionally publishes a related editor's note. Corrections appear in the *Times* almost always on page 2, and research has shown they are very widely read. Much that appears as a correction relates to trivial inexactitude; but the mechanism has been established, and even skeptical press insiders consider it a commendable development. If the major newspapers and magazines—those with the "important" circulations and prize-winning staff members who have built deserved prestige and influence—more openly and expeditiously allowed the citizen his or her right to confront (or at least answer) the accuser, there would be in all likelihood fewer libel actions even if there was no appreciable increase in the popularity of the press. The disrespect for the press, however, among those segments of the public who follow the news and care about public policy could and should be diminished by systematic accountability.

If a reporter or an editor or a television newscaster is said to be accountable, he or she can be called to judgment and expected to give reasonable answers. The very definition of the word *account* is a reckoning properly requested and given, a statement explaining conduct to legitimately designated parties. That the purveyors of news will never win popularity contests is a timeworn assumption. That they may win more respect by genuinely holding themselves to established standards—the standards to which they hold Congress, corporations, and other American institutions and professions in both their reporting and their editorials—is neither timeworn nor merely an assumption. The challenge for the press is not only to establish ethical standards but to see to it that they are perceived to be operational.

Normative ethics beyond the basic demand for accuracy and fairness, which are not always demonstrable, become difficult to define. Ethical codes are often lyrically cobbled together but remain emblematic and impractical. The lawyers warn that published codes can be used against the publisher in libel actions. Similar reservations inhibit the coverage of the media *by* the media. The reluctance of "members of the club" to criticize other members is inherent, and when they do report on the mistakes or incompetence of fellow practitioners, they are often accused of self-decoration—if not treason. When neither honor nor some kind of rough justice is achieved, there is not much incentive. If the not-quite-a-profession called journalism pays too little attention to moral obligations, its young recruits will drift away from ethical judgments because such calculations will appear to be little more than personal opinions without a basis in reliable principles. Useful standards can and have been set by reporters and editors, publishers and producers. The individual conscience and experience have taught journalists what *ought* to be said and done, but the individual cannot decree what *will* be said and done.

Ethical principles are not yet a match for careerism and compromise. News organizations from the top down will convey a commitment to high and honorable standards, to best ethical performance, only if proprietors and managers, publishers and editors, producers and anchors, are convinced that integrity is a sensible long-range investment even if they have to go it alone. A good example of going it alone in the interest of principle comes from a memorandum sent by Steve Brill, who was president of American Lawyer Media, to his colleagues at *Court TV*—a cable service that covers important trials. In regard to a request for coverage of the Woody Allen–Mia Farrow hearing, Brill said, "We also told the judge that consistent with our long standing policy, we would not, even if allowed, show any testimony of children or any testimony pertaining to explicit sexual matters or any testimony about the medical or emotional lives of the children that was unduly personal. . . . I hope other news organizations— including the print media—will do the same (and not do it live and not put all the lurid details in the tabloids), but I'm not confident that all will, and (as with using the names of rape victims without their consent) I'm not going to let their editorial decisions dictate ours."[3]

Social scientists have repeatedly found that there is little correlation between ethical *beliefs* and ethical *behavior*. But individuals who learn to analyze and express their beliefs precisely and then learn how to apply those beliefs to specific problems are far more likely to *act* according to those beliefs. For journalists a written ethical code is comforting, high-minded, and impractical. It may be employed as a shield—"We do things right, read our code." Or at best it is a reminder—often eloquently composed—of ineffable ideals.

Richard Clurman observed tartly, "As the press grew into the news media in the second half of the Twentieth Century, they overwhelmed other conventional centers of American power. To politicians and public officials on every level—from President to aldermen—it was how the media reported and commented on them that determined their fate."[4] As for the public at large, the readers and the viewers, the media have often seemed so indifferent to fair play that trust has eroded. The sharpest skepticism centers on being able to talk back, to remonstrate with editors who may be faceless and nameless, or to confront byline reporters who "stand by the story," won't answer the phone, are out of town, or at best suggest the offended party write a letter that he or she has no reason to believe will ever be published. In regard to that skepticism, the possibilities of news councils should be constantly revisited. Despite the record, changing times make intelligently conceived monitoring councils a potentially valuable resource for the media and the public.

In the next century the mass communications print and electronic news organizations with the greatest influence on public opinion and electoral decisions will be owned by a small group of conglomerates. If profit-seeking overwhelms responsibility among these corporations, the role of the press in a free society will change for the worse. Should the short-term bottom-liners triumph, the trend will be, predictably, toward more sensationalism, entertainment, and soft journalism. If fiduciary responsibility is recognized and supported by management, the press can benefit from the economic strength of being owned by large corporations: It can expand global coverage, hire and appropriately compensate the best educated and talented people, and sustain the capacity to be a sentinel for the public interest.

Not only are the credibility of and open discussion in the media essential to public judgment, but without those conditions public participation will slacken. People may indeed lose interest in self-government. If an informed and active electorate is the nerve system of democracy, it will have to survive the fragmentation of American society, already projected by demographers. In 2050, barring nuclear war or rampant plagues, it is estimated that the number of human beings living on this planet—will grow to more than 10 billion—twice the population in 1995.[5] In that clamorous universe the globalization of American interests will require an understanding of political, environmental, scientific, and spiritual developments that only responsible mass communications can provide on a widespread basis. If nations and political structures are to live together in relative peace on our crowded earth, the international media will be their schoolroom and their mediator. What individual minds will do with reported facts and given opinions will vary according to the emotional and intellectual climate.

The American press has, with all its faults, been the best in the world—technically and editorially—for over 100 years because it has remained free and, by and large, independent. Its leadership position will be confronted in the next century by social, technological, and political ferment, but the greatest threat to America's press comes from within—from its sense of itself. The press has by its very nature defined its own place in society. If it does not clearly define and accept its responsibilities and keep its standards strong under the lens of self-examination, intramural criticism, and public accountability, news will become just another commercial enterprise—selling itself as entertainment in print and on the tube—with little meaningful substance between them. At the end of the day, if news or information on significant public issues is perceived to be so faulty or inadequate that it becomes a "public danger," how long will constitutional protection endure?

EPILOGUE: PATHFINDING

If to please the people, we offer what we ourselves disapprove, how can we afterwards defend our work?

—George Washington, speaking at the
Constitutional Convention in Philadelphia, 1788

Bidding farewell to his students at Chicago in 1951, Robert Maynard Hutchins, the man who had helped to institute the Great Books course to celebrate Western civilization, described a gloomy future in which there would be "nobody speaking and nobody reading." He explained it this way: "Astronomers at the University of Chicago have detected something that looks like moss growing on Mars. I am convinced that Mars was once inhabited by rational human beings like ourselves, who had the misfortune, some thousands of years ago, to invent television."[1]

Early on, Hutchins had foreseen the technology boom and the "intellectual wasteland" of the visual age. He may not have reckoned on the full onslaught of entertainment that television would impose on every aspect of life in the second half of the twentieth century, but he understood its effects. America would be described as the "best entertained and least informed nation in the Western World."[2]

Technology has not been a significant problem for media companies. Both print and electronic news have had little difficulty adopting inventive means of distribution from the telegraph to the satellite. The more complicated task was to keep an established audience. *Life* magazine had to surrender to television. Network television's enormous audiences were fragmented by cable and VCR. Now the computer minces the market for the traditional media into even smaller pieces. This may have a positive effect on entertainment, perhaps on children's programming, and even on general education, but the electorate—the "public" that forms opinions and chooses its public officials—needs help from the serious media.

Thinking of the media as a monolithic force is foolish, but facile judgments are invited when journalists behave, as Eugene McCarthy once described them, like blackbirds on a telephone wire: One moves to a lower wire and all the rest follow. Sometimes it becomes a feeding frenzy. There are, of course, birds of different feathers, and they are not all frenzied. But if journalists are to be regarded as reliable and fair, they will require an ethos that makes ethical consciousness automatic. There *are* lines and boundaries they should not cross. That awareness of boundaries needs the elucidation of a continuous process voluntarily entered into. To remain at arms length, reporters may have to choose between self-aggrandizement and trust. Some commentators in print and on talk radio have trouble with another kind of separation—between healthy skepticism and virulent disrespect. Speech, whether sick or healthy, is protected by the First Amendment, but how long will the public feed on fear and loathing? And with what effect on self-government? Civility has no such strident defenders. "There is no question," Woody Allen reportedly observed, "that there is a moral and ethical world out there. The question is how far is it from midtown, and how late does it stay open."

What is not widely in place is the watchdog for the watchdogs—journalists who can write freely about the transgressions of other journalists without fear of being ostracized or accused of betrayal. Biting the hand that feeds is not happily undertaken. Only when there are other hands that applaud because taking the high ground produces public trust, and ultimately public loyalty, will the ethos change. The bean counters are the least likely to wait it out. The steady, methodical process of reviewing each important public interest story and each editorial decision calls for tough questioning and much patience. Is this what we want to say? Is this what we *ought* to say? After the early headlines, the handouts, and the media events, there can and should be a *second wave* of journalism—follow-up, setting the record straight. In the financial world, it is called "due diligence." No less a precaution should apply to the people's business. But without a bright line between responsibility to the citizens who read, who listen, who watch, and the commercial interests of the proprietors, diligence is meaningless.

Suggestion: a different form of *quarterly results*. News organizations could check their lead stories of the previous three months and report on the *consequences* of media attention—exoneration, prosecution, reform, progress, outrage. Voluntary correctives can be competitive. When top-flight newspapers, television newscasters, and Internet suppliers find their competitors striving for rectitude and accepting responsibility for mistakes, the movement toward institutionalizing ethical standards—without legislative coercion—could become an inexorable tide. The V-chip and the network violence-rating system may be regarded as evasive action to avoid congressional piety, but the challenge for the expanding news business is to identify, as best it can, the divide between public interest and private rights—then create the mechanisms for *keeping* them separate. An intellectual M-chip (for Meiklejohn) would be helpful. No one has spoken more clearly and cogently than he did on the difference between the information and commentary necessary to an informed electorate and those activities that are intrinsically private or commercial. Meiklejohn said: "The guarantee given by the First Amendment is not then assured to all speaking. It is assured only to speech which bears, directly or indirectly, upon issues with which voters have to deal—only, therefore, to the consideration of matters of public interest."[3]

In the past few years, there has been significant intramural criticism concerning journalists whose appearances on television talk shows make them more famous than the public officials they scrutinize. Some reporters have become pancaked pundits, others mere shouters. All of them will claim (and not always disingenuously) that they can keep a wall between their often highly paid public roles and their personal responsibility as observers and interpreters of the political and cultural process. They will have to if they are to be entrusted with the task of separating fact from fiction. The news media will not flourish in public purpose or in private enterprise if they deliberately violate their promises and principles. To avoid that breakdown, the media have to subscribe to a set of beliefs and maintain them—not merely for the sake of appearances but as common sense. Becoming a "public trust" takes time and determination, but that achievement will be an investment worth making for news companies, particularly those that are part of a larger, multifaceted corporation. Without a commitment to responsibility, news operations slip into the ephemeral area of triviality and disguised entertainment.

In contrast, the corporations that protect their news divisions from short-term business adjustments can create an enterprise that will benefit the larger society and engender confidence in the goods and services provided by other divisions under the same management. A flagship news operation can operate with enlightened self-interest. There aren't many well-navigated flagships on the journalistic high seas, but those that set sail each day with a commitment to quality are vital to the safety of democracy—and will enhance the corporate balance sheet. A quality news organization can and does attract advertising revenue. News credibly and competently delivered will also provide that unquantifiable element called integrity. A virtuous reputation in the global marketplace is valuable in itself, and only independent news reporting can countervail the charge that the First Amendment is being used to reinforce concentrations of private power in the hands of conglomerates that control cable television, telephones, and computer networks. The power to *distribute* news is potentially the power to *select* content. The journalism that brings to the body politic the ideas, the actions, and the consequences of public policy cannot be left to the forces in a marketplace because too many voices will go *unheard* and too many voices representing special interests *will* be heard. The danger is not so much from the conscious effort of management to shape the news but from the culture of a vertical corporation that influences the decisions of editors and reporters to serve the best interests of the bottom line.

Can a watchdog also be a celebrity? Fame and fees, book contracts and lecture tours, are seductive. Journalists are no less interested in money than are doctors and lawyers. Regular appearances on the TV screen unavoidably create celebrity. If the mass media reporters are viewed as vassals of special interest groups and the entertainment business—collectively as part of international conglomerates, individually as performers under bright studio lights—the most important institution able to provide political enlightenment for a mass audience loses public confidence. That prospect should concern everyone who cares about democracy in the coming era of borderless cyberspace.

Critics are always long on diagnosis, short on treatment. So what can be done? To start with, we can explicitly employ some of the ideas reported earlier in this book:

- Collaborate with the nation's universities and colleges in designing curricula tailored for working journalists in every community. These can be concentrated seminars lasting days or weeks on those subjects least understood by the public or most rapidly changing. Such educational opportunities will do for journalists what *they* must do for audiences unable to tap or not interested in isolation journalism called up on computer screens. News organizations and foundations should subsidize the cost of such programs and the hiring of more Ph.D.s. In 1898 the *Journalist*, a trade paper, reported that most of the large newspapers in New York City had at least ten college graduates on their staffs. In 1998 a college degree will not be good enough for many key positions. There may be and ought to be in the media a thriving market for Ph.D.s to help interpret economics, environmental problems, science, medicine, and law, among other areas of information.
- Managers of news enterprises should devise and encourage forums on journalistic standards, focusing on how the obvious can be made commonplace and how the lip service given to *accuracy* and *fairness* can be transposed into practical day-to-day decisions. Adherence to an agreed ethical practice should be an important factor in job references and promotions. Newspapers, news magazines, and TV stations can get help in this area from nonprofit organizations

such as the Poynter Institute, the Freedom Forum, and the Nieman Foundation, among others. At issue here is the inherent capacity of computers to provide swift and unretractable misinformation or deliberate distortion—a capacity that is greater today than ever before. What is vanishing in America is that almost tactile news— small papers passed from one person to another, read aloud in taverns and inns, poured over in family sitting rooms, and remarked on from the pulpit, its contents discussed and debated locally among people who know each other. Nineteenth-century Americans waited impatiently for the post and clamored for copies of newspapers. In the South, poor white farmers actually complained that the slaves in the plantation houses had more access to sparse newspapers than they did. The shift from such closeness between limited news and hand-to-hand circulation to national TV around the clock, and now Internet, places an inescapable burden on the responsible press. Somehow, in the morass of competing information systems, there must continue to be those high-quality newspapers, magazines, and newscasts that will attract an audience of educated people. It is that audience, taken as a group and given its ability to help shape public policy, that the media of the next century must satisfy. It is that audience that will eventually question whether democracy can survive if manufacturing public consent is an unregulated private enterprise.

- Accountability is the external face of internal resolve. It cannot be meaningful unless it begins at the top, and it cannot be credible unless it is systematic and candid. Those people who believe they have been wronged by the media should be given an opportunity to make their case and to face their accusers in one manner or another. Ombudsmen can provide a point of contact, or an "office of accountability" might be established to deal with complaints and redress bona fide grievances. The key factor will be *response*. Accountability needs the same robust muscle tone that Justice Brennan advocated for a free press. Correction and clarification require consistent frankness and visibility.
- Journalists long ago gave up on the "objectivity" strategy. Because no reporter can be totally objective, the attempt to report a story as if the writer were a tabula rasa—collecting random facts while carrying no intellectual or philosophical baggage—distorted the news with neurotic neutrality. The challenge of informed interpretation, as the best alternative, is to stay as close as possible to balanced truth-telling, whatever the reporter's personal views. Evenhandedness does not preclude values. In the 1920s it was Henry Luce who

advocated stories that combined "intelligent criticism, representation, and evaluation of the men who will hold offices of public trust."[4]

- For the news consumer who cannot rise above stereotypes, there will always be a convenient bumper sticker about the press—in recent times most likely some variation of "too liberal," although "too conservative" is not ruled out. The public looks for corroboration of a received opinion on special interests—abortion, taxes, law and order, race, and immigration, to name a few. When confronted with contradiction, the viewer or reader must reexamine (possibly reaffirm) his or her position or dismiss the messenger as biased. Circumspection and thoroughness are among the safeguards for the media. Diversity of opinion (and writers) on editorial and op-ed pages or in the casting of television panels is the best evidence of fair play. Individual reporters will experience reality differently and describe it differently. The commonality ought to be a good-faith effort to get it *right* (not necessarily *first*)—to inform, not merely entertain.

- Indisputably, at the center of all journalism in whatever form, there are and always will be *words*—morally charged or deliberately malicious, shaped by spin or sodden with ignorance. Words evoke ideas, and ideas, as Justice Holmes informed us, are incitements. Photographs, video pictures, and digital imagery may convey powerful impressions, but without captions or narration, those impressions are incomplete, inexact, or erroneous. Words are the voices of memory, making the past available. Henry David Thoreau, in the early 1840s, was visited in Concord, Massachusetts, by a reporter who wanted to get the transcendentalist's view of a new device called the telegraph. "The President of the United States," the reporter said excitedly, "sent a message to the Mayor of Baltimore in a matter of minutes." Thoreau, the story goes, pondered this news soberly and then asked, "What did the President say?"[5]

- To choose some events or some public figures as more interesting or more significant than others, we must depend on those values we have been taught or have learned through experience—another function of memory. It has been said that to understand is to explain and to explain is to justify. The more a journalist knows, the less difficult (at least in terms of conscience) is his or her choice of facts—and the *words* that describe their *meaning*. Unlike a musician, reporters have no score to follow. If they create their own score, over time, with reliability and sparkle, they should be suitably recognized internally and externally.

- Since the deep-running principles journalists ought to support and share are vulnerable to situational ethics (choose your own flavor), the rehearsing and revisiting process is vital. Journalism—taken here as the reporting and interpretation of those events and issues the electorate needs to understand—must examine, discuss, and employ enduring standards on a day-to-day basis as part of a working experience that is no less important than getting the facts or beating the competition. Ethical standards are like seat belts—you have to decide to use them. Immanuel Kant advised: "A rule does not oppress me, or enslave me, if I impose it on myself consciously—accept it freely—having understood its value."[6]
- Values compete in the marketplace. The goals of various social groups are not all alike. People must choose between ultimate values, and such choices will be more wisely made if they are based on perceived truths that have lasted for a long time and become integrated into people's sense of themselves. Awakening and reawakening the public to these moral beliefs have not been natural pastimes for journalists—nor have they been for politicians, lawyers, financiers, or others whose work affects public affairs. They should be, however, a *requirement* for the sentinel over all our liberties because despite contradictions and anomalies, the constitutionally protected Fourth Estate has undertaken the surveillance of those who govern or judge or administer public institutions—presumably in the public interest. That surveillance surely must include the press itself—over and over again. Perhaps, after fifty years, another Hutchins Commission should be summoned.

Looking Ahead

However "called up," reliable news coverage will have to be reported and edited by fallible human beings. News events and public policy ruminations in various legislatures and cultural institutions will be reported by the men and women of the news media on site. The fragmentation of delivery systems will have unpredictable economic effects, but the competence and ethical judgment of those who gather and organize information for public consumption will face the same challenges and responsibilities that have been part of the American experience since the beginning of political life in the New World.

If journalists become mere cogs in a corporate wheel, individual conscience and judgment will seem unnecessary. The reality is that anyone can be a journalist simply by declaration. The image of fast-talking, disreputable hacks barking into stand-up telephones faded out with black-and-white movies. But the free-booting, freelancing modern version can chase down a story, interview a public figure, and produce anything from a piece of the truth to a porridge of semifictional innuendo. If some editor buys it, the writer has become, voilà, a journalist. Trash and flash are as permanently on the record as first-rate documented reporting.

I return to the theme with which this book began: Responsible journalists cannot always take the long view when the deadline is daily or weekly, but the best of them can look at least to the middle distance, where consequences begin. If reporters allow pervasive cynicism to cloud their vision, if they mistrust all public officials as scoundrels without considering what they may have accomplished, the "adversary culture" will set the media agenda. Harsh, negative journalism is corrosive. It might not damage the user, but it will certainly discourage public service. Between liberal condescension and the self-righteous anger of right-wing demagogues, there is the "quality" press that often reveals the hollowness on both sides. The best evidence of the success of the journalistic elite is the regularity with which the major newspapers, magazines, and networks are accused of bias by the left *and* the right.

A 1996 survey of 240,000 college freshmen conducted by the UCLA Higher Education Research Institute found that only 29 percent thought it was important to follow the political news. Only a third of them believed that "promoting racial understanding should be a priority." About the same number believed that an individual can do little to change society. The slide downward into apathy has been accelerating since the 1960s. The media must be held accountable for a significant share of this disconnection. If news and commentary come to the public in strident, partisan terms, a turnoff is inevitable—and dangerous for democracy. People know, because of their own experiences, that very few issues are black and white. Ask them to consort with simplistic views expressed with absolute, high-volume certitude and they will soon turn away.

Aristotle's golden mean placed the truth somewhere between the outer edges, and not necessarily in the middle. Journalism seeks the truth without specific entrance requirements, without knowledge of standard texts, and without a supervisory body watching over its practices. The rules can be prescribed only internally, often by individual choice, if the press is to remain free, independent, and trusted.

Because journalism does not provide an oath of office or codified obligations, there has been less institutional feeling, or loyalty, than a professional status might inspire. If the large news organizations—or the large corporations that *own* news organizations—were to voluntarily form an independent monitoring agency with a limited mandate, as is the case in Britain, there might be defined benchmarks, at least regarding accuracy and fairness and corrections. Such an agency might also change attitudes. The notion inside the media that any criticism from the outside is *interference* has deep roots, but survival runs deeper. Moral ambiguity is the fashionable description of what ails the media when it allows facts and fiction—a mixture of reality and pseudoreality based on staged events—to comingle without a clear distinction between the two. Will such practices erode public support for traditional First Amendment protection? Of course they will. The serious news organizations should continue their effort to establish voluntary restraints and standards that can be convincingly displayed to the public. Not all consumers care; that makes it even more important that the press define its values and live by them. The unsubstantiated charges of wrongdoing leveled against public figures by innuendo or drawn from second- and thirdhand gossip are pernicious and self-defeating. Politicizing the news, or the appearance of it, discounts the hard work of uncovering serious misuse of political power. Using tabloid sleaze by attributing it to tabloids will soil the responsible press no matter how sanctimoniously reported. Respectable news organizations should distance themselves from the junk dealers or risk the distrust (if not the disappearance) of their audiences.

"Democracy is a device," George Bernard Shaw slyly proclaimed, "that ensures we shall be governed no better than we deserve." Without a varied, independent, and responsible press, the people will not understand what they have; nor will they know whether they deserve better.

NOTES

INTRODUCTION

1. James Madison to W. R. Barry, August 4, 1822, in G. Hearst, ed., *Writings of James Madison* (Washington, DC: Library of Congress, 1910), vol. 9, p. 103.

CHAPTER ONE

1. General George Washington to "the Members of the Volunteer Association and other inhabitants of the Kingdom of Ireland who have lately arrived in the City of New York," December 2, 1783, in John C. Fitzpatrick, ed., *The Writings of George Washington* (New York: Macmillan, 1938), vol. 27, p. 254; John Quincy Adams to Baron von Furstenwaerther, June 4, 1819, in Moses Rischin, ed., *Immigration and the American Tradition* (Indianapolis, IN: Bobbs-Merrill, 1976), originally reprinted in *Niles Weekly Register* (Massachusetts), April 29, 1820, p. 157.

2. Theodore Roosevelt, *Metropolitan* 20, memorial edition (October 1915):328.

3. William F. Buckley Jr., *Happy Days Were Here Again* (New York: Random House, 1993).

4. Thomas Jefferson, *Jefferson Papers* (Washington, DC: Library of Congress, November 4, 1823), vol. 225.

5. Warren Burger, cited in Christopher S. Lentz, "The Fairness in Broadcasting Doctrine and the Constitution: Forced One-Stop Shopping in the 'Marketplace of Ideas,'" *University of Illinois Law Review* 271 (1966):306.

6. Walter Lippmann, *Public Opinion* (New York: Macmillan, 1965), p. 183. Also see his *Liberty and the News* (New York: Harcourt, Brace & Howe, 1920), pp. 54–55, 73–76.

7. Thomas Patterson, *Out of Order* (New York: Vintage Books, 1994), p. 25.

8. Sissela Bok, *Lying* (New York: Vintage Books, 1989), p. 246.

9. Regarding the Pulitzer prize, see *Columbia Journalism Review,* November/December 1991, p. 86.

10. William Hocking, *Freedom of the Press: A Framework of Principle* (Chicago: University of Chicago Press, 1947), p. 182.

11. Alexander M. Bickel, *The Morality of Consent* (New Haven: Yale University Press, 1975), p. 79.

12. Lippmann, *Public Opinion*, p. 229.

CHAPTER TWO

1. Forrest McDonald, "Bill of Rights: Unnecessary and Pernicious," paper delivered at the United States Capitol Historical Society symposium, Washington, DC,

March 14, 1991; see Robert Allen Rutland, *The Birth of the Bill of Rights* (Chapel Hill: University of North Carolina Press, 1955), pp. 190–216.

2. Stanley Elkins and Eric McKitrick, *The Debate on the Constitution* (New York: Library of America, 1993), p. 62.

3. Richard D. Brown, *Knowledge Is Power* (New York: Oxford University Press, 1991), p. 12; R. B. Kielbowicz, *News in the Mails, 1690–1863* (Minneapolis: University of Minnesota Press, 1984), pp. 190–210; David D. Hall, "The Uses of Literacy in New England, 1600–1850," in William L. Joyce et al. (eds.), *Printing and Society in Early America* (Worcester, MA: American Antiquarian Society, 1983); Carl Kaestle, "The History of Literacy and the History of Readers," *Review of Research in Education* 12 (1985):1–50.

4. *Near v. Minnesota* 283 U.S. 697 (1931).

5. Justice Brennan, *New York Times v. Sullivan*, 376 U.S. 254 (1964).

6. Zechariah Chafee, *Free Speech in the United States* (Cambridge, MA: Harvard University Press, 1921), pp. 33, 506–509. See *Harvard Law Review* 70 (1957): 1341–1343.

7. Alexander Meiklejohn, *Political Freedom: Free Speech and Its Relation to Self-Government* (New York: Oxford University Press, 1948), pp. 24–28; Meiklejohn, "The First Amendment Is an Absolute," *Supreme Court Review*, 1961, p. 246.

8. Meiklejohn, *Political Freedom*, p. 21.

9. Cited in Gerald Gunther, *Learned Hand: The Man and the Judge* (New York: Knopf, 1994), p. 549.

10. Quoted in *Papers of John Adams*, vol. 1 (Cambridge, MA: Belknap Press, 1977).

11. Carl Van Doren, *The Great Rehearsal* (New York: Time, 1965), p. 6.

12. Ibid., pp. 157–158.

13. On September 18, 1787, a woman named Mrs. Powel "asked Dr. Franklin, 'Well, Doctor, what have we got—a republic or a monarchy?' 'A republic,' replied the Doctor, 'if you can keep it.'" Recorded by James McHenry, one of Washington's aides, in his diary (*American Historical Review* 11 (1906):618.

CHAPTER THREE

1. *New York Times v. Sullivan*, 376 U.S. 254, 276 (1964).

2. *New York Times*, March 29, 1960, p. 15; Kalven, "The *New York Times* Case," pp. 198–201.

3. Harrison Salisbury, from a series of articles in the *New York Times*: "Fear and Hatred Grip Birmingham," April 12, 1960.

4. Oliver Wendell Holmes, cited in Lawrence H. Tribe and Michael Dorf, *On Reading the Constitution* (Cambridge, MA: Harvard University Press, 1991), p. 9; *State of Missouri v. Holland*, 252 U.S. 416 (1920).

5. Taylor Branch, *Parting the Waters: America in the King Years* (New York: Simon and Schuster, 1988), pp. 288–289.

6. *New York Times v. Sullivan*, 376 U.S. 254 (no. 39, October 1963); *NAACP v. Alabama*, ex rel. *Patterson*, 377 U.S. 288 (1964).

7. Harry Kalven Jr., "The *New York Times* Case: A Note on the Meaning of the First Amendment," in *Supreme Court Review,* 1964, pp. 191–197; also see Kalven, *A Worthy Tradition* (New York: Harper & Row, 1988).

8. *New York Times,* March 19, 1960.

9. Kalven, "The *New York Times* Case," pp. 198–201.

10. Anthony Lewis, *Make No Law* (New York: Random House, 1991), pp. 113–126.

11. Kalven, "The *New York Times* Case," pp. 191, 194–197, 221.

12. Alexander Bickel, *The Least Dangerous Branch: The Supreme Court at the Bar of Politics* (New Haven: Yale University Press, 1963), p. 267.

13. This article is cited in Lewis, *Make No Law,* p. 25.

14. *Alabama Journal* (Montgomery newspaper), February 1, 1961.

15. Conversation between T. Eric Embry and Anthony Lewis in Lewis, *Make No Law,* p. 26.

16. *Beauharnais v. Illinois,* 343 U.S. 250, 251, 266 (1952); *NAACP v. Alabama,* 377 U.S. 288 (1964), p. 310; *Alabama Supreme Court,* 656, 674–676, 686 (1964); H. Kalven, *The Negro and the First Amendment* (Chicago: University of Chicago Press, 1965), p. 3; see also further background on Alabama laws and rulings in Kalven, *A Worthy Tradition.*

17. H. Salisbury, *Without Fear or Favor* (New York: Times Books, 1980), pp. 21, 26, 384; ACLU Amicus Brief, *New York Times v. Sullivan.*

18. Lewis, *Make No Law,* p. 35.

19. Kalven, "The *New York Times* Case," pp. 195–196.

20. Lucas A. Powe Jr., *The Fourth Estate and the Constitution* (Berkeley: University of California Press, 1991), p. 87.

21. *New York Times v. Sullivan;* Herbert Wechsler, *Media Law Reporter* 16, April 11, 1989.

22. Lewis, *Make No Law,* pp. 106–107.

23. Kalven, "The *New York Times* Case," p. 201.

24. Ibid., p. 193.

25. Ibid.

26. Lewis, *Make No Law,* pp. 118–119.

27. Wechsler brief quoted in Lewis, *Make No Law,* p. 117.

28. *New York Times v. Sullivan,* 376 U.S. 270.

29. Ibid.

30. Kalven, "The *New York Times* Case," p. 205.

31. Alexander Meiklejohn, *Political Freedom* (New York: Oxford University Press, 1960), pp. 26–28.

32. *Kingsley Pictures v. Regents,* 360 U.S. 684, 688–689 (1959); see Potter Stewart, "Or of the Press," *Hastings Law Journal* 26, 1975, pp. 631, 633–634; also see *Redrup v. New York,* 386 U.S. 767 (1967). *Redrup* became a kind of descriptive catchall term used to express a view of obscenity without arriving at a decision or to reverse an obscenity opinion without giving a reason.

33. Kalven, "The *New York Times* Case," pp. 197, 221.

34. "Justice Black and First Amendment 'Absolutes': A Public Interview," *NYU Law Review* 37, 1962, p. 549.

35. Conversation between Kalven and Meiklejohn during the summer following *New York Times v. Sullivan*. Alexander Meiklejohn was then ninety years old. See Kalven, "The *New York Times* Case," n. 125, p. 221.

CHAPTER FOUR

1. Harrison Salisbury, *Without Fear or Favor* (New York: Times Books, 1980), pp. 57–63; Seymour M. Hersh, *The Price of Power* (New York: Summit Books, 1983), pp. 326–330.

2. Robert McNamara, interview with Francis Cairncross, *Observer* (London), 1968.

3. Alexander Bickel, *The Morality of Consent* (New Haven: Yale University Press, 1965), p. 68.

4. Sanford Ungar, *The Papers and the Papers* (New York: Columbia University Press, 1989), p. 41.

5. Daniel Ellsberg, open letter to Harvard classmates, 1965.

6. Daniel Ellsberg, "Ellsberg Talks," interview with *Look* magazine, October 5, 1971.

7. Daniel Ellsberg, article in *Harvard College Class of 1952, Fifteenth Anniversary Report.*

8. Cited in *New York Times*, October 4, 1969.

9. Ungar, *The Papers and the Papers*, pp. 66–68; Salisbury, *Without Fear or Favor*, pp. 57–63, 82, 228; Hersh, *Price of Power*, p. 328; Daniel Ellsberg, telephone conversations with the author in 1991 and 1992.

10. Floyd Abrams, "The Pentagon Papers a Decade Later," *New York Times Magazine*, June 7, 1981; court affidavit cited by Ungar, *The Papers and the Papers*, p. 67.

11. Ungar, *The Papers and the Papers*, p. 68.

12. Salisbury, *Without Fear or Favor*, pp. 327–329; R. Woodward and S. Armstrong, *The Brethren* (New York: Simon and Schuster, 1979), pp. 139–150.

13. Salisbury, *Without Fear or Favor*, pp. 57–63.

14. Foreign Relations Committee hearings, May 13, 1970. Quoted in Ungar, *The Papers and the Papers*, pp. 74–75.

15. *New York Times*, May 14, 1970.

16. *Washington Post* story on the hearings, May 14, 1970.

17. Quoted in the *New York Times*, August 7, 1970.

18. *New York Times* letter column, November 26, 1970.

19. Ungar, *The Papers and the Papers*, pp. 80–81.

20. Salisbury, *Without Fear or Favor*, pp. 259–262.

21. Ibid., pp. 292–294; Ungar, *The Papers and the Papers*, p. 82; Ellsberg, telephone conversation with the author in November 1992.

22. Salisbury, *Without Fear or Favor*, pp. 121, 126–127; Hersh, *The Price of Power*, pp. 328–329.

23. Salisbury, *Without Fear or Favor*, pp. 243–247.

24. Ibid., pp. 121, 126–127.

25. Ungar, *The Papers and the Papers*, p. 106.

26. Salisbury, *Without Fear or Favor*, pp. 223–228, 235–236; Hersh, *Price of Power*, p. 386.

27. *Time Magazine*, July 5, 1971, and July 12, 1971.

28. Salisbury, *Without Fear or Favor*, pp. 223–228; Hersh, *Price of Power*, pp. 383–389.

29. Salisbury, *Without Fear or Favor*, pp. 243–247; Hersh, *Price of Power*, p. 386.

30. Salisbury, *Without Fear or Favor*, pp. 243–247.

31. Abrams, "The Pentagon Papers Case," p. 22; Salisbury, *Without Fear or Favor*, pp. 259–262.

32. Salisbury, *Without Fear or Favor*, pp. 259–262; Ungar, *The Papers and the Papers*, pp. 124–125.

33. Salisbury, *Without Fear or Favor*, pp. 292–294; Ungar, *The Papers and the Papers*, pp. 124–125.

34. Salisbury, *Without Fear or Favor*, p. 294; Ungar, *The Papers and the Papers*, p. 144.

35. Erwin Griswold, "Secrets Not Worth Keeping," *Washington Post*, op-ed, February 15, 1989; Lucas A. Powe Jr., who was Justice Douglas's clerk at the time, in *The Fourth Estate and the Constitution* (Berkeley: University of California Press, 1991), p. 102.

36. Salisbury, *Without Fear or Favor*, pp. 336, 337–339, 347–348, 445–446; *New York Times v. United States*, 403 U.S. 713, pp. 749–750, 752–753, 763; Abrams, "The Pentagon Papers Case." Also see Richard Nixon, *RN: The Memoirs of Richard Nixon* (New York: Grosset and Dunlap, 1978), pp. 510–514.

37. Salisbury, *Without Fear or Favor*, pp. 322–323; *New York Times v. United States*, 403 U.S. 713, p. 728.

38. *New York Times v. United States*, 403 U.S. 713, 749, 750, 753–763; Salisbury, *Without Fear or Favor*, pp. 292–294; Ungar, *The Papers and the Papers*, p. 166.

39. *United States v. Washington Post*, 446 F2d 1327, 1330 (D.C. Cir, 1971).

40. *Time Magazine*, July 26, 1971; Salisbury, *Without Fear or Favor*, pp. 292–294; *United States v. Washington Post*, 446 F. 2d. (1971), pp. 1327–1330.

41. *New York Times v. United States*, 403 U.S. 713, p. 728.

42. Ibid., pp. 728–763.

43. Ibid.

44. *New York Times v. United States*, 403 U.S. 713 at 749–750, 753–763 (1971); see Abrams, "Pentagon Papers Case," for an excellent overview.

45. *New York Times v. United States*, p. 752.

46. Ungar, *The Papers and the Papers*, pp. 297–299.

47. Bickel, *The Morality of Consent*, p. 61.

48. Ibid., p. 60.

49. Judge Robert Bork, opinion given at Washington, DC, Circuit Court of Appeals, *Ollman v. Evans*, December 6, 1984.

CHAPTER FIVE

1. Richard D. Brown, *Knowledge Is Power* (New York: Oxford University Press, 1989), pp. 40–41; N. K. Risjord, *Jefferson's America, 1760–1815* (Madison, WI: Madison House, 1991), pp. 31, 42–45; Bernard Mayo, *Jefferson Himself* (Charlottesville: University Press of Virginia, 1992); *World of the Founders* (New York:

New York State Commission on the Bicentennial of the U.S. Constitution, 1990), pp. 10, 20.

2. Brown, *Knowledge Is Power*, p. 127; J. H. Shera, *Foundations of the Public Library: The Origins of the Public Library Movement in New England, 1629–1855* (Chicago: University of Chicago Press, 1949), pp. 50–54; Carl Bridenbaugh, *Cities in Revolt: Urban Life in America, 1743–1776* (New York: Knopf, 1986), pp. 179, 380; Risjord, *Jefferson's America*, p. 14; Robert M. Calhoun, "Religion and Individualism," in William Graebner and Leonard Richards, eds., *American Chameleon* (Kent, OH: Kent State University Press, 1991), pp. 58–59.

3. Benjamin Franklin, *Autobiography* (New York: New American Library, 1961), pp. 115–116, 131–134. Also see Benjamin Franklin, *An Apology for Printers*, vol. 1 of Leonard W. Labaree et al., eds., *The Papers of Benjamin Franklin* (New Haven: Yale University Press, 1959), pp. 194–199.

4. Franklin, *Apology for Printers*, pp. 194–199.

5. *Pennsylvania Gazette*, June 10, 1731, regarding the *General Magazine*, vol. 2 of *The Papers of Benjamin Franklin*, pp. 263–265.

6. Jack N. Rakove, "The Structure of Politics at the Accession of George Washington," in Richard Beeman, Stephen Botein, and Edward C. Carter II, eds., *Beyond Confederation: Origins of the Constitution and American National Identity* (Chapel Hill: University of North Carolina Press, 1989), pp. 290–291; John Fenno to Joseph Ward, June 6, 1789, in *The Joseph Ward Papers*, Chicago Historical Society.

7. The material that follows to the end of this chapter is drawn from Benjamin Franklin Thomas, *Memoir of Isaiah Thomas* (Boston: Albany Munsell, 1874). Further information was provided by Clarence Brigham, *History and Bibliography of American Newspapers, 1690–1820* (Worcester, MA: American Antiquarian Society, 1947); Dwight Teeter, "Press Freedom and Public Printing: Pennsylvania, 1775–83" *Journalism Quarterly* 45 (1968):445–446. It should be noted that Congress often helped publishers at the end of the eighteenth and early nineteenth centuries because newspaper printing facilities were needed to circulate official government announcements—and occasionally to print currency.

8. Henry J. Merry, *Montesquieu's System of Natural Government* (West Lafayette, IN: Purdue University Studies, 1970), p. 85.

CHAPTER SIX

1. Edmund S. Morgan, *American Slavery, American Freedom* (New York: W. W. Norton, 1975), p. 376.

2. Dúmas Malone, *Jefferson the Virginian*, vol. 1 of William Peden, ed., *Jefferson and His Time* (Boston: Little, Brown, 1948), pp. 163, 391; Thomas Jefferson, *Notes on Virginia*, ed. William Peden (Chapel Hill: University of North Carolina Press, 1955), pp. 150–165.

3. Morgan, *American Slavery, American Freedom*, p. 6.

4. Curtis P. Nettels, *The Emergence of a National Economy, 1775–1815* (New York: Rinehart & Winston, 1962), p. 19.

5. Morgan, *American Slavery, American Freedom,* pp. 381–387; Julian Boyd, ed., *The Papers of Thomas Jefferson* (Princeton: Princeton University Press, 1950), vol. 2, pp. 275–276; vol. 23, pp. 398–399, 632–633.

6. C. Van Doren, *The Great Rehearsal* (New York: Time Life Books, 1965), pp. 186, 278.

7. Morgan, *American Slavery, American Freedom,* p. 371; John Trenchard and Thomas Gordon, *Cato's Letters* (New York: DaCapo Press, 1970); J. R. Pole, *The American Constitution: For and Against* (New York: Hill and Wang, 1987), pp. 17, 24.

8. H. R. McIlvaine, ed., *Journals of the House of Burgesses of Virginia* (Richmond: n.p., 1910), p. 121; Clarence S. Brigham, *History and Biography of American Newspapers, 1690–1820* (Worcester, MA: American Antiquarian Society, 1947).

9. William Stith, *The History of the First Discovery and Settlement of Virginia* (Williamsburg, VA: William Parks, 1747), pp. 130, 131, 160, 161.

10. R. A. Brock, *Official Records of Robert Dinwiddie* (Richmond, VA: The Society, 1883–1884), pp. 100–105, 234–236; Morgan, *American Slavery, American Freedom,* p. 376.

11. Thomas Jefferson, *Notes on the State of Virginia,* ed. William Peden (Chapel Hill: University of North Carolina Press, 1955), p. 162; Norman K. Risjord, *Jefferson's America, 1760–1815* (Madison, WI: Madison House, 1991), p. 179.

12. James T. Schleifer, *The Making of Tocqueville's "Democracy in America."* (Chapel Hill: University of North Carolina Press, 1980), pp. 242–243.

13. L. H. Butterfield, ed., *Letters of Benjamin Rush* (Princeton: Princeton University Press, 1951), vol. 1, p. 454. Rush published a pamphlet denouncing slavery in 1773 and two years later became secretary of a Quaker antislavery society (Risjord, *Jefferson's America,* p. 184).

14. C. Vann Woodward, *American Counterpoint* (New York: Oxford University Press, 1983), p. 27; Max Weber, *The Protestant Ethic and the Spirit of Capitalism* (London: Oxford University Press, 1930), pp. 175, 182.

15. Cited in Pole, *The American Constitution,* pp. 14–19, 21–24; Woodward, *American Counterpoint,* pp. 25–32, 35–40.

16. Melancton Smith, speech of June 21, 1788, cited in Jonathan Elliot, ed., *The Debates of the Several State Conventions,* 2nd ed. (Philadelphia: n.p., 1901), vol. 2, pp. 243–251.

17. Pole, *The American Constitution,* p. 11; Gordon S. Wood, "Interests and Disinterestedness in the Making of the Constitution," in *Beyond Federation: Origins of the Constitution and American National Identity* (Chapel Hill: University of North Carolina Press, 1987), pp. 77–81, 93–96, 100–103; Herbert J. Storing, *The Complete Anti-Federalist* (Chicago: University of Chicago Press, 1981); Cecelia M. Kenyon, *The Antifederalist* (Indianapolis: University of Indiana Press, 1966); Kenyon, "Men of Little Faith," *William and Mary Quarterly* 12, no. 1 (January): 155.

18. Wood, "Interests and Disinterestedness," pp. 102–105.

19. Quoted in Ira Glasser, *Visions of Liberty* (New York: Little, Brown, 1991), p. 60.

20. John Locke, "Of Political or Civil Society," in Peter Laslett, ed., *Two Treatises of Government* (New York: Cambridge University Press, 1988), p. 322.

21. Arthur S. Way, trans., *Euripides* (New York: G. P. Putnam, 1912, reprint 1919), vol. 3, pp. 238–245. "The highest, useless rich, aye craving more; The lowest, poor, aye on starvation's brink, A dangerous folk, of envy overfull. . . . But of the three, the midmost saveth states, Who keep the order which the state ordains."

22. Thomas Jefferson, letter from Paris, January 25, 1786, to John Jay, in *Writings of Thomas Jefferson* (New York: G. P. Putnam, 1894), vol. 5, p. 436.

23. Edmund Randolph to James Madison, March 27, 1789, in *James Madison Papers, Library of Congress,* Washington, DC.

CHAPTER SEVEN

1. Richard O. Curry and Lawrence B. Goodheart, eds., *American Chameleon* (Kent, OH: Kent State University Press, 1991); Robert E. Shalhope, "Individualism in the Early Republic," in *American Chameleon,* pp. 66–67; Kenneth Lockridge, *Settlement and Unsettlement: The Crisis of Political Liberty Before the Revolution* (New York: Oxford University Press, 1981); Gordon Wood, "Interests and Disinterestedness in the Making of the Constitution," in *Beyond Confederation* (Chapel Hill: University of North Carolina Press, 1987), pp. 69–79.

2. Norman K. Risjord, *Jefferson's America, 1760–1815* (Madison, WI: Madison House, 1991), pp. 97–100; essays by Carl Becker, J. N. Clark, and William E. Dodd in *The Spirit of '76 and Other Essays* (Washington, DC: Brookings Institution, 1927); Bernard Mayo, *Jefferson Himself* (Charlottesville: University of Virginia Press, 1992), p. 75.

3. Risjord, *Jefferson's America,* pp. 158–159; Stanley Elkins and Eric McKittrick, *The Age of Federalism* (New York: Oxford University Press, 1993), see introduction and p. 672; Thornton Anderson, *Creating the Constitution: The Convention of 1787 and the First Congress* (University Park: Pennsylvania State University Press, 1984), p. 64.

4. Risjord, *Jefferson's America,* p. 160; John C. Fitzpatrick, ed., *Writings of George Washington* (Westport, CT: Greenwood Press, 1970), vol. 6, pp. 107–108; C. Van Doren, *The Great Rehearsal* (New York: Time Life Books, 1965), p. 51; Max Farrand, ed., *The Records of the Federal Convention of 1787* (New Haven: Yale University Press, 1987).

5. Wood, "Interests and Disinterestedness," pp. 76, 81–93; Elkins and McKittrick, *The Age of Federalism,* pp. 48–55.

6. Wood, "Interests and Disinterestedness," p. 79; Drew McCoy, *The Illusive Republic: Political Economy in Jefferson's America* (Chapel Hill: University of North Carolina Press, 1980), p. 97.

7. Shalhope, "Individualism," pp. 67–70; David Fischer, *The Federal Party in the Era of Jeffersonian Democracy* (New York: Harper & Row, 1965), pp. 3–5.

8. Merrill D. Peterson, ed., *Thomas Jefferson's Writings* (New York: Library of America, 1984), pp. 1304-1310.

9. Linda Kerber, *Federalists in Descent: Imagery and Ideology in Jeffersonian America* (Ithaca: Cornell University Press, 1970), p. 21; also see *Scourge of Aristocracy* (American Antiquarian Society, Worcester, MA), vol. 1, p. 21, and vol. 2, pp. 46–47, 1798.

10. Wood, "Interests and Disinterestedness," pp. 96–99; C. M. Newlin, *The Life and Writings of Hugh Henry Brackenridge* (Princeton: Princeton University Press, 1932), pp. 71, 79–86; Noble E. Cunningham, *The Jeffersonian Republicans, 1789–1801* (Chapel Hill: University of North Carolina Press, 1967), pp. 29–34; Jonathan Elliot, ed., *The Debates in the Several State Conventions on the Adoption of the Federal Constitution* (Philadelphia: n.p., 1896), vol. 2, p. 260.

11. Charles S. Hyneman and Donald S. Lutz, eds., *American Political Writing During the Founding Era, 1760–1805* (Indianapolis: University of Indiana Press, 1983), vol. 1, p. 60; Shalhope, "Individualism," p. 73.

12. Rhys Isaac, *The Transformation of Virginia, 1740–1790* (Chapel Hill: University of North Carolina Press, 1986), pp. 131–133; William Findley, *A Review of the Revenue System Adopted by the First Congress* (Richmond, VA: Dobson, 1794), pp. 114, 127.

13. Benjamin Austin, *Constitutional Republicanism in Opposition to Fallacious Federalism* (Boston: Adams and Rhoades, 1803), pp. 3, 16, 33; G. Warner, *Means for Preservation of Public Liberty* (New York: Greenleaf and Judah, 1797), pp. 13, 14.

14. Russell J. Ferguson, *Early Western Pennsylvania Politics* (Pittsburgh: University of Pittsburgh Press, 1938), pp. 39–40; Donald H. Stewart, *The Opposition Press of the Federalist Period* (New York: State University of New York Press, 1969), pp. 103, 389–390.

15. Shalhope, "Individualism," p. 80.

16. Philip Foner, ed., *The Democratic-Republican Societies, 1790–1800* (New York: Greenwood Press, 1976), pp. 3, 7, 8, 11, 26.

17. Quoted by Gordon S. Wood, "The Democratization of Mind in the American Revolution," in *Leadership in the American Revolution* (Washington, DC: Library of Congress, 1974), pp. 63–88.

18. Shalhope, "Individualism," p. 84; R. Bushman et al., *Uprooted Americans: Essays to Honor Oscar Handlin* (Boston: Little, Brown, 1979), pp. 99–124.

19. James Winthrop, "Letters of Agrippa," *Massachusetts Gazette*, December 14, 1787; Madison to Jefferson, October 17, 1788, in Julian P. Boyd, ed., *Papers of Jefferson* (Princeton: Princeton University Press, 1950), vol. 14, p. 18.

20. Wood, "Interests and Disinterestedness," p. 109.

21. Alexander Hamilton, *Federalist 84*. It should be noted that the public opinion Hamilton referred to was not molded by large circulation or independent newspapers. The audiences were small, and many public officials owned or controlled a subservient journal. Matthew Lyon, for example, was a rough-edged entrepreneur who emigrated from Ireland and acquired considerable wealth during the Revolutionary War. He succeeded in winning an election to Congress from Vermont with the help of his own weekly newspaper, the *Farmer's Library*. His fame was assured in Congress when he spat in the face of Connecticut's representative Roger Griswold, who promptly secured a wooden cane and inflicted a severe beating on the bombastic Vermonter. In October 1798, Lyon suffered a greater loss when he was jailed for four months and fined $1,000 on charges of sedition. His fortunes, however, then changed for the better, even while he was in prison. Using, again, a newspaper he owned, *Scourge of Aristocracy*, he campaigned for reelection and tri-

umphed as "a friend of the working man." (Elkins and McKittrick, *Age of Federalism*, pp. 7, 10, 11).

CHAPTER EIGHT

1. Max Farrand, *The Records of the Federal Convention of 1787* (New Haven: Yale University Press, 1966), vol. 2, p. 587; Bernard Schwartz, "Experience Versus Reason: Beautiful Books and Great Revolutions" paper presented at the U.S. Capitol Historical Society, 1991, Washington, DC; James Winthrop, "Fourteen Conditions for Accepting the Constitution," letter to *Massachusetts Gazette*, February 5, 1788. Winthrop signed the letter "Agrippa"; it was the eighteenth in a series.

2. Thomas Jefferson to James Madison, December 1787, in J. Boyd, ed., *The Papers of Thomas Jefferson* (Princeton: Princeton University Press, 1950), vol. 12, pp. 339–342; Henry Adams, *History of the United States of America During the Administration of Thomas Jefferson and James Madison* (New York: Library of America, 1967).

3. Centinel [Samuel Bryant], *Independent Gazetteer*, January 23, 1788, p. xii; Bernard Schwartz, *The Great Rights of Mankind* (Madison, WI: Madison House, 1992), p. 162; Carl Van Doren, *The Great Rehearsal* (New York: Time Books, 1965), pp. 47–50.

4. John Stuart Mill, *On Liberty* (New York: Penguin Classics, 1988), pp. 110–111.

5. Irving Brant, *James Madison: The Virginia Revolutionist* (Indianapolis: University of Indiana Press, 1950), pp. 111, 112; see Schwartz, "Experience Versus Reason."

6. J. Alexander, *A Brief Narrative of the Case and Trial of John Peter Zenger*, ed. S. Katz (Cambridge, MA: Belknap Press of Harvard University, 1963), see introduction; David Anderson, *The Origins of the Press Clause* (Los Angeles: UCLA Law Review, 1983), pp. 445, 482–483; Leonard Levy, *The Emergence of a Free Press* (New York: Oxford University Press, 1985), p. 182. Professors Lucas A. Powe Jr., David Anderson, and David Rabban have extensively researched and written on the subject of the press clause of the First Amendment. They have arrived at conclusions that differ from those of Leonard Levy, a distinguished and influential constitutional scholar. The issue is over the intentions of the Framers in regard to prior restraint and sedition. Levy believed that seditious libel remained a central part of legal tradition after independence. The conflict is summarized by Powe in *The Fourth Estate and the Constitution* (Berkeley: University of California Press, 1991), p. 27: "The sovereign people needed information and the ability to discuss freely how their government was performing. It is no surprise that they, with 'Cato,' saw a free press as a 'bulwark of liberty,' essential to their newly created constitutions. Levy asks us to believe that revolutionary Americans were operating with one view of sovereignty at a constitutional level and with a different one at a practical level. A far more economical position is that revolutionary Americans were consistent, that changes in sovereignty resulted in changes in the scope of the press." Also see *New York Times v. Sullivan*, 376 U.S. 254 (no. 39, October 1963).

7. Prosecutions under the Sedition Act were directed unabashedly toward the major opposition newspapers. The *Aurora* of Philadelphia, the *Boston Independent Chronicle*, the *New York Argus*, the *Richmond Examiner*, and the *Baltimore Examiner* were all forced to cease publication. J. Smith, *Freedom's Fetters* (Ithaca:

Cornell University Press, 1956), pp. 21–26; Anderson, *Origins of the Press Clause,* pp. 515–516; William Van Alstyne, "Constitutional Power and Free Speech: Levy's Legacy Revisited," *Harvard Law Review* 99 (1986):1089; Stanley Elkins and Eric McKittrick, *The Age of Federalism* (New York: Oxford University Press, 1993), pp. 704–706.

8. Lester J. Capon, ed., *The Adams-Jefferson Letters* (Chapel Hill: University of North Carolina Press, 1959), vol. 1, p. 279.

9. Cited in Forrest McDonald, "'Bill of Rights' Unnecessary and Pernicious," paper presented at the U.S. Capitol Historical Society Symposium, March 14, 1991, Washington, DC. The acts are cited in O. John Rogge, *The First and the Fifth: With Some Excursions into Others* (New York: DaCapo Press, 1971), pp. 76–77.

10. Rogge, *The First and the Fifth,* pp. 76–77; *Stanley v. Georgia,* 394, and *United States v. 37 Photographs,* 402 U.S. 363 (1971).

CHAPTER NINE

1. B. Schwartz, *The Great Rights of Mankind* (Madison, WI: Madison House, 1992), pp. 133–142; J. R. Pole, *The American Constitution: For and Against* (New York: Hill and Wang, 1987), pp. 115–125; Bernard Bailyn, ed., *The Debate on the Constitutions* (New York: Library of America, 1990), pp. 595–597, 623–626, 673–688, 695–697, 701–703.

2. Kenneth R. Bowling, "New York City, Capitol of the United States, 1785–1790," in *World of the Founders* (Albany, NY: New York State Commission on the Bicentennial, 1990), pp. 1–20; Thomas E. V. Smith, *The City of New York in the Year of Washington's Inauguration, 1789* (New York: New York Library, 1889), pp. 183–188.

3. James Madison, *Notes of Debates in the Federal Convention* (New York: Library of America, 1993); Philip J. Cooper, "Freedom of Information," *Public Administration Review,* 1986; Sydney I. Pomerantz, *New York, An American City, 1783–1803, A Study of Urban Life* (Port Washington, NY: n.p., 1938), pp. 102–104, 148–161.

4. C. Brigham, *History and Bibliography of American Newspapers, 1690–1820* (Worcester, MA: American Antiquarian Society, 1947), p. 136, chaps. 1, 2.

5. Ibid., chaps. 1, 2; Frank Luther Mott, *American Journalism, A History: 1690–1960,* 3rd ed. (New York: Macmillan, 1962).

6. Brigham, *History of American Newspapers,* chaps. 1, 2; J. C. Miller, *The Wolf by the Ears* (Charlottesville: University of Virginia Press, 1991), pp. 188–202; Bernard Mayo, *Jefferson Himself* (Charlottesville: University Press of Virginia, 1992), pp. 80–87.

7. *American Minerva* (New York), December 9, 1793.

8. Noble Cunningham Jr., *The United States in 1800: Henry Adams Revisited* (Charlottesville: University of Virginia Press, 1988), pp. 47–50; *Gazette of the United States* (Philadelphia), September 10, 1800; *Maryland Gazette* (Annapolis), April 13, 1800.

9. Jefferson to Spencer Roane, September 6, 1819, in Paul L. Ford, ed., *The Writings of Thomas Jefferson* (New York: G. Putnam, 1897), vol. 12, p. 136; Thomas

Jefferson, inaugural address, March 4, 1801, in American Antiquarian Society, ed., *Early American Imprints, 1801–1819,* 3rd ed. (Worcester, MA: American Antiquarian Society); David Fischer, *The Revolution of American Conservatism* (New York: Macmillan, 1965), pp. 201, 215–217.

10. Jefferson, inaugural address, March 4, 1801; Harry B. Weiss, "A Graphic Summary of the Growth of Newspapers in New York and Other States, 1704–1820," *Bulletin of the New York Public Library* 52 (1948):182–196.

11. S.N.D. North, *History and Present Condition of the Newspaper and Periodical Press of the United States* (Washington, DC: GPO, 1884); Cunningham, *The United States in 1800,* pp. 21, 54; Noble E. Cunningham, *The Process of Government Under Jefferson* (Princeton: Princeton University Press, 1978) pp. 294–315.

12. James Gilreath, ed., *American Book Distribution* (Worcester, MA: American Antiquarian Society Proceedings 95, 1985), pp. 538–541; Jesse H. Shera, *Foundations of the Public Library: The Origins of the Public Library in New England, 1629–1855* (Chicago: University of Chicago Press, 1949); Samuel Miller, *A Brief Retrospect of the Eighteenth Century,* 2 vols. (New York: New York Public Library, 1803), vol. 1, pp. 388, 324–325; vol. 2, p. 393; *The Monthly Magazine and American Review* (New York: T & J Swords, 1799), vol. 1, p. 342.

13. Alfred McClung Lee, *The Daily Newspaper in America* (New York: Macmillan, 1937), pp. 705–750; "2 Cents Here, 2 Cents There, It All Adds Up," *Yale Record,* November 1947. The author of this book was one of the perpetrators.

14. Whitelaw Reid, "Journalism as a Career," in *American and English Studies* (London: Smith and Elder, 1914), vol. 2, pp. 220–225.

15. North, *Newspaper and Periodical Press,* pp. i–iv.

16. Phillip Knightley, *The First Casualty* (New York: Harcourt Brace Jovanovich, 1975), p. 19.

17. North, *Newspaper and Periodical Press.*

18. Donald S. Lutz, "The Origins of the United States Bill of Rights," paper prepared for the United States Capitol Historical Society Symposium, Washington, DC, March 14, 1991; Irving Brant, *The Bill of Rights: Its Origin and Meaning* (New York: Bobbs Merrill, 1965), chaps. 5, 6; Francis N. Thorpe, ed., *The Federal and State Constitutions* (Washington, DC: GPO, 1907).

19. Jack N. Rakove, "The Structure of Politics at the Accession of George Washington," in *Beyond Confederation* (Chapel Hill: University of North Carolina Press, 1987), pp. 267–273, 278–279; James Madison, *Federalist 53*; Madison to Jefferson, October 8, 1788, in Hutchinson, ed., *Papers of Madison,* Library of Congress, Washington, DC., vol. 11, p. 276.

CHAPTER TEN

1. Senator Hiram Johnson, speaking to his colleagues in 1917.

2. Phillip Knightley, *The First Casualty* (New York: Harcourt Brace Jovanovich, 1975).

3. Ibid., p. 20.

4. "History of the Times," *London Times,* vol. 2, p. 373.

5. Gary Wills, *Lincoln at Gettysburg* (New York: Simon & Schuster, 1992), p. 145.

6. Ibid., introduction.

7. J. Cutler Andrews, *The North Reports the Civil War* (Pittsburgh: University of Pittsburg Press, 1955), p. 640.

8. Archibald Forbes, *Memories and Studies of War and Peace* (London: Cassell, 1890), p. 7; F. Lauriston Bullard, *Famous War Correspondents* (London: Sir Isaac Pittman, 1914), p. 47; *New York Times*, November 7, 1861.

9. Andrews, *The North Reports the Civil War,* pp. 49, 71; Gerald J. Baldasty, *The Commercialization of News in the Nineteenth Century* (Madison: University of Wisconsin Press, 1992), pp. 6–8, 213–214, 245; *Chicago Daily Journal*, April 22, 1924 (regarding Wilbur Storey of the *Chicago Times*); R. Ogden, ed., *The Life and Letters of Edwin Lawrence Godkin* (New York: Macmillan, 1907), pp. 204–205.

10. O. Gramling, *AP: The Story of the News* (New York: Associated Press, 1940), p. 49; Andrews, *The North Reports the Civil War*, p. 71; *Journalism Quarterly* 6, no. 1, p. 4; Knightley, *The First Casualty*, p. 25.

11. R. S. Thorndike, *The Sherman Letters* (New York: n.p., 1894), p. 189.

12. David P. Conyngham, *March Through Georgia* (New York: Sheldon, 1865); William Graebner and Leonard Richards, eds., *The American Record* (New York: Knopf, 1982), vol. 1, p. 333.

13. John J. Pullen, *The Twentieth Maine* (London: Eyre and Spottiswoode, 1959), pp. 154–157.

14. Mary Boykin Chesnut, *A Diary from Dixie* (Boston: Houghton Mifflin, 1949), p. 400.

15. C. Vann Woodward, *American Counterpoint* (New York: Oxford University Press, 1983), p. 158.

16. Graebner and Richards, *American Record*, pp. 341–357; C. Vann Woodward, *The Strange Career of Jim Crow* (New York: Oxford University Press, 1974), pp. 17–21; Woodward, *American Counterpoint,* pp. 157–159. Also see V. Jacque Voegeli, *Free but Not Equal* (Chicago: University of Chicago Press, 1967).

17. Edmund S. Morgan, *American Slavery, American Freedom* (New York: W. W. Norton, 1975), p. 331; Sydney E. Ahlstrom, *Religious History of the American People* (New York: Doubleday, 1975), vol. 2, pp. 91–115.

18. Richard D. Brown, *Knowledge Is Power* (New York: Oxford University Press, 1989), p. 283; Ira Glasser, *Visions of Liberty* (New York: Little, Brown, 1991) pp. 193, 196.

19. Woodward, *American Counterpoint*, pp. 140, 144; Walter M. Merrill, *Against the Grain: A Biography of William Lloyd Garrison* (Cambridge, MA: Harvard University Press, 1963).

CHAPTER ELEVEN

1. Thomas C. Leonard, *News for All* (New York: Oxford University Press, 1995), pp. 33–36, 164–167; Gerald J. Baldasty, *The Commercialization of News in the Nineteenth Century* (Madison: University of Wisconsin Press, 1992), pp. 59–74; J. Lincoln Steffens, "The Business of a Newspaper," *Scribner's Magazine* 22 (1897):447–467; Wendell Smith, "Product Differentiation and Market Segmentation as Alternative Marketing Strategies," *Journal of Marketing* 21 (1956):3–8; Jean M. Converse, *Survey Research in the United States: Roots and Emergence, 1890–1960* (Berkeley: University of California Press, 1987), pp. 89–90.

2. James MacGregor Burns and Peter A. Meyers, "A Common Market Called America," *IBM Magazine*, September 1987, pp. 13–15; Alfred McClung Lee, *The Daily Newspaper in America* (New York: Macmillan, 1937), pp. 705–750. Statistical data: Clarence S. Brigham, *History and Biography of American Newspapers, 1690–1820* (Worcester, MA: American Antiquarian Society, 1947); and S.N.D. North, *The Newspapers and Periodical Press* (Washington, DC: GPO, 1884).

3. C. Vann Woodward, *American Counterpoint* (New York: Oxford University Press, 1983), pp. 107–136; William Lloyd Garrison, *Liberator*, March 6, March 13, and April 19, 1857; Leonard, *News for All*, pp. 67–73.

4. James Aronson, *Packaging the News* (New York: International, 1971), pp. 48–49; W. S. Savage, *The Controversy over the Distribution of Abolition Literature, 1830–1860* (Washington, DC: Association for the Study of Negro Life and History, 1938), pp. 13, 92; William L. Barney, *The Secessionist Impulse: Alabama and Mississippi in 1860* (Princeton: Princeton University Press, 1974), p. 163.

5. James Madison, "Property," *National Gazette*, March 29, 1792.

6. Jung further stated: "The European, thoughtless of the spiritual heritage that belongs to him, cannot live unpunished among the negroes in Africa; because, unnoticed, their psychology gets into him, and unconsciously he becomes a negro. There is no fighting against it. There is in Africa a well-known technical expression describing this condition, namely, 'going black.' It is not mere snobbery that an Englishman should rank those born in the colonies, even though the best blood may run in their veins, as 'slightly inferior.' Facts support this view. The strange melancholy and longing for deliverance which characterized imperial Rome, and which found so striking an expression in Virgil's *Eclogue*, was a direct result of slave influence." *Contributions to Analytical Psychology* (New York: Harcourt Brace, 1928), p. 173.

7. Abraham Lincoln to Horace Greeley, editor of the *New York Tribune;* reproduced in G. Wills, *Lincoln at Gettysburg* (New York: Simon & Schuster, 1992), pp. 167–168. Also see Abraham Lincoln, *Speeches and Writings,* Don E. Fehrenbacker, ed. (New York Library of America, 1984), vol. 2, pp. 357–358.

8. Leonard, *News for All*, pp. 67–79; Woodward, *American Counterpoint*, chap. 5; Eileen S. Kraditor, *Means and Ends in American Abolitionism: Garrison and His Critics on Strategy and Tactics, 1834–1850* (New York: Pantheon, 1969); Leon F. Litwack, *North of Slavery: The Negro in the Free States, 1790–1860* (Chicago: University of Chicago Press, 1961); V. James Voegeli, *Free but Not Equal* (Chicago: University of Chicago Press, 1967).

9. Litwack, *North of Slavery*, pp. 91–97.

10. Greeley's editorial comments, written in 1859, are cited in C. Vann Woodward, *American Counterpoint*, p. 164. Senator Henry Wilson's remarks on race are cited in Litwack, *North of Slavery*, pp. 269–272.

11. W.E.B. DuBois, *Black Reconstruction in America, 1860–1880* (New York: Harcourt Brace, 1935), p. 191; William L. Barney, *The Road to Secession* (New York: Praeger Press, 1972), pp. 6–17.

12. Aronson, *Packaging the News*, pp. 47–49; L. F. Palmer, "The Black Press in Transition," *Columbia Journalism Review*, Spring 1970.

13. Dorothy Sterling, ed., *We Are Your Sisters* (New York: W. W. Norton, 1984), p. 130; Shirley Yee, *Black Women Abolitionists* (Knoxville: University of Tennessee Press, 1992), regarding Mary Ann Shadd Cary, p. 33.

14. Merrill D. Peterson and Robert C. Vaughan, eds., *The Virginia Statute for Religious Freedom: Its Evolution and Consequences in American History* (New York: Cambridge University Press, 1988), p. 208; Cushing Strout, "Walling In and Walling Out: American Politics and Religion Before the Second World War," paper prepared for symposium Religion and Public Policy in America, Baylor University, May 1992, pp. 15–16.

15. Strout, "Walling In and Walling Out," pp. 15–17.

16. A. James Reichley, *Religion in American Public Life* (Washington, DC: Brookings Institution, 1985), pp. 199–203, 212–213; James E. Wood, ed., *The First Freedom and the Bill of Rights* (Waco, TX: Baylor University, 1990), pp. 20, 27; Strout, "Walling In and Walling Out," pp. 17–20.

17. Gilbert H. Barnes and Dwight L. Dumond, eds., *Letters of Theodore Dwight Weld, Angeline Grimke Weld and Sarah Grimke, 1822–1844* (Washington, DC: American Historical Association, 1934), vol. 2, p. 717; also see William Graebner and Leonard Richards, eds., *The American Record*, vol. 1 (New York: Knopf, 1982); James Brewer Stuart, *Holy Warriors, the Abolitionists and American Slavery* (New York: Hill and Wang, 1976).

18. Woodward, *American Counterpoint*, p. 151.

19. Ibid., pp. 150–153; Lorman Ratner, *Powder Keg: Northern Opposition to the Antislavery Movement, 1831–1840* (New York: Basic Books, 1968); Litwack, *North of Slavery*, pp. 216–230; Larry Kinkaid, "Victims of Circumstance: An Interpretation of Changing Attitudes Towards Republican Policy Makers and Reconstruction," *Journal of American History* 57, June 1970, pp. 48–66.

20. Kai Erikson, conversation with the author.

21. George W. Julian, *Speeches on Political Questions* (New York: New York Public Library, 1872), p. 199.

22. Fawn M. Brodie, *Thomas Jefferson: An Intimate History* (New York: W. W. Norton, 1974), p. 582.

23. Graebner and Richards, *The American Record*, chart on p. 316.

24. Richard Lacayo and George Russell, *Eyewitness: 150 Years of Photojournalism* (New York: Time, 1995), p. 14.

25. Cited in *DeBow's Review* 36 (September 1867):250.

26. *Independent* (Connecticut), April 4, 1867.

27. Quoted in the *Independent* (Connecticut), November 21, 1867.

28. *New York Times*, October 19, 1867.

29. *Raleigh Daily Sentinel*, March 11, 1868.

30. Everette Swinney, "Enforcing the Fifteenth Amendment, 1870–1877," *Journal of Southern History* 28, May 1962, pp. 210–211; Robert A. Horn, *National Control of Congressional Elections* (Princeton: Princeton University, 1942), pp. 143, 154–155, 183–187.

31. Woodward, *American Counterpoint*, p. 149.

32. Ibid., pp. 190–211; Charles Wynes, "Lewis Harvie Blair, Virginia Reformer," *Virginia Magazine of History and Biography* 62, May 1962.

33. Charles Wynes, ed., "Lewis Harvie Blair, Virginia Reformer, The Uplift of the Negro and Southern Prosperity," *Virginia Magazine of History and Biography* 72, January 1964, pp. 3–18; *New York Independent* articles published in a series during summer 1887 (New York: New York Public Library); Woodward, *American Coun-*

terpoint, p. 204, quotes one of Blair's articles: "The remedy proposed is not a bread pill or some soothing syrup, but is a radical and far reaching one, and is no less than the abandonment of the principle of separate schools, which principle is an efficient and certain mode of dooming to perpetual ignorance both whites and blacks in thinly settled sections."

34. Quoted in the *Independent* (Connecticut), November 21, 1867.

35. Henry C. Dethloff and Robert R. Jones, "Race Relations in Louisiana, 1877–1898," *Louisiana History* 9, Fall 1968, pp. 305, 306–308; William Ivy Hair, *Bourbonism and Agrarian Protest: Louisiana Politics, 1877–1900* (Baton Rouge: Louisiana State University Press, 1969), p. 115; Otto H. Olsen, *Carpetbaggers' Crusade: The Life of Albion Winegar Tourgée* (Baltimore: Johns Hopkins University Press, 1965).

36. Edmund Wilson, *Patriotic Gore: Studies in the Literature of the American Civil War* (Boston: Little, Brown, 1962) p. 537.

37. *Plessy v. Ferguson*, 163 U.S. 559–61 (1896).

38. Ibid.; Olsen, *Carpetbaggers' Crusade*, pp. 298–317; *Dictionary of American Biography* (Washington, DC: Library of Congress), vol. 8, p. 269; *Richmond Times*, January 12, 1900.

39. *Richmond Times*, January 12, 1900; Otto Olsen, *The Thin Disguise: Turning Point in Negro History: Plessy v. Ferguson, a Documentary Presentation, 1864–1896* (New York: Macmillan, 1967), pp. 74–77, 78–80, 103–108; Dethloff and Jones, "Race Relations in Louisiana," pp. 307–317.

CHAPTER TWELVE

1. C. Vann Woodward, *American Counterpoint* (New York: Oxford University Press, 1983), p. 257.

2. Ibid.; Eugene D. Genovese, *The World the Slaveholders Made* (New York: Pantheon, 1969), pp. 96, 101, 131, 199; Pierre L. Vanden Berghe, *Race and Racism: A Comparative Perspective* (New York: Wiley, 1967), pp. 25–37; Philip Mason, *Prospero's Magic: Some Thoughts on Class and Race* (London: Oxford University Press, 1962), pp. 27–33; C. Vann Woodward, *The Strange Career of Jim Crow* (New York: Oxford University Press, 1966), pp. 27–28.

3. Isaiah Berlin, *Four Essays on Liberty* (London: Oxford University Press, 1984), p. xliii.

4. Bernard Schwartz, *The Great Rights of Mankind* (Madison, WI: Madison House, 1992), p. 36.

5. President Andrew Jackson denounced the abolitionist newspapers and pamphlets in his 1835 message to Congress as "incendiary publications." That same year more than 1 million antislavery publications were mailed or carried out of New York City and Boston. Many of these were burned in southern states by postal and legislative officials. Leonard L. Richards, *Gentlemen of Property and Standing: Anti-Abolition Mobs in Jacksonian America* (New York: Oxford University Press, 1970), pp. 13–15, 90–92; Frank Gatell, ed., "Postmaster Huger and the Incendiary Publications," *South Carolina Historical Magazine* 64, 1963, pp. 193–201; Slave ads: William Graebner and Leonard Richards, *The American Record* (New York: Knopf, 1982), p. 290.

6. Charleston *News and Courier*, 1898, Yale University Library, film An C38, no. 2256; Woodward, *The Strange Career of Jim Crow*, pp. 67, 96.

7. Richards, "Gentlemen of Property and Standing," pp. 55–59; Richard B. Kielbowicz, *News in the Mail: The Press, Postoffice, and Public Information, 1700–1860s* (New York: Greenwood Press, 1989), pp. 66–67; *DeBow's Review*, a leading southern periodical and militant defender of slavery in the 1840s and 1850s, was printed in northern print shops. Proslavery propagandists, often backed by government and business, could arrange wider circulation than the abolitionist press—"a despised minority in the North." From Thomas C. Leonard, *News for All* (New York: Oxford University Press, 1995), p. 73.

8. Historian Edgar Gardner Murphy, quoted in Woodward, *The Strange Career of Jim Crow*, p. 108; William H. Pease and Jane H. Pease, "Antislavery Ambivalence," *American Quarterly* 17 (1965):682–695.

9. Ira Glasser, *Visions of Liberty* (New York: Little, Brown, 1991), p. 195.

10. Commented on in the *Nation* and *Atlantic Monthly*, as cited in Woodward, *The Strange Career of Jim Crow*, pp. 72–73; *New York Times*, May 10, 1900; W. R. Brock, *An American Crisis: Congress and Reconstruction, 1865–1867* (London: Saint Martin's Press, 1963), p. 149.

11. L. Snyder and R. Morris, eds., *A Treasury of Great Reporting* (New York: Simon & Schuster, 1962), p. 236.

12. James Creelman, *On the Great Highway* (Boston: Lathrop, 1901), pp. 177–178; W. A. Swanberg, *Citizen Hearst* (New York: Scribners, 1961), pp. 177–178; Phillip Knightley, *The First Casualty* (New York: Harcourt Brace Jovanovich, 1975), p. 56. A number of books have been written about the press and the Spanish American War. Some of these authors examine the effect of tabloid journalism on foreign policy and the mobilization of public opinion. The conclusions vary, and conventional assumptions regarding journalistic propaganda are challenged. Three examples: Charles Brown, *The Correspondents' War: Journalists in the Spanish American War* (New York: Scribners, 1967); Joseph E. Wisan, *The Cuban Crisis as Reflected in the New York Press, 1895–1898* (New York: Columbia University Press, 1934); Marcus M. Wilkerson, *Public Opinion and the Spanish American War: A Study of War Propaganda* (Baton Rouge: Louisana State University Press, 1930).

13. Richard Harding Davis, *A Year from a Correspondent's Notebook* (New York: Harper, 1898), p. 113; R. W. Stallman and E. R. Hagemann, eds., *The War Dispatches of Stephen Crane* (London: Peter Owen, 1964), pp. 7–10.

14. Stallman and Hagemann, *The War Dispatches of Stephen Crane*, pp. 196–199; Snyder and Morris, *A Treasury of Great Reporting*, p. 247.

15. Winthrop D. Jordan, "Modern Tensions and the Origins of American Slavery," *Journal of Southern History* 27 (1962):18–30; Charles E. Wynes, *Race Relations in Virginia, 1870–1902* (Charlottesville: University of Virginia Press, 1961), pp. 148–150; 68–83; Woodward, *The Strange Career of Jim Crow*, p. 70.

16. Former Governor Oates was shocked by the viciousness of Jim Crow in 1901, but earlier he had supported strict segregation and had encouraged disenfranchisement by whatever means necessary. He may have believed violence was not one of those means.

17. Gunnar Myrdal, *An American Dilemma* (New York: Pantheon, 1972), p. 997.

18. Virginius Dabney, *Foreign Policy Reports* 1 (March 1, 1943):178.

19. Mark Ethridge, publisher of the *Louisville Courier-Journal*. Dabney and Ethridge were cited by C. Vann Woodward in lectures given at the University of Virginia in 1954. Professor Woodward informs me that he made no specific notes regarding the two quotations because he had not expected the lectures to be published as a book. The sentiments expressed by both men were commonly held in the South and not always disdained in the North—even among the intelligentsia. Both these distinguished journalists moderated their views over time. Ethridge, writing for the *Nieman Reports* in 1960, spoke of the "obligations to fight the black-heartedness of organized prejudice and repression." (*Nieman Reports* 14, no.4).

CHAPTER THIRTEEN

1. Akhil Reed Amar, "The Bill of Rights and the Fourteenth Amendment," *Yale Law Journal* 101 (April 1992): 1279.

2. Leonard Levy, *Emergence of a Free Press* (New York: Oxford University Press, 1985), p. 199; "Correspondence Between Chief Justice Cushing (Massachusetts) and John Adams," *Massachusetts Law Quarterly* 27 (October 1942):12–15. See William Cushing to John Adams, February 18, 1789, quoted in Levy, *The Emergence of a Free Press*, p. 199.

3. Richard A. Schwarzlose, "Postwar Protectionism," in *The Nation's News Brokers* (Evanston, IL: Northwestern University Press, 1990), vol. 2, pp. 10–14; Alvin F. Harlow, *Old Wires and New Waves: The History of the Telegraph, Telephone, and Wireless* (New York: D. Appleton-Century, 1936), pp. 285–305; James D. Reid, *The Telegraph in America, Its Founders, Promoters, and Noted Men* (New York: Derby Brothers, 1879), pp. 515–520.

4. John Trenchard and Thomas Gordon, *Cato's Letters* (New York: DaCapo Press, 1971), pp. 246–247. Madison in *Federalist 51* identified the two principal concerns about republican government—self-serving government officials and majority actions that would deny a minority or individuals basic rights. Free speech and free press had to protect the minority in what has been called "the structural role" of the press in a democratic society, that is, a forum for public discussion. "Representative," however, means representing majority views. The role of the press as a mediator between these two concerns was apparent, but was a role rarely performed. To be a mediator between the government and the people inevitably encountered the problem of giving voice to minority or dissenting views, along with majority sentiments. Madison feared misrepresentation more at the state level than at the federal. He wrote in *Federalist 55*: "Had every Athenian citizen been a Socrates, every Athenian assembly would still have been a mob," in Alexander Hamilton, James Madison, and John Jay, *The Federalist Papers*, ed. Garry Wills (New York: Bantam Books, 1982), p. 281.

5. A. R. Amar, "The Bill of Rights as a Constitution," *Yale Law Journal* 100 (1991):1151: "Publishers prosecuted under the Alien and Sedition Acts in the late 1790s tried to plead their First Amendment defense to jurors. The judges, after all, had been appointed by the very same (increasingly unpopular) Adams administration that the defendants had attacked in the press.

"This episode contrasts sharply with today's practice, where friends of the First Amendment often seek to limit the power of juries on speech questions such as obscenity *vel non,* by appealing to Article III judges. Since the First Amendment's center of gravity has (appropriately in light of the later Fourteenth Amendment) shifted to protection of unpopular, minority speech, its natural institutional guardian has become an insulated judiciary rather than the popular jury."

6. Sir William Blackstone, *Commentaries on the Laws of England* (Oxford: Clarendon Press, 1769), p. 151.

7. Alexander Meiklejohn, "Reflections," in *Free Speech and Its Relation to Self-Government* (New York: Harper and Row, 1948), p. 78.

8. Robert Hutchins, from a debate with Brent Bozell, January 22, 1964. Cited in *Dialogues in Americanism* (Chicago: Henry Regnery, 1964), p. 85.

CHAPTER FOURTEEN

1. Alexander Meiklejohn, "The First Amendment Is an Absolute," *Supreme Court Review*, 1961, p. 251.

2. R. Schwarzlose, *The Nation's News Brokers* (Evanston, IL: Northwestern University Press, 1989), pp. 237–242; Victor Rosewater, *History of Cooperative News-Gathering in the United States* (New York: D. Appleton, 1930), good overview of the subject up to 1930; William L. Scott and Milton Jarnigan, *A Treatise upon the Law of Telegraphs* (Boston: Little, Brown, 1868).

3. Charles Dudley Warner, *Harper's Monthly*, April 1897; also see Warner, "Better Newspapers," *Journalist*, May 1, 1897, p. 14.

4. S.N.D. North, *History and Present Condition of the Newspaper Periodical Press in the United States* (Washington, DC: GPO, 1884), see tables and statistics; Allan R. Pred, *Urban Growth and the Circulation of Information: The United States System of Cities, 1790–1840.* (Cambridge: Harvard University Press, 1973), table 2.1.

5. "The Press and the Telegraph: The Ramifications and Oppressions of Two Gigantic Monopolies," *New York Daily Graphic,* September 15, 1874, p. 6.; Schwarzlose, *The Nation's News Brokers,* pp. 82–91.

6. Oswald Garrison Villard, *Some Newspapers and Newspapermen* (New York: Knopf, 1926), p. 99; *Journalist,* April 12, 1884.

7. Alvin F. Harlow, *Old Wires and New Waves* (New York: Appleton-Century, 1936), p. 322.

8. *Proceedings of the New England Associated Press:* Smith to Pulitzer, October 1884; Smith to Clapp, November 1884. Both in *Joseph Pulitzer Papers,* Columbia University Library, New York.

9. *Journalist,* August 16, 1884, p. 6; November 8, 1884, p. 5; November 29, 1884, p. 4.

10. Schwarzlose, *The Nation's News Brokers,* pp. 188–189; Gerald J. Baldasty, *The Commercialization of News in the Nineteenth Century* (Madison: University of Wisconsin Press, 1992), pp. 88–94, 150–157.

11. Joe Alex Morris, *Deadline Every Minute: The Story of the United Press* (New York: Doubleday, 1957), pp. 19, 23, 25, 29, 39, 118–120; Oswald Garrison Vil-

lard, "Some Weaknesses of Modern Journalism," *University of Kansas News Bulletin*, November 2, 1914; Villard, *The Disappearing Daily* (New York: Knopf, 1944), p. 6; Robert M. Desmond, *Windows on the World: The Information Process in a Changing Society, 1900–1920* (Iowa City: University of Iowa Press, 1980), p. 126; Rollo Ogden, "The Press and Foreign News," *Atlantic Monthly* 86 (September 1900):390–391; Thomas C. Leonard, *News for All* (New York: Oxford University Press, 1995), p. 103.

12. *The Service of the Associated Negro Press* (annual), 1920.

13. Walter Lippmann, *Public Opinion* (New York: Macmillan, 1922), pp. 339, 441.

14. Alfred McClung Lee, *The Daily Newspaper in America* (New York: Macmillan, 1937), p. 166; Charles A. Dana, *The Modern American Newspaper* (New York: D. Appleton, 1895), p. 20.

15. Daniel Pope, *The Making of Modern Advertising* (New York: Basic Books, 1983), p. 30; J. Lincoln Steffens, "The Business of a Newspaper," *Scribner's Magazine* 22 (1897):447–467.

16. Jason Rogers, *Newspaper Maker* 4 (November 26, 1896).

17. Whitelaw Reid, "Journalism as a Career," in *American and English Studies* (London: Smith, Elder, 1914), vol. 2, pp. 193–199, 200–230.

18. John Tomisch, *A Genteel Endeavor: American Culture and Politics in the Gilded Age* (Palo Alto, CA: Stanford University Press, 1971), pp. 1–2, 8; Arnot Reid, "The English and the American Press," *Nineteenth Century* 22 (August 1887): 529–538, 691.

CHAPTER FIFTEEN

1. Douglas Wilson, "Thomas Jefferson and the Character Issue," *Atlantic Monthly*, November 1992, p. 74.

2. *North Star* (Rochester, NY), 1847–1851, Sterling Memorial Library, Yale University, film An F873; continued as *Frederick Douglass' Paper*, Sterling Memorial Library, Yale University, film An 873 until 1860.

3. Review by Carmen Fields for *Nieman Reports* 45 (Winter 1991):63.

4. Anthony Trollope, *The Warden* (New York: Penguin Classics, 1984), pp. 123–124.

5. E. L. Godkin, "Newspapers Here and Abroad," *North American Review* 150 (February 1890):197–204.

6. Ibid.

7. Richard Watson Gilder, "The Newspaper, the Magazine, and the Public," *Outlook* 61 (February 4, 1899):319–321.

8. J. W. Keller, "Journalism as a Career," *Forum* 15 (August 1893):691–704.

9. W. S. Lilly, "Ethics of Journalism," *Forum* 7 (July 1889):503–507.

10. Editorial, *Dial* 15 (August 16, 1893):79.

11. Whitelaw Reid, "The Future of the Newspaper," *Nation* 95 (June 25, 1879): 432–433; Charles Anderson Dana, "The Modern American Newspaper," in *The Art of Newspaper Making* (New York: D. Appleton, 1895), p. 20; George W. Alger, "Sensational Journalism and the Law," *Atlantic Monthly* 1 (February 1903): 148.

12. Whitelaw Reid, "The Practical Issues in a Newspaper Office," in *American and English Studies* (London: Smith, Elder, 1914), vol. 2, p. 199.

13. Charles Dudly Warner, "Newspapers and the Public," *Forum* 9 April 1890: 201.

14. W.H.H. Murray, "An Endowed Press," *Arena* 2 (October 1890):553–559.

CHAPTER SIXTEEN

1. James McGregor Burns, *The Workshop of Democracy* (New York: Knopf, 1985), p. 224; "Hearst-Pulitzer Feud Cost Millions, Ended in Draw," *Editor and Publisher,* June 27, 1957, pp. 82, 84.

2. Don Seitz, *Training for the Newspaper Trade* (Philadelphia: Lippincott, 1916), pp. 89–92; Frank Luther Mott, *American Journalism: A History, 1690–1960,* 3rd ed. (New York: Macmillan, 1962), pp. 521–539; Charles Anderson Dana, "The Modern American Newspaper," in *The Art of Newspaper Making* (New York: Appleton, 1900), pp. 1–20; Elizabeth Banks, "American Yellow Journalism," *Nineteenth Century* 44 (August 1898):328–340; John Henderson Garnsey, "The Demand for Sensational Journals," *Arena* 18 (November 1897):686; Charles Dudley Warner, "Better Newspapers," *Journalist,* May 1, 1897; Harry Thurston Peck, "A Great National Newspaper," *Cosmopolitan* 24 (December 1897):209–220.

3. Alexander Meiklejohn, *Free Speech and Its Relation to Self-Government* (New York: Oxford University Press, 1948), pp. 24–27, 49.

4. H. L. Mencken, *American Mercury* 2 (October 1924):155–159; Mencken also spoke of the mass audience as *"homo boobus"* and collectively as "the booboisie." Also see "Journalist Groups Arguing Their Need for Strong Ethics Codes," *American Society of Newspaper Editors Bulletin,* December 1987.

5. E. L. Godkin, editorial, *Nation* 66 (May 5, 1898):336.

6. E. L. Godkin, editorial, *Nation* 26 (September 1901):238.

7. Allan Forman, editor, *Journalist,* May 1, 1897, p. 12.

8. Editorial, "The Decay of American Journalism," *Dial* 22 (April 16, 1897): 238.

9. J. H. Garnsey, "The Demand for Sensational Journals," *Arena,* November 1897, p. 682.

10. Delos F. Wilcox, "The American Newspaper: A Study in Social Psychology," *Annals of the American Academy of Political and Social Science* 16 (July 1900):76–77, 86–88.

11. George W. Alger, "Sensational Journalism and the Law," *Atlantic Monthly* 91 (February 1903):148–150.

12. Don C. Seitz, "The American Press" (six parts), *Outlook* 143: part 1 (January 6, 1926):20–22; part 2 (January 13, 1926):66–68; part 3 (January 20, 1926):110–112; part 4 (January 27, 1926):136–138; part 5 (February 3, 1926):176–177; part 6 (February 10, 1926):209–210; Also see *Editor and Publisher,* June 27, 1927, pp. 182–184.

13. Brendon Piers, *The Life and Death of the Press Barons* (London: Secker & Warburg, 1982), p. 451; Joseph Pulitzer, "The College of Journalism," *North American Review* 178 (May 1904):641–680.

14. Pulitzer, "The College of Journalism."

15. George Harvey, *Journalism, Politics and the University* (New Haven: Yale University Press, 1908).

16. Will Irwin, *The Making of a Reporter* (New York: Putnam, 1942), pp. 71–72. Irwin was prophetic, iconoclastic, and courageous. He was, of course, accused of fouling his own nest.

17. Robert E. Park, "The Yellow Press," *Sociology and Social Research* 12 (1924):3–11.

CHAPTER SEVENTEEN

1. Robert Hutchins et al., *A Free and Responsible Press*, ed. Robert D. Leigh (Chicago: University of Chicago, 1974), pp. 76–78. Fuller discussion of this report can be found in Chapters 19 and 20. The Commission on Freedom of the Press was urged by Archibald MacLeish to emphasize the notion of accountability, but several commissioners argued that responsibility was a better prescription because the requirement to be accountable suggested some outside supervision, whereas striving to be responsible required personal and internal commitment.

2. Merle Thorpe, *The Coming Newspaper* (New York: Henry Holt, 1915), pp. 2–5; "First National Newspaper Conference," *Outlook* 101 (August 17, 1912): 847–848; Hamilton Holt, "A Plan for an Endowed Journal," *Independent* 73 (1919):301–303. The earliest code was written by Willis E. Miller and adopted by the Kansas Editorial Association in 1910. The emphasis of subsequent codes was always on doing the right thing in regard to social actions and, therefore, on the effects of news reporting. There was little interest in the intellectual aspect, a philosophical discussion of principles that might endure and were right with or without social connection (Clifford G. Christians, "Fifty Years of Scholarship in Media Ethics," *Journal of Communication*, Autumn 1977, pp. 20–23). Also see N. A. Crawford, *The Ethics of Journalism* (New York: Knopf, 1924), pp. 183–240.

3. Ralph Pulitzer, "The Profession of Journalism—Accuracy in the News," speech given at Columbia University School of Journalism, 1912.

4. James Melvin Lee, *A History of American Journalism* (Garden City, NY: Garden City, 1917–1923), pp. 408–409; *New York Times*, July 7, 1917.

5. Lucy Maynard Salmon, *The Newspaper and Authority* (New York: Oxford University Press, 1923), pp. 428–467.

6. Oswald Garrison Villard and Martin Weyrauch, "Are Tabloids a Menace?" *Forum* 77 (April 1927):493.

7. Samuel D. Warren and Louis D. Brandeis, "The Right to Privacy," *Harvard Law Review* 4 (December 15, 1890):196.

8. Ibid.

9. Upton Sinclair, *The Brass Check: A Study of American Journalism* (Pasadena, CA: author, 1920).

10. Frederick Lewis Allen, "Newspapers and the Truth," *Atlantic Monthly* 129 (January 1922):50; Leon Harris, *Upton Sinclair: An American Rebel* (New York: Crowell, 1975), p. 180.

11. H. L. Mencken, editorial, *American Mercury* 2 (October 1924):155–159.

12. Curtice N. Hitchcock, "Review of *The Brass Check*," *Journal of Political Economy* 29 (April 1921):337–347.

13. Nelson A. Crawford, "The American Newspaper and the People: A Psycho-

logical Examination," *Nation* 115 (September 3, 1922):251–253; and Crawford, *The Ethics of Journalism*, pp. 33, 99.

14. Clarence Darrow, comments at American Society of Newspaper Editors Committee on Integrity of the Press annual meeting, Washington, DC, 1928. *Problems of Journalism: ASNE Proceedings* (annual) 1, 2 (1928):54–63, 65–72.

15. Silas Bent, comments at American Society of Newspaper Editors Committee on Integrity of the Press annual meeting, Washington, DC, 1928. *Problems of Journalism: ASNE Proceedings* (annual) 1, 2 (1928):161.

16. H. L. Mencken, *American Mercury,* October 1924, pp. 155–159; "Rockefeller Money Backs Scientific Probe of News Methods and Sources," *Editor and Publisher,* September 6, 1924, p. 3.

17. Isaiah Berlin, *Four Essays on Liberty* (Oxford: Oxford University Press, 1984), pp. 173–174.

18. Quoted by John Stuart Mill, *On Liberty* (New York: Penguin Classics, 1988), p. 105.

19. Alexander Meiklejohn, "Reflections," in *Free Speech and Its Relation to Self-Government* (New York: Harper and Row, 1960), p. 40.

20. The infant son of renowned airman Charles Lindbergh and his writer wife, Anne Morrow, was kidnapped in the autumn of 1932 from the Lindbergh home in New Jersey. The death of the child, the pursuit of the kidnapper, and the trial of the accused man, Bruno Hauptmann, were reported and commented on stridently, distortedly, and with reckless speculation and invasion of privacy. Said critic of the press Silas Bent: "They outdid themselves and one another in verbosity and vulgarity."

CHAPTER EIGHTEEN

1. *Economist,* January 8, 1993.

2. Edmund B. Lambeth, *You Can't Print That: The Truth Behind the News* (Bloomington: Indiana University Press, 1986), p. 81.

3. Ibid., quoting Curtis MacDougall in *Qualitative Studies Division of the Association for Education in Journalism Newsletter* 7 (Fall 1980):6; also see Margaret Blanchard, *Exploring the First Amendment* (New York: Longman, 1986), pp. 81–86, 120.

4. Everette E. Dennis and Claude-Jean Bertrand, "Seldes at Ninety: They Don't Give Pulitzers for That Kind of Criticism," *Journalism History* 7 (Autumn/Winter 1980–1981).

5. Kent Cooper, *The Right to Know: An Exposition of the Evils of News Suppression and Propaganda* (New York: Farrar, Straus and Cuddahy, 1956), pp. xiii, 314; "The Press in the Contemporary Scene," *Annals of the American Academy of Political and Social Science* 219, special issue, 1942.

6. "Death of Liebling," editorial, *New York Times,* December 1963. The *Times* suffered its share of his barbs.

7. I was the *Life* reporter who covered the death of William Randolph Hearst.

8. From my personal notes made while in the room where Hearst died.

9. A. J. Liebling, *The Press* (New York: Ballantine, 1975), p. 36.

10. Walter Lippmann, "Journalism and the Higher Law," in *Liberty and the News* (New York: Harcourt Brace and Howe, 1920), p. 11.

11. Walter Lippmann, "What Modern Liberty Means," in *Liberty and the News*, p. 38.

12. Ibid., p. 104.

13. Ronald Steel, *Walter Lippmann and the American Century* (London: Bodley Head, 1980), p. 214; Walter Lippmann and Charles Merz, "A Test of the News," *New Republic* 23 (August 4, 1920):1–40; Walter Lippmann, *The Phantom Public* (New York: Macmillan, 1930), p. 53; Lippmann, "Two Revolutions in the American Press," *Yale Review* 20 (March 1931):437–439.

14. Walter Lippmann, *Public Opinion* (New York: Macmillan, 1965), p. 11.

15. Ibid., p. 65.

16. Aristotle, *Politics,* Book 1, ch. 5.

17. Lippmann, *Public Opinion,* p. 19.

18. Ibid., pp. 261–262.

19. H. L. Mencken, *The Portable Curmudgeon,* ed. Jon Winokur (New York: New American Library, 1987).

CHAPTER NINETEEN

In finding much of the information in this chapter, Marion Tuttle Marzolf's excellent history of journalism critics, *Civilizing Voices: American Press Criticism, 1880–1950* (New York: Longman, 1991), has been particularly helpful.

1. Silas Bent, *Ballyhoo* (New York: Boni & Liveright, 1927), p. xiv; also see pp. 265, 371–372, 371–379. Similar themes are examined in Simon M. Bessie, *Jazz Journalism: The Story of the Tabloid Newspaper* (New York: Dutton, 1938).

2. Bayard Swope, comments in *Problems of Journalism: ASNE Proceedings* (annual) (1923):118.

3. Eric W. Allen, "Newspapers Need Criticism," *Editor and Publisher,* September 8, 1923, p. 1. Allen was president of the American Association of Schools and Departments of Journalism.

4. William Rivers, *The Opinion Makers: The Washington Press Corps* (Boston: Beacon Press, 1965–1967), p. 42.

5. Walter Lippmann, *Liberty and the News* (New York: Harcourt, Brace and Howe, 1920), pp. 18–19, 104, 439–440; "Lippmann Sees Passing of Popular Press," *Editor and Publisher,* April 18, 1931, p. 30.

6. Frank E. Gannett, "Sensational Newspapers Near End of Vogue Here and Abroad," *Editor and Publisher,* January 17, 1931, p. 41. The end was far from "near," and the same applies today.

7. Harry Chandler, "Our Day of Responsibility," *Editor and Publisher,* April 11, 1932, p. 7.

8. Herbert Brucker, *Freedom of Information* (New York: Macmillan, 1949), pp. 32, 70, 265–273.

9. Lester Markel, "Lester Markel Thinks Press Neglects Interpretive Role," *Editor and Publisher,* April 3, 1948, p. 61.

10. Reinhold Niebuhr, "The Role of Newspapers in America's Function as the

Greatest World Power," in Ralph D. Casey, ed., *The Press in Perspective* (Baton Rouge: Louisiana State University Press, 1963), pp. 40–44.

11. Ronald May, "Is the Press Unfair to McCarthy?" *New Republic* 128 (April 20, 1953):8–12.

12. Elmer Davis, *But We Were Born Free* (New York: Bobbs-Merrill, 1952), p. 175.

13. This phrase and its implications arise frequently in the literature of press evaluation during the 1930s and 1940s. The term evolved into the concept of social responsibility, articulated by the Hutchins Commission in 1947.

14. Ben Bagdikian, *The Media Monopoly* (Boston: Beacon Press, 1983), pp. 182–185. Bagdikian's analysis was an important compilation of insights regarding press responsibility. It resonates frequently in the articles and books that appeared subsequently in the continuing examination of press performance.

15. Bagdikian, *Media Monopoly*, p. 132.

16. Roy Hoopes, "When Ralph Ingersol Papered Manhattan: The Saga of *PM*, a Revolutionary Newspaper," *Washington Journalism Review*, December 1984, p. 25. Stone had worked for the experimental newspaper *PM*, started by former *Time* editor Ralph Ingersoll in New York City in 1940. The paper attempted to publish without advertising, political bias, or the influence of financial backers. It lasted eight years.

17. William A. Tillinghast, "Newspaper Errors: Reporters Dispute Most Source Claims," *Newspaper Research Journal*, July 1982, pp. 15–23.

18. *Editor and Publisher*, March 21, 1945, p. 58; Edwin Emery and Michael Emery, *The Press and America*, 5th ed. (Englewood Cliffs, NJ: Prentice Hall, 1984), p. 440. Also see William Weinfield, "The Growth of Daily Newspaper Chains in the U.S.," *Journalism Quarterly* 13 (December 1936):357.

19. Carl W. Ackerman, "Nineteen Charges," *Problems of Journalism: ASNE Proceedings* (annual) (1933):54.

20. Willard Grosvenor Bleyer, "Journalism in the U.S.: 1933," *Journalism Quarterly* 10 (1933):296–302; Emery and Emery, *The Press in America*, p. 218; Leo Rosten, *The Washington Correspondents* (New York: Harcourt Brace, 1937), p. 217.

21. Gerald W. Johnson, "Freedom of the Newspaper Press," *Annals of the American Academy of Political and Social Science* 200 (November 1938):74.

22. "The Press and the Public," *New Republic*, March 17, 1937, pp. 78–90.

23. "Faith in Power of Editors Shaken," *Literary Digest*, December 19, 1936, p. 42.

24. George Steiner, review of Harry Ashmore's *Unseasonable Truths*, *New Yorker*, October 23, 1989, p. 142. *Unseasonable Truths* (Boston: Little, Brown, 1989) is a biography of Robert Maynard Hutchins.

25. Ibid., p. 143.

26. Robert Hutchins, *A Free and Responsible Press* (Chicago: University of Chicago Press, 1974), p. v.

27. Ibid., p. vi.

28. Ibid.

CHAPTER TWENTY

1. John Adams to James Lloyd, February 11, 1815. Cited on title page of Commission on Freedom of the Press, *A Free and Responsible Press* (Chicago: University of Chicago Press, 1947).

2. Discussion records of the Commission on Freedom of the Press, University of Chicago Library Archives, box 1, folder 2.

3. "Luce Interview," *Editor and Publisher,* April 8, 1944, p. 7.

4. "Journalism Teachers Parry with Hutchins," *Editor and Publisher*, January 3, 1948, p. 10.

5. "Report Aimed Directly at Owners—Hutchins," *Editor and Publisher,* March 29, 1947, p. 8; "Forrest Accuses Group of Damaging Prestige," *Editor and Publisher,* March 29, 1947, p. 11.

6. A. J. Liebling, "The Wayward Press," *New Yorker,* May 14, 1960.

7. Marshall Frady, *Wallace* (New York: World, 1968), pp. 125, 169; Wayne Greenhaw, *Watch Out for George Wallace* (Englewood Cliffs, NJ: Prentice Hall, 1976), pp. 116–117.

8. All references to the commission on this and the following pages are taken directly from the Midway reprint of Commission on Freedom of the Press, "A General Report on Mass Communication: Newspapers, Radio, Motion Pictures, Magazines and Books," in Robert D. Leigh, ed., *A Free and Responsible Press* (Chicago: University of Chicago Press: 1974). The report was issued collectively by the members of the commission and was signed by all of them. The Midway reprint's editor was director of the commission staff.

9. Edmund Burke, according to Thomas Carlyle, was the first politician to describe the "estates" of government. Justice Potter Stewart cites the quotation in his essay "Or of the Press," *Hastings Law Journal* 26 (1975):631–634.

10. Commission on Freedom of the Press, "A General Report," pp. 13–14.

11. Commission on Freedom of the Press, "Requirements" (Part 2), in *A Free and Responsible Press* (Midway reprint).

12. Margaret Blanchard, "The Hutchins Commission: The Press and Responsibility," *Journalism Monographs* 49 (May 1977):51–52; Jerilyn S. McIntyre, "Repositioning a Landmark: The Hutchins Commission and Freedom of the Press," *Critical Studies in Mass Communications* 4 (October 1987):6–10; For further background: Philip Schuyler, "Government News Gag, Press Freedom Problem," *Editor and Publisher*, April 1944, p. 7; "Hutchins Chastises Editorial Writers," *Editor and Publisher,* November 27, 1948, pp. 6, 50.

13. Frank Hughes, *Prejudice and the Press* (New York: Devon Adaire, 1950); "An Offer to Hutchins," *Editor and Publisher,* November 27, 1948, p. 38; "News, Public Property, Cornerstone of Free Press," *Editor and Publisher,* September 3, 1949, pp. 3, 41.

14. Commission on Freedom of the Press, "A General Report," p. 130.

CHAPTER TWENTY-ONE

I am particularly indebted, regarding many sections of this chapter, to the insights of Lucas A. Powe Jr. (*The Fourth Estate and the Constitution* [Berkeley: University of California Press, 1991]).

1. J. Elliot, ed., *Debates on the Federal Constitution* (Philadelphia: J. B. Lippincott, 1907), pp. 528, 569–570. Madison's comment was part of his *Report on the Virginia Resolutions. Annals,* 5th cong., 2nd sess., pp. 2160–2161; and 3rd sess.,

pp. 3003–3014; Leonard Levy, *The Emergence of a Free Press* (New York: Oxford University Press, 1985), pp. xii, 284–349; David Rabban, "A Historical Historian," *Stanford Law Review* 37 (1985):851–854; David Anderson, "The Origins of the Press Clause," *U.C.L.A. Law Review* 30 (1983):529–533. Rabban and Anderson differ strongly with Levy, as has been previously noted. The divide is over Levy's emphasis on prior restraint as the dominant theme of press-clause history.

2. John Thomson, *An Enquiry into the Liberty and Licentiousness of the Press* (1801), reprint (New York: DeCapo Press, 1970).

3. Ira Glasser, *Visions of Liberty* (New York: Little, Brown, 1991), pp. 118–123.

4. Ibid.

5. *Debs v. United States*, 249 U.S. 211 (1919).

6. Lucas A. Powe Jr., *The Fourth Estate and the Constitution* (Berkeley: University of California Press, 1991), pp. 70–71; D. Rabban, "The First Amendment in Its Forgotten Years," *Yale Law Journal* 90 (1981):514; *Schenck v. United States*, 249 U.S. 214 (1919); *Frohwerk v. United States*, 249 U.S. 204 (1919); D. Rabban, "The Emergence of Modern First Amendment Doctrine," *University of Chicago Law Review* 50 (1983):1265.

7. Chief Justice Vinson in *Dennis v. United States*, 341 U.S. 494, 509 (1951). This formulation was first written by Judge Learned Hand regarding alleged subversive speech and was adopted by the chief justice.

8. Rabban, "The Emergence of Modern First Amendment Doctrine," p. 1205. Some of the material here comes from my personal notes made while attending a seminar on the Bill of Rights conducted by Professor Akhil Reed Amar at the Yale Law School in fall 1993.

9. Ira Glasser, *Visions of Liberty*, p. 125.

10. John Stuart Mill, *On Liberty* (New York: Penguin Classics, 1988), p. 79.

11. Justice Holmes to Zechariah Chafee, June 12, 1922, quoted in Rabban, "The Emergence of Modern First Amendment Doctrine," p. 1265.

12. Learned Hand to Oliver Wendell Holmes, November 25, 1919 (*Holmes Papers*, Harvard Law School, vol. 43, p. 30), quoted by Anthony Lewis in *Make No Law* (New York: Random House, 1991), p. 75.

13. *Kovacs v. Cooper*, 336 U.S. 77 (1949), p. 95.

14. Quoted in Rabban, "The Emergence of Modern First Amendment Doctrine," pp. 1232, 1265–1296; Rabban, "Ahistorical Historian: Leonard Levy on Freedom of Expression in Early American History," *Stanford Law Review* 37 (1985): 795–828; Z. Chafee, *Free Speech in the United States* (Cambridge, MA: Harvard University Press, 1941); P. Murphy, *The Meaning of Freedom of Speech* (Westport, CT: Greenwood Press, 1972), p. 18; Gordon Wood, "Ideology and the Origins of Liberal America," *William and Mary Quarterly* 44 (1987):628–634.

15. Justice Holmes, writing in *Schenck v. United States*, p. 52; Rabban, "Emergence of Modern First Amendment Doctrine," p. 1232; Alfred Bettman to Z. Chafee, October 27, 1919, quoted in Rabban, p. 1296.

16. *United States v. Schwimmer*, 279 U.S. 644–653 (1928).

17. Quoted in Rabban, "Emergence of Modern First Amendment Doctrine," p. 1320.

18. Justice Brandeis opinion on *Whitney v. California*, 274 U.S. (1927), *William and Mary Law Review* 29 (1988):653, 686. Also see V. Blasi, "The Checking Value

in First Amendment Theory," *American Bar Foundation Research Journal* (1977): 521.

19. Brandeis in *Whitney v. California*, pp. 374–377.

20. From *Gitlow v. New York*, 268 U.S. 652 (1925).

21. Justice Oliver Wendell Holmes's dissent in *Gitlow v. New York,* pp. 672–673.

22. Quoted in Rabban, "Emergence of Modern First Amendment Doctrine," p. 484; Z. Chafee, "Freedom of Speech in Wartime," *Harvard Law Journal* 32 (June 1919):932–934, 947, 967–968.

23. Anthony Lewis, *Make No Law,* p. 85.

24. *Whitney v. California*, 274 U.S. 357, 374–377 (1927). Also see Blasi, "The Checking Value in First Amendment Theory," p. 653.

25. For the Brandeis adaptations of Greek philosophy, see ibid., pp. 686–689; quoted in *Independent Gazetteer*, November 9, 1782.

26. Blasi, "The Checking Value in First Amendment Theory," pp. 696–697.

27. Akhil Reed Amar, "The Bill of Rights and the Fourteenth Amendment," *Yale Law Journal* 101(1992):1197; Bernard Schwartz, *The Great Rights of Mankind* (Madison, WI: Madison House, 1992), p. 65.

28. Dwight Teeter, *A Legacy of Expression: Philadelphia Newspapers and Congress During the War for Independence* (Madison: University of Wisconsin School of Journalism, 1966), pp. 239–240.

29. Gordon Wood, "Interests and Disinterestedness in the Making of the Constitution," in *Beyond Confederation* (Chapel Hill: University of North Carolina Press, 1987), pp. 73–76; also see Gordon Wood, *The Creation of the American Republic, 1776–1787* (Chapel Hill: University of North Carolina Press, 1969); Stanley Elkins and Eric McKittrick, *The Age of Federalism* (New York: Oxford University Press, 1993), pp. 10–12; Herbert Storing, ed., *The Complete Anti-Federalist* (Chicago: University of Chicago Press, 1981), vol. 2, pp. 136–213.

30. J. Trenchard and T. Gordon, *Cato's Letters* (New York: DaCapo Press, 1971), pp. 246–247, 253.

31. Jefferson to Abigail Adams, September 11, 1804, in Paul Ford, ed., *The Writings of Thomas Jefferson* (New York: G. Putnam, 1897), p. 311.

32. Alexander Meiklejohn, "The First Amendment Is an Absolute," in *Free Speech and Its Relation to Self-Government* (Washington, DC: Supreme Court Review, 1961), pp. 250–251.

33. Ibid., p. 252.

34. Chafee, *Free Speech in the United States*, p. 32.

35. Ibid.

36. Meiklejohn, "The First Amendment Is an Absolute," pp. 254–256.

37. Ibid., p. 263.

38. Ibid., p. 258.

39. Ibid., pp. 256–259. Brandeis in *Whitney v. California* had advised that "public discussion is a political duty."

CHAPTER TWENTY-TWO

1. John Locke, "Second Treatise of Civil Government" (1690), chap. 5, sec. 27, in Ernest Rhys, ed., *Of Civil Government, Two Treatises* (New York: Dutton, 1936).

2. Lucas A. Powe Jr., *The Fourth Estate and the Constitution* (Berkeley: University of California Press, 1991), p. 125; D. Laycock, *Modern American Remedies* (Boston: Little, Brown, 1985), pp. 591–613.

3. Richard Clurman, "Two Reforms," in *Beyond Malice* (New Brunswick, NJ: Transaction Books, 1988), p. 266.

4. Powe, *The Fourth Estate and the Constitution*, p. 138; *New York Times,* December 18, 1983; B. Brewin and S. Shaw, *Vietnam on Trial* (New York: Atheneum, 1987), pp. 352–353.

5. Clurman, *Beyond Malice*, pp. 190–191.

6. Fred Schauer, "Public Figures," *William and Mary Law Review* 25:905, 911–912, 927.

7. Rodney Smolla, *Suing the Press* (New York: Oxford University Press, 1986), p. 242; Floyd Abrams, "Why We Should Change the Libel Law," *New York Times Magazine,* September 29, 1985, p. 34.

8. Powe, *The Fourth Estate and the Constitution*, p. 139.

9. Advertising billboard used in California in 1950 by a company called Mad Man Muntz, which was selling a new device called television.

10. Randall Tobias, "In a Quick Switch, Lilly Names a New Chief," *New York Times,* June 26, 1993, p. 17.

11. *NBC v. United States,* 319 U.S. 192 (1943).

12. In a letter to Lucas Powe Jr., Richard Salant, then president of CBS News, reported that Whitehead's droll comment had been made at an informal breakfast with news reporters.

13. Owen Fiss, *Yale Alumni Magazine,* October 1991, p. 63; also see Fiss, *Yale Law Journal* 100 (May 1991):2106.

14. Lewis Lapham, "Editor's Notebook," *Harper's,* September 1992, p. 9.

CHAPTER TWENTY-THREE

1. *Red Lion Broadcasting v. FCC,* 395 U.S. 367 (1969). In effect, the FCC was given reassurance of its right to discipline radio stations found guilty of political broadcasts outside the mainstream without permitting so-called opposition views under what was known as the fairness doctrine.

2. Alfred Sikes, "My Turn," *Newsweek,* January 14, 1991, p. 8.

3. Quoted in Fred Powledge, *The Engineering of Restraint* (Washington, DC: Public Affairs Press), vol. 34.

4. Lucas A. Powe Jr., *American Broadcasting and the First Amendment* (Berkeley: University of California Press, 1987), p. 199.

5. *United States Code Annotated* 47, supplement (1986):531–532.

6. *Economist,* August 7, 1993, p. 16.

7. Stephen Carter, *Yale Law Journal* 93, no. 581 (1984):600.

8. *Beauharnais v. Illinois* 343 U.S. 250, 286 (1952), dissenting opinion.

9. C. Edwin Baker, "Advertising and a Democratic Press," *University of Pennsylvania Law Review* 140, no. 6 (June 1992):2097.

10. John Tebbel and Mary Ellen Zuckerman, *The Magazine in America, 1741–1990* (New York: Oxford University Press, 1991), pp. 365–373.

11. Walter Dean Burnham, *The Current Crisis in American Politics* (New York: Oxford University Press, 1982), pp. 183, 188–189; Michael McGerr, *The Decline of Popular Politics* (New York: Oxford University Press, 1986).

12. Erik Barnouw, *The Sponsor* (New York: Oxford University Press, 1978), pp. 84–86, 137.

13. Alexander Bickel, *The Morality of Consent* (New Haven: Yale University Press, 1975), p. 105.

14. *Associated Press v. United States,* 326 U.S. 1 (1945), p. 20.

15. Owen Fiss, "Why the State?" *Harvard Law Review* 100 (1987):781–788.

16. Bickel, *Morality of Consent,* p. 82.

17. Ibid., p. 86.

CHAPTER TWENTY-FOUR

1. Richard Clurman, *Beyond Malice* (New Brunswick, NJ: Transaction Books, 1988), p. 30.

2. Ibid., p. 266.

3. Steve Brill, memorandum to the staff of *American Lawyer* and of the cable television program *Court TV* in 1993.

4. Clurman, *Beyond Malice,* p. 32.

5. Paul M. Kennedy, *Preparing for the Twenty-First Century* (New York: Random House, 1993), p. 23.

EPILOGUE

1. Cited in Jack Smith, *Los Angeles Times,* September 14, 1988, pt. 5, p. 1.

2. Neil Postman, *Amusing Ourselves to Death* (New York: Penguin Books, 1985), p. 106.

3. Alexander Meiklejohn, "The First Amendment Is an Absolute," in *Free Speech and Its Relation to Self-Government* (Washington, DC: Supreme Court Review, 1961), p. 79.

4. Quoted in W. A. Swanberg, *Luce and His Empire* (New York: Charles Scribner's, 1972), pp. 142–143. See also Robert T. Elson, *Time, Inc.* (New York: Atheneum, 1968); Herbert Brucker, "The Glut of Occurences," *Atlantic Monthly,* August 1935, p. 204.

5. Cited in Frank McCullough, *Nieman Reports,* no. 2 (Summer 1995):56; Bradford Torrey and Francis H. Allen, eds. *The Journal of Henry D. Thoreau* (Boston: Houghton Mifflin, 1949); Walter Harding, *The Days of Thoreau* (New York: Knopf, 1965).

6. Cited in Isaiah Berlin, *Four Essays on Liberty* (London: Oxford University Press, 1984), pp. 153–154. Berlin analyzes Kant's theory of voluntary obedience thoroughly in his essay in the context of related doctrines embraced by the ancient Greek philosophers and Enlightenment European philosophers. He cites Edmund Burke, who proclaimed the individual's right to be restrained in his own interest, because "the presumed consent of every rational creature is in unison with the predisposed order of things" (pp. 147–148).

SELECTED BIBLIOGRAPHY

Abernathy, M. Glenn, and Barbara Perry. 1993. *Civil Liberties Under the Constitution*. Columbia: University of South Carolina Press.

Adair, David. 1974. *Fame and the Founding Fathers*. New York: W. W. Norton.

Adler, Renata. 1986. *Reckless Disregard*. New York: Knopf.

Ahlstrom, Sydney E. 1972. *A Religious History of the American People, vols. 1 and 2*. New Haven: Yale University Press.

Altschull, J. Herbert. 1984. *Agents of Power*. New York: Longman.

Andrews, J. Cutler. 1955. *The North Reports the Civil War*. Pittsburgh: University of Pittsburgh Press.

Appleby, Joyce. 1984. *Capitalism and a New Social Order: The Republican Vision of the 1790s*. New York: New York University Press.

Armstrong, William M., ed. 1974. *The Gilded Age: Letters of E. L. Godkin*. Albany: State University of New York Press.

Ashmore, Harry S. 1989. *Unseasonable Truths: The Life of Robert Maynard Hutchins*. Boston: Little, Brown.

Bagdikian, Ben H. 1983. *The Media Monopoly*. Boston: Beacon Press.

Bailyn, Bernard, and John B. Hench, eds. 1980. *The Press and the American Revolution*. Worcester, MA: American Antiquarian Society.

Baker, C. Edwin. 1994. *Advertising and a Democratic Press*. Princeton: Princeton University Press.

Baker, Richard Terrill. 1954. *A History of the Graduate School of Journalism*. New York: Columbia University Press.

Baldasty, Gerald J. 1992. *The Commercialization of News in the Nineteenth Century*. Madison: University of Wisconsin Press.

Barker, Ernest. 1958. *The Politics of Aristotle*. New York: Oxford University Press.

Barnouw, Erik. 1966. *A Tower in Babel*. New York: Oxford University Press.

Beard, Charles A. 1927. *The Economic Origins of Jeffersonian Democracy*. New York: Macmillan.

Beeman, Richard, Stephen Botein, and Edward C. Carter III, eds. 1987. *Beyond Confederation: Origins of the Constitution and American National Identity*. Chapel Hill: University of North Carolina Press.

Berger, Meyer. 1951. *The Story of the New York Times, 1851–1951*. Boston: James R. Osgood.

Berlin, Isaiah. 1956. *The Age of Enlightenment*. Boston: Houghton Mifflin.

Beschloss, Michael R., and Strobe Talbott. 1993. *At the Highest Levels*. Boston: Little, Brown.

Bickel, Alexander M. 1965. *The Morality of Consent*. New Haven: Yale University Press.

Blanchard, Margaret. 1986. *Exporting the First Amendment*. New York: Longman.

Bleyer, Willard G. 1927. *Main Currents in the History of American Journalism.* Boston: Houghton Mifflin.

Blumler, Jay G., and Denis McQuail. 1969. *Television and Politics.* Chicago: University of Chicago Press.

Bogart, Leo. 1989. *Press and Public: Who Reads What, When, Where and Why in American Newspapers,* 2nd ed. Hillsdale, NJ: L. Erlbaum.

Bok, Sissela. 1989. *Lying: Moral Choice in Public and Private Life.* New York: Vintage Books.

Boorstin, Daniel. 1948. *The Lost World of Thomas Jefferson.* New York: H. Holt.
_____. 1973. *The Americans: The Democratic Experience.* New York: Random House.

Boyd, Julian P., ed. 1950. *The Papers of Thomas Jefferson.* Princeton: Princeton University Press.

Brant, Irving. 1950. *James Madison: The Virginia Revolutionist,* 5 vols. Indianapolis: University of Indiana Press.

Brigham, Clarence S. 1947. *History and Bibliography of American Newspapers, 1690–1820.* Worcester, MA: American Antiquarian Society.

Broder, David S. 1972. *The Party's Over: The Failure of Politics in America.* New York: Harper & Row.

Brodie, Fawn M. 1974. *Thomas Jefferson: An Intimate History.* New York: W. W. Norton.

Brogan, Patrick. 1985. *Spiked: The Short Life and Death of the National News Council.* New York: Twentieth Century Fund.

Brown, Richard D. 1989. *Knowledge Is Power.* New York: Oxford University Press.

Brucker, Herbert. 1937. *The Changing American Newspaper.* New York: Columbia University Press.

Buckley, William F., Jr. 1990. *Gratitude.* New York: Random House.

Carlson, Oliver. 1942. *The Man Who Made News: James Gordon Bennett.* New York: Duell, Sloan and Pearce.

Cater, Douglass. 1959. *The Fourth Branch of Government.* Boston: Houghton Mifflin.

Catledge, Turner. 1971. *My Life and the Times.* New York: Harper & Row.

Chafee, Zechariah, Jr. 1947. *Government and Mass Communications,* vols. 1, 2. Chicago: University of Chicago Press.

Christians, Clifford G. 1977. "Fifty Years of Scholarship in Media Ethics." *Journal of Communications.*

Christians, Clifford G., Kim B. Rotzoll, and Mark Fackler. 1983. *Media Ethics, Cases and Moral Reasoning.* New York and London: Longman.
_____. 1987. *Media Ethics.* New York: Longman.

Clark, Charles E. 1994. *The Public Prints: The Newspaper in Anglo-American Culture, 1665–1740.* New York: Oxford University Press.

Clurman, Richard M. 1988. *Beyond Malice.* New Brunswick, NJ: Transaction Books.

Cobb, Irvin S. 1941. *Exit Laughing.* New York: Bobbs-Merrill.

Cohen, Bernard. 1963. *The Press, the Public, and Foreign Policy.* Princeton: Princeton University Press.

Cooke, Jacob E., ed. 1961. *The Federalist*. Middletown, CT: Wesleyan University Press.

Cooper, Kent. 1942. *Barriers Down: The Story of the News Agency Epoch*. New York: Farrar and Rinehart.

Cose, Ellis. 1989. *The Press*. New York: William Morrow.

Crawford, Nelson A. 1924. *The Ethics of Journalism*. New York: Knopf.

Creelman, James. 1901. *On the Great Highway*. San Francisco: Lothrop.

Croateau, David, and William Hoynes. 1994. *By Invitation Only*. Monroe, ME: Common Courage Press.

Crouse, Timothy. 1974. *The Boys on the Bus: Riding with the Campaign Press Corps*. New York: Ballantine Books.

Cunningham, Noble E., Jr. 1967. *The Jeffersonian Republicans, 1789–1801*. Chapel Hill: University of North Carolina Press.

_____. 1978. *The Process of Government Under Jefferson*. Princeton: Princeton University Press.

_____. 1988. *The United States in 1800: Henry Adams Revisited*. Charlottesville: University of Virginia Press.

Curry, Richard O., and Lawrence B. Goodheart, eds. 1991. *American Chameleon*. Kent, OH: Kent State University Press.

Dahl, Robert A. 1989. *Democracy and Its Critics*. New Haven: Yale University Press.

_____. 1990. *After the Revolution?* New Haven: Yale University Press.

Dana, Charles. 1900. *The Art of Newspaper Making*. New York: Appleton.

Davis, David B. 1975. *Slavery in the Age of Revolution*. New York: Oxford University Press.

Dennis, Everette, E. 1992. *Of the Media and People*. New York: Sage.

Diamond, Edwin. 1985–1990. *The Changing Face of the News*. Boston: MIT Press.

Dionne, E. J., Jr. 1991. *Why Americans Hate Politics*. New York: Simon & Schuster.

Downie, Leonard. 1976. *The New Muckrakers*. New York: New Republic Books.

Dreiser, Theodore. 1922. *Newspaper Days*. New York: Liveright.

Edsall, Thomas Byrne, and Mary D. Edsall. 1991. *Chain Reaction: The Impact of Race, Rights, and Taxes on American Politics*. New York: W. W. Norton.

Edson, C. L. 1920. *The Gentle Art of Columning*. New York: n.p.

Elkins, Stanley W. 1963. *Slavery: A Problem in American Institutional and Intellectual Life*. New York.

Elkins, Stanley, and Eric McKitrick. 1993. *The Age of Federalism*. New York: Oxford University Press.

Elliott, Osborn. 1980. *The World of Oz*. New York: Viking.

Emerson, Thomas I. 1970. *The System of Freedom of Expression*. New York: Random House.

Epstein, Edward Jay. 1973. *News from Nowhere: Television and the News*. New York: Random House.

Evans, Harold. 1994. *Good Times, Bad Times*. London: Phoenix.

Fallows, James. 1986. "The New Celebrities of Washington." *New York Review of Books*, June 12.

Farrar, Ronald T., and John D. Stephens. 1971. *Mass Media and the National Experience*. New York: Harper & Row.

Foner, Erik. 1944. *Tom Paine and Revolutionary America*. New York: Wiley.

Ford, Paul L., ed. 1897. *The Writings of Thomas Jefferson*. New York: G. Putnam.

Friendly, Fred W. 1967. *Due to Circumstances Beyond Our Control*. New York: Random House.

Gans, Herbert J. 1979. *Deciding What's News: A Study of CBS Evening News, NBC Nightly News, Newsweek and Time*. New York: Vintage.

Glasser, Ira 1991. *Visions of Liberty*. New York: Little, Brown.

Godkin, E. L. 1890. "Newspapers Here and Abroad." *North American Review* 150, February.

_____. 1895. "Journalistic Dementia." *Nation*, March 14.

Goldstein, Tom. 1985. *The News at Any Cost*. New York: Simon & Schuster.

Goodwin, H. Eugene. 1983. *Groping for Ethics in Journalism*. Ames: Iowa State University Press.

Graebner, William, and Leonard Richards, eds. 1982. *The American Record, Vol. 1—to 1887*. New York: Knopf.

Greene, Theodore. 1970. *America's Heroes*. New York: Oxford University Press.

Greenfield, Jeff. 1982. *The Real Campaign: How the Media Missed the Story of the 1980 Campaign*. New York: Summit.

Greider, William. 1992. *Who Will Tell the People?* New York: Simon & Schuster.

Griffith, Thomas. 1974. *How True: A Skeptic's Guide to Believing the News*. Boston: Atlantic Little, Brown.

Gunther, Gerald. 1994. *Learned Hand: The Man and the Judge*. New York: Knopf.

Halberstam, David. 1979. *The Powers That Be*. New York: Knopf.

Hausman, Carl. 1990. *The Decision-Making Process in Journalism*. Englewood Cliffs, NJ: Prentice-Hall.

Hess, Stephen. 1981. *The Washington Reporters*. Washington, DC: Brookings Institution.

Hocking, William. 1947. *Freedom of the Press: A Framework of Principle*. Chicago: University of Chicago Press.

Hofstadter, Richard. 1948. *The American Political Tradition and the Men Who Made It*. New York: Vintage.

Hulteng, John L. 1976. *The Messenger's Motives*. Englewood Cliffs, NJ: Prentice-Hall.

Hynds, E. 1980. *American Newspapers in the 1980s*. New York: Hastings House.

Irwin, Will. 1911. "The American Newspaper, VI: The Editor and the News." *Colliers*, April 1.

_____. 1942. *The Making of a Reporter*. New York: Putnam.

Jamieson, Kathleen Hall. 1988. *Packaging the Presidency*. New York: Oxford University Press.

Jensen, Merrill. 1940. *The Articles of Confederation: An Interpretation of the Social, Constitutional History of the American Revolution, 1774–1781*. Madison, WI: Madison House.

Johnson, Haynes. 1991. *Sleepwalking Through History*. New York: W. W. Norton.

Juergens, George. 1966. *Joseph Pulitzer and the New York World*. Princeton: Princeton University Press.

Kaplan, Justin. 1974. *Lincoln Steffens*. New York: Simon & Schuster.

Knightley, Phillip. 1975. *The First Casualty*. New York: Harcourt Brace Jovanovich.

Kurtz, Howard. 1993. *Media Circus*. New York: Times Books.

Lacayo, Richard, and George Russel, eds. 1995. *Eye Witness: 150 Years of Photojournalism*. New York: Time.

Ladd, Everett. 1978. *Where Have All the Voters Gone?* New York: W. W. Norton.

Lambeth, Edmund B. 1986. *Committed Journalism: An Ethic for the Profession*. Bloomington: Indiana University Press.

Lamont, P. Lansing. 1965. *Day of Trinity*. New York: Atheneum.

Langford, Gerald. 1961. *The Richard Harding Davis Years*. New York: Holt.

Lasch, Christopher. 1978. *The Culture of Narcissism*. New York: W. W. Norton.

Lasswell, Harold D. 1934. "Propaganda." In *Encyclopedia of the Social Sciences*. New York: Macmillan.

Lee, Alfred McClung. 1937. *The Daily Newspaper in America: The Evolution of a Social Instrument*. New York: Macmillan.

Leigh, Robert D., ed. 1974. *A Free and Responsible Press*. Chicago: University of Chicago Press.

Leonard, Thomas C. 1995. *News for All*. New York: Oxford University Press.

Levy, Leonard. 1985. *The Emergence of a Free Press*. New York: Oxford University Press.

Lewis, Anthony. 1991. *Make No Law*. New York: Random House.

Lichter, Robert. 1988. *The Video Campaign: Network Coverage of the 1988 Primaries*. Washington, DC: American Enterprise Institute.

Lichter, S. Robert, Stanley Rothman, and Linda Lichter. 1986. *The Media Elite*. New York: Adler & Adler.

Liebling, A. J. 1975. *The Press*. New York: Ballantine Books.

Lindblom, Charles E. 1977. *Politics and Markets*. New York: Basic Books.

Lippmann, Walter. 1965. *Public Opinion*. New York: Free Press.

Lockridge, Kenneth A. 1974. *Literacy in Colonial New England: An Enquiry into the Social Context of Literacy in the Early Modern West*. New York: W. W. Norton.

Lutz, Donald S. 1984. "The Relative Influence of European Writers on Late Eighteenth Century American Political Thought." *American Political Science Review*, March.

MacDougall, Curtis. 1938. *Interpretative Reporting*. New York: Macmillan.

MacIntyre, Alasdair. 1966. *A Short History of Ethics*. New York: Macmillan.

Malcolm, Janet. 1990. *The Journalist and the Murderer*. New York: Knopf.

Marzolf, Marion Tuttle. 1991. *Civilizing Voices: American Press Criticism, 1880–1950*. New York: Longman.

Mayer, Martin. 1987. *Making News*. New York: Doubleday.

Mayo, Bernard. 1992. *Jefferson Himself*. Charlottesville: University Press of Virginia.

McCulloch, Frank. 1984. *Drawing the Line*. Washington, DC: American Society of Newspaper Editors.

McCullough, David. 1992. *Truman*. New York: Simon & Schuster.

McGinniss, Joe. 1969. *The Selling of the President*. New York: Trident Press.

McLuhan, Marshall. 1964. *Understanding Media*. New York: McGraw-Hill.

Mecklin, John. 1965. *Mission in Torment*. New York: Doubleday.

Meeker, Richard H. 1983. *Newspaper Man*. New York: Ticknor & Fields.

Merrill, John C. 1974. *The Imperative of Freedom: A Philosophy of Journalistic Autonomy*. New York: Hastings House.

Mickelson, Sig. 1972. *The Electric Mirror: Politics in an Age of Television*. New York: Dodd Mead.

Mill, John Stuart. 1988. *On Liberty*. New York: Penguin Classics.

Miller, John Chester. 1991. *The Wolf by the Ears: Thomas Jefferson and Slavery*. Charlottesville: University of Virginia Press.

Minow, Newton. 1987. *For Great Debates: A New Plan for Future Presidential Television Debates*. New York: Priority Press.

Mitgang, Herbert, ed. 1956. *Abraham Lincoln: A Press Portrait*. Athens: University of Georgia Press.

Mitroff, Ian, and Warren Bennis. 1989. *The Unreality Industry*. New York: Birch Lane.

Morgan, Edmund S. 1975. *American Slavery, American Freedom*. New York: W. W. Norton.

_____. 1977. *The Birth of the Republic, 1763–89*. Chicago: University of Chicago Press.

Mott, Frank Luther. 1943. *Jefferson and the Press*. Baton Rouge: Louisiana State University.

_____. 1962. *American Journalism: A History, 1690–1960*, 3rd ed. New York: Macmillan.

Moyers, Bill. 1971. *Listening to America*. New York: Dell.

Moynihan, Daniel Patrick. 1951. "The Presidency and the Press." *Commentary* 51, March.

Negroponte, Nicholas. 1995. *Being Digital*. New York: Knopf.

Neuman, W. Russell. 1986. *The Paradox of Mass Politics: Knowledge and Opinion in the American Electorate*. Cambridge: Harvard University Press.

North, S.N.D. 1884. *The Newspapers and Periodical Press*. Washington, DC: Government Printing Office.

Page, Benjamin. 1978. *Choices and Echoes in Presidential Elections*. Chicago: University of Chicago Press.

Patterson, Thomas. 1994. *Out of Order*. New York: Vintage Books.

Pelikan, Jaroslav. 1965. *The Christian Intellectual*. New York: Harper & Row.

Polanyi, Michael. 1959. *Personal Knowledge*. Chicago: University of Chicago Press.

Pole, J. R. 1987. *The American Constitution: For and Against*. New York: Hill and Wang.

Powe, Lucas A., Jr. 1987. *American Broadcasting and the First Amendment*. Berkeley: University of California Press.

_____. 1991. *The Fourth Estate and the Constitution*. Berkeley: University of California Press.

Pred, Allan. 1973. *Urban Growth and the Circulation of Information: The United States System of Cities, 1790–1840*. Cambridge: Harvard University Press.

Rabban, D. 1985. "The Ahistorical Historian: Leonard Levy on Freedom of Expression in Early American History." *Stanford Law Review* 795, p. 828.

Ramelkamp, Julian S. 1967. *Pulitzer's Post-Dispatch, 1878–1883*. Princeton: Princeton University Press.

Ranney, Austin. 1983. *Channels of Power: The Impact of Television on American Politics*. New York: Basic Books.

Rawls, John. 1971. *A Theory of Justice*. Cambridge: Harvard University Press.

Reston, James. 1967. *The Artillary of the Press*. New York: Harper & Row.

_____. 1990. *A Theory of Justice and Its Critics*. Palo Alto, CA: Stanford University Press.

Riesman, David, Nathan Glazer, and Reuel Denney. 1961. *The Lonely Crowd*. New Haven: Yale University Press.

Risjord, Norman K. 1991. *Jefferson's America, 1760–1815*. Madison, WI: Madison House.

Ritchie, Michael. 1994. *Please Stand By*. Woodstock, NY: Overlock Press.

Roberts, Chalmers M. 1973. *First Rough Draft*. New York: Praeger.

_____. 1977. *The Washington Post: The First Hundred Years*. Boston: Houghton Mifflin.

Robinson, Michael, and Margaret Sheehan. 1983. *Over the Wire and on T.V.* New York: Russell Sage Foundation.

Roshco, Bernard. 1975. *Newsmaking*. Chicago: University of Chicago Press.

Rosten, Leo C. 1937. *The Washington Correspondents*. New York: Harcourt Brace.

Rovere, Richard. 1959. *Senator Joe McCarthy*. New York: Harcourt Brace.

Rubin, Richard L. 1981. *Press, Party, and Presidency*. New York: W. W. Norton.

Rusher, William A. 1988. *The Coming Battle for the Media*. New York: William Morrow.

Sabato, Larry. 1991. *Feeding Frenzy*. New York: Free Press.

Sabine, George H. 1961. *A History of Political Theory*. New York: Holt, Rinehart & Winston.

Salisbury, Harrison E. 1980. *Without Fear or Favor*. New York: Times Books

Sanford, Terry. 1981. *A Danger of Democracy*. Boulder: Westview Press.

Schlesinger, Arthur M., Jr. 1992. *The Disuniting of America*. New York: W. W. Norton.

Schudson, Michael, 1978. *Discovering the News: A Social History of American Newspapers*. New York: Basic Books.

_____. 1995. *The Power of News*. Cambridge: Harvard University Press.

Schwartz, Bernard. 1992. *The Great Rights of Mankind*. Madison, WI: Madison House.

Shaw, David. 1977. *Journalism Today*. New York: Harper's College Press.

Sheehan, Neil. 1988. *A Bright Shining Lie*. New York: Random House.

Siebert, Fred S., Theodore Peterson, and Wilbur Schramm. 1963. *Four Theories of the Press*. Urbana: University of Illinois Press.

Sigal, Leon V. 1973. *Reporters and Officials*. Lexington, MA: D. C. Heath.

Smith, Culver. 1977. *The Press, Politics and Patronage: The American Government's Use of Newspapers, 1789–1875*. Athens: University of Georgia Press.

Smith, Hedrick. 1988. *The Power Game*. New York: Ballantine.

Sperber, A. M. 1986. *Murrow, His Life and Times*. New York: Freundlich.

Swain, Bruce M. 1978. *Reporters' Ethics*. Ames: Iowa State University Press.

Swanberg, William A. 1961. *Citizen Hearst: A Biography of William Randolph Hearst*. New York: Scribners.

Syrett, Harold C., ed. 1961–1975. *The Papers of Alexander Hamilton*, 10 vols. New York: Public Library.

Talese, Gay. 1986. *The Kingdom and the Power*. New York: Dell.

Tebbel, John. 1972. *A History of Book Publishing in the United States*. New York: Bowker.

Teeter, Dwight. 1966. *A Legacy of Expression: Philadelphia Newspapers and Congress During the War for Independence*. Madison: University of Wisconsin School of Journalism.

_____. 1968. "Press Freedom and Public Printing: Pennsylvania, 1775–1783." *Journalism Quarterly* 45.

Thayer, Lee. 1980. *Ethics, Morality and the Media*. New York: Hastings House.

Tocqueville, Alexis de. 1945. *Democracy in America*, 2 vols. New York: DaCapo Press.

Trenchard, J., and T. Gordon. 1971. *Cato's Letters; or Essays on Liberty, Civil and Religious, and Other Important Subjects*. New York: DaCapo Press.

Tribe, Laurence H., and Michael C. Dorf. 1991. *On Reading the Constitution*. Cambridge: Harvard University Press.

Trollope, Anthony. 1986. *The Warden*. New York: Penguin Classics.

Ungar, Sanford J. 1989. *The Papers and The Papers*. New York: Columbia University Press.

Van Doren, Carl. 1948. *The Great Rehearsal*. New York: Time Life Books.

Veit, Helen E., Kenneth R. Bowling, and Charlene Bickford, eds. 1991. *Creating the Bill of Rights*. Baltimore: Johns Hopkins University Press.

Washington Post. 1974. *Of the Press, by the Press, for the Press (and Others, Too)*. Washington, DC: *Washington Post*.

Weaver, Paul. 1974. "The Politics of a News Story." In Harry M. Clor, ed., *The Mass Media and Modern Democracy*. New York: Rand McNally.

Whiteside, Thomas. 1975. "Shaking the Tree." *New Yorker*, March 17.

Wicker, Tom. 1978. *On Press: A Top Reporter's Life in and Reflections on American Journalism*. New York: Viking.

Williamson, Chilton. 1960. *American Suffrage from Property to Democracy, 1760–1860*. Princeton: Princeton University Press.

Wills, Garry. 1981. *Explaining America*. New York: Doubleday.

_____. 1992. *Lincoln at Gettysburg*. New York: Simon & Schuster.

Wilson, Edmund. 1962. *Patriotic Gore*. New York: Oxford University Press.

Wise, David. 1973. *The Politics of Lying*. New York: Random House.

Witcover, Jules. 1978. *Marathon: The Pursuit of the Presidency, 1972–1976*. New York: New American Library.

Wood, Gordon S. 1969. *The Creation of the American Republic, 1776–1787*. Chapel Hill: University of North Carolina Press.

Woodward, Bob. 1987. *Veil: The Secret Wars of the CIA, 1981–1987*. New York: Simon & Schuster.

Woodward, C. 1974. *The Strange Career of Jim Crow*, 3rd rev. ed. New York: Oxford University Press.

_____. 1983. *American Counterpoint*. New York: Oxford University Press.

Yankelovich, Daniel. 1981. *New Rules*. New York: Random House.

ABOUT THE BOOK AND AUTHOR

Sentinel Under Siege traces the evolution of the media in the United States and its capacity to examine and regulate itself, from its earliest colonial roots to the modern explosion of digital technology.

Once the Bill of Rights was enacted in 1791, the press became the first and only commercial enterprise explicitly protected by the U.S. Constitution. This book is concerned with the legal content given to freedom of the press by the Supreme Court and the fitful attempts of media criticism—both intramural and external—to build a greater sense of responsibility among the practitioners.

Stanley Flink, former correspondent for *Life Magazine* and writer/producer at NBC and CBS, is concerned less with the people's right to know than with the people's *need* to know. Only a competent, responsible press—whatever its means of distribution—can perform the role of watchdog over official abuse of power, business corruption, and political distortions. But the acquisition of so many newspapers, magazines, and broadcasting facilities by corporate conglomerates threatens a new kind of prior restraint on an independent press—the conflicts of interest; the power of advertising; the unspoken self-censorship of reporters and editors, print or electronic, based on the perceived predilections of their employers; and the financial interests of related companies.

Flink believes that responsible journalism can also be economically viable in the twenty-first century because the mass communication of reliable news reporting, and media accountability, will be vital to the democratic process. Unless the news media persistently seeks the high moral ground of public service, the first casualty will be an informed electorate. The second may well be constitutional protection.

Stanley E. Flink, former correspondent for *Life Magazine* and writer/producer at NBC and CBS, is adjunct associate professor of journalism at New York University Graduate School. A graduate of Yale University, he was the founding director of Yale's Office of Public Information.

INDEX

Abernathy, Ralph D., 31, 36
Abolitionist movement, 84–85, 98,
  117–119, 122, 124–127, 286(n5)
Abrams, Floyd, 59–60, 234
Accountability, 216, 258, 266, 292(n1)
Ackerman, Carl W., 205
ACLU. *See* American Civil Liberties
  Union
Adams, Abigail, 230
Adams, Henry, 104, 105, 114
Adams, John, 7, 25, 75, 87, 151, 209,
  219
Adler, Mortimer, 207
Advertising
  ethics and, 235
  news media content and, 249–255
  in newspapers, 121, 122, 130,
    161–162, 187, 197, 250–251
  prohibition against false, 181
  taxation of, 153
African Americans
  abolition of slavery and, 21, 113,
    117–119
  colonial slavery and, 80, 81–83, 85
  military service of, 147
  newspapers published by, 135, 136,
    166–167
  nineteenth-century racism and,
    116–118, 122–125, 127–128,
    131–139, 287(n7)
  racism in the South and, 30
  voting rights for, 34, 35, 132, 143,
    144
Agence Havas, 157
Agnew, Spiro, 58
Alabama Supreme Court, 36
Alger, George, 170, 176
Allen, Ethan, 92
Allen, Frederick L., 183

Allen, Woody, 263
Alter, Jonathan, 180
Amar, Akhil Reed, 150, 228, 297(n8)
Amendments to the Constitution
  Thirteenth Amendment (1865), 21,
    113, 117, 119, 132
  Fourteenth Amendment (1868), 21,
    109, 132, 134, 142, 149–153,
    227–228
  Fifteenth Amendment (1870), 132,
    228
  Nineteenth Amendment (1920), 22,
    151
  See also Bill of Rights; Constitutional
    law; First Amendment
American Anti-Slavery Society, 119,
  126
American Bar Association, 66, 185
American Civil Liberties Union
  (ACLU), 22, 221, 222
American Counterpoint (Woodward),
  117, 123
American Dilemma, An (Myrdal), 147
American Indians, 22
American Lawyer Media, 259
American Mercury, 185
American Newspaper Publishers
  Association, 205
American Revolution, 89, 123
American Slavery, American Freedom
  (Morgan), 78
American Society of Newspaper Editors
  (ASNE), 184–185, 198, 206, 210,
  215
American Weekly Mercury, 71
Anderson, David, 238, 280(n6)
Andrews, J. Cutler, 113
Annenberg Washington Libel Reform
  Project, 239